Passion Made Public

*In memory of my father, Donald Graham Henderson,
and for my mother, Alaine Marsh Henderson,
whose intelligence, love of language, and enduring vitality
never cease to amaze.*

Contents

Acknowledgments ix

Introduction 1

ONE
Elizabethan Contexts
33

TWO
Elizabeth's Watchful Eye and George
Peele's Gaze: Court Drama, Female Power,
and the Lyric of Praise
85

THREE
"Unhappy Dido":
Marlowe's Lyric Strains
120

FOUR
Shakespeare's Laboring Lovers:
Lyric and Its Discontents
167

FIVE
Legacy
214

Works Cited 251

Index 267

Acknowledgments

The poetic plays discussed within *Passion Made Public* are not the only writings that have reshaped labor and love. This book's composition and production have relied on plenty of each, and like most such loving labors become tributes to extensive collaboration and friendship as well. My ardent hope is that the love has not been lost amid the labor.

Much of my inspiration has come from my teachers. At William & Mary, I benefited especially from the rigorous dedication to learning and literature evinced by Robert Fehrenbach and my thesis advisor, Katherine Hill-Miller. When I was a graduate student at Columbia, Martin Meisel, Edward Tayler, and Bernard Beckerman took me seriously before I did myself, and Kathy Eden and Michael Seidel treated me like a colleague before I had earned that privilege. Professors Tayler and Beckerman were unstintingly generous and encouraging as my original dissertation advisers, and David Scott Kastan matched them during the latter stages of that project.

I am indebted to those who helped improve this book. I thank those valiant souls who read the manuscript in its entirety: Lynda Boose, Nancy Coiner, Margreta de Grazia, Kathy Eden, John Elder, Carla Freccero, David Scott Kastan, Sandy Martin, Martin Meisel, Jay Parini, Douglas Peterson, and Maureen Quilligan. Their thoughtful comments have helped immeasurably. Among those who read and commented upon chapters in their various stages and forms, I am particularly grateful to Jan Albers, Louise Fradenburg, Virginia Jackson, Paul Monod, David Price, and Yopie Prins. My readings have been enriched as well by insights shared in extensive conversations with colleagues and friends, most memorably with Julia Alvarez, Ric Burns, Alison Byerly, Susan Cook, Patricia Donahue, Kim Hall, Susan Heath, Terry Hummer, Susan Manning, Pat Skantze, Lola Van Wagenen, and Judy Yarnall. Part of chapter 3 originated as a talk for the Conference on Women and Sovereignty (held at the University of St. Andrews in Scotland and sponsored by the Traditional Cosmology Society) and was published in the volume *Women and Sovereignty,* ed. Louise Olga Fradenburg (Edinburgh University Press, 1992); thanks to all involved in those projects. Special thanks to Ann Lowry of the University of Illinois Press for her professionalism and cordiality in supervising the acquisition of this manuscript, and to Pat Hollahan for being the copyeditor from heaven. Eternal gratitude to my sister Joyce for helping with the index.

Grants from Middlebury College, the Ada Howe Kent fellowship program, and the American Council of Learned Societies helped me to complete the project, as did a summer of research assistance from my student Laurie Greco. Amidst the unexpected twists and turns of a career, I have been cheered by the support of friends too numerous to list here; for this relief, much thanks. Help at key moments came from colleagues both far and near, including Stanley Fish, Susan Fraiman, Susan Frye, Clark Hulse, David Lee Miller, Ann Van Sant, Matthew Wikander, and Susan Zimmerman, as well as many at Middlebury. A broader academic community, including my "aunt" Sara Withers, parents of former students, and the significant others of faculty friends, have provided wise counsel. And to the students of literature who for more than a decade have animated my delight in teaching and learning, my warmest thanks. I especially appreciate the generosity of the faculty and students in the Theater Department and the Women's Studies Program at Middlebury, who have encouraged me to share in their vitality and to pursue a more inclusive vision of education.

Finally, there are the acknowledgments that defy categorization. Among those mentioned above are several rare individuals whose labors have helped shape not only a book but a life. To their names I add and give precedence to those of Devon Jersild, Michael Krass, and my family: Joyce Henderson and William Pierce; Geoffrey Henderson; and Alaine Marsh Henderson. Their encouragement and love has helped me to discover not only a room but a mind of my own; I can only hope to reciprocate.

Introduction

When Romeo and Juliet first act on their erotic desires at Capulet's ball, they do so in extended sonnet form. Romeo attempts to elevate his courtly request to kiss the hand of his new acquaintance by using religious metaphors, a move familiar to readers of quattrocento Italian sonneteers:

> *Romeo [to Juliet]* If I profane with my unworthiest hand
> This holy shrine, the gentle sin is this,
> My lips, two blushing pilgrims, ready stand
> To smooth that rough touch with a tender kiss.
> (1.5.92–95)

But unlike Dante's Beatrice or Petrarch's Laura, Romeo's ladylove joins in the sonneteering, using a strategy characteristic of Shakespeare's witty women: she reinterprets this bold stranger's metaphor so as to redirect his behavior, momentarily checking his most brash physical intimacies while maintaining the pleasures of verbal intercourse ("For saints have hands that pilgrims' hands do touch, / And palm to palm is holy palmers' kiss" [98–99]). What marks this sonnet as distinct from others in the play (most obviously the choral prologues to acts 1 and 2, but also several formal set-speeches within the narrative) is its bantering dialogue after the ritualized octet, capped by the shared split-line finale to a protracted quatrain:

> *Juliet* Saints do not move, though grant for prayers' sake.
> *Romeo* Then move not while my prayer's effect I take.
>   Thus from my lips, by thine, my sin is purged.
>   [*Kissing her.*]
> *Juliet* Then have my lips the sin that they have took.
> *Romeo* Sin from my lips? O trespass sweetly urged!
>   Give me my sin again.
>   [*Kissing her again.*]
> *Juliet*   You kiss by th' book.
> (1.5.104–9)

The book of Romeo's poetic training, if not his kissing manual, is clearly Petrarch; while the genre in which he versifies, as this movement to banter and action just as clearly signals, is drama. Conventional Petrarchan poetry was "a language compounded of hyperbole, more or less witty conceits, word-play, oxymorons and endless repetition, usually focused on the versifier's unrequited love (real or imagined) for a disdainful or otherwise unattainable mistress" (ed. 11). Romeo's earlier appearance in act 1 made obvious that he was in love not only with the unattainable cruel fair (at that moment one Rosaline, a Capulet who never appears onstage) but also with the fashionable courtly poetry of love—fashionable at Shakespeare's English court, as well as in his fictionalized "fair Verona (where we lay our scene)" (1.1.2). Having entered the play spouting a Petrarchan sestet, Romeo now calls out his tropes in honor of another lovely Capulet. The dramatic shift undermines his lyrical lines.

To recognize Romeo's amatory shiftiness does not automatically signify, however, that the style itself is either inflexible or the object of mockery. Petrarchism, the style derived from the sonnets addressed to Laura in the *Rime Sparse,* dominated western European lyrical practice during the sixteenth century.[1] Skillful poets imitated Petrarch's use of sonnet form and rhetorical tropes to represent struggles between heart and mind, desire and frustration, body and soul; lesser talents merely echoed the mannerisms. As Joseph Fucilla observes, "This literary mannerism soon became an object of ridicule, and the term 'Petrarchistic' acquired a derisive connotation because of it, undeservedly casting a pall of opprobrium upon the movement as a whole" (Preminger 613). Dismissals based on the mere presence of Petrarchism persist in twentieth-century dramatic criticism as well, even among those who recognize the complexity of staged poetry; S. L. Bethell used this criterion to pronounce *Romeo and Juliet* "not one of Shakespeare's best; he uses too freely the conventionally conceited manner of Petrarchan love poetry" (135; see also Baxter, Hibbard). Especially to a modern audience conditioned to distrust conventional, "unoriginal" speech as insincere, the self-consciously literary first conversation between Romeo and Juliet seems a signal for skepticism. In concert with Romeo's recent expression of infatuation with Rosaline, nearly identical in its form and conceit (cf. 1.2.88ff.), the exchange gives us reason to pause and wonder (as indeed Juliet wonders of Romeo) whether Shakespeare is toying with our hopes of true love. Harry Levin wittily observes that Romeo resolved to come to the feast carrying a torch, which "may have burned symbolically, but not for Juliet" ("Form" 3). But should our querulousness necessarily extend beyond reasonable doubts regarding the sincerity of a young lover, and evoke skepticism about the potential of Petrarchism to represent anything more than frivolousness onstage?

Because Romeo and Juliet have become the most famous of all young lovers, crossed by the stars more than themselves, most audiences may move quickly to delight in the wit and parrying, not caring for this scene's literary antecedents or its complex messages in context. Nevertheless, if we attend to that potential for distrust a moment longer, we confront an attitude that Shakespeare's drama makes part of its subject; an attitude, moreover, that has contributed to the general disregard for, and scholarly denigration of, some artful poetry by his less familiar contemporaries. What is it in the language of lips and hands, of rough and smooth, of love's pilgrims that so often suggests trifling indulgence? Some answers come obviously, and inspire the smiles that aptly accompany attention to the lyrics of many an ephemeral pop song; but others draw us into richer considerations of minds and cultures, of generic functions and gendered societies. Like the love of Romeo and Juliet, it gets serious fast. Richard Lanham remarks, *"Romeo and Juliet* depends on our seeing the Petrarchan rhetoric as such, else we will mistake the kind of play it is, a play where death authenticates the game" (142). And as with Romeo's death speech, which again invokes the tropes of Petrarchan sonneteering but in a tomb that transforms their meaning, when we look at the cultural stage on which such lyricism is performed, the perspective shift creates a rich and complex drama.[2]

Working inductively from the particulars of Elizabethan texts we will discover more artful significance than deductive (and reductive) judgments about court drama and amatory lyric might lead us to expect. This chapter introduces the method as well as the matter of *Passion Made Public* by analyzing the particulars of poetic representation as prologue and primary source for larger contextual judgments. Attention to the details of Romeo and Juliet's first exchange suggests several lines of inquiry applicable to the study of all lyrical drama: what is the significance of the gender positioning within this representation? what are the associations between gender and lyric poetry that influence our criticism of the representation? and what interpretive strategies do we employ when viewing this lyric poetry within a stage performance? The three subsequent introductory sections examine the assumptions that may inhibit or license our attempts to answer these questions.

Having outlined the motives and territory for exploration here, I then set forth to analyze the nexus of associations among gender, performance, and lyric operative within Elizabethan poetic drama. From this analysis emerges a pattern, a correlation between the specific uses of lyric poetry in performances and the claims and attitudes displayed within those performances regarding female authority and the rhetorical powers of the male poet. This associative pattern, moreover, has often been replicated uncritically in the critical history of Elizabethan lyric and drama, to the detriment of both our artistic appreciation and our cultural self-knowledge. These emergent patterns and the diverse performative capacities of Elizabethan lyric constitute the matter of *Passion Made Public*.

Wherefore Art Thou Lyrical?

Juliet's closing quip invoking "th'book" glances beyond young Montague's opportunistic facility with his pilgrim conceit to underscore her own formal participation as a rhymer in the courtly love game. It also indicates the exceptional significance and artistry of this literary exchange within Shakespeare's particular dramatic narrative. The sonnet's vocal mutuality clearly unites the lovers against the background noise of Capulet's ball; at the same time, Juliet's refusal to be seduced (both here and in the famous "balcony scene" [2.2]) by poetic borrowings alone, unsubstantiated by binding legal language to come in the form of a marriage oath, distinguishes this romance from a simple repetition of the courtly tradition.

During the sonnet, Romeo and Juliet coexist apart from the other Veronese in their own lyrical world of erotic infatuation. As lovers from warring families, the youths embody paradox and desire, the latter often in conflict with reason in Petrarchan sonnets. Within this play's narrative, however, the usual battle arguably is inverted, as they rebel against the *un*reasonableness of the Veronese feud, a political backdrop of obscurely motivated violence. Here the sonnet form epitomizes Shakespeare's complicated inversion of value, elevating the lovers above Tybalt (who "storms" to Capulet to bombast out a few lines of blank verse and some unmemorable couplets in anger at Romeo's intrusion) and Capulet (whose comically choppy blank verse dominates the exchange).[3] In contrast, the lovers' interplay of rhymes and Neoplatonic conceits makes them sound, if not exactly serious, all the more gentle, charming, and well-matched.

Although this lyrical vision corresponds with the scene's general celebration of harmony through song and dance, the lovers' exchange remains surreptitious, a half-successful gesture at a private, apolitical moment during the short respite (demanded by Prince Escales) from "civil" war. The other characters remain earthbound or bloody-minded, and the lovers will not appear together again in a public scene—not even in masks—while they live. Lyricism, then, is presented as an alternative discourse outside the political reality of Verona, an escape from its bloody force.

At the same time, Juliet's skeptical voice signals quite a different attitude from the escapism of traditional courtly love narratives, which usually involved illicit or unrealized desire. Unlike the invisible Rosaline, Juliet is both seen and heard, and her active presence as a woman in love transforms both sonnet and story. She initiates much of the plot's forward motion, most significantly demanding marriage instead of courtly love. This was not the universally expected response from a fair lady in sixteenth-century romance narratives, although the fictions of Spenser, Sidney, and Shakespeare himself were working to make it so: to make normative a coincidence between female desire and the patriarchal social structure of marriage. The idealization of marriage as a happy ending, a means of formal closure so familiar from Shakespeare's comedies and most subsequent western bourgeois romance, will of course be foiled in *Romeo and Juliet* by social corruption and violence, to produce the most popular of love tragedies. But that idealization remains intact. As in much public Tudor-Stuart drama, being able to choose the beloved man, rather than the arranged one, constitutes female rebellion; it is assuredly *not* a matter of preferring no marriage at all.

Yet, ironically, the lyric tradition of sonnets derived from courtly literature of extramarital desire—often sublimated but seldom leading to holy matrimony (Spenser's *Amoretti* being the exception that proves the rule). Moreover, the popularity of sonnetizing during the 1590s, which repeatedly spurred Shakespeare to represent this form onstage, was clearly connected with the courtly culture of Elizabeth Tudor, the Virgin Queen famously averse to wedded bliss. Is Shakespeare's use of the sonnet simply an extension of courtly lyricism into popular narrative so as to entertain the public theater audience, or is he appropriating, and even challenging, the virtues enshrined at court? Consider Romeo's invocation of Juliet as the sun:

> Arise, fair sun, and kill the envious moon,
> Who is already sick and pale with grief
> That thou, her maid, art far more fair than she.
> Be not her maid since she is envious,
> Her vestal livery is but sick and green
> And none but fools do wear it. Cast it off.
>
> (2.2.4–9)

Shakespeare seems to be creating a new goddess, in the likeness of a marriageable fourteen-year-old, to supplant the courtly worship of the aging Elizabeth as the moon goddess Cynthia. As Louis Adrian Montrose has explored, we certainly see the Faerie Queene in an odd light in *A Midsummer Night's Dream,* the comic counterpoint to this play ("Shaping"). In *Romeo and Juliet* we similarly seem to be witnessing some dramatic wit at the expense of the "cult" of virginity associated with a temperamental queen, whose standards of behavior so often made Cynthia's revels difficult for lovesick lords and ladies-in-waiting. Moreover, the very heart of this tragedy lies in the inability of the young lovers, trapped within the hostile court culture of Verona, to unite their private domain of amatory discourse with a public, legal assertion of their bond through marriage.

The pilgrim sonnet in *Romeo and Juliet* exemplifies just one case among many in which Elizabethan lyric discourse enriched, beautified, and complicated contemporary drama. In plays by George Peele and Christopher Marlowe that were more directly aimed at a court audience, and indeed in other Elizabethan plays by Shakespeare such as *Love's Labour's Lost,* lyricism functions variously; those plays raise issues similar to those cursorily suggested here, but imply quite distinct attitudes toward the relationships among courtly love, female sovereignty, and poetic authority. *Passion Made Public* reveals the significance of these artistic choices, focusing on the interrelations between the theatrical representation of lyric and the diverse, subtle social commentary dramatized on the Elizabethan stage.

Kenneth Muir boldly asserts that this "greatest period of the lyric coincided with the finest period of drama," and that "in no other period of our literature have so many good lyrics been written by so many different poets" (*Elizabethan* 41). Why did the Elizabethan period become the great age of verse drama? Leaving aside the vexations of literary evaluation for a moment, what did it mean, culturally and aesthetically, that an exceptional number of poets succeeded in writing both plays and lyric poems? Why did playwrights include lyrical poetry in their narrative dramas? And what was the network of relationships between such lyric poetry and its social contexts?

In addressing these sweeping questions, this book examines the intersections—rather than oppositions—of past and present, lyric and drama, public and private, art and politics, poetry and spectacle, and, especially, male and female. During the later sixteenth century, female political authority, a popular literary vogue, and professional theater interacted to develop a rhetoric and setting for love lyrics; this in turn expanded the meanings and horizons of such poetry. *Passion Made Public* conveys the vitality and complexity of this poetry because (especially though not entirely due to Shakespeare's legacy) it plays a major role in English-speaking culture, shaping and revealing historically based attitudes toward love, art, and women's agency.

Gendering the Subject

"Gender" and "genre" share the same etymology, from the Latin for "kind," "class," "birth," or "origin"; although they thus assert their naturalness (and hence their inevitability), both words refer to ways we choose to divide up our world in order to make sense of it. A central category in this book is gender, the cultural roles and associations accompanying the presumed biological difference of sex. When discussing lyricism predominantly in the Petrarchan, courtly love tradition, we find that issues of sexuality and power embrace; the resulting association between amatory lyric poetry and characterization of the feminine has had complex and enduring consequences. Another reason for emphasizing gender here is the important role of the queen as an audience for (and minor author of) lyric poetry. Not only was Elizabeth Tudor the first English queen to reign successfully and independently for a substantial length of time; she also played a direct role in the creation of a socially oriented lyric poetry.[4]

When Elizabeth ascended to the throne in 1558, her sex was a source of anxiety and amazement for most of her subjects; forty years later, it had become a source of mythology, in one of history's most successful cases of political image-making. Her sex had a widespread and obvious impact on courtly art, be it the cause for eulogy in *The Faerie Queene* or the cause for frustration in the Petrarchan poetry of Gascoigne or Ralegh. Yet the notion that Elizabeth played any significant role in altering the status of women, even within the aristocracy, has usually been dismissed because of her unique position as sovereign (an idea she promoted linguistically by blurring her own gender identity and stressing her exceptional role). The popular accounts of Tudor history resound with this truism; as Lady Antonia Fraser concludes, "Queen Elizabeth was not noted for her advancement of the female sex" (405). At the same time, many of the poems and dramas addressed to the queen by her male courtiers did in fact emphasize her "feminine" attributes as an aspect of her control over them. This transfer of a female realm of authority from the erotic and poetic into the public and political complicates the definition and terms of "power." To what extent did the artistic veneration of Elizabeth extend into a cultural recognition of value in what was perceived as "the feminine"? More particularly, what was implied by representing her power as being distinctively female, and did this rendering modify the theoretical content and borders of Tudor conceptions of "woman"?

Complementing several feminist and historicist studies, *Passion Made Public* analyzes the relationship between the queen's remarkable position as an unmarried woman and the artworks by men struggling to address and place her in relationship to men.[5] It is the specific interplay of lyrical performance with this gendered encounter that encourages a fresh regard for the rich complexity of amatory lyric and its social context. While it is true, as Nancy Vickers observes, that much erotic praise is "the product of men talking to men about women," "a legacy shaped predominantly by the male imagination for the male imagination" ("Heraldry" 209), at the court of Elizabeth much was also written directly for her as female audience and judge. The lyric convention of addressing one's beloved, an implied audience sometimes entirely fictional and sometimes not, was given weight and immediacy when poems were recited in performance before the official state ladylove. Scholars have recognized that women in the audience played a role, at least a small supporting one, in shaping representations of gender on the seventeenth-century public stage; if true there, how much more overtly so when a courtier such as George Gascoigne or George Peele wrote for his female sovereign.[6] This desire to address a particular audience obviously does not erase the playwright's own investment and mark in the collaborative cultural production, but surely complicates our reading of poetic voice and agency.

Thus when we look at court pageants and particular plays by Peele, Marlowe, and Shakespeare, the potential impact of the queen as audience demands attention alongside the characterization, both laudatory and critical, of queens, as these considerations intersect with lyric poetry. The explicit association of lyric poetry with exceptional female power, I propose, first encouraged its inclusion in theatrical fictions, yet also accounts in part for the mockery and diminution of such lyricism in England by uneasy courtiers and academic critics alike. As much as re-presenting the culture, lyrical drama commemorates what people thought they thought, what they wished they thought, what it pleased them to think. And whether or not she wished to do so, Elizabeth clearly provoked new and complicated thoughts about a woman's place.

Obviously, the conditions and fates of women is a vast topic requiring study from many angles, including the archival and material, and the view provided by preserved artworks is necessarily a tiny peephole; despite the limits in scope, it nevertheless furnishes a particularly intense and self-consciously manipulated perspective. Exploring gender representation in lyrical drama demands special attention not only to the artistic fiction-making involved in representing particular queens but also to the multiple aspects of queenship which made Elizabeth exceptional as a woman (including the spiritual and legal sovereign "body" which theoretically transcended femininity); nevertheless the conflicts and possibilities evoked by Elizabeth's human "body natural" were not lost on the artists of her day. Adapting the theory of the king's two bodies to a queen, as Theodora Jankowski (building on the insights of Marie Axton) has remarked, "did not resolve the sometimes rival claims of these bodies" (61). Plenty of tensions and paradoxes remained, providing material with which court authors grappled as they strove to celebrate their sovereign; their art in turn provided rich literary fodder for professional playwrights to reshape in addressing a wider public audience.

The complex representation of queens within certain Elizabethan performances also suggests the importance of attending to the more extensive issue of gendered subjectivity in male responses to Elizabeth's sovereignty. Carol Thomas Neely suggests we "over-read, . . . read to excess, the possibility of human (especially female) gendered subjectivity, identity and agency, the possibility of women's resistance or even subversion" ("Constructing" 15). If we do this knowingly and with a specific goal in mind, we will surely distort our gaze just as thoroughly as our cultural predispositions already skew it, and might well wonder if we should bother to pretend to be reading "another's" text at all. Behind this plea for excess in reading, however, lies the weight of a larger debate regarding the historically denigrated status of women as knowers. Seen in this context, Neely's comment calls attention to the need consciously to counter cultural assumptions, to read against the grain, if one is to see and hear those who have traditionally been excluded from agency and power.

Some of the most influential theorists of the subject in an ideological framework, such as Althusser and Foucault, "are either unconcerned with gender or unable to conceive of a female subject" (de Lauretis 19). Even those whose theories are politically radical often presume the possibility only of a masculine subject (a few, including some subgroups of feminists, do so consciously, regarding the very concept of the subject as bound inextricably with "Eurocentric," "phallocentric" thought). One result of this assumption, observable in several new historicist studies of early modern England, has been to focus scholarly attention on the rebellious (male) courtier's resistance to the hegemonic power of the court system headed by a (female) sovereign, as a desperate gesture at freedom for the subject. As soon as one attends to gender more than parenthetically, the limitations of such analysis become clear. More ironically, those with the expressed desire to scrutinize the constraints created by male dominance sometimes end up replicating the erasure of female subjectivity, because of their exclusive focus on the perceived limitations of the masculine position.[7] Prominent new historicists have now begun to address the possible reductiveness in their methods, as well as the need for emphasis on the complex and variable relationships between society and texts, culture and poetics. The multiple connotations of the word "subject" illuminate these relationships; they move us beyond a single political model for situating the sovereign and the subject representing her, and for evaluating the significance of that representation. As a woman denied full subjectivity but as a sovereign its source for others, Elizabeth was often the subject matter of artwork by her political subjects. By attending to the verbal and conceptual complications of subjectivity, we can more adequately place the text, its author, and its audience within culture, as well as more fully accounting for the tensions and shifts within the scripts of lyrical plays.[8]

Supplementing a historical setting of these plays within a "public" political paradigm with readings that are indebted to theorists who foreground gender allows the truth each model reveals to put pressure on the others. Feminist film criticism offers useful terms for countering a monolithic concept of social power, in its analysis of the relationships between the visual object of the gaze and the viewer as subject (as explored in chapters 2 and 3). Similarly, feminist poetic analysis investigates how authors employ literary tropes and traditions as subject matter, primarily through a strategy of negotiation that allows them to "respond to the assumptions encoded into dominant cultural forms and systems of representation" (Jones 2). These complementary analytic emphases help to reveal the dynamic complexity of defining power and privileged positions in dramatic performance, and help to demonstrate how Elizabethan lyrical drama sometimes innovatively, sometimes anxiously represents female authority. The book's conclusion considers the legacy of these representations, particularly emphasizing the tensions between Shakespeare's incorporation of female desire in comic plots culminating in marriage, and the defiantly virginal image of England's Elizabeth. The repeated juxtaposition of Shakespeare and Elizabeth in nineteenth- and twentieth-century history and drama, both as intimates and as competitors, becomes more comprehensible when viewed as the intersection of different versions of authority; many authors clearly have felt the need to reconceive the relationship between these two emblems of Britain's glory in ways consonant with subsequent artistic, political, and sexual values.

This gendered image-making complicates historicist analysis of the politics of sovereignty and subjectivity, and exposes the false choice between romanticizing monarchy and romanticizing rebellion. When looking at a popular queen and much-venerated artists, deciding who is the subject and which view has been dominant depends mostly on the angle of analysis (literary, political, religious, historical). There is no obvious, unchanging "injustice" played out, but instead a drama of competing interests. Hence drama, as a literary and performative form, provided an ideal forum in which to represent these cultural concerns, and provides an ideal genre for us to examine in pursuit of greater historical and aesthetic understanding.

Theater is always and in all aspects collaborative, even when some participants wish it were otherwise. As playwrights often discover to their disgruntlement, theirs is not the only perspective enacted; in a sense they are not the only "author." Lyrical dramas "produced" by male poets, then, reveal both the possibilities and the limits inherent in their perspective, even as regards their own works in performance. *Passion Made Public* thus looks carefully at the texts of men who can gender subjectivity as exclusively male only in their imaginations (if there), and explores those texts as partial signs of a larger cultural collaboration in which they play one rich part. Without trying to find rose-colored glasses, one can remove the blue shades that sometimes characterize traditional scholarship; one can experiment with troublesome but useful bifocals. This helps us to examine the interplay between author and patron, between author and audience, and between male courtiers and a female sovereign, without automatically identifying with only one side.

A quick look at a relevant new historicist essay about George Gascoigne (who will figure prominently in the next chapter) may clarify my stress on the need for a complicated balance, and my assertion that even much excellent contemporary scholarship overtly sympathizes with male authorial rebelliousness. Richard McCoy, a creative and thoughtful reader, published one of the best and most influential articles on Gascoigne in 1985 (after his study of Sir Philip Sidney entitled *Rebellion in Arcadia,* and before his book on thwarted would-be warriors at Elizabeth's court, *The Rites of Knighthood*); he entitled it "Gascoigne's '*Poëmata castrata*': The Wages of Courtly Success."

The Italian phrase, drawn from a preface to Gascoigne's collection *The Posies*, is used by McCoy to signify the poet's gradual loss "of his virility and poetic authority" (49)—two terms repeatedly linked in this piece. In McCoy's view, the author's decline resulted in large part from his catering to an audience, and a female one in particular. The titular phrase, which the poet announces as borrowed from a distinguished Italian author (hence carrying a typically ironic claim to shared authority, despite its literal anxiety), refers to Gascoigne's censoring by divines and other readers, and the "gelding" is limited to the author's expurgation of some "filthie phrases." Although McCoy concedes the phrase is "hyperbolic" (32), he then applies it to Gascoigne's later work in its entirety. The hero is the struggling poet, the villain becomes the royal court. That court is of course run by a woman; moreover, it is Elizabeth (not the divines and gentlemen who actually criticized and perhaps censored Gascoigne's published work) who rhetorically frames McCoy's article, smothering the artist. She appears in the opening discussion of the Kenilworth pageants to mock and disturb the poet (although McCoy admits that she treated Gascoigne kindly—it was his own indecorous action that "clearly shattered his authorial composure and control" [29]); and she returns in the article's final lines to symbolize his ultimate humiliation: "he remains there, fawning below the Queen's powerful mace and yearning for the security of weakness. Courtly success had its rewards, but the costs to Gascoigne's self-esteem and art were also palpable" (52). The equation of male self-esteem and artistry is explicit, and the fear of female power could not be more overtly rendered: the critic appears to assume that we will share feelings of pity at seeing this man "below" a woman as she wields the phallic symbol of sovereignty.[9] Creative autonomy and completeness being gendered masculine, it comes as no surprise that Gascoigne is represented as having a chance "to become his own man again, free to speak his own voice" only when he tries to return from the court to a male patron, Lord Grey (48). The syntax makes it unclear whether Gascoigne alone or McCoy as well assumes that servitude in the employ of a man is less degrading.

This description shares the language and assumptions of much literary criticism, both in its preoccupation with the poet's "strength" (an emphasis converted into theory by Harold Bloom, whom Elizabeth Bruss [312] called "the Norman Mailer of our speculative prose") and in its deep empathy with the poet's masculine identity. Without in any way denying the frightening power of an early modern sovereign, one may find the critical replication of horror at a woman controlling the poet just as "disturbing" (32) as McCoy finds the threat of (safely metaphorical) emasculation. A frontispiece in which Gascoigne kneels before his monarch—for a marginal gentleman, a position of some honor—becomes a psychodrama in which he "confronts his Queen, as F.J. does his mistress, armed with pen and sword"; "by displaying tokens of poetic and martial potency he sought [*sic*] to forestall threats of emasculation and debasement" (47).[10]

This is not a matter of searching for a momentary lapse or an ambiguous line taken out of context. The tendency to adopt a male poet's or male character's perspective—even in recent historicist work of such a sophisticated and insightful kind as McCoy's—suggests the continuing need to supplement such a perspective with one more attuned to the ironies and complexities of gendered subjectivity.[11] Simply noticing gendered representation is not enough; indeed, as in this article, it may reinforce stereotypical images if unaccompanied by a self-consciously "roving eye" on the subject.

To take the queen seriously as a female audience is to see the intersection of stereotype and exception, and of politics and poetry. Catherine Gallagher, discussing the historical development of the concept of the female subject, remarks that "It is an odd but indisputable fact that the seventeenth-century women whom we think of as the forerunners and founders of feminism were, almost without exception, Tories" (24). Identification with the fantasy of absolute power may have provided one basis for advancing the female self; women turned from a "*roi*" to a "*moi*" *absolu*. If such thoughts could be prompted among those loyal to the Stuarts, it is hardly farfetched to posit that with Elizabeth on the throne, a few women may have momentarily realized that at least in one sense *le roi, c'est moi;* some men certainly worried about it. Viewing the sovereign as a static symbol of repression alone, and the court by extension as a place of untempered, bad-faith groveling and cringing, effectively and falsely removes these complications of gender or else views them solely from the male courtier's perspective. This in no way denies the importance of class analysis (indeed, it is an awareness of class and social hierarchies that makes the image of Gascoigne kneeling before Elizabeth something besides a man below a woman), nor does one thereby excuse or legitimate repression because the royal torturer happens to be female. Those who emphasize the aristocratic self-interest in courtly love literature, such as Frank Whigham and Leonard Tennenhouse, have brought a legitimate concern to light.[12] My purpose here is to complement these concerns and the work of those who look at the lives of the less "exceptional," by re-viewing the subjects and objects of poetry with an eye attentive to the representation and fate of the powerful female.

Re-viewing the Critical History

This task is particularly pressing when the literary category under analysis is love lyric. A long heritage endures, of trivializing lyric precisely because of its association with "the feminine"—even given the stereotyped and limited representation of women therein. To modify a cliché, all this leaves the poetry between a Medusa and a soft place. The next chapter presents some examples of Elizabethan raillery aimed at songs and sonnets (often directed at amateur aristocrats and "poetasters" by those struggling in the new profession of author); a longer critical heritage of such insults also persists. Sometimes the very enterprise of praising a beloved woman is attacked, as if such writing transferred her perceived unworthiness or weakness to the male poet. More often, stereotypically "feminine" adjectives are used to bury art, "masculine" ones to praise it. Just a few examples suffice to capture the tone. Ben Jonson is characteristically forthright and witty in deprecating the "feminine" aesthetic: "Others there are, that have no composition at all; but a kind of tuneing, and riming fall, in what they write. It runs and slides, and onely makes a sound. Womens-*poets* they are call'd: as you have womens-*taylors.* 'They write a verse, as smooth, as soft, as creame; / In which there is no torrent, nor scarce streame.' You may sound these wits, and find the depth of them, with your middle finger. They are *creame-bowl,* or but puddle deepe" (*Timbre,* in Herford and Simpson 585). Carew's elegy for John Donne praises the poet's "manliness" explicitly; not only was Donne the husband of poetry but he "Committed holy Rapes upon our Will" as he "[drew] a line / of masculine expression" (388–90). Similarly, in looking back at their English predecessors Wordsworth sought a "manly" style while Coleridge praised Shakespeare's "will" and "force" (Holmes et al. 202, 222). In one of the more amusing passages from his lectures on Shakespeare, as summarized by his student Collier, Coleridge seems to become excited with his own analogy: "The Wit of Shakespeare was like the flourishing of a man's stick when he is walking along in the full flow of animal spirits. It was a sort of overflow of hilarity, which disburdened us, and seemed like a conductor to distribute a portion of our joy to the surrounding air by carrying it away from us. . . . He would now proceed to a most serious charge against our Poet, which was that of indecency and immorality" (Foakes 72). The ejaculatory fantasy suggested by this "man's stick" comically undermines Coleridge's abrupt shift to a moral defense, though still serving the critic's desire to associate the poet with (properly sublimated) "manliness."

Among twentieth-century critics, these inherited associations of gender and genre recur, sometimes in unexpected and perhaps unintended ways. Despite his own sympathetic attention to poetry by women, Yvor Winters's influential notion of "serious" lyrics as expressed in "Aspects of the Short Poem in the English Renaissance" tends to exclude those directed toward women as audience, in favor of those poems which ignore or reject women: Sidney's sonnets to Stella show "his incurable tendency to softness in diction" and "charming triviality," whereas his renunciations of earthly love are better, the "most serious of his sonnets." Winters finds that authors with a "Petrarchan polish," including Spenser, write poetry that "lacks weight," "intellectual substance," and "moral grandeur"—unwittingly echoing Renaissance criticisms about the nature of women (29–34). In discussing the "plain style in love," Winters regards the object of "unaffected" aspersion in Sir Thomas Wyatt's "Blame not my lute" to be an "affected lady," although he notes elsewhere that the lover might seem arrogant from the lady's perspective (10–11). The moral themes cited in "good" serious poems are "the faithlessness of women" and "the vanity and heartlessness of women," whereas the courtly sonnets praising women are viewed here as mindless, empty, and, repeatedly, "trivial" (8).

The association of things soft and fluid with femininity obviously survives, rewritten as praiseworthy by theorists of *l'écriture féminine* but also persisting as a source of male fear and female victimization. Nor have "sentimental" and "strong" become gender-free terms in our culture at large. Of course, many "feminine" styles and forms, like "lady scribblers" themselves, historically have been spurned—the former even or especially by liberal partisans of social change for women, such as Mary Wollstonecraft.[13] While such labels have been applied to different works at different times, as society's definitions of gendered attributes shift, the association of English Petrarchist lyric poetry with the feminine was clear in the sixteenth century and has endured, both as descriptive of its presumed audience and its subject matter and as a means of derogation. "Effeminate" Petrarchism has sometimes been opposed to the moral rectitude of "plain stylists" (an influential critical category, including Donne, Ralegh, Jonson, and Greville—at least three of whom usually wrote in a manner far from any layperson's conception of "plain"). "Strong lines," masculine force, austerity, stoicism, and anti-Petrarchist satire are often perceived to be more mature, realistic, and serious. Perhaps we all want to be—like Gascoigne in the frontispiece with his sword unsheathed?—on the "cutting edge." The consequent ironies can be amusing (given manly Sir "Water" Ralegh's fluidly oceanic worship of Elizabeth as Cynthia, for example, in a poem often obscure but nevertheless firmly located within the Petrarchan tradition); nevertheless, many modern scholarly judgments do indeed follow in the spirit of many English courtiers and poets. They chafe against what is perceived to be an "unnatural" and (in the pejorative sense) "artificial" situation regarding gender and power in Petrarchism, an inversion of "mastery."

The same legacy of discounting courtly love lyricism for its effeminacy permeates drama and its criticism. Coleridge tried to determine the chronological order of Shakespeare's plays on the assumption that only a young man would focus on love poetry, thus inaccurately separating the stylistically linked, lyrically influenced plays written in the mid-1590s. He relies on their increasingly critical representations of Petrarchist eros to locate them across three major categories: "Youthful Plays" (including *Love's Labour's Lost* and *Romeo and Juliet*), "Manly Plays" (including *A Midsummer Night's Dream*) and finally "Mature Plays" (into which he uneasily fit *The Merchant of Venice* as well the tragedies and romances). Despite this cautionary example, Shakespeare's perennially successful lyrical plays of the mid-1590s are still labeled "immature" by many, although written after at least seven other successful plays.[14] Tales of revenge, love turned to hate, war, and masculine empire-building bestride the theatrical world like a Colossus, like Atlas upholding the Globe. Love comedies and court mythology remain diversions, and even an extremely popular tragedy such as *Romeo and Juliet* is frequently found wanting, its tonal mixture deemed improper. There are many reasons for these appraisals, and all is not reducible to the role of gender bias; nevertheless, the disposition to trivialize does go with the feminine territory. Critical attempts to address this oddity understandably turn to "serious" contexts outside the plays (cultural rituals, political subtexts) to argue for their dramatic significance. *Passion Made Public* considers these contexts, but also concentrates on the dramatic "framing" of lyrical verse within the play—its elevation or trivialization by the poet-playwright, the metaphors and adjectives associated with it—as a crucial part of the story, another matter for serious reflection. Taking seriously Stephen Greenblatt's term "cultural *poetics*" (emphasis added), we can learn much by attending to those poetic details within literary representation that differentiate various uses of lyricism within Elizabethan courtly drama.

The particular possibilities and limits of Petrarchism were not lost on Elizabethan poet-playwrights. "Language most shewes a man: speake that I may see thee," wrote Ben Jonson in his *Timbre, or Discoveries* (Herford and Simpson 625). In the comedies of Jonson and his contemporaries, verbal style often revealed character in an obvious, exaggerated way. Petrarchan "poetasting," the use of this fashionable mode of discourse by would-be courtiers, was a popular target for mockery on the Elizabethan stage, from Shakespeare's Proteus through Jonson's Bobadil to his Sir Amorous La Foole. The stereotype of the shallow, "simpering" Petrarchan lover (to borrow an insult from Shakespeare's Rosalind in *As You Like It*) has encouraged modern scholars of drama to be dismissive of all such speakers on sight.[15]

Yet as Ben Jonson himself dramatized, what we "see" through speech is more often a shadowy refraction than a transparent reflection of a character's intention, personality, or significance. Love poetry that at first glance appears only the idle amusement of literate courtiers may become the site of something more, a game with many cultural and aesthetic functions. The very popularity of that game undermines the monolithic interpretation of its meaning. Moreover, because this courtly love situation presumed the reversal of standard gender roles (the man becoming — at least superficially and temporarily — his beloved's "servant"), sometimes disdain for staged Petrarchism on aesthetic grounds appears to veil other anxieties; during the reign of a female monarch who manipulated erotic language for political ends, such unease could become particularly acute.

Even critics who have seemed sympathetic to Elizabethan courtly lyricism hardly present untroubled support for those analyzing its gender dynamics and associations. C. S. Lewis's magisterial praise for the Elizabethan "Golden Age" is deeply embedded in a discourse of imperialism and privilege, whose highest praise is to laud and "enrich the very meanings of the words *England* and *Aristocracy*" (Lewis 1).[16] It likewise replicates much of the gendered subtext to that discourse. In his refreshingly direct way, Lewis remarks with approval that the golden poet plays "the strong, simple music of the uncontorted line" and fills the poem "with all that is naturally delightful — with flowers and swans, with ladies' hair, hands, lips, breasts, and eyes, with silver and gold, woods and waters, the stars, the moon and the sun." Nevertheless, "Honey cloys and men seek for drier and more piquant flavours" (65). More explicitly, in countering the common complaint that Samuel Daniel's exquisite lines are vacuous, Lewis marshals manliness; Daniel "can at times achieve the same masculine and unstrained majesty which we find in Wordsworth's greatest sonnets" (530). But Lewis's primary strategy for exalting golden poetry — and not just sonnets but also stage lyricism — is to make explicit the gap between fiction and fact, Neoplatonic idealization and actual sexual relations:

> Most of the Golden poetry was not primarily intended to reflect the actual world or to express the personality of the poet. Shakespeare himself might well have agreed with Professor Stoll that his great heroines are not such women as we [*sic*] may ever hope to meet. The poets of that age were full of reverence—for Gods, for kings, for fathers, for authority—but not of our reverence for the actual. Fortune (which in some contexts we call "history") was a blind hussy, a strumpet. To adorn external Nature with conceits and mythical personifications was as legitimate as to tie a ribbon round the neck of one's own kitten . . . ; for we are of a higher birth than nature and her masters by divine right. (Lewis 322)

Obviously discrepancies existed in Elizabethan culture between fantasy and experience, and in a broader historical context feminist critics such as Theweleit and Vickers have vividly stressed the potential for degradation of actual women that may interweave with erotic praise in fiction. Nevertheless, Lewis's reduction of all such idealized representations of women to a study in distance ignores other possible functions, including images of empowerment apparent to later women writers and readers.[17] Lewis's plural subject is of course male, and female figures range from the poet's self-created "celestial mistress" to a "hussy, a strumpet" (by implication, more like the "actual" women one meets)—with feminized nature, undeniably "actual" but needing control, duly trivialized by comparison to a domestic and immature pet.

More recently, specific debates about subjectivity and Petrarchan poetics have complicated readings of Renaissance love sonnets, though not always in ways that decenter these assumptions about what constitutes poetic seriousness and worth. Reinterpretations attentive to gender tend to emphasize the absence of an active female poetic presence rather than the possibilities for female empowerment in the address to and representation of the beloved. In Petrarch, John Freccero argues, the laurel is an emblem of a mirror relationship based on "the poetic lady created by the poet, who in turn creates him as poet laureate," and of the circularity which "forecloses all referentiality" with "self-contained dynamism." Corresponding to the sin of idolatry, this poetic strategy makes the reified sign an object of worship; whereas signs are allegorical, pointing to an absence which implies significance yet to come, idols desperately attempt to render presence and evade temporality by realizing significance in the here and now. Freccero argues that "in order to create an autonomous universe of autoreflexive signs without reference to an anterior logos—the dream of almost every poet since Petrarch—it is necessary that the thematic of such poetry be equally autoreflexive and self-contained." Moreover, the "idolatrous love for Laura, however self-abasing it may seem, has the effect of creating a thoroughly autonomous portrait of the poet who creates it" (27). For Petrarch, "The exterior quest has become an internal obsession" (28). Seen in this light, the subjectivity Joel Fineman stressed in Shakespeare's sonnets is yet another strategy, within the Petrarchan poetic tradition, for wresting authority away from social "self-fashioning" and external agents, an assertion of fractured and unidealized self-mastery impossible at court.[18]

Feminist rereadings, denying the legitimacy of Petrarchism's association with the feminine while sharing Freccero's emphasis on the poetry's narcissistic self-enclosure, have also encouraged a negative view of amatory lyricism onstage. The idealized lady becomes merely a linguistic trope, her possible referentiality inconsequential and her specter delusive. Barbara Bono calls Orlando's impulse to lyric in *As You Like It* a "pathology" which can lead to misogyny ("Mixed" 201), while Sara Eaton castigates this "rhetoric of Courtly Love" as a cause of tragedy in her analysis of Middleton and Rowley's *Changeling* (238). Like Bono, Eaton draws on the rich observations of Nancy Vickers, who rightly called attention to strategies of domination and dispersement of the female body in Petrarch's lyrics; her essays astutely analyze the blazon's attempt to overmaster its putative object of praise. Mark Breitenberg similarly invokes Vickers's analysis to discredit significant variety in the dynamics of masculine desire over the course of *Love's Labour's Lost,* despite obvious poetic shifts and the reversal in the direction of that desire vis-à-vis women (not to mention the attitudes directly expressed toward them).[19] Vickers's feminist critique, while powerful in itself and helpful in considering the psychosocial effects of poetic speech, is often used automatically and exclusively to label all courtly love rhetoric as misogynist and homosocial; this submerged formalist attack comes from a very different position than the earlier tradition of masculinist criticism, but it sometimes carries similarly dismissive consequences for the poetry. The blazon, after all, is but one important feature of Petrarch's influential lyric practice. It is true that Petrarchism could serve as a defensive weapon against obscure objects of desire, a way to further objectify the threat of an Other through a rhetorical "*sparagmos*"; it is also true that in England, and not just in Faerieland, Petrarchan idealism sometimes reinforced concepts other than misogyny—including the legitimacy of some forms of female political power. By looking at a number of texts with some care, I hope to counter the tendency toward blanket condemnation of Petrarchism at first sight (no matter which interpretive school is served), favoring an approach more sensitive to the diversity and variation of courtly love tropes onstage.[20] Like any popular mode of expression, the rhetoric of courtly lyric was molded variously; indeed, this capacity for play and adaptation was a crucial factor in its popularity in many media during the 1580s and 1590s.

More sweepingly, the valid and laudable desire to include women's stories in fields other than the romance (the "erotic plot," as Miller and Heilbrun call it) has led to some feminist devaluation of conventional love poetry. Yet in dismissing the erotic plot and its lyric expression, one loses many of the positive images of women's agency in early modern imaginative literature. "Good" women are, if not entirely erased, most often reduced to ideologically proper silence or removed to religious pedestals far from the earthly realms of social power. Furthermore, the alternative poetic attitudes toward women represented in male-authored drama are often more disturbing and demeaning than Petrarchan excess; they range from Mercutian mockery to abuse and threats of physical violence. In Shakespeare's *Two Gentlemen of Verona,* when Proteus's courtly wooing (including the arrangement of troubadours to sing "Who is Sylvia?") fails, his subsequent "strategy" in the woods is attempted rape. To label such voices and acts of masculine aggression as merely the reaction caused by Petrarchan idealization is too simple and often unsupported by narrative or dramatic context; it resembles antifeminist arguments blaming the women's movement for backlash and violence against women. This is not to deny that modern poets and inheritors of the Petrarchan legacy should be skeptical and critical of it. But given that such impoverished dichotomies constituted the prevailing attitudes toward "the woman's part" in Renaissance ideology and art, Petrarchan lyricism hardly seems the villain of the piece, nor the proper first object for dismissal when looking at art in its historical context.

The dramatic uses of courtly love rhetoric are too various and complex to be equated with a single social position; this does not mean, however, that *Passion Made Public* is any less involved in the intellectual task of women's studies and cultural criticism than are these feminist critiques and comparable material historicist ones. While we, like Shakespeare's female impersonators onstage, may recognize the falseness of much "sugared" lyric, we may still discover that it could be a locus of female influence and voicing (the queen herself penned at least one such lyric, and as a youth had employed a Petrarchan simile when urgently petitioning her brother the king).[21] Most specifically, Elizabeth's monarchy suggested to women as well as men that the lyric could participate in public realms of discourse, and hence that the erotic and the socially ambitious were not mutually exclusive categories. At least at this historical moment and provisionally, we may beneficially supplement the critiques of Petrarchan self-enclosure with some attention to Petrarchan lyric's mixed possibilities for female representation on the stage. To take Petrarchan lyric and lyrical drama seriously is one way of taking the absence or presence of women in art seriously, for these were literary works in which early modern women counted, as much as they ever could on earth—in the erotic plot and the lyric mode.[22]

Locating the Language: What's in a Lyric?

> Western wind, when will thou blow?
> The small rain down can rain,—
> Christ, if my love were in my arms
> And I in my bed again!
>
> (Hebel and Hudson 42)

The anonymous sixteenth-century lyric "Western Wind" is a poem whose tensions and balance—between longing and restraint, bodily desire and referential abstraction, observation and emotion, landscape and inscape—match Romantic notions about what lyric does, notions seemingly self-evident because they still dominate our ideas of this genre. Thus "Western wind" often becomes the starting point for a history of the English lyric (as well as the title of an anthology of lyrics), and attention focuses on those poems leading neatly from it to Keats, Dickinson, and Stevens. We may take its artfulness for granted, while dismissing other, more alien examples of short poetry as failed or trivial. In this book, I therefore highlight the immediate social performance of Elizabethan lyric poetry, often excluded from lyric analysis in the Romantic-New Critical tradition. In the process, I also reexamine some familiar verses and their conventions, in a context that should extend their resonance and significance.

In a recent overview of English lyric written for Methuen's *Critical Idiom* series, David Lindley nicely summarizes many of the attempts and problems in defining lyric, concluding with an appeal for scholars to be historically specific in using the term, while acknowledging the impossibility of restricting the use of such a popular word (especially in its adjectival form) in general use.[23] In the next chapter, I survey Elizabethan conceptions of lyric and scrutinize a selection of lyrics which carried sociopolitical messages during the first twenty years of Elizabeth's reign, sometimes at odds with contemporaneous critical pronouncements. But as a preface, it may be helpful to list here a number of the basic assumptions about lyric poetry still current in post-Romantic culture. Among the commonplaces familiar to students of literature are: a lyric is a short poem, usually in the first person (interpreted as the author or as a persona); lyric poetry explores the private emotions and experiences of the speaker; lyric poetry is about language, a self-referential and enclosed world; it attempts to slow down the experience of time; it derives from and tries to approximate music; lyrics are the words of a song; a lyric is love poetry; it evokes the beautiful, the transcendent, the imaginary, rather than being constrained by the earthly and particular; lyric poetry is not narrative; lyric poetry is not dramatic; lyric poetry is not political. Obviously not all these statements are totally compatible, but all have some critical weight.

Many of these assumptions were shared in the Renaissance, such as the linkage with song or musicality; this connection dates back to Pindar and the earliest known Greek lyricists, and remains the most vital association in our popular culture. Indeed, the title of this book is borrowed from M. H. Abrams's discussion of such musicality in Romantic criticism, music "constituting the very pulse and quiddity of passion made public" and hence useful in attempts "to define and illustrate the nature of poetry, particularly of the lyric, but also of poetry in general" (50–51). But a number of the other descriptions (especially those concerning privacy and the sublime) derive from the practice and observations of later poets, most notably the turn-of-the-nineteenth-century arguments of Wordsworth and Coleridge, and the reactions they provoked. Not surprisingly, some of their assumptions run counter to earlier practice. Most problematic (then as now) are the negative definitions of lyric. Given that lyric poetry appears on the Elizabethan stage and at court, the enduring beliefs that it is necessarily "antidramatic" and that it rises "above" politics seem anachronistic; the notion that "true lyric" was antithetical to narrative, when applied to the great age of sonnet sequences, can lead to verbal shell games.[24]

In *The Rhetoric of Romanticism,* the provocative Paul de Man asserted that "no lyric can be read lyrically" (261). Current scholars of early modern literature are once more situating texts within a historical framework. Annabel Patterson finds in Ben Jonson's *Under-wood* a lyricism that "is always a sociopolitical construct, a product of its relations; especially in its declarations of independence, and especially in its silences" ("Lyric" 153). By allowing Elizabethan lyric poetry similar complexity in its negotiations between a single "voice" and the social world informing it, we will see emerge a rich relationship between such poetry and the dramatic world in which it is represented. And by resisting the desire to construct concrete boundaries (between lyric and other discourse, between the theatrical stage and the monarch's court) where they did not exist for Elizabethans, we will discern similarly potent interactions among diverse texts, within a cultural matrix headed by an iron maiden.

Generic labels often distinguish only a "family resemblance"—with all the difficulties in definition that metaphor implies (see Miner, in Lewalski 22). The lyrical discourse I examine is for the most part explicitly concerned with love and sexuality. It could also qualify in the often amorphous categorization of lyric as "musical," in the sense of being either mellifluous or capable of musical setting.[25] If not self-contained poems inserted within larger poetic frameworks, the passages are recognizable as lyrical "set pieces": they include refrains and stylistic differences from their linguistic surroundings, tropes and topics of an identifiable lyric tradition, and/or allusions to known lyric poems. These poems and passages participate in a specific literary tradition, very much influenced by familiarity with the love poetry of Petrarch and Ovid. While *Passion Made Public* is not confined to an analysis of Petrarchism per se, it does concentrate on the stage rhetoric of courtly love partially generated by this poetic movement. As will become even more apparent in the specific readings to come, various attitudes about gender are played out through this fashionable discourse, and permeate the critical history of lyrical drama.

Sometimes (though not always) related to assumptions about gender is the premise of a split between private and social realms, between the transcendent imagination and political drudgery, which informs much Romantic and modern thought about the artist. "What," lamented Samuel Taylor Coleridge, "was the favour of a Queen or a Court to such a man as Lord Bacon but mere harlotry?" (Foakes 66). Ironically, such a split appears to be more a product than a precondition of Elizabethan literature, as the example of Shakespeare's *Romeo and Juliet* implies and as will be more fully argued in the final chapter. The overemphasis on this binary opposition as static and irrevocable has until recently impeded, and in the particular case of lyric poetry still impedes, exploration of some of the most interesting questions about Elizabethan literature.[26] Therefore "Elizabethan Contexts," as well as illustrating the ambiguousness of such discrete categories in the lyric practice of George Gascoigne, highlights important sites of generic and ideological interaction in performance: the blurred lines between ritual and drama and between lyrical fiction and political commentary, especially in Tudor pageantry.

My analysis of these artistic intersections also raises a distinct though related concern, seemingly perennial to discussions of (and meditations in) lyric form: the role and meaning of its temporality. Changing Elizabethan ideas about stage time and representation notwithstanding, the techniques of lyric poetry in the art of that period often work to imitate stasis or altered time. But instead of conceptualizing static lyric and narrative drama as opposing forms (only conceivable within a discourse that tends to think of them as *abstract* forms),[27] it may be more helpful to borrow a strategy from Roman Jakobson and imagine them as two axes on a graph: to exploit familiar associations, the horizontal axis could stand for narrative, a forward impulsion over time inherent to performing arts; the vertical axis could stand for the lyric impulse, which the poet Jorie Graham has called "transcendence—the vertical burn" (154). Her association is shared by most who think about genre at all: lyric aspires to get out of earthly time while narrative remains immersed in recording the world in flux. This is analogous to the contrast in Christian theology between *kairos,* the moment of ecstatic contact with God and the eternal, and *chronos,* the time charted by calendars and clocks (see Tayler's *Milton's Poetry*). If we can retain the idea of stasis or "slowed time" without automatically assuming transcendence beyond the physical, this description can capture one distinctive aspect of powerful lyric art. The actual verse in a lyrical drama, then, would create a serpentine line, at times pushing almost to horizontal flatness, at others arching up toward a self-consciously lyrical moment imitating stasis or atemporality. This picture, even though still somewhat reliant on modern conventions about the temporality of lyric and drama, can help us to begin conceptualizing lyrical drama not as a "mutation" (W. R. Johnson's term [149]), nor as "immature" drama, nor as "impure form"—at least not in any negative sense—but as its own "kind," a genre, of shapely (though not necessarily schematically organized) art. Such graphing also allows us to see the intersection of the two categories of representation in fact involved in poetic drama without becoming mired in debates as to which medium is primary (that is, whether such art is defined as a subset of literature or a subset of performance); it represents the tension between two trajectories without positing generic warfare, the win-lose mentality familiar in much scholarship by performance theorists and literary theorists alike.[28]

In the courtly scripts of George Peele, Christopher Marlowe, and William

Shakespeare, lyricism functions variously and beautifully. Attending to the differentiating categories of time, place, and especially gender, the largest portion of this book examines three paradigmatic plays to unveil the motives and resonance of lyric poetry onstage. In his *Arraignment of Paris* Peele asserts the triumph of a social language and chastened lyricism, an assertion clearly and directly rejected by Marlowe in *Dido, Queen of Carthage*. These two tales of Troy, moreover, connect the fate of poetic language quite directly with the fortunes of queenship and the representation of female agency, as if lyric's potency were incumbent upon female sovereignty on earth. Modifying this polarity, *Love's Labour's Lost* dramatizes a tension prevalent throughout Shakespeare's "lyrical period": the playwright adapts and incorporates the opposed stances of Peele and Marlowe to create a drama in which lyricism and its mockery compete within a social world of troubled patriarchy. Shakespeare represents his powerful female speakers as skeptical of Petrarchist discourse, even as he removes that discourse from the public domain of efficacious political exchange. A fascinating and consistent correspondence emerges between the formal functions of love lyric within these dramas and the attitudes toward female figurations of power within their fictional representations. At the same time, as the concluding chapter documents, the associations within these plays reverberate well beyond their particular age and art form to create a powerful, delightful, and in some ways disturbing legacy.

All these plays both employ and comment on the Renaissance tradition of courtly love poetry; to the extent they are Ovidian or especially Petrarchan, it is not a mere quirk but a complex borrowing that transforms the tradition and functions distinctively within the play's narrative fiction. In closely reading these works by outstanding poet-playwrights, one need not reify what Paul Alpers calls the "domain of lyric," or other literary spaces, as truly "outside" their culture; but neither need one deny the enduring power of certain artworks or their careful construction by the artist. The self-consciousness of shaped language participating in an artistic tradition, the "literary" and dramaturgical aspects of writing, can too easily disappear in discussions of social context. The resulting lacuna not only discounts much of what art tries to do but also abandons the subtler social commentary played out through sound and dramatic placement. The rich complexity of Elizabethan lyrical drama appears at this intersection of societal meanings and the artist's craft.

Certain crucial aspects of lyric poetry are peculiarly "of an age," in this case the primacy of Petrarch's influence and the political use of such poetry at court; other aspects outlast many generations. The nature of temporality, the fascination with what lasts and what doesn't, appears to be of enduring interest to poets and philosophers alike; nothing is more perennial than mortality. In less direct ways, Elizabethan concerns with place (occasion) and gender (independent women in power) have endured, even though the particular urgency of Petrarchan queen-worship seems far removed. In illustrating ways in which Elizabethan lyrical drama remains interesting and connects with current cultural tensions, I suggest another reason for listening carefully to Elizabethan lyricism, its messages and its possibilities. Finally, in investigating the artistic and cultural legacy of Elizabethan lyrical drama, we may better understand both our literary critical heritage and its role in shaping how we see the art itself, encouraging skepticism and attentiveness to the bases (especially as they involve gendering) for our own aesthetic judgments.

In this "revaluing," we need not lose the sense of play and humor in most Elizabethan lyrical drama that also made it popular and helps describe it as a genre (in part a result of the ambiguous "placement" of lyric poetry in aesthetic hierarchies, as discussed in the next chapter). Lightness of touch—be it of Romeo's hand or the critic's—does not always imply dismissiveness or unimportance. The poet Robert Pinsky points out in discussing Thomas Campion's lyric, "Now Winter Nights Enlarge," that its "harmonious blending . . . rests on a sense of limit" (5). Much of the delight in Elizabethan poetry comes from a sense of proportion, a knowledge of the limits as well as the enchantments of poetry and the courtly pursuits it celebrates. The ability to recognize limitation without being reduced to triviality is a delicate achievement (for critics as well as poets); it may be an achievement at odds with the American proclivities for size, sincerity in emotion, and cynicism toward language. For those who find Romanticism and its legacy at times self-important and ponderous, one compelling reason to attend carefully to Elizabethan lyric practice is to find out how poets achieved this energetic delicacy and how the poetry worked in its social and aesthetic contexts. At this moment especially, when the gap between textual and popular culture appears to evoke anxiety in many quarters, we may benefit from exploring the uses of rhetoric and poetry in another cultural context, recognizing their ethical and political consequences.

The enduring vitality and significance of Elizabethan poetic performance have become all the more vivid for me as I have transmuted private inquiry into public text. Finally, it must be left to the reader to make public passion personal once more, completing the cultural exchange by determining, in one's own terms, the value and currency of this performance.

Notes

1. See especially Forster, Lever (*Elizabethan*), Kennedy, Marotti, and Roche on Petrarchism. See Whittier on the sonnets and Horwich on parodic Petrarchism in *Romeo and Juliet*.

2. For fuller readings of Romeo's stylistic growth, see my dissertation "Poetic Transformations" (Columbia University 1989); Levin ("Form"); and Gibbons's introduction to the Arden edition. I differ from those who read unironically Romeo's lament that Juliet's beauty has made him "effeminate" (3.1.105)—rather than a vengeful perpetuator of the bloody feud—and who regard his death as a selfish indulgence of passion (see Dickey, Peterson, Seward, and R. Berry). Such readings are consistent with certain moral and religious orthodoxies of Shakespeare's era but not, to my ear, with the play's tonalities.

3. Long ago, Spurgeon (310ff.) traced the light and dark imagery that separates the lovers from the rest (as does, more obviously, their commitment to eros rather than the feuding hatred which the others—including Mercutio—perpetuate). See also McLuskie.

4. See Forster 122–47, Jones and Stallybrass, Yates (*Astraea*), and John King on the textual iconography of Elizabeth, as well as the more general discussions of Elizabeth's court by Javitch and Montrose. Elizabeth's older sister Mary Tudor did of course precede her as a female sovereign, but Mary's reign was brief (1553–58) and marred by the extremity of her attempt to reinstate Catholicism and her unfortunate marriage to Philip II of Spain.

5. Notable current studies focus on Elizabeth's rhetoric and negotiations directly (see Susan Frye and Carole Levin; Ilona Bell has work in progress on Elizabeth's poetry); others look for articulated signs of influence, stressing Elizabeth's importance as a model for female virtue and authorship within poetic tributes by women (such studies include Lisa Gim's work in progress). Many historians, including some feminists, remark on Elizabeth's "unsisterly" treatment of ladies-in-waiting, although Bassnett tries to defend her as a protective believer in chastity; see more persuasively Amussen's discussion of the queen as an "exceptional" woman. On the critical placement of Elizabeth, see also P. Berry and Jankowski. Leah Marcus ("Shakespeare's"), Jean Howard ("Crossdressing"), and Mihoko Suzuki have linked stage heroines with the androgynous queen, and Constance Jordan stresses the associations of Elizabeth as monarch with masculine attributes as an aspect of her exceptional gendering in portraiture. My work supplements these analyses.

6. See Gurr, R. Levin, Howard's "Women," and especially Orgel's complica-

tion of sexual representation in "Nobody's Perfect." My work at many points bears a debt as well as kinship to the influential articles of Montrose.

7. See for example critiques by Bruster, Breitenberg, and Bevington of masculine desire in two works I will be analyzing in depth: Bruster's regarding Marlowe's "Passionate Shepherd," and Breitenberg's and Bevington's regarding Shakespeare's *Love's Labour's Lost*.

8. Jankowski's related study of the representation of queen characters in Renaissance drama explores "both the potential disruption of gender identity that occurs when multiple discourses about women converge in a single character and the contradictions, paradoxes, and occasions for subversion that occur when a woman is placed in a masculine position—such as ruler—and still characterized as female" (9); however, she comes to quite different readings than mine, in part because she does not focus on the messages relayed poetically.

9. The poet's praise of the queen is dubbed "obsequious" (47). McCoy does not explicitly address the gender hierarchy that complicates his notions of a "slave morality," the poet's "pitiful" fate as the queen's servant ("Gascoigne's '*Poëmata*'" 48), and especially the representation of debasement within Gascoigne's writing. McCoy speculates about Gascoigne's debased "self-esteem" and his "sense of diminished virility" (50). Blaming the highly visible sovereign works well rhetorically, and allows empathy with the underdog at court. Nonetheless, when this approach is combined with an unscrutinized Freudian inheritance about gender roles and artistic "potency," problems become apparent.

10. McCoy links this royal "audience" with a fictional scene in Gascoigne's narrative, *The Adventures of Master F.J.*, which the critic describes as both a "rape" and a "comically stylized incident [which] ruffles neither of them [F. J. and his mistress] very much and both even sleep better that night" ("Gascoigne's '*Poëmata*'" 36). The analogy assumes Gascoigne's tone not only toward the queen but toward this "rape" and the larger narrative of F. J., adopting the stance of a sophisticate uninterested in "remorseful solemnity or moral admonition" (38). It is primarily this absence of didactic weight, in fact, that in the critic's view elevates Gascoigne's earlier work above his later penitential tracts.

11. For a related example of taking the male character's part, see Von Hendy's reading of Peele, discussed in chap. 2 below. Nancy K. Miller ("Rereading" 357) calls attention to an aligned "model of double reading, which opposes the 'morally inclined' to the 'strictly intellectual or even perhaps esthetic,' and valorizes the victory of the latter position"—with disturbing consequences for the feminist critic.

12. Discussing the opposition to Elizabeth's marriage to the duke of Anjou, Tennenhouse says that voices objected "on other than simply religious grounds. A greater fear had to do with the integrity of the English nation" (21). He rightly attends to multiple reasons, yet feels the need to hierarchize his concern as "greater" rather than "other." Similarly, he sees that John Stubbes's pamphlet, *The discovery of*

a gaping Gulf wherein England is to be swallowed by another french marriage . . . "announces this nationalist theme" (21). So it does, but it presumes the gendered argument that Elizabeth could not sustain her sovereignty once affiliated with a male as well as the gendered argument about lineal worry (that sovereignty would be subordinated to the male heir of the French line). Both angles are worth noting. Patterson (*Censorship* 58–73) remarks on the dynamics of male rebellion before female authority. See also Howard's appraisal in "New Historicism" and Cohen's critique of the new historicist use of gender; for a critique of heterosexism specifically, see Goldberg's *Sodometries*.

    13. See her attack on novels in chap. 13 of *A Vindication of the Rights of Women*. Laura Levine mentions numerous attacks on the theater, as early as Gosson's, because it "effeminated" the mind (121ff.); this also helps explain why Jonson and other poet-playwrights were at such pains to praise art as masculine.

    14. For Coleridge's comments, as recorded by Collier, see Foakes 132–33; though some of Collier's later publications were notoriously marred by forgery and a creative memory, Foakes gives substantial reasons for crediting his diary entries as well as the gist of his account of Coleridge's lectures. "Maturity" was one of T. S. Eliot's key terms for identifying a classic. In his influential essay "Poetry and Drama," he identified "the dramatic" with a play's narrative line, its fiction. For him, good dramatic poetry "does not interrupt but intensifies the dramatic situation" by being "transparent"; by contrast, he calls "lyrical" those poetic lines which he considered a distraction from the "drama," lines dissociated from character and "remote from the necessity of the action" (*On Poetry* 89, 79, 88). He uses these criteria to praise the "mature" plays of Shakespeare. Elsewhere (*On Poetry* 29) he sees maturation in Shakespeare's movement from "artificiality to simplicity," culminating in *Antony and Cleopatra*. Without engaging that work's putative simplicity, I think it worth remarking that these comments were made by the twentieth century's foremost proponent of the revival of verse drama. A generation trained by Eliot's method and insights duly perpetuated the labeling of Shakespeare's "lyrical phase" as immature. For Calderwood, "Shakespeare's maturing concept of dramatic form" requires the sacrifice of lyrical speakers such as Romeo and Juliet (108); similarly, see Hardison.

    15. Though Bethell recognizes that theater's "multi-consciousness" in part derives from movement between "naturalism" and "conventionalism," he proceeds to dismiss Petrarchism as "unserious" and the style most remote "from actuality" (29) when discussing *Love's Labour's Lost,* erasing the possibility of subtler variations and meanings revealed through this mode of staged lyric. See similar comments by Calderwood on the lyric voice in *Love's Labour's Lost.*

    16. Annabel Patterson analyzed the political agenda of Lewis's model of literary history at an MLA session on early modern periodization (San Francisco, Dec. 27, 1991).

    17. The enlistment of Shakespeare to support the modern professoriat (not even

pretending vice versa) and the movement into the present tense trumpet Lewis's own desires here, to erase recalcitrant history and re-create the past in his own idealized image, one with clear hierarchies.

18. Greenblatt's 1980 volume (*Renaissance Self-Fashioning*) initiated a decade of new historical emphasis on Renaissance (male) subjectivity, an important force to keep in mind when reading McCoy as well as Fineman's complex study, *Shakespeare's Perjured Eye*.

19. Breitenberg ultimately acknowledges the play's complexity, although discounting the class issues of the Nine Worthies' pageant in his effort to sustain a gendered opposition in which wit, homosocial bonding, and erotic desire are presented as if definitively masculine (see chap. 4 below). See Vickers, "Diana Described"; she too extends her observations beyond Petrarch to Shakespeare in "Blazon." Other articles dismissing Petrarchan and courtly discourse as a premise rather than a conclusion include Finke and Silberman. Mary Beth Rose is also critical of what she dubs the "courtly love syndrome" (*Expense* 35). Even when female authors chose to write Petrarchan poetry, critics stress its constraint. Gary Waller attributes the gaps and melancholy in Mary Wroth's poetry to the oppressiveness of Petrarchan lyric per se as a reflection of Court and the "subjection to a language which emphasizes the woman's role as empty, passive, helpless" (268). One might balance this emphasis with Deborah Cameron's more expansively applicable observation: "Men do not control meaning at all. Rather women elect to use modes of expression men can understand because that is the best way of getting men to listen" (105). Ann Rosalind Jones distinguishes three strategies women used in adapting male-authored poetry: imitation, negotiation, and appropriation. Male as well as female authors, I will argue, negotiated subtly and variously with their Petrarchan inheritance.

20. My arguments apply to cultural materialist readings as well as feminist ones. For example, Tennenhouse leaps from a valid observation about one use of Petrarchism at court (" 'Making love to the Queen' was a public and political act, and if carried out successfully, it brought one position and power, signs that the suitor was favored by the queen" [30]) to a sweeping reduction: "When we find such terms as 'fortune,' 'suitor,' 'hope,' 'envy,' 'favor,' 'despair' and 'love' in both letters of clientage and in the poetry coined for the queen *as well as that circulated among members of a court coterie,* then, *it can be nothing else but* a language for negotiating with a patron for the client's position. *Neither allegorical nor secretly encoded,* this is *quite simply* a political language. It is from such a political perspective, I would argue, that we should understand Shakespeare's sonnets" (33; emphasis added). Leaving aside Shakespeare's qualifications as a member of a "court coterie," this categorical *de*personalizing of the Petrarchist vocabulary assumes that a close-knit circle of friends, relations, and associates only ever thought about gaining the queen's favor (or, as he subsequently emphasizes using only the atypical Sir Philip Sidney as his example, maintaining the aristocratic "community of blood" [36]); this monocu-

larity undermines his valid emphasis on gender and aristocratic inheritance, as well as his discussion of Shakespeare's dramatic use of Petrarchist texts.

21. Elizabeth's poem, "On Monsieur's Departure," modifies the internalized struggle of the Petrarchan speaker to capture the frustrations of a queen's suppressed desire (see my forthcoming article "Female Power and the Devaluation of Elizabethan Love Lyrics"). She drew on the same rhetoric when her political position and perhaps her life were at stake, in the petition to King Edward beginning with that familiar figure of speech, the Petrarchan simile: "Lyke as a shipman in stormy weather plucks down the sails for better wind, so did I, most noble King, in my unfortunate chance a' Thursday pluck down the high sails of my joy and comfort" (Harrison 16). Her only other extant letter to King Edward begins in a related way, but applying the simile to him: "Like as the rich man . . . so your Majesty" (15). Nor is this merely a stylistic tic of Elizabeth's; in the collection of extant letters compiled by Harrison, these are the only two written before she herself became queen which begin with this figure of speech, thus suggesting the association with political "special pleading" between the sexes which would so greatly increase during her reign.

22. There was also a substantial body of female-authored sacred poetry and meditations, and of course a venerated place for the feminine in religion; but as far as representation within the earthly realm of history and politics, respected roles for women were rare unless played out through the rhetoric of Petrarchism.

23. Lindley begins by noting the historical conflation between lyric as a *universal* and as a specific poetic *genre* (1–2), as discussed in chap. 1 below: see esp. his first chapter and conclusion.

24. William Archer in 1923 criticized Shakespeare's "impure form" and mistaken desire to unite realistic "imitation" with "lyrical passion"; as an anthology introduction from 1962 remarks, "Archer's words were dead when he wrote them" (Barnet et al. 8). Although one might reasonably believe this ancient battle to be over, one still sees its legacy in much contemporary criticism. W. R. Johnson's otherwise admirable study argues that lyric "beyond itself," incorporated into larger narrative presentations, somehow "infects" the larger genre: "when the lyric poet undertakes to write drama, he does not necessarily become a dramatist. . . . What tends to happen [is that] . . . the invaded genre endures some degree of mutation when lyric purposes usurp its form and ignore its customary objects of mimesis" while "the lyric impulse" is "either diminished or uncannily nourished by its imposture" (149). The idea of "lyrical aggression" waged against the drama, of alien artistic forms engaged in a territorial war that produces mutant forms and sullies or overstimulates pure, chaste lyric, seems less useful than Rosalie Colie's syncretist thesis of *genera mista*.

25. For more specific criteria of musicality see especially Hollander's remarks in *Vision and Resonance,* as well as Ing's more particular interpretation in her standard

study of Elizabethan lyrics, which "begins from the ancient definition of lyric as 'a song for singing'" (15–17). See also Stevens's excellent study of early Tudor music and lyric poetry.

26. Among the most influential studies focused on sixteenth-century England that challenge or complicate this binary opposition, though in some cases at the expense of attention to aesthetic subtleties, see especially the work of Greenblatt, Orgel, Goldberg, Montrose, Javitch, McCoy, Jones and Stallybrass, Marcus, Tennenhouse, Crewe, Belsey, Loomba, Frye, Fumerton (*Cultural*), B. Smith (*Homosexual*), and the essays collected in Dollimore and Sinfield, *Political Shakespeare;* Howard and O'Connor, *Shakespeare Reproduced;* and Drakakis, *Alternative Shakespeares.* In addition to some of these works especially helpful and influential feminist studies applicable to the texts under discussion are the works of Boose, Erickson, Adelman, Neely, Bamber, Novy, Jones, Suzuki, Howard, Kahn, Traub, Mary Beth Rose, Wendy Wall, and the essays in Ferguson, Quilligan, and Vickers, *Rewriting the Renaissance;* Lenz, Green, and Neely, *The Woman's Part;* Schwarz and Kahn, *Representing Shakespeare;* Zimmerman, *Erotic Politics;* Wayne, *The Matter of Difference;* and Hendricks and Parker, *Women, "Race," and Writing.* This book both builds upon and serves as a corrective to recent new historicist and feminist study involving poetic texts.

27. This opposition is a familiar critical move, evident in most studies of Marlowe's *Dido* as well as more broadly influential studies of Shakespeare such as James Calderwood's; see my chaps. 3 and 4. On the play of voices in Tudor writing, essential to the delight in multiple perspectives characteristic of lyrical drama, see especially Levao (*Renaissance Minds*) and Altman.

28. See W. R. Johnson 151–53. For a cogent introduction to the complexities involved in categorizing representations, see Mitchell, "Representation." Styan and Beckerman argued for performance "over" text in the late 1960s and 1970s, allowing needed study of theatricality within the academy but also reinforcing the separation between dramatic and literary studies (always excepting Shakespeare, the Bard for all Reasons); at the same time, the new theoretical focus on textuality prompted explicit preference for the page over stage among literary critics such as Berger (a stance he subsequently modified). The impact of this academic split remains powerful, in the way departments are organized and students trained.

ONE

Elizabethan Contexts

At the start of Elizabeth Tudor's reign, one would hardly have predicted a great age of English poetry—much less that lyrical poetry would vitalize the theater. After a decade that saw three monarchs die and the state's religion change as often as its ruler, this female monarch was greeted heartily by a populace preoccupied more with its survival and future as a nation than with its entertainments. The former Clerk of the Privy Council, Armigail Waad, summarized their state: "The queen poor, the realm exhausted, the nobility poor and decayed. Want of good captains and soldiers. The people out of order. Justice not executed. All things dear. Excess in meat, drink and apparel. Divisions among ourselves. Wars with France and Scotland. The French king bestriding the realm, having one foot in Calais and the other in Scotland. Steadfast enmity but no steadfast friendship abroad" (Pringle 19).

Nor was political turmoil the only hurdle. Even after Elizabeth had survived the Northern Rebellion and papal excommunication, even with uneasy foreign alliances holding and internal dissension crushed, artistic stumbling blocks remained. In 1576 when James Burbage opened the Theatre, the possibility of public drama with literary pretensions must still have seemed farfetched. During the first half of Elizabeth's reign, the distance between the practice of stage production and the Renaissance legacy of neoclassical poetic theory (such as it was) did not augur auspiciously for theatrical lyricism.

Plays performed by professional troupes, such as Thomas Preston's extremely popular *Cambises* (published in 1569), relied on spectacle and broad characters, rather than verse style, for their appeal. Although public plays often included songs, and thus were in that precise sense "lyrical," the songs seem to have served primarily as performative diversions, seldom relating in a specific, integral way to the ongoing narrative fiction or its spoken language. In extant scripts the songs are sometimes omitted or remain unspecified, implying that the particular lyrics were deemed by the printer or author unimportant so long as they set the mood or demonstrated the singer's virtuosity. At other times a subgenre is suggested, as when Cambises demands his queen be put to death and she exits singing a psalm. Which psalm, however, remains unspecified, indicating that while the choice of this category of song in the sixteenth century broadcasts its Protestant context, the precise lyrics are not requisite or integral to its effect. As a rule, one does not find much evidence of the developing literary idioms and topics of love lyrics in early Elizabethan drama, nor do the songs often contribute extensively to the spoken dramatic representation.[1]

In *Cambises,* there are at least occasional hints of a narrative situation appropriate to lyrical verse, of a sort later exploited by Robert Greene in *Friar Bacon and Friar Bungay.* Amidst the bombastic antics of the titular tyrant and various low-life characters, the few moments of song and lyrical description are linked with the courtly lady who becomes Cambises' reluctant queen. She enters during a Mayday festivity, invited to dance by a nameless lord whose speech combines (with care sadly absent elsewhere in the play) smooth alliteration, varied caesura, verbal play, and sensual description:

> The blowing buds whose savory scents our sense will much delight,
> The sweet smell of musk white-rose to please the appetite,
> The chirping birds whose pleasant tunes therein shall here record
> That our great joy we shall it find in field to walk abroad,
> On lute and cittern there to play a heavenly harmony;
> Our ears shall hear, heart to content, our sports to beautify.
>
> (863–68)

But even this rare moment of courtly pastoral and comparative musical elegance is almost immediately destroyed by Cambises' uncivil and possibly incestuous courting, expressed through such comically harsh descriptions of his love's "burning fits" as "my corpse they scorch, alas!" (900, 901). Whereas Greene's later play sustains its lyrical subplot, interweaving the aristocrat Lacy's wooing of Margaret, the fair maid of Fressingfield, with the main plot of the friars' magical competition (as well as Prince Edward's dynastic marriage), in Preston's play the lyrical moment of courtly love is only a passing fancy, undeveloped and inconsequential. The drama's focus and flamboyance lies elsewhere, with the witty Vice figure Ambidexter who "plays with both hands," the "ruffians" Huf, Ruf, and Snuf, and the increasingly maniacal Persian prince. Nor do the interspersed fourteeners and four- and five-stress lines of *Cambises* testify to authorial concern with poetic craft.[2] As J. E. Bernard puts it, "Thomas Preston's prosody was not a matter for stimulating concern to him; most of the time one cannot find a standard [metrical pattern] to fit the linear size" (153). The subliterary status of public "theater," performed in innyards and on temporary stages, did not yet attract authors with poetic or courtly pretensions. Yet those were the people consciously drawing on the Petrarchan lyric tradition and intent on shaping the unruly modern English language into some recognizable (and hence poetically communicative) "metric system."

The poets interested in metrical technique were for the most part aspiring law students at the Inns of Court, or humanist-trained aristocrats. It was at the Inns that the first blank verse tragedies were played, scripted by politically motivated rhetoricians such as Thomas Sackville and Thomas Norton (*Gorboduc*) and self-proclaimed gentleman poets such as George Gascoigne (*Jocasta*). William Webbe and George Puttenham, among the more notable commentators, stressed the importance of addressing a particular, elite audience; they viewed poetry as a way to advance standards of literary authority and to gain political prestige. Their aims differed from those of writers trying to amuse the London shopkeepers and their apprentices who had managed to find time and money for a special trip to a public theatrical performance.[3]

Nevertheless, within the twenty years following the Theatre's opening, *The Faerie Queene,* innumerable sonnet sequences, the plays of Marlowe, and the "lyrical" plays of Shakespeare appeared before the public. Poets had successfully overcome the difficulties both of crafting modern English into flexible, expressive verse and, even more remarkably, of finding integral connections between lyric verse and larger narrative and popular dramatic forms. While one can all too easily create an oversimplified story of artistic progress and improvement, that temptation need not foreclose efforts to understand more fully why such a startling shift in generic practice occurred. In addition to strictly material changes affecting performance conditions and writers, several aspects of aesthetic struggle created theatrically functional lyricism, deriving in great part from three "places" of cultural change: the uncertain place of lyric in Elizabethan critical thinking, which led to many spirited attacks on the genre but also allowed some useful fluidity of function; the literary place or domain that poets—especially aspiring professionals—were striving to create, in which they could give voice to conflicts between desire and authority; and the place of courtly entertainments for Elizabeth, which provided an apt occasion for the "theatrical" performance of love lyrics. In all three sites, notions of gender provided an impetus and a vocabulary for debate in poetic form. Reading the lyricism of an earlier Elizabethan courtier, George Gascoigne, within these contexts reveals both the limits and emergent intersections for lyric and drama within a queen's domain.

Lyric Stresses and Strains: The Vexation of Elizabethan Literary "Theory"

If Elizabethan authors were to incorporate lyric poetry into their narrative drama, they needed not only a command of English prosody but also an aesthetic or commercial rationale for making this choice. For Elizabethan commentators on poetry, however, few connections between lyric and drama were apparent—even the ones that in fact existed, such as the inclusion of songs in theatrical performances. As good scholars and humanists, they adopted terminology from other European cultures, including the Aristotelian categories of epic, drama, and lyric, which poorly fit with most Elizabethan artistic practice. The oft-mocked and (not coincidentally) less socially privileged Gabriel Harvey was one of the few even to acknowledge the power of "generall use and custome" in determining poetic style and prosody, personified as "the vulgare and natural Mother Prosodye" (GGS 1: 121). Most of his courtly contemporaries who theorized were studiously indifferent to their own popular, and often rhetorically feminized, artistic traditions. In *The Arte of English Poesie,* George Puttenham suggested quite openly that only the language spoken at court was worthy of poetic shaping. Even writers who created as well as speculated about poetry declined to meld their theory with their practice; the reader has to do a good deal of interpretive work to make the lyrics of so flexible and artful a poet as Sir Philip Sidney consistent with his pronouncements in the *Apology for Poetry.* Nevertheless, the theorists—broadly defined to include almost anyone who bothered to comment on the meaning or craft of poetry—provide a starting point for understanding Elizabethan conceptions of genre at this formative moment for modern English, and reveal the problems they thought they faced. In struggling for clear distinctions and definitions, those who commented recognized form and style among poetry's primary means of signification, which was an awareness requisite for meaningful inclusion of lyric poetry within a fiction. And ironically, because scholars failed to pigeonhole lyric neatly, they could not prescribe its forms and functions so narrowly as to choke out its life (a fate suffered by classically inspired academic drama of the time).

Seen from the vantage point of Elizabethan commentators, the midcentury had produced little lyric poetry or drama of note. Frequent reversals of direction in state religion and policy were indeed matched by a chaotic shifting among verse forms in mid-Tudor interludes. After the premature deaths of Wyatt and Surrey, very few inventive poets appeared to extend their lyric achievements. No wonder that Elizabethan commentators, reviewing the preceding generation, sought order and uniformity. With new energy sparked by the continental Renaissance and the possibility of stable government, the educated tried to define and exalt—or at least defend—the idea of poetry in modern English. To make it laudable as valid literature and its authors what Sir Philip Sidney dubbed "right poets," commentators often opposed it to unliterary, unedifying popular verse, such as "common" ballads. In the process, newly popular lyric forms such as sonnets (in the loosest sense, usually meaning short love songs) were also disparaged, although they too were part of a self-conscious literary tradition. In "The Anatomie of Absurditie," Thomas Nashe rails against "our babling Ballets and our new found Songs and Sonets, which every rednose Fidler hath at his fingers end, and every ignorant Ale Knight will breath forth over the potte, as soone as his braine waxeth hote" (GGS 1: 326). Nashe's attack on the "new found" no doubt refers to the legacy of Tottel's publication of *Songs and Sonnets* in 1557. Yet this wildly popular collection of lyrics, known as Tottel's Miscellany, included the adaptations of Petrarch by Wyatt and Surrey—a far cry from ballads, and hardly "unliterary." Nashe's "Anatomie" exemplifies the elision of arguments in Elizabethan polemical commentaries, which often slip from formal criticism to attacks based on moral or social claims (a blurring, we shall see, that Shakespeare wittily exploits in *Love's Labour's Lost*). For Nashe, the sonnets are cheapened by their very popularity and accessibility.

Tellingly, these elitist attacks intermingle with gendered denunciation of certain "lowly" subject matter. Nashe vividly reviles "the blazing of Women's slender praises," reserving his praise for poetry that is (like the Inns of Court drama) "a more hidden & divine kinde of Philosophy, enwrapped in blinde Fables and darke stories, wherin the principles of more excellent Arts and morrall precepts of manners, illustrated with divers examples of other Kingdomes and Countries, are contained" (GGS 1: 323, 328). Nashe's denunciation may be a Protestant's alternative attempt to distinguish Christian from pagan poetry through its superior morality, without following the Catholic Italian route of Neoplatonism which creates a continuum (the ladder of love) between praise of earthly women and the divine. But no matter whether the motivation be doctrinal, classist, personal, or some combination thereof, the expression is frankly misogynous. Despite the fact that artists such as Spenser and Peele link Nashe's two opposed topics, the belittling of poetry by association with the feminine endures as a platitude of Elizabethan criticism; this ironic tension becomes one of the shaping factors in the use of love lyric, especially Petrarchan sonnets, in performance.

Nashe is not alone in lambasting popular lyric. In "A Discourse on English Poesy," William Webbe similarly decries "the uncountable rabble of ryming Ballet makers and compylers of sencelesse sonets, who be most busy to stuffe every stall full of grosse devices and unlearned Pamphlets" (GGS 1: 246). The attack implies that love sonnets encourage moral lassitude as well as commonness, a charge Philip Sidney addresses directly. In the *Apology for Poetry,* he notes that detractors of poesy "say the lyric is larded with passionate sonnets, the elegiac weeps the want of his mistress" (58)—hardly ennobling stuff, it is understood. Like Nashe, Sidney then distinguishes between the desired mistress and divine beauty as two subjects of poetic praise; but his rhetorical shifts signal some discomfort with rigid separation of such categories. His writing displays the greatest consciousness of complexity and potential contradiction in the evaluation of lyric.

Sidney tries to distinguish poetry's divine potential to address elevated topics and persuade through reason from the present work of indulgent love poets. Thus he redeems the *idea* of lyric at the expense of actual practice (including his own, considering the erotic focus of his sonnet sequence *Astrophil and Stella*). And yet, he adds, "it be very hard, sith only man, and no beast, hath that gift to discern Beauty" and that "even some of my masters the philosophers spent a good deal of their lamp-oil in setting forth the excellency" of love (58). In this comically grudging aside, he implies a Neoplatonic challenge to the baseness of love lyrics, reminiscent of the arguments for love's nobility Astrophil asserts when not overwhelmed by lust (one moves from the image of a lady to the transcendent idea of Beauty). But in each case, the context is highly ironic, more clearly illustrating the gaps between philosophy and practice than countering the dominant hierarchies of value. Later in the treatise, Sidney tries to redeem "that lyrical kind of songs and sonnets" by changing their topic from women to God, more explicitly moving up the ladder of love as Pietro Bembo instructed in Castiglione's *Il Cortegiano;* foreshadowing the Sidneys' own translation of the Psalms, Philip imagines how good this change would be, "with how heavenly fruit, both private and public, in singing the praises of the immortal beauty, the immortal goodness of that God who giveth us hands to write and wits to conceive" (80). The ancient distinction of lofty and lowly lyrics becomes a matter of deictic topic, of the subject's worthiness to be praised.

In Protestant England, doctrinally shorn of Mariology or saint worship, this shift of topic also entails a shift of gender, as the suspect females in love sonnets are replaced by God the Father in psalms. Sidney would distinguish holy lyrics from the merely imitative works of poets who "coldly . . . apply fiery speeches, as men that had rather read lovers' writings, and so caught up certain swelling phrases" (81). This passage slyly combines several criteria, shifting from a traditional split between elevated and lowly lyric, based on whether the subject matter is sacred or worldly, to a stylistic critique; through this elision all love poets are tarred with insincerity. If Sidney intends an ad hominem attack on a certain school of excessive poets, then his target is obviously courtly Petrarchists. Sidney's charge of self-conscious, vaunting imitation and his humorous inclusion of that most famous stylistic tic, the oxymoron, in its most familiar form (fire and ice) clearly identify his victims. Such Petrarchist-bashing is consistent with his comic attacks in *Astrophil and Stella*. But, as in that sonnet sequence, the mockery extends beyond the particularly uninspired Petrarchan imitators, perhaps even glancing back at Sidney as author. Admitting the validity of those who attack such poetasters and positing no alternative amatory style in the *Apology* despite his own practice, Sidney at least implies the inappropriateness and insincerity of idealistic praise for mere mortal women (as, in a more overtly religious context, Ben Jonson found John Donne's allegorical *First Anniversarie* on the death of Elizabeth Drury "profane and full of blasphemies" but had no problem hyperbolically praising famous men such as Cary and Morrison for his own symbolic purposes). And this from the most influential love sonneteer of his time. Perhaps we should not be surprised at Fulke Greville's report that the dying Sidney requested all his "prophane" poetry be burned.

And yet . . . Sidney does for a moment adopt the position of a female judge when he discusses love poetry, coyly prefacing his attack on Petrarchism with the remark "But truly many of such writings as come under the banner of unresistable love, if I were a mistress, would never persuade me they were in love" (81). In contrast to the putatively self-enclosed dynamic of Petrarchan poetics described by Vickers and Freccero, Sidney—at least momentarily and in theory—recognizes a female audience as the proper and intended addressee of male lyric composition. Yet he does so only in a context that proceeds to dismiss the dominant style of amatory lyric. Although he speaks of the opportunities to praise the "immortal beauty" of God, he ignores the elevating possibilities provided by Petrarchan address to a female sovereign. Of course, given his less than ideal relations with the queen (including and after his attempt to entertain her with his pageant *The Lady of May*) that absence more likely testifies to a political conflict than a specifically gendered aversion. Notwithstanding, the consequences for amatory discourse in his *Apology* remain damaging. Akin to current dismissal of all instances of Petrarchism because of its potential for self-privileging, Sidney as commentator identifies the excess but ultimately fails to distinguish other more ambitious or charitable uses of those tropes—including, perhaps, his own.[4] If even Sir Philip Sidney could not or would not redeem Elizabethan amatory lyric from its lowly and corrupt associations, we should not be surprised at its devalued currency. For writers of "serious" forms such as humanist drama, the assumption that love lyrics were frivolous, profane, and effeminate conspired even more strenuously against their inclusion in theatrical fictions.[5]

Nevertheless, Sidney's wry moments and lyric practice did echo after his death, and provided a model not only for others' recuperation of lyric but for its incorporation into drama. An ability to hear an interplay of voices permeates Sidney's writing; in *Astrophil and Stella,* he can turn his ironic ear upon the sonneteer himself, and at least imply if not represent the position of the beloved. When Thomas Nashe, that castigator of "new found Songs and Sonets," describes Sidney's sonnet sequence in the preface to the 1591 unauthorized edition of *Astrophil and Stella,* he not only applauds the work but does so in terms accordant with the contemporary development of lyrical drama as a significant medium: he describes a "theater of pleasure" in which "the tragicomedy of love is performed by starlight," with the muse Melpomene as "chief actor," the "argument cruel chastity, the prologue hope, the epilogue dispair" (Rollins and Baker 324). And even within earlier commentary lie those countertendencies that would eventually help to license lyricism as a medium for performance.

Most importantly, lyric was one of Aristotle's three categories of literature, and so it was in some sense classical and respectable. David Lindley points out that this use of lyric as a "universal" category alongside drama and epic, part of a "literary trinity" or triumvirate "in the carving up of literature's empire," has often been conflated with "a more specific label for one among many poetic genres" (1); Elizabethan theory certainly exemplifies such muddiness. While one may argue that Aristotle was citing three media in the *Poetics,* few who used his terms were so exact or consistent. Nevertheless, he did provide an authority for more elevated claims for lyric poetry. Instead of explicitly connecting lyric with the subject of earthly love, for example, Puttenham links "lyrique poets" with melodious song. However, he then cites as examples some classical authors who certainly were meant to be read, and some who excelled at love poetry (placing Horace, Catullus, and Callimachus alongside Pindar and Anacreon). Many pages later, he associates "honest love," "the first founder of all good affections," with both a variety of poetic forms and a certain uneven form: love "requireth a forme of Poesie variable, inconstant, affected, curious, and most witty of any others, whereof the ioyes were to be uttered in one sorte, the sorrowes in an other, and, by the many formes of Poesie, the many moodes and pangs of lovers throughly [*sic*] to be discovered" (GGS 2: 46–47). One seeks in vain for examples of the protean, offbeat poetry implied by Puttenham's treatise. His "Poesie variable" simply seems to mean a varied group of poems, such as were gathered in contemporary miscellanies and collections (Tottel, Gascoigne's *Posies, A Paradise of Daintie Devices,* and the like). By mentioning songs and devices here as well as when discussing "lyrique poets," Puttenham undermines his own distinction between a "high" classical form of lyric and the playful, popular world of love songs.

Similarly, although David Lindley cites Michael Drayton as one who "has a fairly clear notion of the lyric genre as being defined by [social] function, form and subject-matter (significantly without any mention of personal voice or feeling)," his actual quotation from Drayton's preface to the *Odes* is less than clear in its placement of lyric, for the poet declares that such verses "are (as the Learned say) divers: Some transcendently loftie, and farre more high than the Epick . . . Others, among the Greekes, are amorous, soft and made for Chambers, as others for Theaters" (6–7). Implying the lowliness of courtly love's chamber music while not definitively ranking theatrical odes, Drayton also treats Aristotle's three universal categories as one moment distinct, the next moment capable of fusion. Moreover, he replicates the association of "amorous, soft" verse with a feminized private territory clearly distinguished from public and transcendent matters.

Such mixed and often contrary views of lyric poetry, coupled with the disparagement of love, presented obvious problems for lyricists who wished to have their nonreligious poetry received with any seriousness. Not that this stopped production. Ironically, the literary poetic form developing most fully during the 1580s, when most of these tracts were written, was the Petrarchan love sonnet. A thoughtful poet such as Sidney was caught in a bind. While this practicing sonneteer wisely avoids condemning the sonnet form per se, his theoretical work shares the dominant Protestant attitude toward the contemporary composition of love lyrics: derogatory. And yet the sonnet was the most notable poetic creation of the Renaissance, and Petrarch among the most important figures in promoting poetry as a noble pursuit.

For those who regarded themselves as advocates for the "renaissance" of classical learning, the appeal of poetry lay primarily in its potential as rhetoric, the art of persuasion through language. Both Italian and English humanists perceived literary style to be a valuable tool in efforts to emphasize the noble and heroic potential of "man" on earth, the active life as well as the contemplative. As A. C. Spearing notes, "one line of argument of the humanists against the scholastics had to do with the need not just to rely on the academic definition of truth but to use the power of words to persuade men to put it into practice," which in turn "may be connected with a general tendency to elevate the dignity of poetry." Indeed, Spearing asserts that the terms "poetry" or "literature" as now understood, implying "verbal structures of intrinsic beauty and lasting value," are themselves—"so far as English is concerned"—Renaissance conceptions (5). He cites the new claims for poetry as an intellectual pursuit made in Petrarch's laureate oration and Boccaccio's *De genealogia deorum gentilium* books 14 and 15, the latter specifically emphasizing how the "veiled language" of poetic fictions makes them "'the object of strong intellectual effort and various interpretation' and thus more highly valued" (7). Boccaccio's claim for poetry as allegory promotes textuality as well, demanding close and extended study; it suggests and reinforces the subsequent importance of printing in providing greater access to texts. These elevating claims provide a defense of poetry but also encourage the debasement of comparatively simple lyrics, at least to the extent that they remain linked to popular song and oral performance.

Nonetheless, the Renaissance emphasis on rhetoric, like the ambiguous placement of lyric in theoretical writings, was in some ways amenable to the inclusion of lyricism in a variety of contexts. In positing slow and careful attention to language, Boccaccio advocated an experience for the reader comparable to that demanded by the more self-consciously literary love lyrics, such as Petrarch's and Shakespeare's sonnets—an experience of slowed time or altered temporality. It was in this area of experiential similarity to elevated literature that Elizabethan love lyrics in fact superseded the dichotomies of high and low art dominating Elizabethan genre theory. And for Shakespeare, who put such sonnets in the lyrical plays *Romeo and Juliet* and *Love's Labour's Lost,* love rhetoric also broke down the division between literary lyric and drama.

The humanist emphasis on poetry as rhetoric also called attention to the role of an audience, and here as in the case of lyric theory something like double vision held sway; but what seems to have held greater sway for Elizabethan poets, as the later sixteenth century wore on, was the body natural on the English throne. In an analogy to the generic theory that split lyric into high and low, the Elizabethan court encouraged a split between two kinds of works addressed to women: in addition to the "low" females Nashe found addressed in babbling sonnets and ballads, a "high" female audience appeared in the person of the queen. Monarchic theory invested the sovereign with a spiritual as well as a physical body, encouraging an analogy between poetic praise of the ruler and of God. As Louis Adrian Montrose (among many) observes, "this analogy of sacred and secular encomia is strengthened when the incarnation of temporal authority and power happens to be a virgin queen who is head of both state and church, and whose personal mythology is contrived to be a national and Protestant substitute for a cult of the Blessed Virgin" ("Celebration" 3).

But because tropes and forms derived from the "low" poetry of earthly love were adapted to compliment the queen, these two audiences, or the tones in which they were addressed, became elided. That is, Elizabeth's gender obscured distinctions between the erotic and the political, the profane and the sacred. It reified the fictive construct of the masterful lady in Petrarchan poetics, hence transforming the relationship between amatory lyric and the political world of state power. The rhetorical categorization of lyric poetry as epideictic oratory designed to praise or blame, in concert with the courtly lyric convention of directly addressing a beloved lady, encouraged poems flattering to Elizabeth; when the reasons for praise extended beyond her exceptional position as sovereign to embrace her womanhood, such praise could logically be extended back to other women.

Certainly this rhetorical situation affected the way courtiers perceived their elite audience. Although the number of women at court was a tiny percentage, the intimate access of ladies-in-waiting to the sovereign invested them with prestige and the appearance of political influence. When courtiers such as George Puttenham and George Gascoigne speak "to the ladies," they are not the alehouse wenches of Nashe's satire. Indeed for Puttenham, the only audience worth addressing contains both men and women, and his order of address reverses the usual hierarchy; he salutes "princely dames, yong ladies, gentlewomen and courtiers" (quoted in Javitch 78). Part of this deference may be attributable to his literary model of Castiglione, but conversely, one factor in *Il Cortegiano*'s applicability was its model of a court with a woman at the top (albeit, in the dukedom of Urbino, the woman's consort was absent rather than nonexistent).

In "Of Proportion," focusing on shape poems, Puttenham provides an example of both formal poetic flattery of Elizabeth and the way such praise can influence the reading of other, more intimate, love lyrics. He includes two column-shaped poems: "Her Majestie resembled to the crowned pillar," and "Philo to his Lady Calia sendeth this Odelet of her prayse in forme of a Piller" (GGS 2: 101). Printed side by side, as they are in Puttenham's text, the two columns are visually almost indistinguishable (see figure 1).

Puttenham instructs us to read the first column upwards, an unconventional mode befitting an unconventional woman, and one which concludes by lifting our eyes to her "crown," literally and figuratively; for the courtly lady, we read downwards, as usual. These instructions are crucial, because otherwise the terms of compliment might seem too closely related. The queen is admired for "Her mayden raigne / And womanhead," among other virtues, while Calia's praise idolatrously begins "Thy Princely port and Majestie / Is my terrene deitie." Moreover, the choppy syntax encourages misreading, if one scans habitually across the page as Puttenham's surrounding text requires; the two poems easily begin to "bleed" and blur. Although the first-person address to Calia does imply a more intimate and less official relationship, the ambiguous referent for this courtly pseudonym could exemplify the use of such monikers in Petrarchist flattery of Elizabeth. "Calia" may be one of many courtly names applied to the queen herself, but conversely, nothing in the text prevents "Calia" from standing for another beloved lady. Either way, the queen's status as exceptional among women is blurred by these parallel, metaphorically related pillars.

With the need to address Elizabeth came a modified attitude toward female audience and love lyric, as well as the adaptation of its rhetoric to political issues; the final third of this chapter (like the subsequent readings) underscores the queen's important influence on lyricism in court pageants and plays. But equally important was a practical perception by poets that lyric could be crafted to express male subjectivity and a range of social concerns. These were the combined potentials of courtly lyric that would eventually encourage dramatists to transpose amatory discourse into stage speech, and to employ it resonantly. The verse of one earlier Elizabethan courtier, George Gascoigne, illustrates how lyric poetry played off and against contemporary theoretical assumptions, resulting in work that is sometimes richer and more sophisticated than the critical commentary

Figure 1.

| Her Maiestie resembled to the crowned pillar. Ye must read upward. | Philo to the Lady Calia sendeth this Odelet of her prayse in forme of a Piller, which ye must read downeward. |

Is blisse with immortalitie.
  Her trymest top of all ye see
    Garnish the crowne,
    Her iust renowne
    Chapter and head,
    Part that maintain
    And womanhead
    Her mayden raigne
    In te gri tie:
    In ho nour and
    With ve ri tie,
    Her roundnes stand
    Strengthen the state.
    By their increase
    With out de bate
    Concord and peace
    Of her sup port,
    They be the base
    With stedfastnesse
    Vertue and grace
    Stay, and comfort;
    Of Albi ons rest,
    The sounde Pillar
    And seene a farre
    Is plainely exprest
  Tall stately and strayt
By this no ble pour trayt

Thy Princely port and Maiestie
  Is my ter rene dei tie,
    Thy wit and sence
    The streame & source
    Of e lo quence
    And deepe discours,
    Thy faire eyes are
    My bright loadstarre,
    Thy speache a darte
    Percing my harte,
    Thy face, a las,
    My loo king glasse,
    Thy louely lookes
    My prayer bookes,
    Thy pleasant cheare,
    My sunshine cleare,
    Thy ru full sight
    My darke midnight,
    Thy will the stent
    Of my con tent,
    Thy glo rye flour
    Of myne ho nour,
    Thy loue doth giue
    The lyfe I lyue,
    Thy lyfe it is
    Mine earthly blisse:
  But grace & favour in thine eies
  My bodies soule & souls paradise.

leads one to expect. Although Gascoigne himself did not synthesize his dual achievements as a neoclassical dramatist and a lyric poet, his best poems suggest important Elizabethan precedents for the staging of lyric. Of special interest in this regard is Gascoigne's ingenious play, while establishing a narrative and social context, with two related aspects of lyric that endure as modern concerns: the rhetoric of temporality and the authority of the gendered first-person speaker.

The Lyric Attitudes of George Gascoigne

Given the limitations of Elizabethan commentary in articulating the aims and functions of lyric, what did poets try to do with it in practice? How did they set the stage for lyrical drama? Some answers are suggested by the poetry of Gascoigne, one of the earliest lyricists to write with an eye to material gain. Unlike the dual pillars of Henrican love lyric, Sir Thomas Wyatt and Henry Howard, Earl of Surrey, George Gascoigne lived on the margins of courtly respectability, closer in status to late Elizabethan professional playwrights than to earlier aristocratic courtly makers. He allowed his substantial collection of poems *A Hundreth Sundrie Flowres* (1573) to be published, followed by the "corrected, perfected, and augmented" version reissued as *The Posies* (1575), and he incorporated love lyrics into larger narratives, such as *The Adventures of Master F.J.* and the royal entertainments at Kenilworth. His poetry evocatively explores temporality and the constraints on his voice; because these concerns become a crucial source of tension and richness in lyrical drama, Gascoigne's poetry thus serves well as an Elizabethan introduction both to those issues as they intersect with gendered representation in lyrical discourse and to the genealogy of functional lyricism in the theater.

In focusing on Gascoigne's poetry as the locus of new narrative and dramatic possibilities for the lyric, I am certainly not denying the important continental and Henrican precedents for the complex rendition of lyric subjectivity; rather, Gascoigne should be located along a historical continuum of lyric practice, with especially important ancestors including Chaucer, Wyatt, and Tottel's collection of *Songs and Sonnets,* as well as Petrarch himself. Tottel's appendage of headnotes to the Petrarchan sonnets of Wyatt and Surrey, specifying (and privatizing) the lover's situation, provided an especially influential model for "discovering" an implicit narrative line within particular lyrics; in concert with an imposed order of arrangement, the headnotes produce a narrative temporality that works against reading the poems as isolated, disjunctive moments. As Jonathan Crewe aptly notes in regard to Surrey's poems, "In supplying running titles for untitled lyrics, Tottel begins (or helps) to construct the sequential romance narrative of the wistful, distinguished, eternally pining Surrey-type: 'The lover for shamefastnesse hideth his desire within his faithfull hart,' 'The lover sheweth how he is forsaken of such as he sometime enjoyed,' and so forth" (50). The importation of such narrative tags into *A Hundreth Sundrie Flowres,* here self-consciously imposed by the poet himself, exemplifies one of several ways in which Gascoigne extends earlier gestures toward the intersection of lyric and narrative tropes.

Whereas Tottel marketed the poetry of aristocrats, Gascoigne marketed himself (to adapt Crewe's description) "for profitable distribution to a by no means exclusive reading public, and for future use by literary upstarts"—including, I would emphasize, those "Shake-scene" playwrighting upstarts.

At the same time, writing in the 1560s and 1570s Gascoigne represented a new Elizabethan generation of lyricists, resembling their queen in selectively remembering their Henrican paternity and claiming to restore order after the chaos at mid-century. Gascoigne's "Certayne Notes of Instruction" stresses the need for metrical regularity to establish some shared system among English poets; he accepts (with regret) the strictest interpretation of iambic regularity: "And surely I can lament that wee are fallen into suche a playne and simple manner of wryting, that there is none other foote used but one: wherby our Poemes may justly be called Rithmes, and cannot by any right challenge the name of a Verse. But since it is so, let us take the forde as we finde it" (*Complete Works* 1: 468). Given his need to include the elementary advice that poets should stick to the same verse form once they have begun a poem (rather than change in midstream), one can sympathize with his desire for metric uniformity. Gascoigne's clearly delineated technique well represents the educated views of his generation, as becomes obvious when reading through Tottel or the *Mirror for Magistrates*. Variation is rare; the pause comes after the second foot in the pentameter line, after the third in the alexandrine, and after the third or fourth in the fourteener. Wyatt's troublesome mixtures of four-stress and iambic pentameter lines had been regularized by Tottel, often ineptly; Surrey provided sonorous examples of sibilant styling in his more regular iambic pentameter; and their followers solidified the iambic foot into the metrical pedestal upon which all poems were to be erected.

Within this context, Gascoigne was hailed by numerous Elizabethan writers as the progenitor of their line, both metrical and ancestral. Puttenham cites "*Gascon*, for a good meeter and for a plentifull vayne" (GGS 2: 65). In their typically qualified and reserved way (consonant with their strict adherence to academic theory and metrical correctness), Gascoigne's critical contemporaries esteemed him as a bringer of order, a formal experimenter, and a poet of intelligence and craft. Thomas Nashe grudgingly acknowledges him as the first Elizabethan verse translator: "Who ever my private opinion condemneth as faultie, Master *Gascoigne* is not to bee abridged of his deserved esteeme, who first beate the path to that perfection which our best Poets have aspired too since his departure; whereto he did ascend by comparing the Italian with the English, as *Tullie* did *Graeca cum Latinis*" (GGS

1: 315). Based on the quantity of praise, William Webbe regards Gascoigne as second only to Spenser among past poets; whereas he simply lists others such as "the olde Earle of Surrey, . . . the L. Vaus, . . . Norton of Bristow, Edwardes, Tusser, Churchyard, Wyl. Hunnis, Haiwood . . . ," Gascoigne is singled out for discussion. He precedes the rest despite chronology, coming directly after Skelton: "next hym I thynke I may place master *George Gaskoyne,* as painefull a Souldier in the affayres of hys Prince and Country as he was wytty Poet in his wryting: whose commendations, because I found in one of better iudgment then my selfe, I wyl sette downe hys wordes, and suppresse myne owne" (GGS 1: 242). Webbe then characteristically defers to Spenser, citing the commentator *E. K.*'s gloss to the November eclogue in *The Shepheardes Calender,* the eclogue which concludes with an elegy to "some mayden of greate bloud, whom he calleth Dido" (Spenser 460). *E. K.*'s praise recalls one of Gascoigne's most suggestive personae, a male appropriation of Philomel whose grounds for complaint, like the mythical Dido's, echo throughout literary history (as well as this book). *E. K.* explains that "Philomele" is the Nightingale: "Whome the Poetes faine once to have bene a Ladye of great beauty, till being ravished by hir sisters husbande, she desired to be turned into a byrd of her name. Whose complaintes be very well set forth of Ma. George Gaskin a wittie gentleman, and the very chefe of our late rymers, who and if some partes of learning wanted not (albee it is well knowen he altogyther wanted not learning) no doubt would have attayned to the excellencye of those famous Poets. For gifts of wit and naturall promptnesse appear in hym aboundantly" (463). Referring specifically to Gascoigne's late elegy "The Complaint of Philomene," *E. K.* moves unselfconsciously from a myth of female victimization to his praise of the "wittie gentleman," foregrounding the compensatory logic of the nightingale's myth: having been violated by a man, "she" receives the gift of beautiful song, which is then assumed by the (male) poet as analogous to—or in the case of Gascoigne's first-person elegy, the same as—his own. Not surprisingly, *E. K.* glosses over the perpetuation of male dominance involved in translating this myth into poetry, instead joining the chorus of theorists who focus on craft and classical training. Nevertheless, this associative move from Philomel to a somewhat ambivalent account of Gascoigne's status aptly calls attention to that author's own poetic use of gender to both represent and quell anxieties about his borderline social position.

A soldier and a gentleman by birth, lacking "some [albeit not all] partes of learning," Gascoigne's social status and luck placed him in an odd limbo between the aristocratic poetasters and academic amateurs on the one hand,

and the now-unknown writers of popular shows on the other. C. T. Prouty explains Gascoigne's limitations as a dramatist in words that apply more broadly to his artistic career: "He was proud of his family and his title of 'Esquire,' and could not, therefore, accept monetary reward for his literary efforts. He could seek patronage, the reversion of an office, or royal employment consistent with his position, but not money. He was '*Tam Marti Quam Mercurio,*' but never a professional man of letters" (172). Twenty years later, he might have "descended" to publishing pamphlets or writing plays for a livelihood, like George Peele or Thomas Nashe. But in the 1560s and 1570s, the profession of author was only in embryo and certainly not respectable enough for a gentleman.[6] Gascoigne instead struggled to be a "professional amateur," a jack-of-all-trades whose writing might indirectly subsidize his life at court through the pleasure it provided his patrons. When this attempt to embody an oxymoron failed, he surreptitiously let his poetry be published in the volume entitled *A Hundreth Sundrie Flowres*. Never one upon whom the gods smiled without irony, Gascoigne found himself embroiled in a scandal over certain "lascivious phrases" and the identities of the characters in his narrative of F. J., as well as over the public circulation of this text (*Complete Works* 1: 3). Two years later he produced the "perfected" revision dubbed *The Posies,* a latter-day *sylva* (divided into "Flowers," "Hearbes," and "Weedes") which includes a wedding masque, two neoclassical plays amidst the "Hearbes," several shorter verse narratives, a coronet of sonnets, "Certayne Notes of Instruction Concerning the Making of Verse," and copious prefatory material, as well as many love lyrics. *The Posies* constituted the most audacious attempt to gain respect for a published poet as worthy craftsman prior to Spenser's publication of *The Shepheardes Calender* in 1579.

In both editions of his poetry, Gascoigne dramatizes tensions that will animate the characters of late Elizabethan lyrical drama: tensions between past and present versions of oneself, and between the roles of truthful speaker and creative personality. Gascoigne presents his own life as poetic source, and cultivates the personas of repentant prodigal and truth-telling social bungler. In the process of this self-fashioning, he employs lyric poetry to express social and emotional conflicts in subtler, more varied ways than contemporary theories of amatory lyric acknowledged. Overtly, he appeals to plain speech and truth-telling rather than flights of fancy and metaphor, yet the adoption of mythical personae such as the Greene Knight and Philomel (both here and in his last works) immediately complicates the picture. Nor does Gascoigne restrict his "truthful" writing to weighty political matters, as many other Inns of Court men (such as *Gorboduc*'s co-author Thomas Sackville, later Lord Buckhurst) did. No doubt Gascoigne's tenuous position at court encouraged opportunism, but it is also true that such somber, statesmanlike writing could not adequately capture his poetic range and temperament. Gascoigne's corpus includes many songs and sonnets, his *Flowres* framed with two narratives containing inset love lyrics; and despite the pat categorization of *The Posies*, which reclassifies most of the amatory verse as frivolous and immoral "Weedes" or flattering "Flowers," he had in fact found a rich medium for exploring the relationship between his youthful and mature selves. Two attitudes toward lyric poetry dominate Gascoigne's commentary in *The Posies*, the volume he openly authorized. The more obvious one has been seized upon by those (such as Yvor Winters and C. T. Prouty) who honor Gascoigne as a "native" or "plain stylist" and a moralist; the other complicates their attempt, supporting Richard McCoy's counterassertion that the "poet's best work resisted the simplicities of plain speech" ("Gascoigne's '*Poëmata*'" 32).[7]

In his prefaces and poems, Gascoigne often presents himself as one who represents the world "as it is." His direct diction, regular metrics, and sparing use of figurative conceits reinforce the impression that he does not greatly embellish or idealize his experience. This dedication to *reportage*, understandable given the low critical regard we have seen for love poetry and amorous fancy, is far more pervasive than the specific pose of repentance in the poet's last works. Sidney, in his *Apology*, was to separate the "historical" from the imaginative poets, favoring the latter as the only "right poets" because they can create golden worlds by ranging solely "within the zodiac of [their] own wit" (14, 20). Gascoigne takes the opposite position in his narrative poem *Dulce bellum inexpertis*, recounting his grim war experiences in the Netherlands. He starts by dismissing the poet's, painter's, and astronomer's definitions of war because "they faine to[o] farre" (*Complete Works* 1: 142). "Let poets lie"; *he*, on the other hand, will "Tell by trustie proufe of truth" that "war is even the scourge of God" (143). The poets are discredited not only for their false romanticizing but also for their rhetoric, which is too packed with classical allusions and the fantastic to serve his empirical, historicist bias. As a narrator, Gascoigne presents himself as a revealer of the truth, unallegorized and unadorned.[8]

Similarly, the poet frequently claims to base his lyrics on experience, plainly but artfully related. The narrative emphasis even in short love lyrics attests to this; so does the frequent appearance of "George" within the poems and "Gascoigne" in their titles (for example, "Gascoigne's Good

Night," "Gascoigne's Good Morrow," and "Gascoigne's *de profundis*"). Such self-presentation can be an effective strategy for keeping moral history, as distinct from moral ideals, in focus, and hence for legitimizing the recreation of one's messy experience as a source of "profite" for the "yong gentlemen" he addresses (*Complete Works* 1: 12). The poet seems to take direct, literal responsibility for his life and words in this brazen world, rather than creating fantasies and veiled allegories of a golden alternative. Yet this use of personal narrative tags, extended from Tottel, is at the same time an important move toward self-conscious "self-dramatization."

Moreover, for a literalist, "George" does show up in some rather odd places, such as "Beautyes barre" (in "The Arraignment of a Lover"). He thus transfers his self-dramatization of lyric subjectivity into a fictive context, creating a precedent for the complex voices of lyrical drama. In this case Gascoigne's poem prefigures George Peele's *Arraignment of Paris* in using a legal court as the scene for a moral debate about eros and power at quite another kind of court. While allegorical journeys are commonplace in medieval literature, here the result is earthbound and public—like late Elizabethan drama—rather than dominantly introspective or religious; what Gascoigne's "Arraignment" nonetheless shares with both later drama and earlier spiritual autobiography is an indirect, figurative method of representing truth claims. The bulk of *The Posies* is in fact neither strictly autobiographical nor historical but imaginative, and the poet frequently toys with his role of bluff George. Mimicking Chaucer, he claims simple "experience" as his authority even when adopting another voice, such as in the Reporter's prologue to "Dan Bartholmew of Bathe."

> To tell a tale without authoritye,
> Or fayne a Fable by invencion,
> That one proceedes of quicke capacitye,
> That other proves but small discretion,
> Yet have both one and other oft bene done
> And if I were a Poet as some be,
> You might perhappes here some such tale of me.
>
> But far I fynde my feeble skyll to faynt,
> To faine in figurs as the learned can,
> And yet my tongue is tyde by due constraint,
> To tell nothing but trueth of every man:
> I will assay even as I first began,

> To tell you nowe a tale and that of truth,
> Which I my selfe saw proved in my youth.
>
> (*Complete Works* 1: 96)

The internal contradiction and irony are as thick in this prologue as in that of the most famous fictional resident of Bath, the Wife whose opening speech these self-consciously literary lines clearly echo. Gascoigne's diction and claim to simple witnessing may be plain, but the authorial stance and truth claims are not.

This literary playfulness is typical, for Gascoigne's "realistic" narrators and framing devices are deeply embedded in poetic tradition. The use of a prose narrative to link love lyrics in *The Adventures of Master F.J.* harkens back to Dante's *Vita Nuova;* the psychological toying with a "split self" suggests Petrarch's influence extending well beyond Gascoigne's adaptation of the *Trionfi.*[9] As both speaker and subject of many poems, Gascoigne does not merely record but filters experience; in his preface "To al yong Gentlemen," he mocks the "ignorant Readers" who might think otherwise, and "understande neyther the meaning of the Authour, nor the sense of the figurative speeches" and hence "take Chalke for Cheese" (*Complete Works* 1: 10–11). Confuting his professions of simply recording his experience (and sheepishly admitting that "the number of loving lynes exceedeth in the Superlative"), he tells "the Readers generally" that, Cyrano-like, "if ever I wrote a lyne for my selfe in causes of love, I have written tenne for other men in layes of lust" (16). Similarly, in his "Preface to the Divines" he acknowledges "the depth and secrets of some conceytes . . . being passed in clowdes and figurative speeches," and hopes that men of learning will understand the multiple levels and fictionality of his poetry. His comments underscore the melding of *prosopopoeia,* conceited rhetoric, and narrative emphasis that will prove serviceable in the creation of lyrical drama.

Despite these witty defenses for writing love poetry, Gascoigne does present many of his lyrics in an ironic context, implying a more pragmatic critique of love poetry: it fails to "get the girl," instead deluding its authors as they praise unworthy beloveds. Such is the fate of his character Dan Bartholmew of Bathe, whose lyrics are framed by a verse narrative showing both the poems and his beloved to be dishonest. The lover himself, not entirely aware of the extent to which his "Goddess" has been untrue, is left frustrated and disconsolate.[10] Jack hath not Jill. Placed at the end of *A Hundreth Sundrie Flowres,* this story serves as a conclusive commentary, with the rueful Reporter rather than the lover getting the last word. The use of a narrative frame to undermine the idealistic love lyricist, although partly an excuse allowing Gascoigne to tell his "immoral" story, foreshadows the more complex mockery of Sidney's Astrophil and Shakespeare's Berowne, who are exposed by the double comeuppance of narrative context and duplicity within their verse. In those later works, it is fundamentally the poetic speaker rather than the beloved lady who turns out to be unworthy, whereas Gascoigne (like Sir Thomas Wyatt) tends to expose the beloved woman at least as much as the unhappy lover. Gascoigne's tack is more traditional and predictable, reinforced by the artistic tendency to sympathize with the male protagonist as well as by the culture's more overt forms of misogyny (stereotyping woman as fickle, untrustworthy, sexually insatiable, etc.). In both cases the use of a narrative frame can serve the perennial attack on love lyric by moralists and also by those realists who associate a less sugared style of linguistic representation with truth; but it also suggests a potentially dialogic play of lyric and satiric perspectives amenable to dramatization.

The particular "realism" of this narrative frame presumes that lovers do tend to be unfaithful and their words untrue; it also may lead readers to presume that the narrator's framing language can approach transparent referentiality or objectivity. But while Gascoigne usually adopts the male subject position unquestioningly, he tends to be more complicated in his response to poetic language, recognizing that every style or stance shapes the object it represents. He presents his "steele glas," in the blank verse satire so named, as a device shaping vision just as the crystal mirror does—albeit with less flattering and seductive results. Plainness is one chosen, not an unmediated or undistorted, view. And indeed Gascoigne's stories as totalities tend to be more compelling and complicated by multiple perspectives than his narrators' bald moral conclusions would imply.[11] As in most drama, the privileged perspective, if it can be discerned at all, is presented obliquely. In consequence, the lyrics contained within his narratives, and the less cynical attitudes toward love and ladies expressed therein, cannot simply be dismissed as false or worthless; they still merit a large place in Gascoigne's representation of memorable experience, as well as constituting a large proportion of his artistic output.

Just as Gascoigne plays with the tensions between lyric and satiric perspectives in his narratives, he also plays with the multiple perspectives afforded by temporal change. Attention to time past is a rich linguistic device to sustain a distance between language and experience, serving to keep unruly, immoral, putatively unimportant experience safely elsewhere. It also complicates the exclusive forward momentum of present-tense narrative often associated with stage time, and, used ambivalently in amatory lyric, can thwart a single vision of time as either decadent or progressive. Whether under his own name or those of poetic intermediaries such as the Greene Knight and F. J., Gascoigne uses temporal distancing to create a role that allows him to attack love poets and be one too. He plays the repentant prodigal, the former poet who sees the error of his whimsy. Tellingly, repentance is not enough to stop the poet from remembering and lamenting his lost past—and not just because it was misspent. This representation creates the ambivalent attitude toward irretrievable youth, and toward the lyric poetry associated with it, that permeates *The Posies*. The prodigal's double perspective and temporal obsession provide Gascoigne with a distinctive situation and set of concerns that give his lyric poetry a range and tension exceptional in his time, and constitute an appealing, enriching counterpoint to episodic narrative sequence. His assumption of a double stance, like a dramatist's distance from his character, encourages the audience both to enjoy the emotions and display of a first-person lyricist and to attend to the ironies of his placement on earth, in time.

In the "Flower" entitled "The Lullabie of the Lover," for example, the poet tries to put the past to bed with a song whose gentleness and irony captures the wistfulness of age rather than the righteousness of the redeemed (or even the frank resignation of the realist found in Lord Vaux's contemporary "The Agèd Lover Renounceth Love," to which Gascoigne refers in his preface [*Complete Works* 1: 11]). As Leonard Nathan has indicated, the poem's form avoids a simple, traditional contrast of age versus youth, with age victorious.[12] Regret resides in the present and its limits in this swan song, not in the remembrance of sins past:

> Sing lullaby, as women doe,
> Wherewith they bring their babes to rest,
> And lullaby can I sing to,
> As womanly as can the best.
> With lullaby they still the childe,
> And if I be not much beguild,
> Full many wanton babes have I,
> Which must be stild with lullabie.
> . . . .
> Next Lullaby my gazing eyes,
> Which wonted were to glaunce apace.
> For every Glasse maye nowe suffise,
> To shewe the furrowes in my face:

> With Lullabye then winke awhile,
> With Lullabye your lookes beguile:
> Lette no fayre face, nor beautie brighte,
> Entice you efte with vayne delighte.
>
> (*Complete Works* 1: 44, ll. 1–8, 17–24)

Taking on "the woman's part," the speaker tries to pacify desire, but his motives seem expedient, based on necessity rather than propriety. One sings a lullaby to calm and comfort a child, not to judge it. This is a far cry from the satiric exposure of desire found in the more charged moralistic scenes of Ben Jonson's plays and Spenser's epic, both of which reveal falseness or putrid female bodies hidden behind cosmetically constructed facades. By contrast, Gascoigne's speaker might as well slowly shut his "gazing eyes" if all he sees is his own lined face, perhaps unable to attract "beautie brighte." Meanwhile, soft sounds lull the critic's reason and evoke sensual beauty; enticing pleasures may be vain, or merely sought in vain, but its placement as the final word of the third stanza gives lingering length to their undeniable "delight." Even if the eyes close on beauty, its memory has not been put to sleep. Likewise in the same poem's fifth stanza, the speaker directly addresses his "loving boy," his phallic sexuality. Wittily recognizing time's power, the poet tells "little Robyn" to rest, "Since age is cold" and he has less "coyne": "Lette others pay which hath mo pence." This fondly fondling farewell to eros appears motivated by time's power, not by rectitude or desire.

The speaker's present stance in this lullaby is hardly invested with righteousness or moral certitude. The repeated word "beguile" refers in both cases to the present moment, obliquely expressing doubt about whether age has any greater claim to wisdom or truth at all. "With Lullabye your lookes beguile": deception lies in *not* looking at the mirror. The poem itself thus becomes implicated in the self-deception, for it is the "Lullabye" we are looking at as we read these words on the page.

> With Lullaby your dreames deceive,
> And when you rise with waking eye,
> Remember then this Lullabye.
>   *Ever or Never*
>
> (*Complete Works* 1: 45, ll. 46–49)

The motto's absolutism, reliant on a single letter, accentuates the fluidity between states in the poem's final lines. Deceiving dreams will be deceived by this song; when the lover wakes, his youthful desires returning after age's calm, he is to remember this dreamlike poem as a sign of an age now past. Just as a lullaby blurs the edges between sleep and waking, Gascoigne's poem blurs what logic regards as categorical oppositions. Age and youth, deception and knowledge, now and then become part of a rhythmical, repeating wave pattern. Gascoigne's poetic method reinforces the link between temporality and morality, in effect undermining changeless codes that reject passion and love poetry categorically—a sort of poetics of situational ethics, later to be dramatized comically by Shakespeare in *Love's Labour's Lost*. Even the attempt to confine passion to one stage of life is vexed, as the poem makes obvious. In this act of composition, Gascoigne thus provides a precedent for the representation of a lyrical voice within a context of change *and* creates a lyric discourse capacious enough to render the complexities of anxious subjectivity in conflict with simple chronological change.

Found among the "Weedes," "The Greene Knight's Farewell to Fansie" similarly mingles moral struggle with poetic play in a lyric form amenable to narrative dramatization. This time Gascoigne strengthens the satiric impulse even as he explicitly differentiates himself from the critical speaker, by parenthetically repeating the third-person pronoun "he" in the refrain. The Greene Knight, a favorite in Gascoigne's gallery of uncouth personae derived from English folk tradition, equates fancy, poetry, and his youth. Like the speaker of "Lullabie," he emphasizes lost hopes rather than the wisdom putatively replacing them. Eight of the ten stanzas in this "Farewell" provide illustrations of different ways "Fansie" deceived the knight, in each case moving from a grand first impression to a final rejection. Thus the third stanza travels from "The glosse of gorgeous courtes, by thee did please mine eye," to "But since I see how vayne it is, *Fansie* (quoth he) *farewell*" (*Complete Works* 1: 380). The sixth stanza declares the Greene Knight's (but not Gascoigne's) farewell to versifying:

> A fansie fedde me ones, to wryte in verse and rime,
> To wray my griefe, to crave reward, to cover still my crime
> To frame a long discourse, on sturring of a strawe,
> To rumble rime in raffe and ruffe, yet all not worth an hawe:
> To heare it sayde there goeth, *the Man that writes so well*,
> But since I see, what Poetes bee, Fansie (quoth he) farewell.
>
> (381)

The poet lingers over the delusions of his past, reserving only a line and vague dismissal to counter their vividness. Despite the disproportion and immorality he imputes to his past writing, the Cowardly Lion-like fun of rumbling "rime in raffe and ruffe" (not to mention the pleasure of public praise) makes it hard to interpret this farewell as inspiring moral fervor or unambiguous joy, in either audience or speaker. A single moralizing stanza at the poem's end hardly balances, poetically, the many attractive illusions lost; and of course, this is still verse, a lyric in spite of itself. The reluctant moralist, the poet as not-poet, creates a voice whose attitude toward lyric and love is far from plainly negative.

Neither "Lullabie" nor "The Greene Knight's Farewell" centers on a courtly love relationship with a specified lady, as most of Gascoigne's more pedestrian Petrarchan "Flowers" do (and many more lyrics would, once the sonnet sequence gained ascendency). Instead, they include love—and especially the poet's sexual vigor—as one of the most pleasurable indulgences in a catalog of loss. These poems achieve a complex tone because of their double attitude toward time's passing, their speaker caught between a happily unwise past and a sadder but wiser present. Which experience and which attitude is "truer" remains moot. But unquestionably, the questionable status of love lyrics becomes an aid in representing ambivalence, allowing the poet to present that which he rejects. He uses verse to remember and recall the experiences which his maturity cannot relive. This potentially tragic position will be developed in the public drama of the 1590s, most notably in Shakespeare's lyrical history play *Richard II*. Narcissistic Richard may "call back yesterday," but only in language; locked in narrative time onstage, he can't juggle these states as if they were purely linguistic constructs.

By regarding Gascoigne as a plain-style moralist, some of his scholarly defenders are forced to disregard much of his poetic practice, including the garden of courtly flowers written to lovely ladies; more importantly, this position tends to overlook his contribution in creating complex and playful lyric poetry of interest to narrative poets, including playwrights. Despite the separation of fancy and history in some of Gascoigne's own narrative works, including his neoclassical dramas, his lyric practice suggests a way to supersede categorical splits which he himself acknowledged to be frustrating. These nostalgic lyrics, containing ethical and temporal tensions rather than simple pronouncements, suggest the capacity of lyric poetry to represent a mind in struggle with itself and its material conditions. Gascoigne's lyric voice thrived in and because of a narrative context, namely the prodigal's realization of his lost youth and the waning of romance. The presentation of that self entails representation of language and the poet changing over time, abetted by the forms and figures of poetry. Moreover, in Gascoigne's narrative poems, lyrics are ironically framed by events in a way foreshadowing satiric scenes in Marlowe's and Shakespeare's plays. It is this legacy of lyric practice, not the profession of plainness, that helps account for the emergent lyrical drama of the late sixteenth century.

The nostalgia characteristic of much of Gascoigne's lyric poetry obviously was not unprecedented in English; most notably, Sir Thomas Wyatt's "They flee from me" plays with the double perspective of the lover for whom "all is changed now." But even Wyatt does not allow his "present" stance to involve so much self-doubt, instead cultivating an image as victim of "newfangleness" and female wiles—the stereotypical fickleness of the other rather than a sign of internal change. It is Wyatt's own unchanging truth and virtue, in theory, that allows him to speak with harsh irony about his betrayers, and by implication undermines the past happiness in love as deception or a dream. This assertion of "troth," Jonathan Crewe points out, is part of Wyatt's dynamic and "crafty" power as a lyricist. Even when he asserts "It was no dreme," his portrait of the past is misty and ambiguous: the animalistic "They" who used to stalk, take bread at his hand, and were tame remain metaphorically unspecific; the "once in special" she, with long, small arms, has the veiled mystery of an erotic fantasy. The lyric presents an unveiling, the removal of illusions to be replaced by the speaker's baffled cynicism and desire for revenge (blame not *his* lute for exposing *her*). Having seen through these desirable but deceptive females, the wronged speaker leaves behind the vanity of love and courtship in favor of moral rectitude. Wyatt's poems often conclude with the defeated lover a sadder but wiser man; moreover, because his poetic "fansie," his role as poet, was never linked with or confined to a time of youth and love, representing that past in poetic form is not in itself ironic.

Nevertheless, whether the glance backward be sad, loving, or ironic, the lyrics of both Wyatt and Gascoigne presume, implicitly, a narrative of desire erased or thwarted. Poetic representation becomes a substitute for desire, a compensation for that loss. In the delicate balance of interest between narrating the change and meditating upon its meaning, Gascoigne finds a resonant voice transferable to a dramatic narrative context. And because so much of emotional life revolves around desire and loss, projecting forward and backward, lyric poetry became a richer medium for thought than contemporary theorists recognized.

Of course, not all lyric poetry looks backward. Some of the most memorable Elizabethan lyrics involve different versions of multiple temporality. It is the breaking up of one perspective through play with time that links the poetry of Gascoigne with Marlowe's lyrical voice in *Dido, Queen of Carthage*, for example, not the specific terms of their temporal obsession. This function of time is not only a thematic but a structural issue, a way to add complexity to narrative sequence. Furthermore, the direction and tone of the temporal gaze often correlates with the representation of the lyric speaker's predominant attitude toward the beloved. Because the stereotypical model of male maturation requires abandonment of the feminine, sometimes the male lyricist's backwards glance indicates reluctance or dramatizes the cost of a culture's demand for gender differentiation. Even more tellingly, the inability or refusal to represent the beloved female as "staying put" in the past may in some cases signal active valuing of, or at least dramatic struggle with, a vital version of "the feminine."

For example, Spenser's *Amoretti* 75 ("One day I wrote her name upon the strand"), as contrasted with Sir Thomas Wyatt's more righteous lyrics of erotic victimization, complicates both temporality and gender positioning so as to create an enduring, almost mutual image of love between male and female. Spenser, unlike the Italian *inamorati* mourning their dead women, refuses to lock his lover safely in the past. Her putative words are reproduced in the second quatrain, put in the present tense and in a voice critical of his "vaine assay." Her expressed doubt about his eternizing enterprise signals his own larger ironic awareness about his role as love poet victoriously vaunting over Time, even as the dialogue provides another way to meld their temporally bound voices together. Of course the poet is ventriloquizing "her" voice, and so one can accurately argue that he in fact retains total authority; nevertheless, it is an oblique rather than directly asserted control, which creates a more complicated gendered literary territory. It implies a larger landscape of contestation with an enduring and vocal Other whose perspective must be considered. In this, Spenser's representation bears more kinship with Shakespeare's subsequent dramatizations of a skeptical female position than with the singular self-assertion often attributed to lyric form. The somewhat ironically collaborative presentation of lovers fittingly complements Spenser's narrative practice in *The Faerie Queene,* where he manages to celebrate (alongside his own authorial achievement, and not without ambivalence) an eroticized and chaste *living* queen.

This is not to say that Spenser's own work ultimately develops in a direction comparable to that of lyrical drama, for Spenser not only stops short of representing Gloriana but also retains a firm hand in writing his narrative on paper, if not in writing that other beloved Elizabeth's name in the sand of *Amoretti* 75. Unlike the rendering of female speakers by court dramatists such as George Peele, Spenser includes female voices fitfully even as he tries to subordinate them to his larger narrative patterns. What remains relevant here is that even in his attempt to include and thereby control female agency in the service of his own poetic authority, Spenser acknowledges an ongoing feminine power that resists or modifies his monovocal shaping, a figure that cannot be neatly placed in the past and that persists as obscurely desirable.

In "Gascoigne's Woodmanship," the location and representation of a female figure similarly complicates the poetic landscape, and directly links the attempt to be reformed and manly with a high price for femininity. With its allegorical female deer (a variation on the conventional dear female) and its glance at God, Gascoigne's poem shares with Spenser's sonnet 67 ("Lyke as a huntsman"), Wyatt's "Whoso list to hunt," and their Petrarchan predecessors the complexity of erotic and Christian imagery combined with a hunting narrative about power and struggle. One hundred and fifty lines long and developed as a tripartite defense of the poet, "Gascoigne's Woodmanship" can only loosely be classed as a lyric; more accurately, it indicates the potential for figurative language and Petrarchan tropes to complicate a longer quasi-narrative piece—a transference of lyric techniques that Gascoigne did not see fit to use in his neoclassical academic dramas, but which later dramatists such as Marlowe certainly exploited. In "Woodmanship," Gascoigne moves away from the plain style through an extended metaphor that finally becomes a self-reflexive commentary on the poetic project itself.

The text presents Gascoigne (in the first person) trying to forestall questions from his patron, Lord Grey of Wilton, about the failure of "your woodman" (i.e., Gascoigne in the third person) at the hunt. A prized deer quickly expands, like the Greene Knight's "Fansie," to encompass all the botched attempts of his past, the hunt figuring his life at court. After an indirect satire in the third person listing those corrupt courtly practices at which he has "failed," Gascoigne shifts back to a direct first-person defense and reappraisal of his past, remembering its joys and profitable experiences as well as his bad luck. But the poem does not end here. Unlike "The Greene Knight's Farewell" and "Lullabie," "Gascoigne's Woodmanship" goes beyond nostalgic lamentation to make a present-tense apologia for the poet using not only a female animal but also, ironically, the kind of consciously figurative language that Gascoigne elsewhere attacks as false fancy. He shifts to an imaginative space in the conditional mood, using the vocabulary of poetic creation and hypothesizing "If" he were to strike a pregnant doe:

> Let me imagine in this woorthlesse verse,
> If right before mee, at my standings foote

> There stoode a Doe, And I should strike hir deade,
> and then shee prove a carrian carkas too . . .
>
> (*Complete Works* 1: 351)

He asks a question which refers both to his fictive action of shooting her and to his actual poetic creation of this imagined scene: "What figure might I finde within my head, / To scuse the rage which rulde mee so to doo?" (351). He rejects the "playne paraphrase" of his critics, who think he lacks skill or luck, just as his poem now rejects the plain style in favor of a grander defense of the poet/woodman. The doe becomes God's reminder of death's suddenness and the speaker's need to reform. Its milk (the product of his own poetic imagination, his ink) teaches a further moral: "Me thinkes it sayth, olde babe, now learne to sucke, / Who in thy youth couldst never learne the feate / To hitte the whytes whiche live with all good lucke" (352). As the figure of the wise fool, the babe nourished by his Lord in heaven as well as by Lord Grey of Wilton, Gascoigne turns his shortcomings into a superiority of grace over those whose success is merely worldly.[13] He does so by employing the devices of a fanciful poet, not a reporting historian, once again complicating his relationship to those "lies" which filled his youth, and to the lyric poetry he continued to write.

The mediating figure, the scapegoat, is a nursing female. Given the associations of love lyric with the feminine, the deer's "white ink" becomes all the more suggestive. As when he takes on the role of a male Philomel, Gascoigne conceives of a feminine aspect to poetic creation; but rather than being spurred to modify his masculine ideal, he physically sacrifices the female to enlarge himself metaphorically—sucking his virtue from her very corpse. Although its presence is vividly rendered as bodily suffering, here the feminine stays safely distanced for Gascoigne, an attribute of what remains a dumb animal of another species rather than a thinly disguised metaphor for a "venerated" earthly woman. In part, Gascoigne's rare excursus into extended figurative language serves as a way to legitimate his unwitting, "unsporting" violation of the female. Ironically, his poetry transforms the doe's body into a sign of his worthiness rather than shame before another male. (Similarly the allegorical persona of Satyra/Philomel, raped and mutilated by her brother-in-law, is adopted by the male poet as he addresses his predominantly male readership in "The Steele Glas"—another poem dedicated to Lord Grey.) The distance between plain "honest" description and metaphor, often cited by Gascoigne as a reason for his simplicity when discussing male violence performed as acts of war, now re-covers the poet's culpability in this scene of his own violence to a female figure. Gender difference helps to reenfranchise Gascoigne as poet despite his lengthy confession of his distressed social position. The hunting conceit may have been enough to keep the poet from worrying much about his shifting style and moral stance here; if not, sixteenth-century social theory, nicely epitomized in the poet's desire to please his double "Lord," could reassure him of his rightful superiority.[14]

Both the doe's carcass and the poetic recollection of time past become Gascoigne's means to transcend personal limitations, taking him beyond intransigent events into a realm of reinterpretation. In "Gascoigne's Woodmanship," this process also moves him beyond one-directional satire to a negotiation between the self and its social location. Unlike Sir Thomas Wyatt's "Mine own John Poins," an earlier commentary on court corruption which leaves the speaker starkly separated from court "In Kent and Christendome," Gascoigne finds a space for personal redemption within his social milieu; his allegorizing poetic "fansie" creates a rationale for continued social performance rather than retreat from the political world. This dynamic anticipates George Peele's dramaturgical movement from a vexatious pastoral landscape to an allegorized court of chastened lyricism and sublimated eros in *The Arraignment of Paris*, although that work carries very different messages about gender and power.

In the poems discussed here, Gascoigne uses the poet's resources to produce something more than a moral or a simple story. Irony and sentiment are blended to complicate the poet's attitude toward time and a gender-differentiated society. The traditional ties between "fansie," lyric poetry, and youth allow him to take many positions within one poem: Gascoigne invokes the mature moralist, the youthful, versifying subject of his lyrics, and the regretful penitent who nevertheless continues to write lyric poetry. This last subject position, like a metaphor, connects the opposed selves of past and present. Poetic fictions and figures here become more than ornaments or illusions; they furnish paths to a fuller portrait of male subjectivity within a courtly society.

Not until Gascoigne was close to death did repentance grow to be more than one ironic aspect of his prodigal personality. In his last works, appeals to experience and defenses of love disappear from his writing—and so does the space of lyric poetry. In *The Elizabethan Prodigals*, Richard Helgerson charts how the poet takes on a prodigal's voice as "justification" for his prior immorality in *Master F.J.*, and then rejects even that defense of his youth, turning instead to precept alone in his (mainly prose) prodigal-son play, *The*

Glasse of Government.[15] Tellingly, the versifying represented within that play's action is not even the product of a poet's imagination or self-description, as *The Posies* had been. Instead, the verse recited is a schoolboy's dry exercise in memorizing a hierarchical set of moral rules. Erotic tensions and gender roles have simultaneously been simplified, creating an emotional chasm between the sexes. The representative of love is now a bawd, Pandarina, who counsels her niece the "harlot" in a parody of the schoolmaster's good advice: "I pray you learne these three pointes of me to governe your steppes by. First *Trust noman* how faire so ever he speake. Next *Reject no man* (that hath ought) how evil favored so ever he be. And lastly *Love no man* longer than he geveth, since lyberall gyfts are the glewe of everduring love" (*Complete Works* 2: 25). Love has been reduced to bodily acquisition and commerce, and words of love are utterly discredited by all parties. The tensions of Gascoigne's own lyrics fail to find a place in his academic drama.

In playing the prodigal, as Helgerson notes, Gascoigne is fashioning himself after yet another aspect of Petrarch—his moralizing at the end of a literary career, as in the *Epistle to Posterity:* " 'Youth led me astray, young manhood corrupted me, but maturer age corrected me and taught me by experience the truth of what I had read long before: that youth and pleasure are vain. This is the lesson of that Author of all times and ages, who permits wretched mortals, puffed with vain wind, to stray for a time until, though late in life, they become mindful of their sins' " (as quoted by Helgerson 12). "And for Petrarch, as for the Elizabethans," Helgerson adds, "love and poetry were a part of youth and its vanity" (12). Perhaps influenced by G. K. Hunter's analysis of mid-century humanism in his study of John Lyly, Helgerson sees in Gascoigne's penitence a reaction to the times. Certainly the poet was one of a generation shaped by dynastic turmoil, religious bloodshed, and the consequent revision of humanist goals. Helgerson cites Roger Ascham's (atypically extreme) rejection of experience as a source for learning—a stance that not only obliterates the prodigal's claim to authority but also by extension may explain the refusal of some later theorists to take into account artistic practice as a source for learning what poetry and drama should or might do. A similarly extreme attitude appears in the work of Gascoigne's last year; but, as his lyrics demonstrate, it does not adequately describe the way he spent most of his poetic life, the voices in which he wrote most often, the manner in which he "composed himself."

What Gascoigne's last works do indicate is the enduring difficulty of negotiating between Elizabethan lyric theory and practice, and the complex work of gender in that negotiation. As well as venting his spleen at court corruption (perhaps motivated by the perceived indignities of poetic service that McCoy emphasizes), Gascoigne expresses righteous sorrow at his treatment as a poet by taking on the voice of the nightingale in "The Steele Glas." He published that satire together with an elegy begun "twelve or thirtene yeares past," "The Complaint of Philomene" (*Complete Works* 2: 177). In *The Posies,* he had compared "A straunge passion of a Lover" to this bird as well as to the lark, emphasizing the masochistic pleasure of Petrarchan love:

> And as fayre *Philomene* againe,
> Can watch and singe when other sleepe:
> And taketh pleasure in hir payne,
> To wray the woo that makes hir weepe.
> So sing I now for to bewray
> The lothsome life I lead alway.
>
> (*Complete Works* 1: 42)

In "The Steele Glas," by contrast, the speaker Satyra makes only passing allusion to "my reckles youth mispent," instead emphasizing his/her virtuous ancestry from the allegorical parents "Playne dealyng" and "Simplycitie" (2: 144). Moreover, s/he presents her/his muse the nightingale's "happy noble hart" as heroic and praiseworthy, which "No dole can daunt, nor feareful force affright . . . Whom worthy mindes, always esteemed much, / And gravest years, have not disdainde hir notes" (143). In posing as a Philomel figure, Gascoigne emphasizes his victimization by others rather than his power as singer, although he stresses the worth of the song. He presents himself, appropriately given his persona, as more sinned against than sinning.

> This worthy bird, hath taught my weary Muze,
> To sing a song, in spight of their despight,
> Which worke my woe, withouten cause or crime . . .
> Then helpe me now, O byrd of gentle bloud,
> In barrayne verse to tell a frutefull tale,
> A tale (I meane) which may content the mindes
> Of learned men, and grave Philosophers.
>
> (2: 143)

In blank verse, "barrayne" of rhyme, he tells a moral tale to serious men. Gone is most of the playful duplicity and lyrical nostalgia for pleasure; indeed, in this allegory it is the courtly "Galant" "*vayne Delight*" who plays the role of the rapist Tereus, and only Slander says that the victimized speaker courted Delight (145, 146).

Gascoigne's reversal of the power of voice, professing to be the silenced feminine victim who transmutes physical ravishment into a metaphorically ravishing aesthetic power, becomes a vehicle to express what he regards as his aesthetic and sociopolitical strangulation at court. Along with the satire's battering blank verse, the violence of this mythical drama as the originary scene for poetic expression gives "The Steele Glas" a sharper, angrier edge than we witnessed in his nostalgic lyrics in *The Posies*. At one moment, Gascoigne does anticipate an amused response to his professions of innocence, and wittily evades responsibility, this time for writing seductive love poems, by once again bending gender:

> But that my Lord, may playnely understand,
> The mysteries, of all that I do meane,
> I am not he whom slaunderous tongues have tolde,
> (False tongues in dede, & craftie subtile braines)
> To be the man, which ment a common spoyle
> Of loving dames, whose eares wold heare my words
> Or trust the tales devised by my pen.
> I n'am a man, as some do thinke I am,
> (Laugh not good Lord) I am in dede a dame,
> Or at the least, a right *Hermaphrodite*:
>
> (2: 144)

Drawing upon the association of love lyrics with the feminine, Gascoigne uses the figure of the hermaphrodite to make himself something more, rather than less, than a man. Through this moment of rhetorical play, the speaker seeks to avoid the charge of being a victimizing male by becoming Other, without being quite so preposterous as simply to reverse his sexual position — *and* without carrying the humiliation associated with being feminine from the allegorical to the literal level of biography. The sense of being attacked for being *too* male and this means of escape, played out in gendered terms, echo beyond the specific charge; but they gain credence only if we differentiate between the symbolic gendering of these power struggles and the actual biological sex of the courtly agonists here allegorized. Although McCoy dwells on Elizabeth's role as censor, those who criticized Gascoigne's published artwork for aesthetic and moral reasons also included male literary commentators, wounded courtiers, and the "divines" he addresses in prefaces to his lyric collection. His appropriation of the female position calls attention to two ironic gaps that resonate throughout the late Tudor period: first, between gender as a reflection of biological difference (sex) and as a way of defining social power through hierarchical positioning; and second, between the theoretical presumption of male dominance and the monarchic system which had temporarily awarded supreme power to a woman. Unless we attend to both these gaps, we risk perpetuating a vision that equates male dominance with poetic freedom and honest speech; or we may ignore and discredit the multiple strains poets struggled to express.

Even when Gascoigne becomes a social moralist in "The Steele Glas," the power of song remains a singular compensation for this disembodied, unempowered speaker. He may have felt himself marginal and unheard amidst courtiers of high birth and greater political savvy, but his representation of his mistreatment becomes a means to a voice of protest, not an end in itself. It also helps adapt into modern English an antique poetic tradition linking birds, especially nightingales, with the lyricist's self-definition. Depending on one's level of sympathy and sense of his accuracy in opposing those he casts as the rapist Delight/Tereus, one may regard Gascoigne as the forthright moral poet triumphing over the base mishandlers of worldly authority, as the artful strategist using femininity and passive aggression to justify his work and question social values, or as the self-exalting egoist superficially co-opting the woman's part to one-up his male poetic competitors. Not coincidentally, this range of interpretations is also applicable to many Petrarchan sonneteers, with their seemingly submissive, self-effacing complaints. Gascoigne uses the devices of that tradition in the service of his blunt persona, speaking the truth, struggling against a sophisticated court: against critics and backbiters, and sometimes against his own "immoral" emotions as a poet loving beauty and sensual delights. In his pageant writing, we shall see that he also struggles with the paradox of "female power" suppressing his male desire.

Theories about which poetic messages mattered or were moral influenced the shaping of a lyricist's voice, as did the poet's own temperament and sense of a literary tradition; so too did one's sociopolitical position, especially at court. The tensions with his court surroundings expressed in Gascoigne's lyrics and verse narratives become more pronounced and are dramatically rendered in the pageants he penned for performance before the queen. Such royal entertainments provided an especially important place for the development of generic interaction and gender-conscious poetry.

When an elderly Queen Elizabeth visited Harefield Place in 1602, very near the end of her life, she was greeted by two actors representing Place (a brick house) and Time (a green-robed, yellow-haired figure with an hourglass). As June Osborne relates, "The hour-glass was stopped, not running, to signify that time stood still at the Queen's welcome" (96). Like this wistful theatrical tableau, lyric often gestures at a world stopping or outside time, sometimes by juxtaposing various temporal perspectives, sometimes by elaborating the single moment. This act of will and verbal fiction also reverberates politically, whether the lyric is presented as a partial view or as an improved alternative to what is usually regarded as "reality." In representing the queen of England during the last quarter of the sixteenth century, this aspect of lyric art was frequently invoked, and, like Elizabeth's carefully controlled image in portraiture, became an increasingly distant representation as the woman aged and decayed. These two temporal perspectives or realities, a lyrical idealism and a transient, often satiric materialism, became the stuff of drama for Marlowe and Shakespeare.

Alongside Time, Place in a specific sense mattered for those who wrote lyrics to be performed as part of court entertainments. Just as a dramatic performance may seem more obviously foreign because of its rootedness in a lost setting rather than because of its temporal distance, Place was presented as the more problematic category at Harefield. It was Place, dressed in widow's weeds, who lamented when the queen was leaving: "Time can go with you, Persons can go with you; they can move like Heaven; but I, like dull Earth, must stand unmoveable. I could wish myself like the enchanted Castle of Love, to hold you here for ever" (Osborne 96). Once again, the language of magic and love is invoked to create a desired landscape, the Castle of Love—but only as a wish, a hypothetical fiction stated in the conditional. Material reality often seems more recalcitrant, and less capable of rhetorical manipulation, than time itself (albeit Time's ability to "move" beyond Harefield, the envy of plaintive Place, would hardly console its royal listener as she approached death; Time's hollow victory signaled the ultimate failure of lyrical stasis, and provided the queen with an unwelcome companion). Place defies our imaginative attempts to deny change or difference far more concretely than does time.

To consider the place of courtly entertainments in creating lyrical drama requires reconstructing the physical conditions as well as the times in which lyric voices were heard. Drama usually posits an imaginative landscape in addition to the actual performance spot, and so the interweaving of those places can become just as complex as is the play of temporality in Elizabethan love lyrics performed onstage. In court pageantry, connections between the conditions of performance and the fictionalized landscape were intimate and inescapable. Furthermore, the placement of the desired or rejected female within those fictive and actual landscapes became a particularly meaningful source of play when the show was designed for a queen as primary audience. Entertainments for Elizabeth thus provided a location in which lyric poetry could and did function significantly within a social and dramatic context as a means of political address, and constituted a vital source for the subsequent transference of lyric into publicly performed theatrical fictions.

Gascoigne's self-presentation as a constrained male Philomel nicely evokes the potential complexities and limits of courtly aesthetic exchanges from the perspective of the pageant author, or "deviser"; he was obviously in the inferior, "female" position of power in relation to his biologically female audience. While Elizabeth as an image-conscious sovereign encouraged Petrarchist worship, she also worked to control the expanded functions of lyric as political commentary by refusing to watch what displeased her. Yet the pageants also provided writers with a rare opportunity for generic experimentation. The external constraints of genre theory and the poet's social role made the figure of Elizabeth as female "beloved" all the more important for those trying to expand the perceived uses for lyric poetry into theatrical performance. When Sir Thomas Wyatt had referred to his would-be beloved as "Caesar's" in the Petrarchan sonnet "Whoso list to hunt," the sovereign played no other role than inhibitor, the role of many a king in narratives of illicit courtly love. (On numerous occasions, Henry VIII also adopted the stereotypical role of poet/suitor himself, further eclipsing his "courtly makers.") But when entertaining a female sovereign, by contrast, poets found a new location for lyric which involved a more immediate, complicated interplay between political advice and erotic discourse—and one obviously demanding measured and respectful address to the "beloved."

The Queen in Performance and the Progress of Lyric

In court pageantry, the frivolous love lyric became serious by merit of occasion. During the early years of Elizabeth's reign, attempts to ensure the royal succession by persuading the queen to marry (including Inns of Court plays such as *Gorboduc*) failed repeatedly; faced with the reality of a woman heading the body politic indefinitely and in her own right, the court needed new myths, an ideology to justify the nearly unprecedented. Since Elizabeth indeed "played" the inaccessible lady, the language of Petrarchan sonneteering had a certain applicability, and became an elegant way to plead for more than ladylove. As Puttenham's verse columns indicate, this created an important and unconventional possibility for written lyric poetry, one that allowed Petrarchan addresses "To the Ladies" a place in the "serious" public world of traditionally male statecraft. The so-called cult of Elizabeth, developed during the 1570s and early 1580s, also provided a performance situation for lyric in which the poem became more than a frivolous (or immoral) "posie." In the pageants emerges a present-tense, incipiently dramatic conflict for which lyric poetry provides an especially appropriate rhetoric.

Here too Gascoigne's work illustrates the developing use of lyrical tropes. In court entertainments, he found an ideal stage upon which to combine his own lyric persona and narrative of the prodigal with Petrarchan praise of the courtly lady Elizabeth (though, as we shall see, not always with ideal results). Gascoigne even saw fit to publish his account of *The Princely Pleasures at Kenilworth,* a spectacular series of pageants in which he had a major hand. Dubbed by the historian J. E. Neale the entertainment par excellence (*Queen Elizabeth* 214), it was created for the queen's visit to the castle of Robert Dudley, Earl of Leicester, in 1575, the same year that *The Posies* was published. Such courtly amusements could be quite important for their devisers artistically and politically, as social gestures at the center of state power. Gascoigne's contribution to this mode at Kenilworth illustrates the pageant's amenability to the kind of cross-generic interplay that literary drama did not accommodate in the 1560s and 1570s.[16] Working within a less rigidly prescribed form than the neoclassical Inns of Court plays, yet faced with a highly sophisticated and literate audience presided over by the queen, Gascoigne and his fellow devisers included lyrics in a variety of forms and contexts "onstage."

Court pageants provided a medium acceptable to the gentlemen who were rethinking English prosody in light of their knowledge of classical and continental meters. Moreover, they could employ their craft with more formal freedom than in scholarly drama because pageants were by comparison subliterary, overtly occasional pieces. The interaction between performers and royal audience in such shows allowed exceptional license, both poetic and political, if the deviser could handle himself gracefully. Of course, this particular situation, fraught with political meaning and weight, could also limit the range of acceptable speech and action. In the pageantry of two of the most gifted wordsmiths, Gascoigne (*Kenilworth*) and Sidney (*The Lady of May*), various frustrations about the queen's marital and foreign policies vie for attention with the artistry of their scripts. Indeed, her opposition to Sidney's desire for an interventionist continental policy, personified in his pageant by the active forester Therion whom the author clearly favors to win the Lady of May, led the queen to make narrative nonsense of his conclusion by honoring the more passive rival, the shepherd. Elizabeth refused even to watch a section of Gascoigne's entertainment that lobbied too vigorously for a royal marriage. Notwithstanding, their entertainments testify to a functional place for performed lyric at court, as well as its use in pressing ritualistic spectacle in the direction of court drama. Here lyricism comes to embody one perspective in conflict with others.

The pageant was formally amenable to lyric pieces, in that it was created through a series of tableaux, comparatively static moments within a larger performance. With the greater impulse toward dramatic narrative in the pageants of the late 1570s, devisers played with the tension between stasis and action, and between lyric and drama as conventionally conceived, in ways that foreshadow Shakespeare's lyrical drama on the public stage. At the time, Inns of Court drama was still essentially declamatory and allegorical, partaking of the medieval aesthetic of "narrative conceptual symbolism into which the formulas of classical art had been frozen" (as E. H. Gombrich [9] describes Italian painting before Giotto). A shift analogous to the "spatial" breakthrough in the visual arts of the quattrocento took place in English drama between the 1560s, with its relatively undeveloped, allegorical characterization in works such as *Jocasta* and *Cambises,* and the 1590s, with its emphasis on action and change (both in characters and ideological perspective) in works such as *Edward II* and *Romeo and Juliet.* The pageants furnish a locus for investigating and describing that historical shift from formalized ritual to a fluid play of perspectives within its social and aesthetic context.

Prior to the 1570s, the roles of poetry and oratory within court pageants varied greatly according to the occasion and type of entertainment. Often these shows were written predominantly in Latin, with sporadic English verses ranging in form from rime royal to doggerel or poulter's measure. A hastily composed royal entry for Edward VI in 1547 pirated verses a century old, indicating the general inattention given to pageant as well as theatrical prosody at mid-century (and their relative stasis in verse style, as opposed to the dynamic changes of the subsequent forty years). During the queen's visit to Cambridge in 1564, by contrast, the scholars put great emphasis on their orations and verses—hardly surprising given a community of academicians. Orations, however, were a far cry from the "light" verses composed for the queen's amusement at Kenilworth. Alice Venezky observes that for royal entertainments at the nobility's country estates, "formal oration disappeared altogether, being quite inappropriate to the atmosphere of myth, music and enchantment"; it was replaced by "welcoming lyrics," either songs or poems (79). This is not universally true and may not be a function of place entirely, for Sidney's *Lady of May* includes a parodic oration by a schoolmaster, and Peele even includes a formal oration in *The Arraignment of Paris* that is quite appropriate to the myth and music of his court drama. Nevertheless, the general emphasis in court pageantry certainly shifts during the 1570s, from weighty school rhetoric to pastoral and lyric verse.

Pageants, including royal entries and Lord Mayor's shows as well as entertainments for the queen in "progress" among her towns and her peers' estates, were organized according to predominantly spatial rather than temporal patterns. Elizabeth's coronation entry into London guided her across the town from one pageant car (or platform) to another. At each place, an allegorical show was performed, either as tableau, recitation, or physical action (such as the much-discussed offering of the English Bible to Her Majesty). The narrative string tying the shows together was the queen herself, the audience to whom all the festivities were directed. As in the medieval cycle plays, a central authority linked many stories and stage-bits; but in post-Reformation England, that center was the queen's political presence rather than the Bible's scriptural authority. Obviously, the religious aspects of performance had not disappeared, for the queen as mystical sovereign and as Supreme Governor of the Church of England had a crucial spiritual function for her people; nevertheless, instead of reenacting past narratives of Christian history, the theatrical "script" invoked that past to serve and enrich a current political event. Thus the artistic emphasis, if not the ideological basis for celebration, shifted from a shared belief in inherited religious doctrine to shared participation in the developing monarchic nation-state.

As a living woman rather than the disembodied Word, Elizabeth was not only granting a royal audience but was also "subjected" to being an audience member—albeit an unpredictable and active one. Her female body may in fact have encouraged greater attention to her physical presence and greater boldness in giving advice on the part of the devisers. The pageant scenes at her coronation entry sent quite specific messages to the queen; Sydney Anglo notes that the show was "indeed following the practice *laudando praecipere,* and . . . [was] doing so to a degree unprecedented in English pageantry" (358). This instruction occurred when the queen was young and her ability to control spectacles was less clear than it would become. At one stop, Elizabeth saw the figure of Deborah, whose import according to Anglo was a persuasion to "virtuous, discreet, and considerate behaviour" (352); although this does not strike me as the most obvious signification for the militant prophetess of Judges, she was indubitably being presented as an exemplar for her royal observer. The pageant car itself had a table bearing verses in English and Latin, and a child dressed as a poet bade the queen farewell in typical pageant hexameters as she passed on to Westminster:

> And for this hope they pray, thou mayst continue long,
> Our Quene amongst us here, all vice for to supplant,
> And for this hope they pray that God may make thee strong
> As by his grace puissant, so in his trueth constant.
>
> (353)

Just as in the presentation of the English Bible, this moment in the procession makes clear the desire of her fellow audience members that Elizabeth become a strong and constant leader of the Protestant faith. This tradition of giving moral advice to the prince, even on ritualistic occasions of celebration, provides a precedent for the less benign messages of later devisers. Nevertheless, the queen remains at the theatrical center and, as God's surrogate on earth, in command. Both politically and aesthetically, the queen gave meaning to the pageant, as she moved through the space between pageant cars. Without her, the artwork becomes incoherent.

At Leicester's Kenilworth estate, a stop on the queen's midlands progress more than fifteen years later, she determined the entertainment's own progress—by this time in a more overtly dramatic and imperious manner. She was not the only one contending for authority. All the episodes of the entertainment revolved around the queen, yet the devisers' narrative, written at the behest of Leicester, not only involved her as audience but demanded she play a crucial role within the fiction.

The Kenilworth entertainment stretched out over the queen's week-and-a-half visit. On Saturday, July 9, the first segment introduced various local spirits, including a porter, the Lady of the Lake, and a poet; they spoke verses (the third in elevating Latin) written by different authors. With the arrival on Monday of the ivy-draped Savage Man, recognizable kin to the Greene Knight of *The Posies,* Gascoigne entered the entertainment as actor as well as author. To call the subsequent week of pageantry a "narrative" perhaps inflates the importance of a unifying storyline, for the entertainment still contained a number of separable episodes; nevertheless, the recurring presence of Gascoigne's wild man figure as well as the Arthurian Lady of the Lake, and a central motif of captivity requiring royal delivery, connected the verse and shows in a more complete way than had appeared in earlier pageants. At least three times during the major "fictional" sequences (if one includes the planned but unpresented "Zabeta" skit penned by Gascoigne, as well as the stories of the Lady of the Lake and Deepe Desire), passages written in lyric forms focused on the location and pleas for freeing of captives.[17] Moreover, in his segments Gascoigne shifted the emphasis toward a coherent fiction particularly appropriate to his poetic persona.

He did so without sacrificing the nonfictional, political demands of the pageant form. Gascoigne quite openly pleads Leicester's case, pressuring the queen to marry him. He portrays Leicester as her ultimate captive, hence merging the realms of fiction and politics. Predictably, Leicester is presented as captivated by her erotic, not her political, power; given the fearsome arsenal he had stockpiled at Kenilworth and his notable self-promotion, perhaps this is not so much a displacement as an acceptable version of the truth. Dudley was no stranger to this kind of performance diplomacy, having in 1561 played in a Pallas/Perseus masque offered at court (along with *Gorboduc*) which contained advice on royal marriage and succession. Dudley had been assigned the role of Pallaphilos; even then, Marie Axton observes, lawyers were channeling political hopes into revels iconography (40–41).[18] The would-be king performed much the same role fourteen years later at Kenilworth, when his chances of becoming royal consort were wildly improbable.

By creating shows that illustrate the queen's power to imprison and release, complementing Dudley's role as Deepe Desire, Gascoigne and his collaborators set up a romance narrative that is simultaneously a forum for political commentary. They did so, moreover, in a way which allowed multiple opportunities for performed lyric poetry. Both the lyric form and the lyric subject of love were decorous in these entertainments, since the queen reveled in the interplay between courtship, as we now use the term, and courtiership, one of its contemporary meanings.

In addition, Gascoigne's use of his own lyric persona, the semicivilized Greene Knight, was encouraged by the pageant structure, as Venezky recognizes: "Since the Sovereign's part in these episodes was limited to her mere appearance upon the scene, the showmakers especially favored for their greeting a device found in the pastoral and romance, wherein a wild man is tamed through the influence of a pure and virtuous lady" (80). This pastoral plot provides the poet with a narrative appropriate to his lyric voice and situation, as the queen becomes the agent of Gascoigne's own reform, his prodigal's return. Not that this silences his complaints or advice. Philippa Berry believes that the phallic wild man with his "dynamic masculine energy" introduces "an implied challenge to royal authority" (94–95), and it is certainly true that Gascoigne argues on Leicester's behalf at Kenilworth. But the narrative also emphasizes Gascoigne's desire to be accepted and "tamed" by the queen's beneficent presence, a desire to be worthy of her divine grace translated into erotic imagery. Artistically, Gascoigne's exceptional move was to combine the lyric persona we have seen in *The Posies* with formal lyrics of royal praise within a loosely narrative performance, thereby creating an entertainment which hovers in the space between pageant and lyrical drama.

During his first appearance as the Savage Man, Gascoigne immediately melds the factual and fictional landscapes, as well as two senses of courtly love, in his verse. In a poulter's measure apostrophe to Jupiter, he asks why all these (actual) lords have assembled. Although he cannot go to court, he claims to have been drawn here, for no man "But needes must mount, if once it see / a sparke of perfect grace" (*Complete Works* 2: 96). That "sparke" is obviously her grace the queen, and the poet rises to meet her (using a verb that encourages the potentially scandalous elision of sexual and religious vocabularies). An ensuing echo song just as openly identifies the other main player in this court drama, the earl of Leicester. It takes a rather strained echo line to accomplish this, in answer to the Savage Man's question:

> And who gave all those gifts?
> I pray thee (Eccho) say?
> Was it not he? who (but of late)
> This building here did lay?
> *Dudley*
> (99)

Although inelegantly handled, this is the first documented echo song in English, and its presence highlights Gascoigne's range of experimentation with lyric forms in pageant performance. Including a sophisticated European import such as the echo song complements his uncouth lyric persona of the Greene Knight, and demonstrates the same artful naiveté found in *The Posies*.[19] Unfortunately for him, poetic innovation was overshadowed by his bad luck as a performer; when Gascoigne broke his tree-staff as a sign of obeisance, a piece of wood flew dangerously near Elizabeth. She proclaimed "no hurt, no hurt," but the episode became a memorable testament to the queen's composure rather than the author's composition.

A subsequent episode, performed on Monday, July 18, more directly illustrates the complexities of scripting the sovereign. When the queen had first arrived at Kenilworth, the Lady of the Lake, as guardian since the time of Arthur, had offered the lake to Elizabeth; Her Majesty parried "that she thought it was hers already" (Osborne 76). Now another power struggle surrounded the Lady. Tryton arrives to announce, in broken fourteeners, the capture of the Lady of the Lake by Sir Bruse, Sans pittie, in revenge for his cousin Merlin. The queen alone can save her, and simply by appearing: "Your presence *onely* shall suffice" (*Complete Works* 2: 102–3; emphasis added). Tryton then sounds his trumpet and announces that the crucial "action" has indeed taken place. This episode obviously exploits the queen's unique position in courtly entertainments: she is the point of the drama, but as monarch must not be made to *do* anything in particular. She does not have to perform in order to change a fictional situation; she merely need be present to preside over events, just as her audience "onely"—only and alone—allows the show. As the necessary and sufficient condition for the pageant, she is honored for her power—at least until one considers the particular use to which Gascoigne puts it. She is, after all, being asked to rescue the Arthurian temptress who seduces Merlin and usurps his magical power; this Lady of the Lake, whose story is wisely untold although alluded to by Tryton, is at best a morally mysterious figure, at worst a male fantasy of fearful female sovereignty. More overtly, Elizabeth is drawn (and written) into this fiction, with the deviser giving a specific meaning to her presence not of her own making. Here, perhaps more than in Gascoigne's self-presentation as wild man, dramatic representation carries a potential challenge to the female monarch's beneficence and her control over signs.

The conflicts, and hence danger to ritualistic authority, embedded within this devising may be hidden by the queen's positive role here as liberator. Elizabeth's next "given" role in the entertainment was not so flattering, and so the strain between the queen's and the deviser's control is easier to see— which may be why Elizabeth refused to see it at all. The skit planned was Gascoigne's story of the virgin queen Zabeta. Because of inclement weather (so the author posits in his written account) or because of its unsubtle support for a royal marriage, the episode was cancelled. M. C. Bradbrook declares that it was cut "because it gave too frank expression to hopes on the question of the royal marriage" ("Artist" 29).[20] The queen may also have realized that in this show, as in the later controversy surrounding Shakespeare's *Richard II,* her placement as a character "onstage" (through a most obvious surrogate) would subject her actions to manipulation by *her* subject, the pageant's deviser. When she showed characteristic sensitivity about representation, David Kastan has remarked, "Elizabeth was not merely being paranoid" (464). Gascoigne had gone beyond the ambiguous balance of flattery and potential criticism found in the Tryton skit.

The "Zabeta" text maintains a plausible but extremely fragile fiction that attempts to "cover" political messages verging on impertinence (from the queen's perspective). Mercury brings Diana to find Zabeta, but in doing so the actor was actually bringing another actor into the queen's presence; only because the characters remain semifictional could the performers have refrained from bowing immediately (during the first day's festivities, the Savage Man did bow upon entering the royal presence—but that was when he came to praise Elizabeth, not to advise her).[21] Iris runs in and boldly moves the skit along the borderline between fiction and history, telling the queen she had meant to arrive before the abusive "babling God" Mercury, that "tatling traytor" to the queen's interests; she then launches into her persuasion to marry, a very real court issue, and presents it with reference to the queen's factual past. "Remember all your life, before you were Queen, . . . Were you not captive caught? were you not kept in walles?" asks Iris. She declares that Juno (queenship), not Diana (virginity), helped her then. "How necessarie were for worthy Queenes to wed / That know you wel, whose life alwayes in learning hath been led," Iris boldly continues (119–20). Gascoigne adds a player's caveat to shield his character, however shallowly, by having Iris remind the queen that these words are not her own but those of the offstage (and thus, in dramatic terms, indisputable) Juno. In fact, however, they recall words the queen herself had used nine years earlier on November 5, 1566, when countering a formal request by Parliament that she marry or establish the order of succession. Gascoigne is using the same personal history to make an argument utterly at odds with her own. Elizabeth had emphasized that her captivity and deliverance during her sister's reign had taught her the dangers of naming a "second person": "I am sure there was not one of them [the parliamentary delegation] that ever was a second person, as I have been, and have tasted of the practices against my sister . . . I stood in danger of my life, my sister was so incensed against me: I did differ from her in religion, and I was sought for divers ways. And so shall never be my successor" (Neale, *Elizabeth I* 148). Angered that Parliament should pressure her ("it is monstrous that the feet should direct the head" [150]) she had refused to commit herself to marrying or naming her successor. She repeatedly stressed her distinctiveness, both as one with perilously gained knowledge and as an unmarried yet marriageable woman; but here again at Kenilworth, aspects of her singular, exceptional life were being polarized by Gascoigne, like other male advisors, and represented through the opposition of two goddesses and versions of femininity. It is this sort of challenge through mythological performance that George Peele's *Arraignment of Paris* would soon counter. Elizabeth's method of combat was simpler: censorship by refusing not only the roles suggested by the fiction but also her crucial role of audience.

That the queen later chose to allow a formal farewell from the author of "Zabeta" (Gascoigne in his guise of Sylvanus) shows a modicum of good humor on her part. He did not retreat from urging his entertainment's messages, nevertheless; since he was in the service of Leicester, such tenacity made some sense. The ideas that Gascoigne had been thwarted from relaying in poetic form return in "playne" prose. Taking advantage of the pageant form's amenability to improvisation, Sylvanus alludes to earlier events so as to complicate and develop his narrative. He reports the distress of suitors Elizabeth has "rigorously repulsed, or rather (to speake playne English) so obstinatly and cruelly rejected," who have thus been turned into "most monstrous shapes and proportions" (124–25). Yet another semifiction is created, as the transformed Deepe Desire—né Dudley—begins speaking in poulter's measure from a holly bush (a mode of self-presentation that, in hindsight, surely elicits a smile from even the most humorless scholar). He approaches his finale, after fifty tedious lines of Petrarchan platitudes, by singing these pentameter verses of woe: "If death or dole, could daunt a deepe desire, / If privie pangs could counterpeise my plaint: / If tract of time, a true intent could tire . . ." Untiring perhaps for the singer and his original audience, the deadly regularity of his alliterative verse makes reading this scene doleful indeed. The entertainment concludes on a glum note: "O farewell life, delightfull death farewell, / I dye in heaven, yet live in darksome hell" (130). Petrarchan oxymora serve quite directly to emphasize Leicester's unfortunate position (physically as well as politically on this occasion) due to Elizabeth's foreign policy and her unconventional attitude toward marriage. For Leiceister and Gascoigne, the only happy solution to their real-life drama would be an action by the queen, and despite their lyric pleas she does not allow herself to be written into *that* Circean script. Gascoigne repeatedly asks for, and even tries provoking, a drama based on Elizabeth's own life narrative of captivity and liberation, while the queen's will and the conventions of courtly entertainment keep the events at Kenilworth inscribed within the realm of a lyrical pageant.

But not easily. The savage man employs lyric to praise Elizabeth and honor her power, yet he also talks back, threatens, and is silenced only by the sovereign's active intervention; though not in the way they hoped, Leicester and his devisers did induce the queen to act. It is unlikely that they expected Elizabeth to change her mind and policies exactly to match theirs because of a few lyrical appeals, but they did manage to involve her in their performance of thwarted desires. Rather than simply affirm her policy, the Kenilworth pageants dramatize a conflict of wills and perspectives. Axton notes that Kenilworth contains not only the pressures to marry, but also two scenes (the freeing of an enchanted suitor and of an imprisoned virgin) suggesting total disengagement from courtly desire as an alternative for frustrated subjects (63). Such scenes can be read as obliquely challenging Elizabeth's unequivocal control, or at least as quite backhanded compliments to her absolute sovereignty. Perhaps just as disturbing to her, they signal the frustration and fading desire of her most personally devoted subject, "Robin" Dudley, to continue enacting scripts of sublimated eros, scripts that were helping to consolidate and sustain her power as female sovereign. The "Zabeta" skit hints at the vulnerability of her female body natural by evoking her adolescent captivity, rather than just lamenting the uneasy thrall and physical discomfort of doting suitors. Financed by an aristocratic "servant" whose desire for military involvement on the Continent challenged Elizabeth's chosen foreign policy, the pageant reflects the complicated political and personal strains underlying "light" courtly fictions. The poetic messages and elaborate shows of Kenilworth, performed in spaces where the "stage" was itself a fiction, gesture at the tensions implicit in these marginal artworks—potential political dramas that might be played out as formal theater or as state crises.

Whether one highlights the subversive glimmers or their artful containment in this particular text, lyrical poetry and Petrarchan rhetoric were clearly becoming vehicles within court entertainments for politely expressing conflict with or surrounding the sovereign. Howard Cole has distinguished devising from drama in terms of intention, based on whether scenes are created for the queen or for "art's sake."[22] This dichotomy, even if it does not dismiss the pageant altogether, seems to miss precisely what is interesting about Kenilworth: the use of lyric tropes to represent tensions and ideas soon to be elaborated in the fictions of lyrical drama. The Kenilworth entertainment illustrates the increasing pressure toward dramatic conflict within court pageants during the 1570s (extended most notably in Philip Sidney's *Lady of May*). Here the conflict rooted in political tensions between the female sovereign and her male "suitors" was played out in lyric and spectacle.

This version of conflict, as the speeches of Deepe Desire make painfully apparent, drew on the ready-made rhetoric of Petrarchan lyric poetry, the oxymora and mistress-servant language of that dominant mode of erotic literature. The fiction of Gascoigne's pageant similarly exploits the developing connection between lyric tropes and the immediate political situation, most notably by using captivity and deliverance from "thralldom" as a unifying motif, and by including his lyric persona as the marginal, uncouth, plain speaker struggling for favor. While the specific moniker of "Greene Knight" derives from English literature, Gascoigne's other name here, Sylvanus, belongs to the European pastoral tradition popular with the more sophisticated court writers at this time. These versions of the Savage Man are in practice almost interchangeable, a case of syncretism again illustrating the irony in Gascoigne's professions of artless "simplicity." Equally interesting, as regards his developing claims of poetic authority, are the implications of this choice of persona in performance. For the mere presence of a savage man speaking "freely" before the queen circumvents hierarchy and decorum, the conventional ideas of how much should be said by whom and how. This persona allows a mere gentleman (albeit under the protection of an earl) to evade the court's rigid structure of birth and office but, because of the general recognition that this is a holiday guise and still signifies his liminality, does not immediately provoke indignation or a deaf ear. Elizabeth may have censored Gascoigne's "Zabeta" skit, but she did not silence her woodsman; nor did she inhibit distribution of his "Zabeta" text, unlike those who protested against Gascoigne's earlier erotic publications for being scurrilous and inflammatory. Because Elizabeth's fictions focused on a mythology of love, the poet could effectively incorporate pastoral and lyric tropes into his semifictive narrative, adding his own twists to the tradition (albeit keeping it "cleaner" than he had in *The Adventures of Master F.J.*). Integrating his lyric roles of inept savage man and prodigal, Gascoigne even managed the "improvisatory" addition of awkward tree-chucking at Kenilworth—though he omitted that *truly* artless moment from his published account. Like the other differences between that text (whose publication was another exceptional case of authorial self-assertion) and Robert Laneham's contemporary account, this omission attests to the care and pride with which Gascoigne presented his "simple" self and his art as a deviser of lyrical performance.[23]

This chapter has set forth some of the key contexts—the limits, experiments, and struggles—that inform the aesthetic work of late Elizabethan playwrights in "staging" courtly poetry. Despite lowly associations of lyric poetry with the profane, the unlearned, and the feminine, Elizabethan commentators failed to pigeonhole all such poetry, and occasionally acknowledged its nobler potential. The queen's continued presence as the "woo-able" object of praise and the source of authority, moreover, provided incentive for courtiers to pursue those elevating possibilities. As they employed Petrarchan tropes in their political as well as marital suits, the boundaries between high and low lyricism at times became faint indeed. Erotic and political territories merged in the elite court entertainments for Elizabeth, which while often categorized as a form of "private" theater were in many ways quite public performances.

Gascoigne's poetic practice in *The Posies* also blurred the boundaries of public and private, as his personal follies and shortcomings became the occasion for satirizing social corruption (particularly in "Gascoigne's Woodmanship" and "The Steele Glas") and his prodigal past was transformed into an exemplum—published along with the intimate amours of fictive courtiers such as Dan Bartholomew and F. J. In playing with multiple perspectives and rhetorical attitudes in lyric form, and in employing temporal and gender differences to represent tension within the lyrical "speaker," Gascoigne's poetry suggests the dramatic potential for a lyric voice in a narrative context. It also reveals the tensions between the poetic placement of female figures as victimized enablers of male voicing and the veneration of an exceptional, powerful courtly woman—a tension aggravated when that woman is the queen. More directly, his work as a courtly deviser anticipates much of the lyrical practice of the fin-de-siècle playwrights; his *Princely Pleasures at Kenilworth* employs lyrical tropes within a social narrative, suggesting conflicts more fully explored in the self-contained fictions of public theater.

The Theatre itself was built the same year that Gascoigne died, but the possibilities of his work were not immediately translated to that stage. There was a mediating stage—both physical and temporal—at court, performed upon by youthful actors who embodied the crossing of sexual boundaries: as actors, between child and man, and as characters, between woman and man. In George Peele's courtly play *The Arraignment of Paris,* they brought to life the possibilities explored in the lyrics addressed to Queen Elizabeth and in the Kenilworth pageantry. At least in sixteenth-century England, it took boys as well as men, and a female rather than a male monarch, to produce a "mature" lyrical drama.

Like Peele's play, Marlowe's *Dido, Queen of Carthage* was also performed at court by a troupe of boy actors. The use of boys encouraged associations with the feminine (including yet going far beyond the particular ramifications of cross-dressing the "woman's part"). Moreover, because the boys tended to be adept choristers as well as actors, their productions spotlighted song and lyrical recitation.[24] Thus the boys' companies also helped provide the craftsmanship and motivation required for transferring courtly lyricism to a theatrical stage "proper." The lyricism they made fashionable was then transferred to a wider audience by poet-playwrights, who moved from writing for "private" court productions to "public" theaters more frequently than scholars sometimes emphasize. Such was certainly the case for both George Peele and Christopher Marlowe. In their plays, the narrative representation and fate of mythologized queens progresses through lyrical verse in an unprecedented manner. And with Shakespeare's lyrical plays, that poetry and its social signification are fully transformed to please the paying customers in Southwark.

Notes

1. Even in early university plays, the lyrics of most songs do not carry particular significance within the fiction; see J. E. Bernard and Sanders et al. on early Elizabethan versification and drama.

2. Of the fourteener, probably the most popular stage line at this time, Potter remarks: "To make the lines scan, the writer is now forced to pad them out, to subtract definite articles, and to use an excessive number of inversions; the result is the style of *Cambises* and *Horestes*" (Sanders et al. 237). Poulter's measure (alternating fourteeners and hexameters) could be just as unwieldy.

3. See Javitch on Puttenham's courtly theory, May for a more precise definition of courtier poets, and Gurr on the theatrical audience. In contrast to the laxity of versification in public plays, the academic dramatists often held themselves to absurdly severe standards; according to Ascham's *Scholemaster,* Watson refused to have his *Absolon* performed abroad because he had lapsed into a few anapests. Alexander Neville, translator of Seneca's *Oedipus,* lamented the "groseness of our owne Countrey language, which can by no meanes aspire to the high lofty Latinists stile" (Platz 10), and even the pragmatic Gascoigne accepted (with regret) iambic regularity. See Axton on the topical links between Elizabeth and the Inns of Court drama.

4. On the rhetorical complexities and gender in the *Apology,* see Margaret Ferguson's *Trials;* see also Levao ("Sidney's"). One wonders what Sidney would have made of Donne's combination of Petrarchan praise with religious meditation in the very poem Jonson attacked, the *First Anniversarie* being among the most ambitious transformations of Petrarchism (see Martz 211–48).

5. Gascoigne's tragedy *Jocasta,* for example, rarely hints at his interest and ability as a lyricist, although several moments in its narrative suggest a suitable setting

for a lyrical evocation of the past as found in *The Posies* (see Henderson, "Poetic" chap. 2). For more on the inhibiting factors of courtesy theory, see Whigham and Javitch.

6. Cole summarizes: "To write verses is commendable, to live by them is base, and to write professionally for professionals is basest of all" (115). Literary ability was an educated gentleman's accomplishment, not the basis for a specialized trade or income; thus Gascoigne did not wish to let others think he would publish. An indication of his precarious status appears in the letter to the Privy Council "Against Georg Gascoyne yt he ought not to be Burgess": "Item he is a common Rymer and a deviser of slaunderous Pasquelles against divers personnes of greate callinge" (cited by Prouty 61). See Wendy Wall's related discussion of Gascoigne (chaps. 2 and 4).

7. See Peterson and Baxter on the plain style; the term, attentive to the moralizing impulses in sixteenth-century literary criticism, was an apt corrective to C. S. Lewis's discounting of "drab" poetry. I cite the standard edition of Gascoigne by Cunliffe, which includes *The Posies,* but take into account the differences between that edition and the earlier *Flowres* where relevant.

8. McCoy ("Gascoigne's '*Poëmata*'" 50) sees court-inspired "evasion" in *Dulce bellum* when Gascoigne does not name those who performed badly but does name the good nobles, merchants, and soldiers; but this ignores the satiric convention, especially favored by Juvenal and Ben Jonson, that the poet shows his own authority by naming only the good. In this way he demonstrates his power to perpetuate or withhold fame, as well as his moral discernment. Thus Gascoigne's naming is a sign, not of diminished "potency" or authority but quite the reverse (as well as a useful convention for those wishing to avoid lawsuits and censorship).

9. See Kennedy on Petrarch's rhetorical strategies; the poet-lover has a double or split perspective, with one part of the self observing the plight of another part, further complicated by the double audience of actual and implied reader. Especially relevant here is Crewe's dense and astute analysis of "anterior forms" and poetic self-construction in Wyatt, Surrey, and Gascoigne.

10. Gascoigne, *Complete Works* 1: 131. The "Reporter's conclusion" tells of Dan Bartholmew dying, saved only by a last-minute message from his lady, written in blood; but a rosy romance finale is undermined by the narrator's further revelation that Dan B.'s "Goddess" was a false idol. The ending leaves Dan Bartholmew bent by doubts and grief.

11. For more detailed analysis of the ironies in *The Adventures of Master F.J.,* see McCoy ("Gascoigne's '*Poëmata*'") and Hedley; focusing on the rhetorical trope of *allegoria,* Hedley observes that "[t]he narrator's analogy from 'common experience' and F. J.'s metaphor from the tradition of *amour courtois* are competing bids for 'mastery,' in [Kenneth] Burke's sense of that word, over the situation of adulterous courtship" (152).

12. See Peterson's and Nathan's readings. The poem presents its farewells in an order similar to the Renaissance idea of desire's psychological progress, moving from eyes to will to sex.

13. Winters found "Woodmanship" Gascoigne's best poem, and called attention to the Christian interpretation of its moral allegory (17–18); more recently, Jane Hedley has similarly praised it, emphasizing Gascoigne's "rhetorical dexterity in manipulating an allegorical vehicle at hand" (154). See also Peterson's reading, which differs greatly from mine, and Crewe's sophisticated analysis, which sees the antioedipal gestures of Gascoigne's self-presentation ultimately undermined by the linkage of Jehovah and the deer as parental figures within this "primal scene."

14. See Vickers ("Blazon") and Stephanie Jed (*Chaste Thinking*) on the figure of Lucrece as the originary sacrificial figure undergirding the construction of Italian humanist rhetoric. See also W. Wall, chap. 4.

15. Helgerson emphasizes Gascoigne's actual repentance in life and narrative, complementing my stress on the important and complex role of lyricism in Gascoigne's "earlier" writings—which includes, significantly, all his works published up until a year before his death.

16. See Dieter Mehl on the dumb show and static characterization; the accounts and examples of early Tudor pageantry in Anglo and civic pageantry in Bergeron; Bruce Smith's analysis ("Landscape") of country-house entertainments; and Queen Elizabeth's progresses as collected in Nichols.

17. On Saturday, July 9, Elizabeth arrived; she stayed more than a week, hunting and seeing a folk play as well as viewing the elaborate entertainments of the first day, Monday week, and the following Wednesday; for dating, see the discussions in P. Berry (95–99) and Osborne (74–80). The primary sources are Robert Laneham's letter to Master Humphrey Martin, and Gascoigne's own account of "The Princely Pleasures," included in Nichols and here cited from Cunliffe's standard edition of Gascoigne's *Complete Works*. See Susan Frye and Wendy Wall for careful analysis of the dense political context and discussion of the various versions in which the pageants circulated.

18. Mortimer Levine similarly discusses *Gorboduc* as an early "tract" in the succession debates. Dudley hoped for political advancement of this radical Protestant agenda through his personal wooing.

19. For more on this echo song, see Lowenstein (63–66). P. Berry links the "phallic sexuality" of the wild man figure with Leicester, attributing Gascoigne's role of Sylvanus to this source despite his contemporaneous lyric self-presentation as the Greene Knight in *The Posies*. She ignores this echo song, which along with Dudley's speech as "Deepe Desire" certainly signals the attempted "literary displacement of erotic desire" in the Petrarchan mode (albeit not particularly elegantly) that she claims "had not yet been completely formulated" (99).

20. Axton (63–66) and others agree, although P. Berry, who wishes to stress

Elizabeth's growing association with chaste Diana, discounts the seriousness of this marriage proposal (99). Certainly the odds of acceptance were slim, but then Leicester was not known for his common sense or practicality.

21. "Zabeta," according to Nichols, plays on a Latin version of "Elizabeth" also mentioned (1: 502–3): spelled backwards, the name resembles Ahtebasile, e.g., "oh you queen." Rather ironically, Zabeta became one of Elizabeth's complimentary names; Peele uses it in his pageant *Descensus Astraea* as well as *The Arraignment of Paris* (see chap. 3).

22. Cole also suggests that more open contemporary allusions in prose after Kenilworth may be due to that show's precedent (482).

23. Pageants were often anonymously composed, and previously had not been a medium for literary self-advertisement with the public. Those authors of earlier pageants who are known tended to be permanent servants of the court and schoolmasters; Gascoigne, with less sure patronage and his proclaimed identity as writer/soldier, had a more direct investment in his pageant poetry. He leaves out a country hock dance performed by locals to the great pleasure of the queen, deeming it too simple to bother explicating. As well as signaling a rival's annoyance at their positive reception, and disdain to be considered on a par with rustics, Gascoigne here confirms the value he (like Boccaccio) places on complexity and "literariness," values he helped to transmit to later poetic dramatists.

24. See the substantial recent scholarship on the complexity of cross-dressing, including influential articles by Belsey ("Disrupting"), Rackin, Shapiro, Howard ("Crossdressing"), Orgel ("Nobody's Perfect"), Case (*Feminism* 24–27), and Jardine (as well as rejoinders to her book, such as Katherine Kelly's).

TWO

Elizabeth's Watchful Eye and George Peele's Gaze
Court Drama, Female Power, and the Lyric of Praise

The discursive power of Elizabeth's court extended beyond the parameters of its aristocratic ambitions and love affairs. Just as the queen's progresses brought the court to towns such as Norwich, Worcester, and Warwick, the published texts of courtly shows performed for more than their original audiences, carrying their language, images, and arguments to the growing reading public. Many courtly works of the 1580s, including the Euphuistic prose plays of Lyly, brought the questions and tensions raised by female sovereignty to center stage; when subsequently published, they had an impact well beyond the bounds of the playing hall. In some cases the attempt to represent the queen to herself and her courtiers led to a re-vision of certain aspects of the culture's gender stereotypes that can be read as anticipating (partially and tentatively) the modern project of conceiving female subjectivity. One of the brief, shining moments of Elizabethan court mythology, and a premier example of this novel reflection of female power, is George Peele's lyrical drama, *The Arraignment of Paris*. The forms and rhetoric of lyric poetry are crucial in Peele's construction of a paean appropriate to the queen.

While this middle-class Londoner wrote for a specific audience and may have intended to do no more than flatter his monarch, the representation of gender in his drama goes beyond mere recital of traditional praise for queens.[1] His play reduces the erotic differentiation between the sexes typical of courtly Petrarchism, and explicitly lauds the power of females in a political context, as ultimately bringing peace, cooperation, and wise guidance to an earthly kingdom—rather than keeping Woman in distinct religious or private erotic realms, her common places of praise. Peele's play thus illustrates how Elizabeth's position as sovereign provided a specific occasion for, and indeed demanded, a reexamination of the proper places and power of women. Its gendered image-making through poetry interestingly complicates historicist analysis of the politics of sovereignty and subjectivity.

The text of *The Arraignment of Paris*, published in 1584, is most often remembered as the first English pastoral play and as a five-act drama unusual in its time for its poetic self-consciousness and metrical variety.[2] It presents the Judgment of Paris, but adds a legal twist to this familiar mythological scene: his subsequent arraignment before the Olympian gods on charges of corrupt judgment (due to bribery by Venus, who uses Helen of Troy as bait). The play also includes processions of country gods, a subplot involving the lovelorn Colin and his shepherd friends, and a masquelike finale in which Queen Elizabeth receives the golden apple. Scholars have debated the extent to which Peele creates any unity out of his disparate characters and scenes;[3] clearly the piece partakes of the court pageant's mode of serial tableaux, but it also sustains its fiction through scenic juxtaposition and allusion. Rather than separating exalted and lowly characters, Peele allows gods and shepherds to converse in a more fluid protonational community, interweaving their stories to create a loose but coherent narrative about state power and desire.

The Arraignment of Paris was performed at court by the Children of the Chapel Royal, most likely during the winter of 1581–82 on New Year's Eve or Shrove Tuesday.[4] The historical moment is suggestive, in that the play idealizes Elizabeth's power to create peace at the very time her religious and political policies were becoming more belligerent. By the end of 1581, the international situation for Protestant England was particularly ominous. Philip II had annexed Portugal the year before; Jesuit-educated Englishmen were returning to their homeland illegally, as missionaries; a Catholic resurgence seemed threatening. The Parliament of 1581 reacted with repressive new religious restrictions, supported by most of the Privy Council. Although Elizabeth still officially pursued neutrality and refused direct involvement in the Netherlands, avoiding military commitments on the Continent grew all the more difficult. She made hostile public gestures toward Spain, such as knighting Sir Francis Drake on board the Golden Hind, which had returned, laden with pirated Spanish gold, from circumnavigating the world.

Most ironic, given Peele's representation of the queen as a peaceful unifying force, were two recent enactments of torture, among the more famous cases of the Crown's violent power over subjects who had not been implicated in any direct rebellion against Elizabeth. The first victim was John Stubbes, whose book *The discovery of a gaping gulf* ... (August 1579) warned the queen not to marry the French prince Alençon (later duke of Anjou). Elizabeth was furious enough to demand Stubbes's death, and settled reluctantly for a mild form of dismemberment, the axing of his authorial hand. Then in December of 1581, the Jesuit missionary Edmund Campion was dismembered in a gruesome public spectacle, which included hanging, removing his entrails before death, and quartering. Both men were reputed to have endured their punishments gallantly.

Although a standard punishment for heresy or treason in the sixteenth century, drawing and quartering was often commuted to beheading when the victim was a gentleman; Campion was not only of good social standing but a moral scholar of great eloquence who had been praised by Elizabeth during her 1566 visit to Oxford.[5] International politics demanded some display of power from the Protestant sovereign and radical Protestants may have cheered, but this particular response ran counter to Elizabeth's tolerance of Catholics in earlier years. It may indeed have backfired, illustrating too clearly the violent power of the body politic over the body natural. Certainly it prompted a pamphlet war, including written accounts of Campion's bravery as well as a defense of the government, the *Execution of Justice in England,* from William Cecil's office.[6]

The spectacle of a wellborn Englishman dismembered provides an unsettling prelude, a necessary counterimage, to the complacent spectacle of peace and unity that resolves George Peele's *Arraignment*. In its famed final gesture, Juno, Pallas, and Venus endorse Diana's decision to give the golden apple to the queen. Elizabeth is said to unify the strengths of many in her singular body, re-membering female virtues (obscured by the goddesses' earlier competition) as "shee, / In whom do meete so manie giftes in one / On whom our countrie gods so often gaze / In honour of whose name the Muses sing" (5.1.1167–70). The object of a fictional as well as a courtly audience's admiring gaze, the queen also embodies the abstract virtues of a happy, healthy state, a nation at peace. As at Kenilworth, Elizabeth's double role as source and audience for this performance of the gaze creates a circularity of perspective reliant on her person.

The juxtaposition of Stubbes's hand or Campion's bloody corpse with Peele's poetic tribute provides an illustration of an early modern state's mechanism for discipline and assertion of the Crown's power over the body politic, fitting almost too neatly into a Foucauldian model.[7] The tendency in much recent analysis is to expose such historical tensions, suggesting the necessary connection between dismembering the unruly subject and incorporating state power in the sovereign, and furthermore implying alliance with the doomed subject struggling against monarchic authoritarianism. (In fact, while this anecdote certainly indicates Elizabeth's participation in ruthless mechanisms of social control, political history to some extent supports a view of the queen as personally advocating peace and tolerance; if one looks at variations in the use of state power by a number of early modern sovereigns, including other Tudors, then the specific praise of Elizabeth no longer looks like sheer hypocrisy or an automatic response.)[8]

But this is not the whole story. What may be discounted in these analyses is the double function of power to create as well as suppress (recognized by Foucault), and moreover to create several kinds of knowledge. Sometimes little regard is given to the particularity of the poetic language within its context, its distinctive emphases, as part of the social vision created. The particulars of Peele's poetic representation lead us to attend to other aspects of power besides the state's atrocious apparatus of corporal punishment and control. Instead of viewing power solely as state authority, we may wish to investigate the intersections and relationships among the cultural powers of the sovereign, the author, and patriarchal theory. In its gender play, *The Arraignment of Paris* creates a new space in which to examine the queen's two bodies, another way to "know" female sovereignty going beyond conventional flattery or a counterstatement to the violent potential of Elizabeth's authority. The transformation of Petrarchan tropes to idealize the sovereign illustrates the diversity of potential functions for that rhetoric. The queen's presence as judging audience in this case prompts a final representation of female power as publicly *active* (rather than frustratingly distanced, as in the dominant Petrarchan poetic model) and *benevolent* (rather than exclusively death-dealing, through sexual rejection or the violence of an unruly "woman on top"—fears displaced onto two minor characters, Thestilis and Ate).[9] Peele's artistic response to Elizabeth's own gaze thus ambitiously addresses the peculiar difficulties of venerating a female sovereign and imagining alternative views of female presence and power.

The play underscores the importance of recognizing a variety of competing positions of power or hegemony when analyzing court culture. As Carolyn Porter and others have shown in their analyses of new historicism, power often becomes an amorphous term into which all culture collapses. In the *Arraignment,* the power implicit in gendered social roles intersects with the power implicit in relations between sovereign and subject and between audience and artist. Peele's use of lyric poetry in particular raises questions that challenge easy or static situating of power. The *Arraignment* thus illustrates how Elizabeth's complication of simple gender definitions provided an occasion for, and indeed pressured, male courtier-artists to reexamine the "naturalness" of their culture's ideology of female inferiority.

As has often been noted, *The Arraignment of Paris* finally dissolves into a personal compliment to the queen, naming her as the "Nymphe Eliza" and aligning her with several goddesses represented onstage. It takes fully five acts, however, to reach this figure of the unified sovereign. En route, as it searches for appropriate terms with which to praise a royal woman, the play reexamines human desire and its frustrations from the perspectives of both male and female characters, in ways that reduce the emphasis on sexual difference common to myths and courtly love plots. In the first four acts, *The Arraignment of Paris* exposes the inadequacies of objectifying women as the "cruel fair," that vision of the Other so familiar in Tudor poetry. By presenting equivalent stories of romantic cruelty and abandonment, the playwright suggests that the amorous behavior of the sexes is in fundamental ways similar. Paris's abandonment of his first love, the shepherdess Oenone, takes place in scenes interspersed with the nymph Thestilis's indifference to Colin, and both Oenone and Colin lament their rejection in song.

The ability of Oenone to hold her own in the lyric lamentations alongside Colin Clout (who was at this time the surrogate for England's most impressive contemporary poet, Edmund Spenser) suggests a female as well as male version of voice and subjectivity.[10] Indeed, in the first scene between Paris and Oenone, it is she who commands language as well as song. Paris asks *her* to

> Tell me what shall be subject of our talke:
> Thou hast a sorte of pretie tales in stoore . . .
> In telling them thou hast a speciall grace.
> Then prethee, sweete, afforde some pretie thing,
> Some toie that from thy pleasaunt witte doth springe.
>
> (1.5.235–36, 239–41)

She confidently responds, "Use thou thy pype, and I will use my voyce" (1.5.243). Although she will soon be rejected for a competing singer (Helen of Troy, crooning an Italian aria), Oenone's speech paves the way for a stronger and more successful assertion of female voices in the play's finale.

For a shepherdess to sing and tell a "pretie tale" in itself matches pastoral expectations as well as feminine pastimes, and as such is unthreatening to Paris—but here only because he fails to take her or her lyrics seriously.

In this he resembles some modern scholars who attend only to masculine agency. Andrew Von Hendy, for example, not only ignores Paris's own comments (both those cited above and his subsequent admission that his cunning does not match hers) but even misattributes Oenone's lines and the choice of song to Paris.[11] The text is nevertheless clear; it is Oenone who tells stories of betrayal and then introduces the song: "There is a prettie sonnet then, we call it Cupid's curse: / They that do chaunge olde love for new, pray gods they chaunge for worse" (1.5.282–83). Unlike the audience, Paris cannot yet know that these lyrics will curse his own fickleness: like her song, Oenone will soon become the "toie," easily played and dismissed. Although he vaguely recognizes the song as applicable, "Our musicke, figure of the love that growes twixt thee and me" (287), Paris seems only to hear the harmony of his own notes, not her words. Within two scenes he has "chaunged" Oenone for Helen, the "worse" love in view of its consequences for Troy. As in any well-crafted verse play, the words are designed to resonate, and the use of a song refrain hammers home the dramatic irony; sympathy for Oenone, spurred by her abilities and wit, increases, while we are proleptically distanced from the less articulate, cognizant, and faithful shepherd. Peele reinforces the point once more when in act 3 the abandoned Oenone recalls her lyric refrain: "False *Paris,* this was not thy vow, when thou and I were one, / To raung [range] and chaunge old love for new: but now those dayes be gone" (3.585–86).

The use of song as a means of pleasing yet self-assertive voicing for female characters extends beyond Oenone. (This is not to say that *only* females sing, for indeed part of the function of song will be to link all the earthly lovers, as discussed below.) No doubt Peele's reliance on song partly derives from performance conditions, in that he wrote for a boys' troupe. Nevertheless, the careful use of songs such as Oenone's to advance characterization and narrative not only exploits poetic and gender associations more fully than did earlier interludes but also creates distinctive female voices in advance of praise for the queen. Seen thus, it is hardly coincidental that the only song in Italian belongs to the seductive Helen of Troy.

Helen helps Venus capture Paris's heart, and thus the golden ball, by singing an Italian lyric in which she claims to be a "Diana dolce e rara" deceptively like the figure who will eventually be the play's sovereign goddess. Unwisely (given myths such as that of Niobe), Helen vaunts she can rival the goddess: "Io posso far guerra / A Dian' in fern' in cielo, et in terra" (2.2.507–8). The very presence of a rival to Diana (and to the queen herself, given Elizabeth's frequent identification with that goddess) may seem a challenge or exposure of courtly ritual, and in one sense this is perhaps true. Helen's is the original language of the great sonnet tradition, of Dante and Petrarch and their unqualified idealizations of female beauty as Other; as dramatized here, Helen is connected with the desire of sonneteers, especially with their emphasis on the seductive powers of eye and ear (she even makes war "con Le guardi," with her eyes). She also epitomizes the societal problems created by that desire.[12] For unlike the chaste and unattainable Beatrice or the Diana with whom this play concludes, Helen is legendary for her physical availability; her earthliness works against the ethos of sublimated desire and the use of Petrarchan lyric in its service, so useful to Queen Elizabeth. Thus Helen embodies tensions commonly voiced in the poems of English sonneteers: for the lover, tensions between the use of lyric poetry to praise an idealized image of "woman" and its use to pursue actual earthly women; for the courtier, tensions between the use of lyric poetry to praise the queen, and its use to attain concrete political advancement.[13]

Because a character onstage who is both seen and heard, Helen takes on a subjectivity not possible for the lady as represented in the words of male lyricists; or more accurately, while the ventriloquism of the playwright puts words in "her" mouth, it is "she"—not even a male narrator reciting her words within his own lyric context—whom the audience sees and hears. She is indeed a dangerous figure; while her voice again attests to female power, hers is the stereotypical erotic power to ensnare masculine judgment. To the extent her presence seduces, she may temporarily seem to challenge both the possibility and primacy of sublimated eros at court and also the veneration of any woman's power. But it is not only the fact of her representation by a boy actor that controls this larger threat to Elizabeth's court; rather, it is her clearly delimited role within the play, as she is confined to singing this artful lyric on behalf of Venus and then disappearing. The presence of other commanding female figures prevents her from epitomizing powerful womanhood. Instead, she suggests the particular problems inherent to the stereotypical portrait of the cruel and beautiful Other, that inheritance of the sonneteers' emphasis on physical "fairness" and difference. Helen's failure to sustain her power as a figure in the drama, her replacement by the true Diana onstage and by praise of Elizabeth in Peele's finale, implies a victory over the pragmatic political and sexual goals of Paris-like men, through a fuller idealization of womanhood that neither explicitly and exclusively fetishizes, nor denies, chastity. It is the erotic physicality textualized by Petrarchism, rather than the veneration of women, that will not find its way into royal praise.

Helen's foreign tongue also emphasizes her "strangeness," signaling that she is a distinctively dangerous, usurpatious character with aesthetic and sensual appeal. Her song may have evoked the commonplace English imagery of Italy as a land of intrigue and corruption, and more specifically the fears that had led to Campion's dismemberment: the Protestant image of the pope as Antichrist, falsely pretending to empire, excommunicating the English queen, and authorizing invasions in favor of her licentious Catholic cousin. In a convoluted way, the Tudors' outlandish promotion of a monarchic genealogy back to the Trojans (via Arthur, Brute, and Aeneas) makes Helen's destructiveness somewhat akin to the contemporary foreign threat to the English throne. By specifically claiming to be an all-encompassing Diana, she usurps the mythological space created for and by Elizabeth in court pageants and other tributes. Helen, then, becomes the projection of linguistic, sexual, religious, and national anxieties. When Oenone returns in act 3 to lament in English, one can imagine a tinge of patriotism as well as pity stirring in her support throughout Elizabeth's court, bizarre and illogical though it seem from afar.

Without disproportionately stressing all these associations, one can certainly recognize that the Italian of Helen isolates her from the other earthly singers, whereas the singing of Oenone and Colin—the premier representative of specifically English poetry—links these two rejected lovers. Nor does Peele show any sympathy for Helen's handling by the gods, her victimization being a matter set outside his play's careful boundaries (in direct contrast to Marlowe's *Dido,* which emphasizes the cost of erotic suppression by more powerful forces). Helen's unhappy fate, like Paris's, is not represented, not presented as a reason to resent or lament the power of chaste goddesses. The careful construction of the play keeps Helen and other female figures of questionable repute (Ate and Thestilis) at quite a distance, temporally and physically, from Diana and Elizabeth. This in part precludes the potential danger Philippa Berry sees in Lyly's *Endimion,* of having negative portraits of women "contaminate by their proximity the icon of Elizabeth" (130). As will prove true in the stories of Peele's other earthly lovers, the traditional rhetoric and worries about eros are not merely denied or refused any representation; instead, they are clearly subordinated—and neatly distinguished from the poetic praise of the queen that concludes the play.

Song lyrics in *The Arraignment of Paris* help individuate and give voices to the women; just as importantly, they help reinforce the narrative parallels between certain male and female characters. Of course, from the time of

Ovid's *Heroides,* male poets have taken the voice of lamenting ladies in epistolary verse, and Peele's drama negotiates with poetic tradition in portraying these characters. Oenone becomes an abandoned lover, whereas Colin Clout's love is unrequited, so that in a sense she resembles her ancestress in *Heroides 5* lamenting bitterly after the fact, whereas he shares the thwarted desire for what has not yet been achieved that is characteristic of Petrarch's and Spenser's lyric speakers. But as indicated above, Oenone speaks and sings well before as well as after her rejection, and Peele softens Ovid's portrait by replacing her anger at desertion with lamentation and song; thus he sustains not only unambiguous sympathy and pity for her as victim but also her resemblance to Colin. More broadly, the sequential juxtaposition of these two literary figures onstage serves to emphasize their *shared* experience rather than two different temporal modes or attitudes toward desire. Peele dramatically interweaves the two rejections: in adjoining scenes, Colin's shepherd friends lament both his death and Oenone's abandonment.

When Oenone chastises the shepherds as ones who "whet your wits on bookes. / And wrap [rape] poore maydes with pypes and songes," she suggests an origin for the feminine distrust that dooms Colin (3.3.591–92). The shepherds counter by citing Colin's fidelity, at the same time acknowledging that Paris's "trothles doble deede, / Will hurte a many sheepeherds else that might go nigh to speede" (595–96). Each lover's fate affects others of their gender, a consequence that Thenot spells out even as he contrasts the two men: "Poor Colin, that is ill for thee, that art as true in trust / To thy sweete smerte, as to his Nymphe Paris hath bin unjust" (597–98). The very words of the faithful lovers begin to intersperse, only in part because of conventions (such as their crying out to Venus). In act 3, Oenone not only uses Spenserian archaisms ("ypeirced" [3.4.651]) but also sings to "Melpomene, the muse of tragic songs" (3.4.8), thus invoking the same muse as did the "original" Colin Clout in Spenser's November Eclogue. This complaint follows less than sixty lines after Peele's "revised" Colin apostrophizes Love in a song of broken fourteeners.

The interpenetration of stories, emphasizing the inevitability of romantic pain as well as men and women's parallel fortunes in love, is not confined to the faithful. Venus herself treats both sexes similarly, combining her powers with castigation when she encounters the coldhearted: she scolds and punishes the nymph Thestilis by causing her to become enamored of a "churle," and warns Paris that unfaithful lovers will be punished in hell (after having induced his infatuation with Helen in the first place). Here too, lyric verse plays a crucial role in developing the play's thematics. Colin's death is followed by the songs of Thestilis, now smitten with love for her churl; the shepherds use the figure of echo to mock her with the similarity of her situation and the dead Colin's, adding one vengeful variation of their own. The song concludes:

> *Thest.* Cruell disdaine, soe live thow named.
> *Shep.* Cruel disdain, etc.
> *Thest.* And let me dye of Iphis paine.
> *Shep.* A life too good for thy disdaine.
> *Thest.* Sithe this my stars to me allot,
> And thow thy love hast all forgot.
> *Exit Thest.*
> *Shepherds.* And thow etc.
> *The shepherds carie out Colin.*
>
> (3.5.736–42)

Thus Thestilis exits from the play—so much for her. Titania-like, she has been made to pay for not being responsive to men. Yet in the same act, Oenone pays for being faithfully responsive, as her song reminds the audience, hence erasing any easy solution to the complexities of human desire. Here, as in the case of Helen of Troy, Peele's use of several female figures counters simple misogyny or condemnation of a particular behavior, even as the play represents the anxieties and frustrations of eros.

Perhaps alluding to Gascoigne's Kenilworth prototype, in which Dudley unsuccessfully sought an even stronger alliance with the queen, Peele's echo song emphasizes the failure of romantic love. As if to reinforce this point, the form of the song alludes to yet another exemplary case of love's doom, the cautionary tale of the original Echo. In the published text, an unusual evaluative comment masquerading as a stage direction calls attention to the form's moral wit: "The grace of this song is in the Shepherds Ecco to her verse." In the version of Echo's story narrated at the beginning of act 2, Juno ties the nymph's demise with her collusion in advancing Jove's amorous adventures; "though perhaps shee was a helpe to Jove," "She playde with Juno, so she tolde her thankes: / A tatling trull to come at everie call, / And now foresooth nor tongue nor life at all" (2.1.328, 325–27).[14] Doomed to the ineffectual voicing of Narcissus's words, Echo suffers for using her agency to abet male lust and to betray another female. Thestilis "sins" in refusing Colin's desire, and suffers another kind of echo, one of remonstrance. Unlike them, Oenone loves faithfully—but all three women suffer just the same, each rejected by an indifferent lover. The erotic dilemma remains, and does not appear attributable or generalizable to gendered behavior. Similarly, although perhaps with at least the illusion of choice, Paris will die (outside the scope of the play) for winning the songstress Helen, even as Colin dies because he lacks his love. Peele effectively animates this array of doomed love affairs through his lyric poetry, but such poetry and earthly desire in this pastoral world provide no happy ending for either sex.

Colin and Oenone remain faithful and loving even when hopeless, whereas Paris and Thestilis can both act heartlessly and also share the fate of being victims (perhaps scapegoats) of punitive gods. The distinction between men as active wooers and women as passive victims of love, familiar from many literary narratives, does not materialize. Indeed, it is the utterly passive Colin who, during the third act of the play, literally dies of a broken heart. The unhappy similarity between the romantic fates of men and women holds true as their stories conclude, superseding sexual difference.

Act 3 moves to negative finality regarding the love affairs of the earthbound. The scope of this problem is extended by having several lovers scorned, at least one of each sex. Thus the drama's ability to portray numerous episodes from multiple perspectives enlarges and qualifies male lyricists' traditional self-absorption. In so doing, and despite the severe condemnation of hard-hearted Thestilis, the play portrays with notable sympathy the female as well as male lover. Oenone's continued voice in disillusionment, including her attack on the words of shepherds, anticipates not only Ralegh's reply to Marlowe's "The Passionate Shepherd to His Love" but also the wry and melancholy ladies of Shakespeare. Peele does not locate the source of erotic suffering primarily in the inaccessibility or unworthiness of the desired female.

Through its pastoral removal and sustenance of a fictional world as it confronts eros, the *Arraignment* avoids direct satire or courtly analogy (except to another middle-class poet, Spenser). Unlike Gascoigne's Savage Man and Deepe Desire at Kenilworth, Peele's characters are kept at a safe distance from court as long as the play examines sensual desire. This version of pastoral might seem more akin to Spenser's than Sidney's, as Paul Alpers describes them; rather than having elegant courtiers disguised in shepherds' weeds lament their misfortunes with epigrammatic self-consciousness, Peele presents rustics and lovers who dramatize their mental sufferings through expansive lyrical verse.[15] In his familiar emphasis on the author's subjectivity and literary power, Alpers regards this latter form as more independent and free, establishing a "domain of lyric" in which the poet can investigate "serious" matters without the apologetics characteristic of mid-Tudor courtier lyricists such as Gascoigne (174ff.). But Peele in another sense supersedes these categories (as he does the literary/performance division Alpers also cites), and with them the implicit claim of superiority for the less courtly, authorially independent version. In the first three acts the playwright combines expansive lamentation with formal songs without privileging either (Alpers emphasizes the temporal distancing of the formal songs in Spenser's eclogues), just as the *Arraignment* as a whole combines rustic literary characters with the figure of Elizabeth.

The immersion of this play in a courtly context, then, does not prevent the kind of poetic and cultural interplay Alpers reserves for the lyric domain of *The Shepheardes Calender*; it does, however, require the kind of careful subordination and narrative placement I have highlighted in examining the lovers. Indeed, one could argue that the movement from earthly passions to the public praise of act 5 reverses the emphasis in Spenser's eclogues, finally privileging court speech over the literary fiction. Only after escaping this erotic "underworld," with its metaphoric potential to undermine and satirize courtly love behavior, does the playwright fuse his fiction and the actual performance situation, or refer to the queen as mythologized beloved. Of course, the domains of literary pastoral and courtly allegory remain part of a single aesthetic creation composed by Peele for the queen.

It is only if one presumes authorial goals which are at odds with formal verse and the desires of his audience that the concluding courtly allegory looks less "free"; furthermore, only if the author's constraint is somehow translated into the lyric poetry could it factor into our perception and judgment of the representation itself. In the case of *The Arraignment of Paris,* such presumptions and signs are not easily determined. The finale, as we shall see, has a logic and assurance often absent in court pageantry. But surely if there is a place where authorial subjectivity is at issue, it is in the representation of Colin. The difficulty of determining his significance may best illustrate the allure and instability inherent in viewing Elizabethan lyrical drama as an allegory for the masculine author's subjectivity; this will return us to the play's concluding poetry and narrative with a more watchful eye, considering the roles of audience and performers as they interact with the author's poetic script.

The lovers' stories are poetically connected with the last act's paean to Elizabeth through the passing presence of Colin Clout, the shepherd-poet borrowed from Spenser's *Shepheardes Calender* (published in the winter of 1579). Whereas Oenone's song initiates the positive representation of a female human voice, Colin's appearance foreshadows explicit praise of the queen. Spenser's fourth eclogue, resembling Virgil's fourth in its celebration of a messianic virgin, includes Colin's song "Of fayre Eliza, Queene of shepheardes all" (l. 34), which according to the Argument "is purposedly intended to the honor and prayse of our most gracious sovereigne, Queene Elizabeth" (Spenser 431). The eclogue links nostalgia and pastoral pain with praise of the queen through the personage of old Hobbinol, who, grieving at his loss of the young man's love because of his passion for Rosalind, recites Colin's happy song; not only is the song of female praise doubly removed by speaker but it is also a relic of a happier past.[16] In this regard, Spenser's eclogue partakes of the nostalgia in Gascoigne's framed lyrics. Peele, by contrast, moves his song of praise to a present whose immediacy in time and place supplants the pains of Troy and eros. Having killed off *his* version of Colin Clout in act 3, Peele uses his skills as a playwright to create a more spectacular praise of the queen, not from the male poet's perspective (or his male surrogate's, as in Spenser) but from the empathetic viewpoint of female goddesses.

Before examining that altered view, let me suggest the complex issues which Peele's use of Colin raises about the "power" of poetic authorship, especially in different media. Peele represents Spenser's character faithfully, at least in tone and level of sympathy. Colin is now ignored by Thestilis rather than dismissed by Rosalind, but his role and emotions as the lovestruck pastoral poet are not altered. Thus Peele quite openly announces the kinship between his play and the literary cutting edge, using the work of one whom Richard Helgerson dubs a "self-crowned laureate." In uniting Spenser's specifically English shepherds with figures from classical mythology, Peele reinforces the English claim of descent from the Trojans; he also transfers the bold poetic claims made by *The Shepheardes Calender* onto the stage, implying literary value for his stage poetry on a par with that highly annotated and self-conscious work. A desire to proclaim generic equality may motivate this specific "plagiarism," as much as does thematic interest in two types of love (Von Hendy perceives a Neoplatonic schema operating in the *Arraignment* [93]). Peele need not have chosen Colin Clout as his disappointed lover unless he wished to raise the particular issues of authorship, media, and poetic composition.

Peele does take the rather crucial liberty of changing Colin's narrative fate: he kills him off almost immediately after his entrance. Fulfilling his song's lyrics, Colin proceeds to "dye at Venus foote"; the location may or may not be figurative (he and Venus are offstage at the time) but the death is not (3.1.552). Literalizing the metaphors of courtly love poetry, Venus herself commands Colin's corpse be brought onstage for burial, "And let this be the verse. *The love whom Thestilis hath slaine*" (3.5.671). This startling innovation in character-borrowing, as well as making obvious love's destructive potential, certainly alters the status of the poet.[17] Depending on whether one regards this revised Colin Clout as the surrogate predominantly for a pastoral lyricist (as he is in Spenser's *Calender,* hence standing for that poet) or for the poet as playwright (Peele himself), two different interpretations arise. Because Colin in a sense belongs to both authors, these two emphases may be contradictory in their messages but are not mutually exclusive.

One analogy exists between the death of the lyricist and the "disappearance" in dramatic performance of the playwright as a first-person speaker. Whereas Spenser's persona (so figured explicitly in *E. K.*'s glosses) laments his failure at love and then is silenced, Spenser himself records the lyricist's failure as lover through his own poetry and then moves on to pastures new, retaining his own voice as a first-person narrator throughout the *Amoretti,* "Epithalamion," and at crucial points in *The Faerie Queene.* In contrast, Peele as playwright cannot speak without the mediation and hence complication of a stage character; amidst the variety of verse forms and styles, Peele's "own" voice cannot be heard as distinct. Of course this distancing can be seen as a means to a potentially greater because invisible authority, presenting a narrative creation as if it were impartial truth or necessity. In his concluding scene, Peele brings on "Th'unpartiall dames of destenie" themselves, the three Fates, to endorse his narrative choice of the queen as most fair (5.1.1224). And yet, as one who practiced his art in both media, Peele was surely aware of another kind of rhetorical authority available to the lyric speaker. Even in the Renaissance when lyric conventions did not automatically presume a unique or individuated speaker, poets such as Gascoigne and Spenser were clearly engaged in creating an authorial lyric voice. Spenser's surrogate (who begins by breaking his pipes but somehow can still hang them up in December) merely abandons his music—allowing him to pick up louder instruments later, and even to "come home again." Peele's representation of this lyric speaker as dying points to a crucial difference in medium. Moreover, it anticipates the play's shift of perspective in the last act, which obliterates not only a specific kind of poet but the first-person masculine voice altogether. Peele's play relies on his twofold self-effacement of personal authority; the trade-off for erasing his male poetic presence is invisible authority, a happy ending, and a happy audience. (Eventually, Peele managed to win both ways, attaining the same textual self-assertion as Spenser by having his play published, as well as having been "heard" through performance before the queen. Indirection has its own rewards.)

This reading is grounded in the analogy between Peele and Spenser as male lyric poets, and hence in their shared identification with Colin as surrogate. While Peele's sympathetic, unsatiric tone in representing Colin's fate encourages such a view (as does the playwright's attempt to link his play with the highbrow literature of his day), seen more literally, the irrevocability of Colin's fate—complete with epitaph—separates him from the still-scribbling playwright. This suggests another reading grounded in difference. To the extent Peele identifies Colin Clout with the *non*dramatic lyricist specifically, his violent end may assert the playwright's ability to surpass the single-voiced speaker (just as the choral finale will displace the problems represented for individual earthly lovers). Even the skeptical Sidney does not present the sonneteer's dilemma as fatal, while Peele feels free to "bury" Colin in the dead center of his play. Spenser himself hints that the representation may have been hostile (at least playfully so) when he speaks of Peele in "Colin Clout's Come Home Again": "There eke is Palin worthie of great praise, / Albe he envie at my rustick quill" (ll. 392–93). Whether Spenser is implying a reversal of the generic attack or merely a difference in poetic ability, his barb points to a rivalrous tension not explained by simply conflating both poets with Colin.

Peele's use of Colin Clout suggests a consciousness about generic interplay matching his considerable formal aptitude at versifying, but evades a simple and definitive statement about the court poet as subject. Within the fiction, it is unrequited love that kills Colin, hence linking him not only with the would-be professional poets but also with so many frustrated court "poetasters," dabbling in verse to please the queen or one of her ladies (in either case, a proposition often fraught with anxiety). One can see in Peele's representation of Colin a precedent both for Marlowe's portrait of pyrrhic love in *Dido* and Shakespeare's mockery of the literary lords in *Love's Labour's Lost;* these works share a vision that includes love, poetry, and gender politics, though each author frames the lyricist quite differently.

In Peele's play, the death of the lyricist and the judgment of Paris present obstacles to social harmony, overcome in act 5 only by removing male characters altogether. Through this perspective shift and allied artistic strategies, the play supersedes the competitive aesthetic of most male praise for the beloved, epitomized in the choice demanded of Paris by the Olympian goddesses.[18] Because Elizabeth's power was not merely a literary fiction but a political truth, the use of Petrarchan praise for the venerated lady by her male "servants" often created as many tensions as it solved. In *The Arraignment of Paris,* Peele counters the use of love poetry as a means to emphasize the frustration of particular male courtiers regarding their distanced female monarch, a device familiar in the work of Gascoigne, Ralegh, and Sidney. Instead, while acknowledging the pain of eros, Peele presents men and women united in their experience of desire and disappointment. Moreover, through Helen of Troy, Peele explicitly connects the tongue of Petrarch with the divisiveness and tragic desire inherent in the story of the judgment of Paris. The playwright thus turns elsewhere to find terms of praise for his female sovereign. He turns away from men entirely.

Judgments based on male standards and desires are symbolically dismissed in the fourth act: first, after being arraigned and tried before the gods on charges of misjudgment, Paris is sent offstage to Troy and his tragic fate; then, in response to the demands of Juno and Pallas for a retrial (an appeals court ruling to decide who's the fairest of them all), the male Olympians abdicate their authority in favor of Diana as ultimate judge. The change to a female judge is defended on the grounds of both domain and gender: the initial decision was made "neere Dianas bowre" on Mount Ida, in the earthly realm where mortal queens also hold sway (4.4.1053); and besides, these comically timorous gods admit, it would be folly for males to choose among powerful women. After complaining that women cause men's woe, Apollo presents the lofty rationale which Vulcan deflates:

> *Apol[lo].* . . . Suppresse not then, 'gainst lawe and equitie,
>   Dianas power in her owne territorie:
>   Whose regiment, amid her sacred bowers,
>   As proper height as anie rule of yours.
>   Well may we so wipe all the speeche awaie,
>   That Pallas, Juno, Venus hath to say,
>   And aunswere that by justice of our lawes,
>   We were not suffred to conclude the cause.
>   And this to me most egall doome appeares,
>   A woman to be judge among her pheeres.
> *Mars.* Apollo hathe founde out the onely meane,
>   To rid the blame from us and trouble cleane.
> *Vul[can].* We are beholding to his sacred wit.
> *Jup[iter].* I can commend and well allow of it,
>   And so derive the matter from us all,
>   That Dian have the giving of the ball.

Vul[can]. So Jove may clearly excuse him in the case,
    Where Juno else woulde chide and braule apace.
                                                (4.4.1060–77)

Drawing on the traditional representation of Juno as jealous nag, a familiar negative image of female power, Peele gets his laugh about shrewish wives, but also clears away the male characters for an alternative vision of "woman on top." Diana's "regiment" is as properly called ("hight") rule, and is as lofty ("height"), as any male Olympian's. Thus Peele stresses the presence of a valid, earthly space of female rule and authority, before turning to the queen in particular.

By making Diana the arbitress and by returning from the heavens to earth, Peele alters the Judgment tradition to create a final vision that idealizes rather than transcends present-day England; that distinction would be reinforced by the immediacy of performance. It is not the archpatriarch Saturn who restores this Golden Age, nor even heavenly Astraea, but instead the version of Diana who resides in the world of mortals.[19] This innovation is all the more striking when contrasted with Lyly's *Endimion,* which opposes the moon-goddess Cynthia to the base and earth-based Tellus. Whereas Lyly emphasizes the difficulties created for the male lover of Elizabeth's fictional correlate because of her unattainable otherworldliness, Peele stresses that correlate's ability to connect earth and heaven harmoniously. In act 2, Helen of Troy unwittingly called attention to the attributes of the "true" Diana that make her an appropriate goddess to preside over a happy ending: sovereign in all three realms (*cielo, ferno, terra*), Diana can create a vision of heaven *on earth;* and as the chaste protector of virgins, she helps the other goddesses to dismiss the sexual rivalry caused by their competitive desire to be the fairest object of a male gaze. On a stage cleared of male characters, the fifth act's praise of the nymph Eliza unites an unusual assortment of female deities, heavenly Olympians and infernal Fates combining to sing the praise of an earthly queen. Boundaries blur and realms merge in this paradise of women. The precedence of Diana and the more explicit portrait of Elizabeth as the fairest nymph clearly figure the queen's English court as earthly perfection.

The traditional story of Troy, of male heroism and tragic desire, also recedes before a different image of human power in Troynovant or London—without representing the suffering and violence of that *translatio empirii* as recorded in Tudor historiography. *The Arraignment of Paris* achieves this transformation with an elegance that balances (and, given the narrative structure, outweighs) earlier expressions of anxiety about eros and the poet's fate; Peele's version of poetic self-assertion does not preclude or inhibit his creation of unambiguously celebratory verse for the queen. The first act's chorus to "Ida happie hill," laden with dramatic irony when it introduced the three goddesses to the disruptive judgment scene, is transmuted into a lofty Latin paean, "Vive diu foelix," purged of ambiguity, dissension, or doubt. The landscape regains floral abundance, recalling the world as Flora dressed it in act 1, before the golden apple caused a falling-out:

> . . . Nor doth the milke-white way in frostie night,
> Appeare so faire and beautifull in sight:
> As done these fieldes, and groves, and sweetest bowres,
> Bestrewed and deckt with partie colord flowers . . .
> The dayntie Violet and the holsome Minthe:
> The doble Daisie, and the Couslip queene
> Of sommer floures, do over peere the greene:
>
> (1.3.80–83, 91–93)

Now, Pallas reminds us that when "Zabeta" was born, "Flora with her flowers strewed the Earth" (5.1.1179).[20] In borrowing his name for Elizabeth from Gascoigne's pageant, which favored Juno over Diana in an effort to persuade the queen to marry, Peele reinforces his praise for the queen *not* as consort or the object of male aspirations but as she professed to see herself: chaste and singular, yet fertile. Her distance from men, nevertheless, does not undermine her authority over them, nor isolate her from a community of females—or from lyrical poetry.

Shifts in the cast and verse help both to represent the queen's virtues and to keep Elizabeth free of the complicated passions portrayed in earlier acts. "*Diana describeth the Nymphe Eliza a figure of the Queene*" in a passage reminiscent of Flora's lyrical picture of nature, but in blank verse; the more elevated verse form, discordant at the beginning of the play when spoken by Ate, is pacified in its subject matter and sound (stage direction at 5.1.1137). Now the lyrical description evokes a perfect society as well as natural beauty. With the "pleasaunt shady woods," "Where neither storme nor Suns distemperature / Have power to hurte by cruell heate or colde," "Where whystling windes make musick 'mong the trees," and where the "countrie gods" (such as Flora) would merely be a "disturbance," pastoral retreat gives way to the apex of civilization (1.5.1139–41, 1145–46). Merging topical allusion with paradisic imagery, England transforms into "Elizium," the people are "ycleeped Angeli" (the famous Latin pun about the Angles well placed in this poetic creation of heaven on earth) and the queen is hailed as "*doctis-*

sima, candida, casta" (5.1.1150, 1155, 1215). This "aunciente seat of kinges, a seconde Troie, / Ycompast rounde with a commodious sea" prefigures John of Gaunt's vision in *Richard II* ("This royal throne of kings, this sceptred isle . . . This precious stone set in the silver sea" [2.1.40, 46]), with one crucial difference: Shakespeare's perfect mixture of land and empire, beauty and state, belongs to a mythic, dying past, whereas for Peele the mythology is asserted as present, immediate in time and place (5.1.1153–54). In this Fairyland, Gloriana is idealized but also looks like the woman in the audience:

> She giveth lawes of justice and of peace,
> And on her heade as fits her fortune best,
> She weares a wreath of laurell, golde, and palme:
> Her robes of purple and of scarlet die,
> Her vayle of white, as best befits a mayde.
> Her auncestors live in the house of fame;
> Shee giveth armes of happie victorie,
> And flowers to decke her lyons crowned with golde.
>
> (5.1.1157–64)

In this transformation of a Petrarchan blazon, the speaker Diana "*describeth*," at the same time as she is—through her proclaimed resemblance and linkage with the object of her verse, Elizabeth—being described. The rhetoric approaches a mythic representation of female self-description.[21] Every line recalls Elizabeth's gender as well as her appearance and strengths; she is viewed not only as a decorated body but as an agent who "giveth." Other female figures speak of her and judge her fairest, extending Oenone's earlier powers of speech beyond the erotic into heroic portraiture. The queen's body is colorfully decked, not to fetishize its parts but to compose a regal emblem. Unlike the mannerist distortion of female nudity in the French courtly blazons, which Nancy Vickers astutely reveals as one legacy of Petrarchism, here the body is carefully covered by symbolic clothing that undoes gendered opposition. The gold and purple of State mix harmoniously with flowers and laurels, Beauty and Fame. Rather than erasing the woman to create a king, this passage weds the queen's two bodies: she is a female sovereign who simultaneously gives arms and flowers.

This catalog of praise for Elizabeth, gathering together stereotypically feminine traits with those of a good monarch, surpasses the Petrarchan *sparagmos,* the objectification of the female body by a dismembering male gaze. Peele creates a kind of "anti-blazon," akin to "anti-Petrarchan" lyric in that it employs some of the devices of a conventional poetic tradition to express a very different attitude toward its subject. By reworking tropes inherited from Petrarchan lyricism, Peele invests his regal "subject" with a complicated, multifaceted authority appropriate to her exceptional position.

If all the world were a text, one might initially infer a similarity between the queen's position as unifying sovereign presence here (in antithesis to the rhetorical dismemberment of the traditional blazon) and in the Foucauldian political paradigm. But such sleight of mouth not only denies, irresponsibly, the pain of torture that subjects such as Stubbes and Campion experienced; it also ignores the complexity of Peele's poetic strategy in maintaining variety within the whole, and in sustaining the queen's gendered difference within the praise of her cultural authority. Indeed, the hypothesized correlation between two kinds of dismemberment calls attention to the problems posed by too simply accepting a similar dynamic at work in all epideictic catalogues, and in all renditions of sovereignty. Veneration of the parts need not always and inevitably imply denigration of, or even mastery over, the whole; that much is obvious from religious language, which can easily be enlisted to create the awe requisite for absolutist sovereignty. Nor does the invocation of the sovereign's unifying power automatically imply a monolithic or uniform idealization. What this "anti-blazon" neatly captures is the further kinship between such praise of female sovereignty and less aggressive lyric versions of praise for the beloved. Just as the image of the queen is carefully related, rather than merely contrasted, to the imaging of other female characters, so this catalogue may be placed on a continuum of lyric praise—not simply rejecting physical or stereotypical woman's "parts" but extending such praise into a political context. The queen both gathers and magnifies those attributes of will and beauty seen in other female characters, and thus receives tribute from admiring females in verse that transmutes rather than erases the blazon and lyricism.

The play has moved from Ate to Elizabeth, from a blank-verse prologue in which a female signifies Discord to a portrait of woman as ideal sovereign. While the play's earlier scenes suggest tensions between mortals and gods, and between lovers, the narrative's trajectory celebrates the possibility of resolving problems under female guidance. Especially as compared to contemporary representations of courtly love, gender difference is subordinated until the play's end, when the praise of Elizabeth honors her sex explicitly. The tragic potential of the play, announced by Ate, is finally solved by a very different female power—not only through the gesture of giving the apple to Elizabeth but also through Diana's crucial role as the ultimate judge, with the endorsement of a female chorus.[22] The threatening versions of womanhood presented earlier (interspersed with male infidelity and violence) are absent from the final tableau, their appearance having worked against mere inversion of gender superiority (just as the erotic episodes worked against standard definitions of sexual difference). Poetic changes reinforce the nature of this victory. The Fates' heroic Latin replaces Helen's erotic Italian, signaling all the stereotypical differences those cultures implied: the state over the individual, weight over frivolity, chastity (Vestal or Lucrecian) over sexuality. The only character who used Latin previously was Ate, when she rolled out the ball, also inscribed in Latin, crying "*Fatum Troie*" (stage direction at 2.1.355); she invoked "Th'unpartiall daughters of Necessitie" as allies in her grim mission (*prologus*. 20). Now those Fates do indeed appear, but their Latin does not signal a return to Ate's world of "Lordings," bombast, and militarism, but to a chastened lyric vision combining blank verse, rhyme, and song. In this landscape of women, *The Arraignment of Paris* artfully evades the representation of tragedy promised by the play's beginning. Diana pacifies the three Olympian goddesses who competed earlier, initiating a compromise which does not deny the worthiness and fairness of any. In parallel couplets, as formal and ritualistic as the Latin song, Juno, Pallas, and Venus recognize the queen as their apogee and verbally erase their differences. While most of the play diminishes or refuses to endorse stereotypical contrasts between the sexes, this public celebration of sovereignty occurs in an exclusively female realm—a reversal rather than erasure of traditional gender roles.

Viewed through modern eyes, this peace obviously has its sacrifices and its boundaries; an unhappy courtier time-traveling in the twentieth century might be more inclined to call it "pacification." The absence of female human beings, as well as males of all sorts, indicates the unresolved problem of the actively sexual body. And while the playwright finds a way to get beyond sexualized male praise for the female, he does not present any males participating in the scene of desexualized admiration. Like Sidney in his *Apology*, Peele implies a distinction between the potential of lyric poetry and its (corrupt) practitioners; unlike Sidney, he produces a chastened epideictic lyricism, among women only. While lyric poetry obviously is not the obstacle to harmony, Peele suggests that sexual desire, which apparently blinds men to all other aspects of womanhood, may well be.

Nevertheless, despite the purging of human sexuality from the scene, the most remarkable aspect of the finale to *The Arraignment of Paris* remains its attempt to represent a woman's-eye view, pleasing the queen as audience with praise appropriate from a female perspective. Other female figures speak of and to the queen here, extending Oenone's earlier powers of language, without renewing the problem of personal desire her story had entailed. Nor is Elizabeth herself called on to speak, hence avoiding the problem of coercion or subjugation of the monarch to her playwright's script.[23] Through the queen's presence in itself, but also through her representation in the goddesses' words, singing, and dancing, Peele associates Elizabeth with a vocal, harmonious community of powerful females. Thus he celebrates his monarch not as virago or exception, nor primarily as a perpetual virgin, but instead as the epitome of femininity, the best of several female powers in the play. Indeed, in terms of the actual event, she was the only "true" woman participating in the play, since the roles of the other goddesses were performed by boy actors.[24] As such, she marks the feminine extreme on a continuum of gender identity.

The queen is certainly "different" from the other characters, as Inga-Stina Ewbank has remarked, noting that she defeats the dynamic and potentially tragic world of the play through her "simple, static presence"; she functions, in my paraphrase, like a lyric in a narrative drama. To Ewbank's analysis, I add the emphasis on this "wonder of monarchy" being represented as explicitly feminine, and associated both with justice and state power and with fertility, peace, beauty, and life itself.[25] This is achieved only by representing the queen in language amenable to Elizabeth as female auditor and by offering a magic gesture amenable to her female gaze.

In so presenting this spectacle for the queen, Peele in a sense supplants his own male perspective and takes what is traditionally the "woman's part." He does not present Elizabeth, as most of his and our contemporaries tend to do, by finding an explicit relationship between her image and his own subjectivity, his own male gaze. In its reflection of the queen at twice her natural size, serving as a beautiful yet self-abnegating mirror, this play performs "like a woman." In *A Room of One's Own,* Virginia Woolf wryly observes that this traditional female role as flattering reflector, for all its gross inequity, has boosted the confidence and achievement of men throughout history: "it charges the vitality; it stimulates the nervous system" (36). To the extent that Peele participated in a role-reversed version of this inflation of self, and to the extent that his printed play communicated and energized that image for his countrymen and women, *The Arraignment of Paris* participates in the countercreation of a female subject as worthy sovereign.

By contrast, the scholarly tendency to focus on the succession and Elizabeth's virginity as central to all representations of the queen, while certainly attending to major anxieties of the day and in some cases filling lacunae in scholarship, may replicate the cultural difficulty of looking beyond Elizabeth's sexualized body when discussing her female sovereignty. Louis Adrian Montrose quite reasonably underscores Shakespeare's imaging of Elizabeth as mother, wet nurse, and virgin within *A Midsummer Night's Dream,* and the historian Christopher Haigh adopts the same rhetoric, dubbing the queen a mother to the Church, a nanny to her Parliament, a nagging wife to her councillors, and a seductress to her court. The conventional labels are presented wittily and as sixteenth-century views, though not seriously criticized.[26] Nevertheless, *The Arraignment of Paris* does not praise Elizabeth because of her relations to men or her ability to service them; Peele dismisses such labels of female power along with the gaze of his male characters. His representation of England as fertile and flowering while simultaneously chaste and virginal refuses the binary exclusiveness of succession discourse and, at least figuratively, blurs the conventional categorization of women solely on the basis of their sexual experience.[27] Here again Peele negotiates with traditional representations of his subject matter: while building an image of female sovereignty from terms and tropes familiar to a predominantly male audience as well as the queen, his play represents her power as all-embracing and self-sufficient, not derived from men (not even her father) in any way. This fiction, applied to a human woman, can validly be read as both flattery of a sovereign and violation of part of the ideological basis for England's sex-gender system.

To say this is not to remove tension from Peele's vision, nor to ignore the cost of his happy ending—as he himself represents it, using Colin and Paris—from a man's and a poet's perspective. But the *Arraignment* is by no means a tragic or even a preponderantly melancholy work, in part because it joyously resolves the question of "fairness," and in part because of its pastoral activity and variety, moving between episodes and refusing to focus on the plight of anyone for very long. Moreover, Peele's poetry does not sound squelched or even constrained by the courtly conditions of performance and female political authority (unlike the pageants of Gascoigne and Sidney). While drawing on Neoplatonism in sublimating overt eroticism, the play's final act goes far beyond merely elevating masculine desire the way some Petrarchist poetry does; it also imagines a paradise that is (to transfer the categories of deity to sovereignty) immanent rather than transcendent. Among the salient particulars of the final praise is its emphasis on communal consensus, enacting onstage the queen's ability to replace civil dissension and competition with peace and harmony.

This positive representation of Elizabeth's female political authority, building on and modifying the tropes and figures of lyric poetry, is not confined to *The Arraignment of Paris*. Similar representations appear in later works by Peele and other influential writers. In his Lord Mayor's Show of 1585, printed as "The Device of the Pageant Borne Before Wolstone Dixi," Peele praises the queen as a figure of bounty and harmony, bringing to London "peace and calme" which now "Hath long bin such as like was never seene" (1: 211). Again the reason for respecting the queen's sovereignty goes beyond courtly veneration of a mistress's beauty, to more substantial political praise. Her "regiment" is not monstrous, as in John Knox's famous pamphlet, but "sacred":[28]

> So long as Sunne dooth lend the world his light,
> or any grasse dooth growe upon the ground:
> With holy flame, our Torches shall burne bright,
> and fame shall brute with golden trumpets sound
> The honor of her sacred regiment:
> That claimes this honorable monument.
>
> (1: 213)

Here traditionally masculine public fame is grafted onto the queen's holiness and pacific influence. The claim of immortal fame for the poetic object may be more familiarly associated with sonnets, and indeed several of Peele's phrases resound in Shakespeare: "O she doth teach the torches to burn bright" and the pilgrim sonnet in *Romeo and Juliet;* "So long as men can breathe or eyes can see, / So long lives this, and this gives life to thee" in sonnet 18. A similar tension between epic and lyric rhetoric exists in each author's work, but with opposing emphases. When Shakespeare's vaunts that his beloved in "pow'rful rhyme" will outshine marble or "gilded monuments / Of princes," he supplants public discourse with the personal, and emphasizes his male authorial power to give fame (sonnet 55). Peele's speech uses the tropes of courtly lyric to praise a public version of "fairness," and credits the queen's worthiness regardless of his own poetic ability: fame itself, not the author's verse, shall trumpet; it is her agency, her honor, that "claimes" his tribute.

Moreover, London (or new Troy, in the pageant's language) is allegorized as a woman, reinforcing the positive power associated with the queen. Peele does not always imagine London as female; his narrative poem "A Tale of Troy," for example, genders the city masculine. The pageant representation, then, implies a conscious choice, allowing Peele to stress the kinship between city and queen in a way that is not eroticized by male desire (despite the obvious occasion for such a trope given the site of performance before a new lord mayor, not to mention the tradition of royal entries in which kings "marry" the capital city of their realm). Like his court play, Peele's pageant ends with communal female celebration; here, four nymphs praise the queen directly—without reference to the mayor. The female is invoked not only in traditional guises as a symbolic mediator or giver of sovereignty but also as the recipient of tribute, as the surrogate for the actual possessor of sovereign power.

In *The Rites of Knighthood,* Richard McCoy calls attention to the role of audience composition in altering an author's political angle (see for example his discussion of Samuel Daniel [121]). Lord mayor's shows, semimagical secular rituals designed for a more varied audience than were the country house entertainments for the queen, sometimes do reveal concerns other than those of the court's inner circle. In Peele's case, however, the change of forum does not so much alter as accentuate his praise of female sovereignty. Less is said about the queen's beauty and more about her ability to bring peace and bounty, as seems apt given an audience including substantial London citizens. But even when Elizabeth's watchful eye was not in immediate attendance, her sovereign power "from whome our peace and quietnes proceeds" still exerts its sway over Peele's script (1: 213); perhaps it is not mere coincidence that "Wolstan Dixi" is, according to Horne, the first complete lord mayor's show extant (Peele 1: 154). The allegorical pageant speakers, like the goddesses in act 5 of *The Arraignment of Paris,* unite in paying homage to female London, who (according to the presenter "apparelled like a Moore" and riding a lynx) accepts their various offerings "with humble gesture" (209, 210). This kind of procession may be more familiar as a trope in seventeenth-century country house poems such as Ben Jonson's "To Penshurst"; in this earlier manifestation, not just an aristocratic house but the state's major city is honored and well-managed, providing a colonizing model for national order and cooperation. Performed during the good harvest years of the mid-1580s, the pageant implies no irony in representing "the Country" as happy to present its grain to London. Like the *Arraignment,* Peele's pageant idealizes a current center of English society, using pastoral as a device for allegory rather than for retreat from female authority.

Related transformations of poetic tropes in order to honor Elizabeth's sovereignty occur in other courtly works of the time. In discussing the judgment tradition, Ekeblad cites George Puttenham's 1579 New Year's gift for the queen, laudatory poems which honor wisdom as the preferred virtue (249). These lines also stress the earthly location of sovereignty:

> I am not rapte in Junoe's spheare,
> Nor with dame Venus lovely hewe;
> But here on earthe I serve and feare,
> O mayde Minerva, thine ydoll true,
> Whose power prevayles in warr and peace,
> So as thy raigne can no tyme cease.

Even more notably, in the *Arte of English Poesie* (1589), Puttenham was to write of Elizabeth—using a strikingly odd iconographic simile—that

> Out of her breast as from an eye
> Issue the rayes incessantly
> Of her justice, bountie, and might,
> Spreading abroad their beames so bright,
> And reflect not, till they attaine
> The fardest part of her domaine.
> And make eche subject clearely see
> What he is bounden for to be
> To God, his Prince, and common wealth,
> His neighbour, kinred, and to himself.[29]

The queen's light "beames," issuing from her feminine "center" to "circle" the realm (these being Puttenham's three structuring words for his "Roundell" form) become the precondition for generic-male subjectivity. Lacking the poetic delicacy of Peele, Puttenham's language nevertheless captures how the sovereignty of Elizabeth demanded new formulations of the linkage between femininity, the subjectivity of a royal "I," and the gaze of her "eye." The female breast itself, often praised in the poetic form of the *blason du tétin* as an object for male desire, becomes not only a source of nourishment but a viewing eye, the source and subject of a different sort of "fairness," that of a just sovereign.[30] Moreover, as in the Rainbow portrait of Elizabeth where ears and eyes bedeck the queen's gown, the allegorical quality of Puttenham's use of female body parts transforms the dynamics of the blazon to imagine a female figure of authority both fleshly and symbolic. Peele's work provides a fuller and more elegant precedent for such transformation of female fairness.

In later histories such as William Camden's, the image was perpetuated (often to be used as a chastising counterimage to the contemporary government). Camden's introduction begins with back-to-back praise of Elizabeth as the pattern of princes and the glory of womankind, epitomizing her achievement as a long-lived female sovereign in her own right. She is "The all-glorious, all-virtuous, incomparable, invict and matchless pattern of princes, the glory, honour and mirror of womankind, the admiration of our age, ELIZABETH, Queen of England." Despite cultural assumptions and actual hierarchies, Camden can see a prince mirroring a woman, now to be gazed upon by all who follow—including her male successor (who by implication would do better to gaze on her than be seen himself). The gaze is not one of gendered desire but of "admiration," the wonder appropriate to sovereignty.

Without the (over)viewing eye of Elizabeth as impetus for performance and simultaneously its ultimate judge, the specific vision of *The Arraignment of Paris* would hardly have been realized—although the Wolstan Dixi pageant shows how such a reappraisal of female sovereignty, once developed, could be adapted to other performance venues. Sidney's "misunderstood" pageant *The Lady of May* and Gascoigne's aborted "Zabeta" sketch attest to the queen's shaping role in determining what would be, imaginatively and materially, shown. To recognize this does not automatically reduce Peele's play (and other such praise) to a lackey's servile reflection, nor confine the critical enterprise exclusively to a search for the author's veiled but doomed marks of aesthetic autonomy in the shadow of political authority. It can also suggest a vision of political and aesthetic collaboration, with all the complexity that word connotes when applied to unequal partners—collaboration, moreover, involving the queen in creating an image of a woman's political power as self-sufficient and assertive.

In considering Peele's work and emphasizing its representations of gender, I have stressed Elizabeth's power as creative, counterbalancing the rebelliousness against central authority suggested by foregrounding the dismemberments of Stubbes and Campion, or indeed the poetry of Sidney and Marlowe. These poetic rebels have often been taken as models of emerging individualism and modern subjectivity fighting a monolithic state power whose hegemony creates a compelling tragic vision (as in the work of Stephen Greenblatt during the early 1980s, most influentially). In the process, critics often valorize, or identify with, masculine discontent as more mature and truthful than tamer tributes (just as anti-Petrarchan poetry claims to be more honest and true than its object of parody). Some more recent new historicist studies of Tudor aristocracy and monarchy still do not consider gender as an issue complicating their discussion of political struggle, presuming rather than studying those aspects of "self" being asserted in challenges to the queen's authority.[31] But the very amorphousness of the Crown's power as a concept, as distinct from de facto force, was one of the central problems of Elizabeth's reign; this problem was aggravated by her sex, which made it even more obvious than usual that the sources for political authority did not simply reflect all of the culture's theoretical hierarchies. Dismissal of Peele's work as mere court propaganda ignores his poetic artistry and his investigation of this gendered sovereignty, and to some extent reenacts the more rebellious courtiers' attitude toward female power.[32]

Readings of *The Arraignment of Paris* that ignore the play's totality likewise erase complexity in favor of a single voice of assertion. Sometimes this voice is made explicitly male, as when Howard Baker focuses on Paris's act 4 oration before the gods as the play's distinctive moment—despite the fact that the happy ending does not derive from that speech at all (95–97).[33] Even in Baker's own formalist terms, his focus on Paris's blank verse discounts Ate's Senecan prologue and Diana's culminating praise of Elizabeth, other blank verse tonalities just as crucial to the poetic whole; perhaps overestimating the importance of the title, Baker unironically calls this a "one-man play" prefiguring Marlowe's *Tamburlaine,* hence devaluing the importance and praise of feminine community in favor of masculine individualism. The play becomes one moment in a narrative about the establishment of male subjectivity. Yet as we have seen, Peele's play examines subjectivity and power in quite another way, and uses song and the tropes of lyric poetry— not just the "bumbast" of blank verse—to do so. Like the works of Spenser, *The Arraignment of Paris* draws on a rich courtly love tradition and modifies it, to portray numerous responses to female sovereignty and by extension to other forms of female power in England, in its time, on earth.

Seeing the female as nurturing or peaceful is not in itself radical (especially when she's a queen), and Peele certainly praises Elizabeth's physical beauty; but *The Arraignment of Paris* melds these qualities with political praise for the queen's justice and wisdom quite vigorously. It praises her as a peacemaker with power in the public, earthly realm rather than in exclusively erotic, domestic or religious territories. In watching this representation of herself, Elizabeth unifies the role of the female as the mediator or symbol of sovereignty, found in traditional ceremonies and pageants, with the direct, official power of the king. Thus the play indicates how Elizabeth's sovereignty sparked new interpretations of gender stereotypes, if only or primarily in works performed under her aegis and for her approval. Subsequent publication gave these interpretations greater and more lasting currency.

Because published works were increasingly important as a means by which subjects conceived of their monarch, especially in the north and west of England, the publication of Peele's play in 1584 exemplifies the growing potential of court works to function nationally as what Louis Adrian Montrose calls "shaping fantasies," creating as well as representing cultural attitudes.[34] In this case, the fantasies include a bevy of powerful women ruling the universe and more immediately the state of England, and a representation of the pains wrought by romantic love comparatively free of explicit gender or sexual inequity. The very real presence of Queen Elizabeth as viewing eye conditioned the playwright's own gaze, his view of his artistic "subject"; in turn, the reality of her rule makes the published play more than mere fantasy. *The Arraignment of Paris* becomes a unifying aesthetic spectacle, and not only the converse of the political spectacle involved in punishing unruly subjects. It unites idealized femininity with actual political power in what is, for its time, a progressive though not politically subversive performance. Seen in historical context, this court drama creatively confronts the double perspectives demanded by Elizabeth's gender and her sovereignty. In so doing, it substantiates her shaping role in the creation of positively resonant cultural images of women's political power.

To say this is not to fetishize royalty as a nostalgic form of worship in a fractured culture. Obviously, gender is not the single defining attribute or category of judgment to be considered in reading court works, and in sketching the background of religious violence and the Crown's power to destroy I intended more than an anecdotal aside. Others have explored the seamy relationship between monarchic worship and public torture, and the human cost of establishing the "Elizabethan settlement" is well known. None of this negates the fact that Elizabeth, because of her political power, provided a unique incentive within her culture for reevaluating the feminine. Peele's careful deployment of amatory lyric traditions in his representation of female authority attests to her transformative impact.

Such interconnections of women, lyric poetry, and sovereignty were not always viewed as benign by Elizabethan artists, and the voices of the poetic rebels eventually achieved dominance (if not in the print of their own time, then in the literary histories that ensued). Much of the subsequent public drama reorients attention to masculine political power, placing courtly ladies in a different landscape. Even within the court playing halls of the 1580s, there were rumblings. In Christopher Marlowe's version of Trojan mythology, *Dido, Queen of Carthage,* women, power, and lyrical poetry are associated within a less complimentary narrative. Peele's *Arraignment of Paris* combines two traditions of love poetry, the Petrarchan pining of Colin and the Ovidian complaint of Oenone, in such a way as to emphasize the comparable distress of men and women. Oenone's voice, shorn of the competitive carping at Helen found in Ovid's *Heroides 5*, expresses female agency as well as pain; her unambiguously sympathetic dramatization serves as an apt prelude to the finale's praise of female sovereignty. In Christopher Marlowe's hands, narrative and poetic materials of similar ancestry are used quite differently, and his alternative voices are placed in opposition.

As it did for Peele, the matter of Troy provides the basic plot for *Dido*. Marlowe's only known court drama is drawn primarily (sometimes literally transcribed or translated) from Virgil's *Aeneid*, books 2 and 4. His choice of this epic source places lyric poetry within an heroic context that necessitates its abandonment; love, like Aeneas's dalliance in Carthage, is a pleasing but unmanly interlude for the hero devoted to earthly fame and controlled by the gods. Marlowe alters Virgil's representation crucially, perhaps drawing on the Ovidian complaint of Dido in *Heroides 7*, to create even greater sympathy for this queen (and less for Aeneas). Nevertheless, the messages of *Dido* are by no means as laudatory or clear as those of Peele's *Arraignment*—especially the messages regarding female sovereignty and the cultural fate of love poetry.

Notes

1. For more on George Peele's life and background, see Horne in Peele 1: 3–146.

2. See Benbow's introduction (Peele 3: 7–50) for standard views. Montrose ("Gifts"), while challenging Hallett Smith's reading, also discusses the play within the pastoral tradition. I use the modern spelling of the play's title but otherwise follow Benbow's edition; he divides the script by act and scene, but does not renumber lines accordingly.

3. See Von Hendy, Lesnick, and Welsford.

4. Benbow (Peele 3: 7–12) conjectures a version of the play prior to its 1584 publication date, but he acknowledges that Greg placed it with "no doubt in 1581"; Horne finds biographical evidence pointing to 1582. Daniel substantiated the dates I give through examination of the Master of the Revels' property lists for 1581. The 1581–82 date for me remains illustrative, not causal or necessary to my argument; it points to the growing belligerence of the state, a process that continued into 1584, the year before England finally became involved directly in the Netherlands.

5. See McGrath and Meyer on Campion. His "Brag" (a defense of his mission) was published before his sham trial.

6. Most notably, Thomas Alfield's *True Report of the Death and Martyrdom of M. Campion* was secretly published before 1582; Cecil's defense was countered by William Allen's *True, Sincere, and Modest Defense of English Catholics;* see also Cecil, Haigh (*Reign of Elizabeth*) 9, and MacCaffrey.

7. See Foucault 23–49; he invokes Kantorowicz's influential analysis of the king's double body in discussing power's double functioning (28–29).

8. As many historians note, it is a wonder Elizabeth could withstand the militaristic and fervent religious pressures of her counselors for so long. Read echoes Peele's own praise, as he discusses Drake's 1581 return from his voyage around the world, noting that while such enterprises were in part motivated by the need for investment of accumulated capital, "all these good things" were also "the fruits of peace. And it was Elizabeth who kept the peace, in the face of all kinds of pressure from those immediately around her, at the expense often of the most transparent breaches of faith, to the despair of her counselors, her diplomats, her soldiers and her sailors—nevertheless she kept the peace" (192).

9. See Davis's classic article for more on early modern fears and rituals of gender role inversion. Marcus observes that "The image of a woman in power carried strong associations with anarchy in sixteenth-century England" ("Shakespeare's" 147).

10. Colin Clout was of course a character in John Skelton's poetry earlier in the century, so Peele had Spenser's own precedent in "borrowing" him. While in Peele's play he is referred to simply as Colin, his relationships with Hobbinol, Thenot, and the rest of the shepherds, as well as his role as the prized poet whose voice has been silenced by unrequited love, confirm his identification with Spenser's recent creation. Benbow summarizes the arguments of other critics who have linked the two Colins. This is a topic I will be pursuing in a forthcoming study.

11. Von Hendy asserts that "In deciding what he should play, Paris has raised sinister topics:" and then quotes part of Oenone's long catalogue of betrayal myths (1.5.19–22 in his numbering). He concludes that "Paris' repertoire, both political and amatory, consists of tales of infidelity later corrected by justice" (91). The lines are clearly marked as Oenone's in the Brooke and Paradise edition which Von Hendy uses as his source along with Child's 1910 Malone reprint.

12. The sonnet was without doubt the most popular of those few Renaissance poetic forms not derived from a classical precedent. For the Elizabethans, Petrarch especially made the sonnet an Italian creation.

13. Whereas the Italian idealizations of feminine beauty and love were quite separable from particular women, the English beloved was often represented as an actual known woman, i.e., of the world and the flesh and hence flawed. Even if, like Sidney's Penelope Devereux Rich, the shadowed lady is off limits, the reasons are usually pragmatic; she is hardly an Italian madonna, soon conveyed to the otherworld. Although such a generalization is perforce oversimplifying, this English emphasis is at least partially attributable to the Petrarchan worship of Elizabeth,

who remained earthbound even if sovereign; see Forster's chap. 4, and Jones and Stallybrass. Viguers observes that elsewhere Peele suggests Paris's choice was motivated by "adulterous pride" ("A Tale of Troy," l. 202) and stresses the moral context created by the contrasting songs of Oenone and Helen (484–85).

14. On echo songs and Echo, see Hollander's *Figure of Echo*.

15. According to Alpers, "[t]here are eclogues in Sidney's *Arcadia*, but their motivation is as social and dramatic as the motivation of the lyrics that occur in the narrative itself," whereas in Spenser "[t]he modes and conventions of pastoral . . . free the woeful lover from the assumptions of the courtly lyric of social situation and witty coherence"; thus the freer literary and constraining courtly-social domains are set in opposition, and the literary domain allows "a qualified but nonetheless genuine independence" (see 169–75). Discussing Hallett Smith's reading of pastoral retreat in this pageant, Montrose observes: "What appears to be a contradiction between ambition and pastoralism, between social value and cultural form, may in fact be a subtle rhetorical strategy" ("Gifts" 439).

16. John N. King emphasizes Spenser's double distancing of this song from his narrative voice as significant in the changing iconography of Elizabeth. See also Alpers on the public formality of this song and the November dirge.

17. Cole thinks Colin's death occurs "simply for visual and tonal effects," whereas I regard the stories of these pastoral characters as more than "momentary adornments, pretty pieces by the wayside, neither advancing the main action nor really contributing to the principal theme" (504).

18. Such competition works in two directions: between men, in boasting of their lady's superiority (see Sedgwick passim); and between women, as they strive to be chosen as the man's particular love object.

19. Von Hendy stresses the finale as a Saturnian return to the Golden Age (90–91), equating Diana with Natura (97); he regards chastity as the essence of praise for Elizabeth here. The use of Diana is not part of the Judgment tradition (see Anglo, Ekeblad, and Reeves for other Judgments); rather, it derives from and transforms another Elizabethan pageant rivalry between Juno and Diana. Montrose believes "The most significant innovation in Peele's treatment of the myth is to encompass Diana and the virtue of militant virginity. To proclaim that Elizabeth infolds the excellences of all the goddesses is to perfect the encomium in a manner that is possible only when the prince is a woman" ("Gifts" 436). However, Diana signifies not just a *Trionfo della Castità* (not an entirely novel idea in any case, as Ekeblad shows) but more specifically and embracingly a triumph of female sovereignty as cooperative and pacifying. The earthly locale and immediacy—her immanence—mark a significant shift from Mariology. (Montrose also notes that Diana arbitrates "because the harried male gods think it politic" to have a woman do so, thus crediting those gods' perspective. He concludes that the play discredits Paris's "pastoral perspective"—the operative factor informing that "perspective" being specifically

male heterosexual desire.) For extensive discussion of the figure of Diana, using terminology drawn from Irigaray, see P. Berry, especially chaps. 2 and 3.

20. Montrose asserts that the most common name for menses was "flowers," noting that this adds "a peculiar resonance to certain occurences of the word and of floral imagery in Renaissance texts" ("*Midsummer*" 333); if so, it makes flowers an especially apt symbol of femininity and further compounds the fertile gendering of this earthly paradise.

21. I invoke the title of Vickers's influential article to stress the difference between the use of a verse catalog here and in Petrarch; see also her "The Mistress in the Masterpiece" in Miller, *Poetics*. The difference involves a double impersonation (Peele presenting his words as a goddess's, and the boy actor presenting himself as a female) which is a far cry from actual female self-representation; nevertheless, the change in empathy and posture matters.

22. The concluding tranformation of Ate's disruptive prophecy is reinforced through the visual icon of the golden apple and through the shared use of blank verse. Blank verse is not the play's dominant meter; with the famous exception of Paris's oration before the gods, most of the rest of the play is rhymed, often in fourteeners.

23. Recent studies have emphasized this tension between royal presentation and representation (cf. Montrose, Kastan). Gascoigne's "Zabeta" sketch at Kenilworth exemplifies the dangers in instructive representation of the queen; not coincidentally, Peele uses the name "Zabeta" to praise Elizabeth in a context that shows chaste Diana superior to married Juno (thus reversing the trope that got Dudley, Gascoigne, and several other proponents of a royal marriage into trouble during the 1560s and 1570s).

24. The ironies of boys' company performances before the queen surely contributed to the overt concern with sexuality and queenship in the court drama. This emphasis is not exclusively attributable to homosexual titillation, nor simply a result of more female parts (indeed, it does not necessarily correlate with the number of such parts).

25. Ewbank 138, 141. References to the fertile landscape and the queen's virtues permeate act 5.

26. Haigh frames his discussion by calling attention to the queen's reliance on illusion, viewing her as an actress; he rightly notes that she "had a constant struggle to get men to do what she wanted" (*Elizabeth* 125), but the labels of nanny and nag are surely not hers. Stressing the queen as exceptional or androgynous is the flip side of stereotyping, releasing the individual without challenging the category's portrayal.

27. Montrose hypothesizes that the *Arraignment* belongs to texts "which shadowed the controversial issues of royal marriage and succession" ("Gifts" 440); I believe it shadows other political issues as well, in praising the queen as peacekeeper.

Montrose observes that Peele's offering a gift "fully acknowledges and celebrates the Queen's own choice, her complex transcendence of the simplistic oppositions contrived by her courtiers" ("Gifts" 444)—and by scholars as well. Recent attention to the Alençon courtship (cf. Marcus, *Puzzling*) may lead some to believe it polarized the culture into camps for and against the French marriage even into the early 1590s (when Elizabeth was obviously beyond childbearing and the French prince was long dead). Peele's work shows how mythological figures, images, and even "loaded" names such as "Zabeta" and "Colin Clout" could be transmuted by a new context, given complex new meanings that do not simply repeat or reverse earlier ones.

28. Peele's phrase "the honor of her sacred regiment" is a clear rebuttal of John Knox's 1558 *The First Blast of the Trumpet* . . . , a work that infuriated Elizabeth by denouncing "the monstrous regiment of women."

29. GGS 2: 103. Montrose's mention of the first three lines in a footnote to "Shaping Fantasies" (88) spurred me to analyze this passage.

30. The breast as mystical source of nourishment is not unique to Puttenham, although his graphic juxtaposition with the eye causes an incongruously jarring effect, given the queen's sex; without the simile, one would think immediately of the iconography of the Virgin. This maternal return could be seen as a way of fitting Elizabeth back into a familiar figure of femininity, though because of Elizabeth's refusal of anything but mystical maternity this association remains purely figurative. One might argue that faint allusions to the absent/suppressed mother do not appear coincidentally both here and in Peele's play (possibly hearkening back to Udall's pageantry using the Judgment of Paris before Anne Boleyn), in works making strong claims for "legitimate" female sovereignty independent of the father.

31. McCoy's analysis of chivalric "manliness" and the "militia" faction at court (in *Rites*) never addresses gender as a complicating term (despite Elizabeth's double role as observing ladylove and active monarch). For tragic subjectivity see Greenblatt's *Renaissance Self-Fashioning,* but see also his revised thoughts about "power" in *Renaissance Negotiations* and in Veeser. Tennenhouse's introduction is straightforward about the desire to challenge the institutions of which he is an uneasy member; he tends to refer gender complication to systemic patriarchal issues of "blood," in a very different way discounting the specific problems of sexual difference and stereotypes in favor of inheritance and group identity. Reiss is equally frank about reading Marlowe through the lens of Foucault. Corthell, citing Greenblatt and Althusser, distinguishes the subjectivity of Campion and other recusants: "Catholics were perhaps uniquely situated to experience the problem of the subject in Elizabethan England" (272). For a different perspective on the scholarly wish to rebel, see Gerald Graff's article on "Co-optation" in Veeser.

32. In a more sympathetic vein, Ewbank notes that Peele's writing in a variety of genres for differing audiences "seems largely opportunistic, lacking the kind of inner compulsion which lies behind the work of Marlowe, and even Kyd" (128).

Peele's variety might alternatively be viewed as effective subordination (though not erasure) of an authorial "self."

33. Similarly see Brooke and Paradise (2), and G. K. Hunter's commentary in *Lyly* (155), which draws on Welsford in judging Peele's ending and many other episodes as extraneous to a "central action." Without denying the importance of Paris's oration and other moments of questioning directed at the gods, one may note that the play presents quite a different perspective on self-assertion than appears in Marlowe's *Tamburlaine* or, as I shall illustrate, *Dido, Queen of Carthage*.

34. See Montrose's article of the same name. Ewbank observes that, after being performed as a play "*to* and *for* the queen, it becomes a poem *about* her" in publication (137). Frye pursues the potential of such shifts to reinstate the authority of her masculine subjects. In this case, however, because of the laudatory content of the representation, further distribution does not result in gendered competition, but rather collaboration.

THREE

"Unhappy Dido"

Marlowe's Lyric Strains

> I heard thee speak me a speech once, but it was never acted, or if it was, not above once—for the play, I remember, pleased not the million, 'twas caviare to the general. But it was, as I received it—and others, whose judgments in such matters cried in the top of mine—an excellent play, well digested in the scenes, set down with as much modesty as cunning . . . One speech in't I chiefly loved—'twas Aeneas' tale to Dido—and thereabout of it especially when he speaks of Priam's slaughter . . .
> *Hamlet*, 2.2.430 ff.

Christopher Marlowe was among the upwardly mobile "new men" in Elizabethan England, son of a craftsman but university educated.[1] He seems to have done his best to retain his marginal and fluid status. Moving among the court world of ritual and poetic fictions, the professional world of the London theater, and the political underworld of Her Majesty's secret service, Marlowe acquired the intelligence of a humanist scholar and a spy, the craft of an artist and an agent. It is no surprise that his allegiances are hard to pinpoint, nor that his work challenges the views of those less comfortable with mobility and multiple, perhaps duplicitous, meanings. He was a groundbreaker whose method was unsettling.

Aptly, the rhetoric of eros and its problems particularly dominate Marlowe's single extant play associated with the court rather than the public stage.[2] First performed by the Children of Her Majesty's Chapel, *Dido, Queen of Carthage* exploits its cast's aptitude for displaying more "feminine" emotions and well-spoken, ornate rhetoric, and forgoes any attempt at representing a thunderous boy warrior. Despite the critical tendency to see overreachers and bombast everywhere in Marlowe's work, Aeneas is no

Tamburlaine.³ Whereas the classical Aeneas strains toward his heroic future, this Aeneas mourns for a simpler past and desires a comfortable present. Marlowe shifts the immortal longings onto Dido and her language; it is she who most notably combines heroic vaunting with erotic seduction. This melding of masculine and feminine, heroic and lyric vocabularies is in some ways comparable to Peele's lovingly heroic praise of female sovereignty, but Marlowe's language and its sovereign female speaker are subjected to a very different narrative frame. Dido, inevitably, is doomed. Consequently the play becomes less a *débat* between love and honor (the traditional rendering of this story) and more the analysis of a failed rhetoric of desire.⁴

Marlowe's tragedy strains against two kinds of necessity, the artistic pressure to render familiar literary material "faithfully" and the gods' power to make human beings their puppets—but it finally acknowledges the sway of both. Within the drama, love poetry becomes an alluring voice of failed resistance to material reality. Openly irresponsible, it can violate hierarchies on heaven and earth, unsettling conventional assumptions about gender, heterosexuality, and duty. But the narrative also conveys the triumph of those hierarchies, by portraying over time the failure of a lyrical vision and its female spokesperson. Marlowe refuses his audience a comfortable position from which to evaluate his drama's suppressed rebellion, instead creating a play of tensions. We are tempted to enjoy what we know to be doomed, and forced to see the unpleasantness of what succeeds; like Gascoigne's lullaby singer, the audience may begin to feel the moral order of things disintegrate, and discover that the greatest self-deception resides in seeing the world as it is. Unlike the ritualistic clarity of George Peele's praise of Elizabeth, Marlowe's play concludes with an image startling and destructive: a queen in flames.

Whereas Peele obviously aspired to courtly service in the early 1580s, Marlowe's relationship to queen and court remains vexed and ambiguous—as *Dido*'s ending seems to hint. Marlowe demystified court lyricism by exposing both its falseness and its limits as persuasive oratory, an attack which at least in theory undermined the entire range of courtly fictions—including that of male service to a "woman on top." In the process he cleared space for radically new uses of love lyric within a dramatic world of upheaval; his lyric was an aesthetic tool, deprived of its symbolic magic but not its significance. Through the juxtaposition of poetic styles in his plays, Marlowe found a way both to contain and overgo the courtly version of lyrical drama. As he proceeded to develop his technique in wildly successful public plays, his representation of lyricism had a massive, far-reaching effect.

The Passionate Lyricist
and the Delights of Deferral

To distinguish the rhetoric that Marlowe associated with courtly love, it makes sense to preface this discussion of *Dido, Queen of Carthage* by looking at Marlowe's own love lyric. That "The Passionate Shepherd to His Love" appears to be his single foray into original lyric writing provides evidence of his skeptical (or at least uneasy) attitude toward courtly lyrics. Rather than a Petrarchan sonnet sequence or his own miscellany of "posies," Marlowe's writings of love include the urbane epyllion "Hero and Leander" and the *Elegies,* the first English translation of Ovid's equally urbane and sensual *Amores.* Stephen Orgel (Marlowe, *Complete Poems* 233) calls these *Elegies* "[i]n a sense ... Marlowe's sonnet sequence, the psychomachia of a poet-lover whose love is both his creation and his ultimate monomania, frustration and despair." But the frustration does not derive from his lady's chaste inaccessibility, its usual source in Petrarchan sonneteering; Ovid's Corinna is all too sexually available. Rather, the elegies convey the violence and disturbance of a realized sexual relationship, adulterous and lustful. These poems were the least canonical of Ovid's works, and the licentious violation of Neoplatonic lyric propriety in Marlowe's translations, as well as their being published in a volume with Sir John Davies's satires, may have contributed to their being banned and burned in 1599. Although in the context of Latin literature the *Amores* may not appear exceptionally upsetting, when placed against the moralizing impulses of Elizabethan theory and practice Marlowe's translations flout the conventions used to justify writing love lyrics. They present a speaker psychologically unhinged by love, with sexual violence close to the surface; courtship is neither idealized nor moralized.

"The Passionate Shepherd" also shares the sensuality and wit of Ovid's poetry, with none of the edifying metaphysical overtones of much Petrarchism. Without wishing to deflate this poetic cream puff, I want to show how Marlowe's rhetoric in this poem suggests the aesthetic appeal but also the fragility and self-deceit of lyric pleading, a notion most fully explored in *Dido, Queen of Carthage.* Through this analysis, the distinctiveness of Marlowe's rhetoric and syntax from its "source-rhetoric" in Ovid becomes clearer, as does its dramatic significance in Marlowe's modification of his Virgilian source-narrative. In other words, what *Dido* dramatizes is not antithetical to Marlowe's lyric practice, but rather an extension of its internal dynamics; his love lyric shuns the ethical overlay of Elizabethan sonneteering, and, as transferred to court performance, becomes a device to expose the limits of beauty's power. Rosalie Colie's perception of a sophisticated interweaving in mixed genres applies to Marlowe's poetic practice, a collaboration within and between genres both fulfilling and fraught. Ultimately, Marlowe's lyrical voice contains the seeds of its own undoing.[5]

Marlowe's love lyric is seduction in the future conditional tense. His speaker presents a series of promised pleasures *if* the beloved will "Come live with me and be my love." Marlowe's short poem simultaneously revels in lyric simplicity and reveals that simplicity to be deceptive. In its regular stanzas, its sonorous diction and imagery ("Melodious birds sing madrigals"), its refrain, and its uncomplicated syntax, the poem lends itself to a musical setting. Yet its simplicity, like that of most pastoral, is achieved by subordination—subordinating the obvious constraints of a world outside the poem, and subordinating the conditional nature of the speaker's offer.[6]

The list of pleasures which the shepherd foresees may initially appear to be in the simple future tense, inevitably coming. This impression is fostered by the simple conjunction of addition, "and": "and be my love"; "And we will all the pleasures prove"; "And we will sit"; "And I will make." Only in the fifth stanza does an extra word qualify the addition and complicate the future: "And if these pleasures may thee move, / Come live with me, and be my love" (19–20). The final stanza replaces simple connection with the appropriate form for a hypothetical proposition: "*If* these delights thy mind may move, / *Then* live with me, and be my love" (23–24). What the syntax of the first stanzas avoided finally becomes plain, and with it the motivation for delay: this passionate shepherd must hope that his rhetoric has compellingly obliterated alternative visions, unclenched logic's tight fist, and seduced the beloved's imagination.

Later poets saw the implications of Marlowe's lyric syntax, using it to parodic ends. However, Sir Walter Ralegh's famous answering poem, "The Nimph's reply to the Sheepheard," is less parody than a necessary and implied companion piece. His nymph disarms the shepherd's address by immediately exposing its conditional claims: "*If* all the world and love were young," she begins. Using the seducer's syntax against him, she lists the very different conditions that would lead her to love him. Her ability to imagine alternative futures, as well as the opportunity to voice them through Ralegh's use of *prosopopoeia,* deflates the shepherd's persuasion.[7] Adding insult to injury, "she" uses the same paratactic "ands" in her description as she shifts tenses. Her lines gain matter-of-fact power through present-tense verbs: "The flowers doe fade, and wanton fieldes, / To wayward winter reckoning yeeldes" (9–10). Her description is not merely possible but inevitable in the temporal world of events: "Time drives the flocks from field to fold, / When Rivers rage, and Rocks grow cold" (5–6).

Ralegh's "anti-lyric" follows Marlowe's form throughout, even in his final stanza's recognition in syntax of what has been illustrated already in a less obvious way. The nymph concludes that the cost of this love offer is too high by stating the missing and unrealizable condition that could persuade her:

> But could youth last, and love still breede,
> Had joyes no date, nor age no neede,
> Then these delights my minde might move,
> To live with thee, and be thy love.
>
> (21–24)

Even if there were truth on every shepherd's tongue, he could not counter time except in his words. The transcendent claims of lyrical imagination will not sway a material girl.

Ralegh's poem serves as a reminder that the shepherd's power lies exclusively in poetry's beguiling image of the future, not in his appeal to the beauties of the physical world. Marlowe's lyric requires a future tense which allows the offer of aestheticized pleasures, and asks the listener to accept them as realized by speech rather than testing them against experience. He creates a world in which signifiers have free play, a future reached outside temporal sequence and change. Accordingly Marlowe shifts his emphasis in the final stanzas away from the offered objects to their present persuasive power: "And if these pleasures may thee move" becomes "If these delights thy *mind* may move." His is a world of wild and whirling words, a fantastic, temporally removed verbal construct. The shepherd offers nothing but the apogee of lyric poetry; the seduction is entirely in its telling.

In a sense, my rhetorical analysis of the poem shares as well as highlights the atemporality to which this lyric aspires: the words provide a set of clues to its tone and meaning, unaffected by temporal change. If we read them as an isolated aesthetic performance, the shepherd in a sense succeeds at his exquisite game. But when this rhetoric is placed in a narrative historical context—in dialogue with other poems, within a staged fiction, or set against the commentary of Marlowe's contemporaries—the victory appears less assured. Even within the lyric form, Marlowe teases us to notice this delimited power of his speaker by finally positing the offer in a logical form and referring it to the listener's "mind." He appeals, in other words, to the role of the mind and image in poetic persuasion, precisely the subject of Sidney's concern in the *Apology for Poetry*.

The primary function of poetry, according to Sidney's neoclassical theory, is to create images with sufficient vitality or *energeia* to move the listener to praxis of an appropriate, moral kind; he felt the image gained its peculiar force by negotiating between perception and abstract reasoning. Seen through the lens of his didactic aesthetics, the shepherd is just another inferior courtly love poet, wearing the conventional garb of the pastoral suitor, corrupting the imagination for inappropriate ends. Unlike the tortuous debates between Desire and Reason in Sidney's *Astrophil and Stella*, Marlowe's poem denies any metaphysical weight or seriousness of purpose to his would-be lover. He will have his fun without playing the moralizing game of contemporary sonneteers, and indeed will flaunt his amorality by invoking the same constructs of image and mind found in tracts such as Sidney's; when Marlowe's speaker appeals to the mind rather than the liver, it is to an aesthetic rather than an ethical mind.[8]

In Sidney's hands (and more flippantly, in Shakespeare's parody of the Sidneian sonneteer in *Love's Labour's Lost*), the lover's words emphasize the self-delusion and pain that result from pursuit of immoral aims. Marlowe's attitude toward erotic poetry is quite different in "The Passionate Shepherd" and the *Elegies* (and indeed in "Hero and Leander"), for when not swept along by aestheticizing delight, he recognizes its limits from a pragmatic and logical perspective rather than a moral one. Even in his short lyric of light and sweet sound, Marlowe's rhetoric points toward an exposé always implicit in pastoral: Arcadia is absent—always already lost or an impossible fantasy—even as it is represented. The bleaker subtext of pastoral as pipe dream reappears in Marlowe's plays, represented as the fate of the lyric vision over time, no matter what its imagined landscape.

Marlowe's single-voiced lyric implies its limits through word choice, syntax, and tone, leaving other lyrics such as Ralegh's to articulate the opposition discursively. In the drama, Marlowe employs various rhetorics and theatrical resources to strengthen his commentary. His criticisms of courtly lyricism are again made not on moral or personal grounds but on the basis of such poetry's ineffectuality as social praxis in a destructive universe. Lyrical rhetoric creates a seductive dream, but fails its earthbound speakers.

Dido's Offer and Drama's Sea Change

The syntax, diction, and imagery of Marlowe's lyric poem recur in his plays to create an identifiable rhetoric of eros, which is set against other voices in dramatic conflict. This poetry is not distinguished by stanzaic forms—hardly surprising, given Marlowe's great achievement of establishing blank verse as a flexible medium for drama, capable of containing a variety of voices without chopping up the flow of his narrative. By making lyricism a style rather than a form, Marlowe allows for an integrated rhetorical interchange that carries rich dramatic significance through poetic voice as well as denotation. *Dido, Queen of Carthage* does include stage directions for songs, but the tunes and lyrics are not specified in the text and hence do not remain to carry any rhetorical significance in the play's fiction.[9] They are, however, often sung during scenes that also include the sonorous, seductive rhetoric familiar from "The Passionate Shepherd": for example, Venus woos Ascanius to sleep in 2.1 after she catalogues possible (false) gifts she will give him; and Cupid sings to Dido in 3.1, accompanying the usual arrow as his weapon for infatuating her.

As "The Passionate Shepherd" plays with the insulated aestheticism of courtly pastoral, so *Dido* dallies with the mannered court plays of Peele and his contemporaries, while in some ways claiming for itself greater truth value. Brian Gibbons ("Unstable") and Jackson Cope have pointed out the many attributes this play shares with other courtly shows, including an emphasis on spectacle, scenery, and costume as well as sophisticated play with language and protean shifts of tone and texture. While true, such a list only begins the investigation of how Marlowe uses the devices of the court play to make his own *Dido,* one markedly different from other renditions despite its textual borrowings.[10]

The lyric voice noted in *Dido* has often been described in vague terms and characterized as counterdramatic, as if it were the aberration of an apprentice author.[11] More recently, in a sweeping survey, Douglas Bruster has analyzed the function of lyric borrowing from "The Passionate Shepherd" in *Dido* and many other plays. He does not perforce attend to the particulars that make *Dido*'s version compelling and distinctively Marlovian, subtly but importantly different from other poets' parodies. In foregrounding generic difference between lyric and drama, Bruster also discounts the importance of the lyric speaker's gender; in the case of *Dido,* this once again erases the importance of the figuration of female power (and its limits) from our picture of Elizabethan art. While Marlowe undoubtedly toys with the theatrical potential for ironic framing of the lyric speaker, it is not always, as Bruster claims, the lyric speaker's barely hidden potential for violence that is exposed.[12] As we shall see, when Dido tries to seduce Aeneas, the context hardly encourages us to view her as a potential rapist.

Marlowe's play involves more interplay than warfare, and the dramatic place of lyric strains demands more particularized attention. While "the timeless world created in the rich language of the lyric invitation is almost inevitably discredited in some fashion when it meets a different representational mode" (Bruster 67), the vagaries of such fashion matter. In *Dido*, poetic style serves both as tool and topic for Marlowe's representation of a decidedly dismal picture of female power and desire in history, and a sympathetic as well as ironic treatment of the doomed lyricist.

Dido's first major love speech beautifully displays Marlowe's distinctive lyricism. In this scene, Dido has been wounded by Cupid's arrow and is trying to win Aeneas's love without directly admitting her own. She responds to Aeneas's plea for material aid with a lyrical set piece epitomizing Marlowe's rhetoric of desire, another instance of sensual persuasion in the future conditional:

> Aeneas, I'll repair thy Trojan ships,
> *Conditionally* that thou wilt stay with me,
> And let Achates sail to Italy.
> I'll give thee tackling made of rivell'd gold
> Wound on the barks of odoriferous trees;
> Oars of massy ivory, full of holes,
> Through which the water shall delight to play;
> Thy anchors shall be hew'd from crystal rocks,
> Which if thou lose shall shine above the waves;
> The masts whereon thy swelling sails shall hang,
> Hollow pyramides of silver plate;
> The sails of folded lawn, where shall be wrought
> The wars of Troy, but not Troy's overthrow;
> For ballace, empty Dido's treasury,
> Take what ye will, *but* leave Aeneas here.
> Achates, thou shalt be so meanly clad
> As sea-born nymphs shall swarm about thy ships,
> And wanton mermaids court thee with sweet songs,
> Flinging in favours of more sovereign worth
> Than Thetis hangs about Apollo's neck,
> So that Aeneas may but stay with me.
>
> (3.1.112–32;[13] emphasis added)

This is an artful court-ship. Characteristically, Marlowe uses sensual adjective-noun images to make boat repair into something rich and strange. But whereas Tamburlaine will try to realize similar figures as metaphorical *description* to invest himself with power, here the images remain obviously fantastic metaphors, and subsequent events will reinforce their remoteness from reality. Like the shepherd, Dido is transforming words about matter into (im)pure desire, with no regard for correspondence with her world's limiting forces. She revises history—as Peele's *Arraignment* did—to include "The wars of Troy, but not Troy's overthrow," just as she transforms the particulars of Aeneas's request (oars, sails, etc.) to fit her own wishes. But the revision, unlike Peele's, reveals a queen's profligate desire, a vision in which courting mermaids fling their favors of "sovereign worth" at the sight of a bare-chested sailor. Trying to realize her desired future in the instant through sumptuous language, she expresses the sexual thoughts she overtly denies. Dido's holey oars are more suitable for a sex fantasy than for transportation, as are swelling sails of lawn hanging upon hollow masts. The ship's description builds to the climactic offer, "For ballace, empty Dido's treasury."[14]

Ironically, given that her putative subject is a journey on the fluid seas, Dido's words do not create a trip *to* anywhere else or any more distant future *beyond,* but instead fix the desired future moment. The first part of the speech has been addressed to Aeneas, who is not even going to sail—again reminding us that the seductiveness of this ship is a purely rhetorical construction, allowing the sequence of double entendres that leads Aeneas (and presumably a titillated audience) to Dido, not Italy. Addressing Achates, Dido's suggestiveness becomes explicit and even more outrageous as she undresses the sailors, perhaps enticing gazers of both sexes. As in "The Passionate Shepherd," lyric poetry envisions an erotic paradise whose time and place exist only in language.

Marlowe's lyric poem also reverberates in the terms of this offer, that Aeneas "stay with me"—and be her love (although that part of the condition remains suppressed here). Dido repeats her request as a frame to her speech; she divides her address before turning to Achates with the similar refrain, "Take what ye will, but leave Aeneas here."

Some scholars have posited that Marlowe's erotic style simply derives from his classical sources. Richard A. Martin has pointed to a contrast between Marlowe's epic and lyric rhetoric, with particular reference to *Dido.* He attributes the play between them to Marlowe's combination of sources, with Virgil providing the martial and Ovid the sensual tones. Martin (and others) cite Polyphemus's seduction speech to Galatea in book 13 of the *Metamorphoses* as a locus classicus for Marlowe's lyric voice in Dido.[15]

Certainly Marlowe borrows from Ovid, but he gives his lyric speakers (both in *Dido* and "The Passionate Shepherd") quite a different emphasis.

Polyphemus offers what he already possesses and can share, none of which is particularly unusual for someone living in the country. The lushest language, moreover, describes not what he offers but the loved one herself (in Golding's 1567 translation, the relevant passage begins, "More whyght thou art then Primrose leaf my Lady *Galatee*" [book 13, l. 929]). Polyphemus does have his conditions, even implying that his lovely vision of the beloved only applies if she satisfies him:

> O Galatea, whiter than snowy privet-leaves, more blooming than the meadows, surpassing the alder in your tall slenderness, more sparkling than crystal, more frolicsome than a tender kid, smoother than shells worn by the lapping waves, more welcome than the winter's sun and summer's shade, more nimble than the gazelle, fairer than the tall plane-tree, more shining-clear than ice, sweeter than ripened grapes, softer than swan's down and curdled milk, and, *if only you would not flee from me,* more beauteous than a well-watered garden. (Ovid, *Metamorphoses* 2: 285; emphasis added)

But unlike the passionate shepherd, this speaker is not particularly delicate or skillful, making his poetic lapses the cause for ironic amusement ("softer than . . . curdled milk").[16] As do Marlowe's lyric speakers, Polyphemus slips in the crucial condition after his offers: "Of Chestnutts eeke (if my wyfe thou wilt bee) / Thou shalt have store: and frutes all sortes" (13.962–63). His poetic list nevertheless remains in the present, describing the actual and verifiable. Whatever force Polyphemus has resides in that presence; of course this is also the source, along with some questionable choices of simile, for his comic deflation. He vaunts, "This Cattell heere is all myne owne" (964) — hardly Marlowe's glittering prizes.[17]

Marlowe's poetry is very different, then, in tone and temporality, his witty speakers often transgressive not only of practical limitations but of moral imperatives. He appeals not to acquisitiveness but to unattainable desire, a pull expressed in another possible Ovidean source for *Dido, Heroides 7*. There Dido complains of Aeneas's desertion: "facta fugis, facienda petis" ("what is achieved, you turn your back upon; what is to be achieved, you ever pursue" [l. 13 in the Loeb trans.]). Along with the obvious aestheticizing of nature in Marlowe's lyric, typical of courtly pastoral, the elusive temporal distance of his seductive imagery from the speaker and listener becomes crucial when dramatized. The gap between words and their referents is emphasized onstage by the immediate presence of the characters as embodied by actors and by the absence of any fictional "other place" offstage. Marlowe takes the ambiguity of the future, as psychologically alluring but unreal, and molds it into a source of dramatic conflict. Thus the rhetoric of his sensual appeals to love in *Dido* lends itself to dramatic "testing" over time, during the inexorable sequence of stage events and the imagined passage of time in Carthage.

Furthermore, unlike many other versions of Virgil's story, Marlowe's play dramatizes the earthly relationship between Dido and Aeneas from start to finish. Jodelle's near-contemporary *Didon se sacrifiant,* for example, focuses on her final abandonment, a choice consonant with neoclassical theories of dramaturgy and an awareness of the Ovidian complaint tradition. Marlowe's alternative rendering shifts much of the attention from the queen as pathetic victim to her role as active, if unwitting, participant in her own destruction. Admittedly, because of the gods' intrusive actions and Aeneas's "escape," Dido's active role remains somewhat limited and unthreatening (freeing her from the negative representation often associated with powerful and exotic women in the western tradition, such as the enchantress Circe or the other famous North African queen). The play's structure as a dramatic epyllion nonetheless foregrounds the fate of human lovers locked but struggling in narrative time. As in Ralegh's poem and many later public stage plays, narrative time conspires with the material world to thwart the claims of lyrical vision.

While Dido's seduction speech is masterful eroticism, it is tempered by this dramatic context and by the response of other characters. As voyeurs, the audience can delight in the thick sensuality of the verse while smiling at its extravagance. But in performance her verse is almost immediately displaced by the demands of the fiction and her listeners; the audience waits to see the effects of her speech on the characters onstage. What the audience hears (or rather doesn't hear) is Aeneas's surprising lack of response to this outpouring of desire, for he gives no sign of interpreting the messages beyond her overt declaration that she will help him. Somewhat comically, his first response is to ask "Wherefore would Dido have Aeneas stay?" During the remainder of the scene, he makes three more comments, each a single-line assertion, while Dido flounders between confession of her love and more conventional self-promotion as the unattainable and hence quintessentially desirable queen. In her verbal struggle between expressing and hiding desire, she prefigures Shakespeare's comic heroines (particularly Rosalind):

> it may be thou shalt be my love.
> Yet boast not of it, for I love thee not—

> And yet I hate thee not. [Aside.] O, if I speak,
> I shall betray myself!—Aeneas, speak.
>
> (3.1.169–72)

He does not. Fundamentally unsentimental, Marlowe's wit demands victims.

Aeneas's terseness foregrounds the battle of wills involved in love, immediately qualifying the powers of Dido's lyrical sea-vision. Dido is of course nominally offering material aid rather than sex, and since she is a queen her offer is a powerful one. Yet it also demands Aeneas's consent. Though Dido's speech makes the prospect of staying with her an implied delight, she requires the submission of Aeneas's will to her own, his future to hers. This also means that Dido must create his future, that he must rely on her to sustain or realize the fantasy. The very extravagance needed to ensnare her beloved makes realization difficult, as Dido comes to learn through the play's course. While Aeneas does indeed become enamored, Dido's victory is short-lived. Other powers impinge.

In *Dido,* what defeats lyricism and desire is sheer force in the present tense—what might be called (looking forward to *Tamburlaine*) the heroic voice of power. This is distinguishable from the epic rhetoric of Aeneas's account of the fall of Troy, though the two become conflated if one disregards temporality, and only sees the play as a version of public versus private affairs.[18] While Marlowe's lyric exists as an articulation in the present moment, its reference to a fictional future splits its temporal location (just as Gascoigne's lyric situation split his voice between past and present, and as early in the play Aeneas's grief at Troy's demise splits him between the present and delusive visions of the past). Marlowe's heroic rhetoric, by contrast, addresses the present, its speaker standing singularly alone to declare and enforce his or her status. It is the voice of the gods, of necessity.

This heroic rhetoric is not so impressive in *Dido* as it is in Marlowe's later works, but it nevertheless appears at the crucial moments when Aeneas is confronted with the gods' decree to move on. In the last three scenes (as throughout the story of the lovers), Marlowe diminishes Virgil's appeal to the heroic future and his vision of Aeneas as the preserver of a past society, leading and epitomizing an entire civilization.[19] Instead, the playwright portrays Aeneas as indecisive and torn, completing a sequence in which we have seen him humble, weak, and deluded by grief (2.1), self-effacing in love (3.4), and even dishonest (4.4). Before act 4, Aeneas is passively willing to accept Dido's conditional world; indeed, even after Hermes appears in a dream, Aeneas is held only briefly by the gods' opposing power. He crumbles in the presence of Dido, and agrees to stay.

By contrast, in book 4 of the *Aeneid* Hermes first appears to a waking Aeneas, and his second appearance in a dream is not a second persuasion but merely a bit of strategic advice (giving the hero new information which causes him to speed up his departure schedule). Marlowe alters the significance of this double visit substantially. Only when Hermes arrives a second time, when Aeneas is awake, does the hero recognize that he must indeed go, that the power of the gods to impel him onward is greater than the power of Dido to hold him still. Marlowe thus dramatizes the gradual awakening of Aeneas, from a lyrical dreamworld in which fantastic language both suggests and is constructed from sensory delight into a harsh epic universe in which rhetorical assertion ironically substantiates and validates bodily pain.

This creates a drama less of heroic impulsion than compulsion; we watch Aeneas being pushed offstage by the gods rather than truly choosing a desire "nobler" than erotic love. After Hermes' second appearance, Aeneas acknowledges the power of Dido's competition and openly tells her he is leaving. This second encounter echoes and finally quotes the single farewell scene in Virgil. Marlowe turns to his source to articulate the epic "choice" in Latin—even less a matter of free will in this dramatization than in the original: "Italiam non sponte sequor" (5.1.140). In Marlowe's English, Aeneas speaks tersely, "unpoetically," his halting phrases working to suppress his personal desire:

> *Aeneas.* I am commanded by immortal Jove
>   To leave this town and pass to Italy,
>   And therefore must of force.
> *Dido.* These words proceed not from Aeneas' heart.
> *Aeneas.* Not from my heart, for I can hardly go.
>   And yet I may not stay; Dido, farewell!
>   (5.1.99–104)

Trying to console her, Aeneas syntactically denies the importance of choice for mortals: "O Queen of Carthage, wert thou ugly-black, / Aeneas could not choose but hold thee dear" (5.1.125–26). His final line recalls the condition and conditional now past that allowed the queen her power: "If words might move me, I were overcome" (154). As Dido too soon discovers, a brutal present—the true realm of force—obliterates lyrical language and dreams.

By downplaying the referentiality of heroism beyond present demands, Marlowe diminishes its moral and civilizing claims, its potential as a positive alternative to the lyric's future delights. The only moment when Aeneas envisions a future Troy is when he has decided to *stay* and rebuild it in Carthage, thus merging his public mission and private desires. The sensuality of Dido's earlier speeches is transferred here to a public project, a vision of an eroticized feminine civilization comparable to Egypt in Shakespeare's *Antony and Cleopatra*:

> *Aeneas.* Triumph, my mates, our travels are at end;
> Here will Aeneas build a statelier Troy
> Than that which grim Atrides overthrew;
> Carthage shall vaunt her petty walls no more,
> For I will grace them with a fairer frame
> And clad her in a crystal livery
> Wherein the day may evermore delight;
> From golden India Ganges will I fetch
> Whose wealthy streams may wait upon her towers
> And triple-wise entrench her round about;
> The sun from Egypt shall rich odors bring
> Wherewith his burning beams, like labouring bees
> That load their thighs with Hybla's honey's spoils,
> Shall here unburden their exhaled sweets
> And plant our pleasant suburbs with her fumes.
>
> (5.1.1–15)

This image of civilization is fecund, luxurious, and delightful, a sensuous and beautiful new Troy. The sexuality of sun and scent, of "laboring bees / That load their thighs" all for the sake of creating sweet smells (not even the sweet commodity of honey) resembles Dido's unlikely fantasy, enlarged to a state scale. Like the idealized version of courtly entertainments, such labor is useless, except to please its audience; it appears harmless; it is blissfully aesthetic. It is also the antithesis of empire as glorified in the bloody poetic accounts of patriarchal human history. Thus the Trojans have difficulty finding a name for such a city, and the gods are prompted to intervene, preventing its realization:

> *Iloneus.* But what shall it be call'd? Troy, as before?
> *Aeneas.* That have I not determin'd with myself.
> *Cloanthus.* Let it be term'd Aenea, by your name.
> *Sergestus.* Rather Ascania, by your little son.
> *Aeneas.* Nay, I will have it call'd Anchisaeon,
>   Of my old father's name.
>   *Enter Hermes with Ascanius.*
>   (5.1.18–23)

As Aeneas tries to commemorate his past, to venerate the father whom he loved through his body (carrying him out of burning Troy) as well as spirit, hence uniting personal memory, love, and the material body with the state, duty, and public discourse, Hermes appears to break them violently asunder. He discounts the value of Aeneas's collaborative vision (especially as it also honors a woman) in favor of self-aggrandizing power, accusing Aeneas of having forsaken glory:

> Why, cousin, stand you building cities here
> And beautifying the empire of this Queen
> While Italy is clean out of thy mind?
> Too too forgetful of thine own affairs,
> Why wilt thou so betray thy son's good hap? . . .
> Vain man, what monarchy expect'st thou here?
> Or with what thought sleep'st thou in Libya shore?
>   (5.1.27–31, 34–35)

Marlowe could hardly make the impossibility of integrating lyricism and history more overt. Duty and desire, love of woman and loyalty to son, building cities of delight and seeking dynastic glory, are placed in opposition without the opportunity for logical challenge: this is the unattractive message from the king of the heavens.[20]

The universe is not so benign as Aeneas and Dido would have it. We hear little of the Latin culture to come, and to the extent we bring to bear our knowledge of classical Rome from outside the play (particularly considering Renaissance conceptions of ancient Rome), it hardly resembles the sensual realm of exquisite delights envisioned by Aeneas as Anchisaeon. Epic warriors are "grim" like "Atrides," figures of brute force even when it is decorated as masculine strength or stern virtue. Within the play, Hermes creates no alternative future vision of beauty, but simply assumes a world in which lyric and epic, pleasure and glory are set at odds, where it is necessary to destroy the present—including one's lover—on behalf of one's son.

Whereas the potential beauty of empire remains absent (unpraised in the terms usually applied to Rome and other warrior societies, and unrealized in the terms of Aeneas's vision), Dido's suffering, the cost of heroism, is all too apparent. The final flames of Virgil's *Aeneid* hover around Lavinia's head and in Turnus's fury, premonitions of a new empire; in Marlowe's *Dido*, they instead encompass not only the queen but Anna and Iarbus, obliterating the peaceful civilization of Carthage. In the absence of Virgil's epic context, the sheer bodily destruction of empire building, as well as its erasure of other enticing cultures, creates tragedy rather than glory.[21]

The alternative to desire in the future is force in the present—and in this sphere, Dido is clearly limited whereas the gods are not. The focus on the present moment in Marlowe's representation of heroic motivation reminds the audience that lyric poetry is present only as a signifier: its referents, its fulfillment—though not its verbal appeal—reside in an absent, impossible future.

Dido's Demise

In addition to using the demands of the epic plot and the temporal contrast with present-tense "heroic" speech to highlight the limitations of lyrical persuasion, Marlowe also shows the failure of this rhetoric in Dido's own stylistic shifts. During the scenes of Aeneas's vacillation, her rhetoric necessarily begins to change: "Heaven, envious of our joys, is waxen pale, / And when we whisper, then the stars fall down, / To be partakers of our honey talk" (4.4.52–54). Breathtakingly beautiful and bold, this sentence epitomizes the hyperbolic rhetoric of present power that Elizabethans came to associate with Marlowe through *Tamburlaine,* because of its great success on the public stage. But for Dido, it symbolizes the defeat of her earlier lyric syntax, whose deferral can no longer compete with the gods' present demands. Moreover, even though her words sound strong, this "honey talk" surely drips with dramatic irony for an attentive audience. The play's opening and subsequent scenes with the gods refute her; rather than envying human love, Heaven—indeed, the goddess of love herself—demands the enactment of empire for Aeneas's future glory. Placed in the verifiable present, the gap between poetic description and dramatic experience becomes painfully obvious.

Whereas Tamburlaine continually finds new lands to conquer and new kings to kill, and Jupiter can offer and give an infinity of matter to his favorites, Dido's treasury of pleasures is presented as exhaustible. A flippant shepherd might keep using imaginary offers to woo new nymphs, but for a woman—even a queen—in love with one man over time, the rhetoric of desire has its limits. Having given herself to Aeneas, Dido can now use the future conditional only to offer something other than herself. Therefore she comes to proclaim not her desirability but her superiority over competing forces, the heavens.

Although the audience knows better, her new rhetorical tack temporarily seems powerful: it stirs Aeneas to bombast, to his few lines of forceful talk in the play. The man who not twenty lines earlier protested that he was neither warrior nor king now pledges himself to the power of Dido, not the gods:

> O Dido, patroness of all our lives,
> When I leave thee, death be my punishment!
> Swell, raging seas, frown, wayward Destinies;
> Blow, winds; threaten, ye rocks and sandy shelves!
> This is the harbour that Aeneas seeks,
> Let's see what tempests can annoy me now.
>
> (4.4.55–60)

Like Lear's on the heath, his declamatory speech is impressive as rhetorical display; as a declaration of action within the narrative, its irony is piercing. Aeneas "challenges" nature to do exactly what he wants: to make him unable to move on and thus allow him to avoid even the semblance of heroic choice. Consequently, the vaunting of the last line has the sound of heroic verse but the significance of parody. Even as Aeneas (like Othello) tries to change his occupation, he is caught in a vocabulary and a plot that now require a fighter, not a lover. While the failure of lyricism remains central to *Dido, Queen of Carthage,* Aeneas's speech foreshadows the more embracing despair of Marlowe's later works, in which all systems and rhetorics break down over time. Lyricism's more obvious deferral and fragility make it both an extreme and exemplary case of the problems of language in Marlovian tragedy.

Dido's need to change her rhetoric signals the end of her love story. Her words and desires no longer match decorously. Her offers in response to Aeneas remain equally bold and hyperbolic, but they move from eros to the overtly political, a risky business: "Not all the world can take thee from mine arms: / Aeneas may command as many Moors / As in the sea are little water drops" (4.4.61–63). In her attempt to "make experience of my love"

(64; a phrase that echoes Jupiter's words in the play's opening scene), Dido asserts her power as queen rather than as beloved. Luring Aeneas as a commander, she unwittingly colludes in turning his gaze away from her to his own imperial command.

These ironies culminate in a proposition which Dido asserts will prove her words' truth and her love: the foreigner Aeneas will ride through the streets of Carthage as sovereign lord, physically embodying her esteem. In response to her sister Anna's quite reasonable reservation that the people might object, Dido proclaims her absolute power:

> The ground is mine that gives them sustenance,
> The air wherein they breathe, the water, fire,
> All that they have, their lands, their goods, their lives;
> And I, the goddess of all these, command
> Aeneas ride as Carthaginian King.
> (4.4.74–78)

To read this speech as the author's uncritical assertion of absolutism (as some critics have) seems insensitive to Marlowe's dramaturgy.[22] Were Dido to enact this ceremony, the consequences might well be as politically disastrous as they were for Shakespeare's Antony and Cleopatra (and had been historically for Mary Tudor and Philip of Spain—or might have been for Elizabeth, had she wed the Duc d'Anjou). Anna's skepticism has indicated as much. More to the immediate point, as Dido shifts her authority from her female to her queenly body, she leads Aeneas away from his male sexuality in the cave to his masculine identity as warrior-lord. Because Marlowe bases her lyrical and personal appeal in sexuality, and then sets this appeal at war with larger social structures and history, Dido must abandon that lyrical vocabulary of mutual desire to seek political force. Indeed, in the process of adding the new title of king to her previous list of offers, Dido apotheosizes herself right out of her sexual self into the heavens as "goddess." The condensed syntax of the final two lines allows them to be read as a command to Aeneas as well as to her people, sustaining her power to keep him present at the expense of her desire to be one with him.

Despite this desperate vaunting, Dido herself knows the limitations of her words and offers, and hence reinforces the audience's awareness. As soon as Aeneas exits (now swearing to remain and make Carthage new Troy), she recognizes her inability to "keep the winds / Within the closure of a golden ball," and vainly wishes that "the Tyrrhene sea were in mine arms" (4.4.99–101). For though she could command Aeneas to "Speak of no other land, this land is thine" (83), as long as other lands exist, her force remains rhetorical. She can no more constrain Aeneas than the sea itself. Having shifted from a fantastic future to this instant, she must repeatedly assert her authority every moment to prevent new and different forces from re-moving Aeneas.

Consequently, Dido must now acknowledge the importance of material reality as well, the present time and place. Having just vaulted herself into the heavens, she now descends to tackle the tackling. Denying the efficacy of her words, she is reduced to breaking Aeneas's oars and shredding his sails: "I must prevent him; wishing will not serve" (4.4.104). She would go farther and sink his ships except that the act would anger him, again distinguishing the limits of a lover from the power of a ruthless warrior: because she is not using force as an end in itself but as a means to sustain love, her power is fatally limited. The rhetorics of force and eros do not mix. She must keep Aeneas happy to keep him at all, and to maintain her desired future:

> It is Aeneas' frown that ends my days.
> If he forsake me not, I never die,
> For in his looks I see eternity,
> And he'll make me immortal with a kiss.
>
> (4.4.120–23)

Like Doctor Faustus when he echoes these words to Helen of Troy ("Troy's overthrow" indeed), Dido is doomed by the clock.[23] She must now try to make the beloved *not* act in order to prevent a future of change and loss. She again invokes the conditional future, but now as a negative condition rather than an offer. Speaking to herself, her rhetoric no longer moves the action along, no longer functions as dramatic persuasion. Dido's treasury is indeed empty.

It is no mistake that the syntax of desire returns here, with a twist. The inappropriateness of mixing present-tense force with love has highlighted desire's undeniable connection (at least in Marlowe's world) with the future, and so it is the failure of the lyric vision to sustain itself over time, as the future becomes present, that signals the defeat of love. When Dido's rhetoric was successful, it demanded a future—as does this dramatic narrative. Now she would conserve her gain forever, possess the future and make time meaningless, ending the play. To do so, she would have to stand outside the power of narrative and representation, controlling the show like Elizabeth at a pageant. But Dido is caught in her story; Marlowe, unlike Peele, will not present Troy without its overthrow, or Dido without her death. The demands of the fiction and the playwright overwhelm this queen and her lyrical voice.

In Dido's subsequent pleas to Aeneas (paralleling the form of Hermes' rebukes, without the god's force), she attempts to sustain her identity through working words, but her mode of expression acknowledges her failure; she shifts between the first-person and a selfless third-person reference to herself, her "I" having lost its power. Finally, all that Dido can truly give without qualification is that crumbling self:

> If thou wilt stay,
> Leap in mine arms: mine arms are open wide.
> If not, turn from me, and I'll turn from thee;
> For though thou hast the heart to say farewell,
> I have not power to stay thee.
> (5.1.179–83)

Dido's final offer, her last conditional, recognizes two alternatives rather than persuading her lover to a single, united, fantasy of the future. As the lovers part, language also splits from one to two. The scene's poignance lies in the inadequacy of this starkly honest offer of her physical self and love: silently, Aeneas exits.[24]

Dido's end is swift and inexorable, especially when contrasted with other Renaissance treatments in which the heroine (following Ovid's complaint tradition in the *Heroides*) seems to lament interminably. Marlowe has anatomized the trajectory toward love tragedy; now, with the end of persuasive love speech, the play itself follows Aeneas to the land of silence. Dido briefly indulges in more oceanic word-visions, positing future ploys to reach Aeneas, at which point the syntax and sensual imagery of her initial seduction speech return:

> I'll frame me wings of wax like Icarus,
> And o'er his ships will soar unto the sun
> That they may melt and I fall in his arms;
> Or else I'll make a prayer unto the waves
> That I may swim to him like Triton's niece;
> O Anna, fetch Arion's harp,
> That I may tice a dolphin to the shore
> And ride upon his back unto my love!
> (5.1.243–50)

But this speech is merely self-consoling and self-directed, having lost an appropriate audience, an object of desire to persuade. Dido's fantasies are will-o'-the-wisps, wandering between images ("or else" links them as alternatives, rather than as a steadily accruing metaphoric pattern).

Using her powers as a lyrical poet, Dido has seen too much and too little. In a scene clearly paralleling Aeneas's raving entrance into Carthage (an earlier variation from Virgil that has baffled many critics), Dido acknowledges his exit by retreating into untempered fantasy. What began with her lover's arrival is ending. Dido sees what is not, and tries (as Aeneas did with Achates) to make Anna see similarly: "Look, sister, look . . . See, see, the billows heave" (5.1.251–52). In vain Dido uses the rhetorical figure of *anamnesis* to distort her vision, creating mental images that replace an unbearable future. Anna tells the deluded Dido to give up "these idle fantasies" and "remember who you are" (262–63), much as Dido told Aeneas upon his arrival; but in facing her present emptiness Dido sees no son or lover, only death. Again she connects her loss of power with a lack of visual perception: "What shall I do, / But die in fury of this oversight?" (268–69). Cut off from her lyrical future vision, having lost her grounds of appeal as a poetic speaker and her identity as lover, she proceeds to substantiate her loss by destroying her body. With the companion suicides of Iarbus and Anna, Marlowe wipes out life and desire from the stage world of Carthage, and with them ends the drama.[25]

Olympians Revisited:
Marlowe's Inversion of Power

How do we read Marlowe's erotic tragedy after Peele's chastened celebration? More specifically, how do we read Dido's demise and the fate of her lyrical voice in historical context? The answer partially depends upon how we relate this story to two other "frames": the play's opening scene among the gods, which extends the rhetoric of eros into the heavens; and the courtly occasion of the play's performance, which suggests a complicated relationship between the figure of Dido and Queen Elizabeth.

Because the first scene presents an interplay of erotic and heroic speech on Mount Olympus, it clearly functions as a rhetorical as well as narrative introduction to *Dido, Queen of Carthage*. But the function and fate of those rhetorical voices are not precisely the same as in the Dido story. Indeed, the discrepancies between a god's and a mortal's use of these rhetorical strategies reinforce the necessarily tragic fate of Marlowe's lyrical speakers in the human theater. Scene 1 thus is a frame but not a "mere" frame for the love story; it serves as exposition, a distancing device, and a preview of the story with a crucial difference. Marlowe provides not only the cosmic cause for the earthly action but another scene of eros at war with destiny—making Dido's story exemplary rather than idiosyncratic, and directing the audience to consider the status of love and its poetic expression more generally.

Like the authority Hermes invokes when inducing Aeneas to leave Carthage, the power Jupiter wields in the heavens is in many ways unattractive yet undeniable. Ruling by caprice and lacking any moral superiority or dignity, Jupiter remains as unimpeachable as in Greek mythology. Marlowe's travesty lies in exposing the god's exercise of power to be absurdly disproportionate, as when we hear Jupiter threatening his consort while he fondles his "minion" Ganymede:

> *Ganymede.* [Juno] reach'd me such a rap for that I spill'd
>   As made the blood run down about mine ears.
> *Jupiter.* What? Dares she strike the darling of my thoughts?
>   By Saturn's soul and this earth-threat'ning hair,
>   That, shaken thrice, makes nature's buildings quake,
>   I vow, if she but once frown on thee more,
>   To hang her meteor-like 'twixt heaven and earth,
>   And bind her hand and foot with golden cords,
>   As once I did for harming Hercules!
>   (1.1.7–15)

Swearing by the father whom he destroyed, Jupiter turns heroism into farce by equating the persecution of Hercules with a servant's cuffing. As his citing of precedent indicates, he has the power to execute such absurd punishment. Jupiter's motivation, like that of his human victim Dido, is erotic and obsessive; but unlike hers, Jupiter's desires are unlimited by material reality.[26]

Unlimited—with the crucial exception that he cannot force voluntary love. To do so would be a logical contradiction, the kind of nonsense, in linguistic terms, that even omnipotent gods cannot perform (though an all-too-familiar psychological wish). It seems even Jupiter must play the game of lyric seduction. He makes future conditional offers to use his power, trying to entice Ganymede through deferral and future delight rather than his presence alone. Thus Jupiter will punish Juno *if* she again treats his beloved badly; even threats of violence become part of the lover's rhetorical enticement. Interestingly, in this exceptional case where the lover has the power to enact any offer, Marlowe makes those offers seamier and overtly irresponsible. On earth, where Dido's offers are hypothetical and untestable, the lover's imagination is more benign, rising to the occasion with scenes of beautiful rather than vindictive indulgence. The author again plays with expectations: the spatial hierarchies of heaven and earth seem skewed when one compares the opening scene's childishness with the human lovers' more poignant and expansive moments.

Jupiter stresses his past deeds and his attributes of power, such as the hair (mentioned in the passage above) which is physically present onstage, thus mixing all three temporal realms with an ease unavailable to mere mortals. But this world of possibility is presented as a travesty, neither heroic nor noble. Power is a toy for Olympians, as Ganymede's response to the offer to string up Juno makes apparent:

> Might I but see that pretty sport a-foot,
> O, how would I with Helen's brother laugh.
> And bring the gods to wonder at the game!
> Sweet Jupiter, if e'er I pleas'd thine eye,
> Or seemed fair, wall'd-in with eagle's wings,
> Grace my immortal beauty with this boon
> And I will spend my time in thy bright arms.
>
> (1.1.16–22)

The wider potential for violence in such pleasure is clear in the passing allusion to Helen, whose role in the ruin of Troy will soon be recalled by Aeneas (Ganymede's own words echo in *Doctor Faustus* when the protagonist encounters Helen—or a succubus in the shape of Helen). The importance of violation increases as the seduction continues. Jupiter tosses out offers without concern for their consequences, parallel syntax exposing the absurd disproportion between what is desired and given (and hiding the if-then relationship between the two lines): "Sit on my knee, and call for thy content, / Control proud fate, and cut the thread of time" (1.1.28–29). The god then launches into a typically lush description of sensual delight to come; but unlike the speeches of Dido (or the passionate shepherd), these are accompanied by actions, stage gestures which indicate Jupiter's greater ability to carry through on his offers. Thus Marlowe begins by showing that those with the most power use it with a casualness that looks absurd.

Moreover, Jupiter's gestures, like his offers, are violations: he plucks a feather from Mercury's wing as he proclaims:

> Hermes no more shall show the world his wings,
> If that thy fancy in his feathers dwell,
> But, as this one, I'll tear them all from him,
> Do thou but say, "their color pleaseth me."
>
> (1.1.38–41)

Here indeed is the threat of force in lyric speech, reinforced by the unusual use of the verb "tear" for feather-removal—but the force is directed not, as Bruster argues generally, at the beloved but at an innocent passerby (or lier-by, in Hermes' case). This particular example also emphasizes the great distance between Olympus and earth, foreshadowing the powerlessness that characterizes human love; the threatened feather-bearer, the lowest and most passive character in this heavenly scene, will later appear as the rigid voice of the gods on earth, denying the free will of Dido and Aeneas. By using the same character and poetic voices in a different framework on Olympus, Marlowe sets the stage for a main action in which both tragic pity and admiration are reserved for the human participants.

Whereas Marlowe diminishes the significance of marital violation found in earlier versions of Dido's story (i.e., the "betrayal" of dead Sychaeus), he emphasizes Jupiter's faithlessness.[27] Earthly social contracts have no weight for Jupiter. He gives jewels to Ganymede that are not only his wife's but the very gems "My Juno ware upon her marriage-day" (43). Ganymede clearly enjoys this game, perhaps for the attention and gifts he gets, perhaps for the more unsettling pleasure of upsetting order and violently displacing other gods. He coarsely counteroffers, adding more conditions before he will submit (again, contrasting with the more admirable human lovers, for Aeneas is presented as anything but cunning or greedy): give him yet another jewel or two, "And then I'll hug with you an hundred times" (48). Heavenly love is a tawdry affair.[28]

Jupiter's final line emphasizes the syntactic kinship of this speech with "The Passionate Shepherd." The god has made his love offers employing rich imagery and smooth sounds, compounding delights with the simple connection of addition: "And Venus' swans shall shed their silver down, / To sweeten out the slumbers of thy bed" (36–37). Now that Ganymede is playing along, he bluntly concludes with the obvious but previously unstated condition familiar to the student of Marlowe: "And shalt have, Ganymede, if thou wilt be my love" (49).

Jupiter, then, can combine the rhetorics of future desire and present force, unlike Dido. Whether this disturbs or amuses depends on how seriously the audience members regard the scene, and how much they enjoy the flaunting of hierarchies and conventional notions of morality. Recent critics have made much of the homoerotic preciosity derived from the casting of boys, and in a related argument Roma Gill suggests that Marlowe is mocking anthropomorphic conceptions of the supernatural: the joke is on us for creating god in our own image, and besides, she adds, Marlowe "must" make his gods more human because of staging that demands a boy represent a god.[29] Yet the finale of Peele's *Arraignment of Paris* illustrates how gods' grandeur (or at least beneficence) *could* be signified onstage through spectacle and poetic style. Moreover, Marlowe emphasizes that Jupiter retains active, albeit immoral, power; he is travestied but not disarmed. Thus, as in the drama of another skeptic, Euripides, the gods can be both absurd and disturbing, and are presented without the solace of any less anthropomorphic or irresponsible object of worship. Nevertheless, the exchange contains more impudence than serious critique; the actions in this prelude are few, and of little consequence in themselves. The horror of death by fire is reserved for human victims—as is audience sympathy. Only after the play has presented the human consequences of Olympian distance and indifference does the first scene resonate darkly. Once juxtaposed with the earthly players, the gods look not merely human but smaller than life, far from mystical sovereigns even as they wield absolute power.

The second exchange in this Olympian prelude, between Jupiter and Venus, shifts the attention more directly to humanity and horror, again playing against expectations. That the goddess of love should enter at Jupiter's word "love"—but to chastise rather than encourage seduction—extends the topsy-turvy inversion of this meanly comic heaven. It is Venus who calls attention to life-and-death issues, setting the tragic plot "on course" in the interests of empire for her son (or, as Aeneas will be told, her son's son—the heroic vision ever deferred rather than richly imagined). Even on Olympus, even when the speaker is a god and can realize his fantasies, lyric seduction is superseded and mocked by the dramatic narrative. Venus scorns Jupiter's "toying there / And playing with that female wanton boy, / Whiles my Aeneas wanders on the seas" (50–52). She proceeds to provide an expository narrative about the Trojan in a style verging on parody of Thomas Sackville: an older heroic rhetoric, which her son improves upon when giving *his* account of "Troy's overthrow" (which Shakespeare in turn appears to parody in *Hamlet,* in the artificial language of the Player's speech describing the same event).[30] Thus, with the conventional symbolic system standing on its head, with the god of power sounding like a lover and the goddess of love sounding like an impatient warrior, the Dido story "proper" begins.

Despite Venus's slur at Ganymede as a mere "female" boy, "effeminizing" eros does not initiate this drama's tragic plot. Desire may be used as a tool or weapon by the gods, but it is not the source of earthly suffering. While Jupiter's desire is indeed infantile and irresponsible, it is the stern goddess, with her seemingly rational demand that her human heirs and surrogates thrive, who causes *Dido*'s tragedy. Not only the differences between this picture of Olympian desire and the earthly lovers' powerful scenes to come but also the very structure of the opening scene thus undermine attempts such as W. Craig Turner's to fit this *Dido* into a hierarchical hermeneutic advocating "reason over irrational love." Passion is indeed declared to "unman" Jupiter, but it is the angry Venus who says so and who has rivalrous dynastic reasons for abusing the queen of Carthage. It is the founding of empire that demands and legitimates Dido's abandonment and hence leads to her destruction. Ultimately, the play's criticisms, or at least its representation of responsibility, point outward to a hostile world order rather than inward to the moral shortcomings of its particular passionate protagonists.

The inversions of the opening scene serve to expose and challenge conventions: moral, aesthetic, and, in this exchange, sex-based. Venus makes the case for empire while god the father enjoys his "female" boyfriend. Clearly, we are not to expect a simple allegory of manly heroism easily triumphing over effeminizing desire. The gap between conventional gender associations and the actual positions inhabited by Marlowe's male and female characters, introduced along with the poetic voices on Olympus, continues throughout the play. The workings of sovereignty, on Olympus and in Carthage as in the England where this play was performed, do not mirror patriarchal theory comfortably.[31]

The first scene sets the stage for the play's retelling of a culturally central story about gender roles with a difference, a shifting and shiftiness of perspective. If one argues that women in power are the troublemakers in this story, citing the initiatory bossiness of Venus, one is also questioning the validity of empire and the manly heroism she advocates; conversely, if one were to eliminate the role of erotic desire, the resulting landscape would be bereft of poetic beauty and also of the Olympian patriarch. When taken as a whole, Marlowe's tale seems less a lament for a lost orderly past, when men were heroes and erotic desire was subordinated, than a work of "meta-desire": a play of utopian desire, recognized as impossible, for a universe of desire, in which license and sensuality are not at odds with masculine social identity. To the extent that one can find misogyny in the Olympian margins, it is directed not at female sexuality (a familiar trope in Renaissance drama) but at females in power—or more precisely, at their social position as inhibitors of desire rather than at their sexual difference. Hence, as in its characterization of sovereignty, Marlowe's court drama directly counters the messages and hierarchies of Peele's *Arraignment*.

This last interpretive distinction (reading Marlowe's social critique as directed at the culture's policing agents, in this particular case represented by a female, rather than at women as a sex) is admittedly a subtle one, relying on a careful contextual reading of tropes elsewhere used to attack women as a group. It remains a valid and crucial distinction nonetheless. By linking Jupiter and Dido as lovers, by casting Venus and Hermes as the agents of empire, Marlowe defies the accuracy and naturalness of totalizing gender stereotypes. Additionally, by making Dido an active and sensual wooer, giving her the best lines of poetry, and presenting her downfall with pity (that rare quantity in Marlowe's work, perhaps only to be found more compellingly in his tale of another unfortunate lover, Edward II), the playwright makes her more than a pawn; but by showing her manipulation and limits in contrast with Jupiter, Marlowe directs his criticisms at the order of the gods rather than the ambivalent Aeneas. Her doom by fire, the age-old metaphor of passion made literal, is not so much the usual sign of moral decline or a battle between the sexes. It becomes an image of the pyrrhic fate awaiting a sensualist's utopian rebellion within a hostile political universe.

Disorder in the Court

Or so it seems on the basis of the playscript alone. Does the link between the play's queen and Marlowe's queen, obviously present though hard to decipher, complicate the image of a burning monarch? Or do Elizabeth's mythic associations with goddesses and her notorious role in controlling court amours implicate her alongside Marlowe's perverse Venus? Given that rebelliousness against Elizabeth was often played out in terms of gender struggle and that some of this rebelliousness derived from male unease with her unconventional power, it may at first glance seem contradictory now to stress a difference between two courtly strains, against the female and against the sovereign, in Marlowe's case. But this differentiation is in fact justified and indeed required by the playwright's own unconventional practice. Marlowe carefully and thoroughly reorients the dramatic focus in representing desire, away from the terms of heterosexual Petrarchan lyricism and the courtly system in which the two rebellious strains were elided. In one sense, this radical shift of emphasis became the greatest challenge of all, implying the comparative triviality of Elizabeth's lyric mythology; but in terms of a direct attack or defense of the queen's authority based on gender attributes, Marlowe's art appears to leave that vexed field entirely. Rather, Marlowe focuses his conflict on the discomfiting indifference of the powers-that-be to human desire. These observations can be substantiated by looking at the details that seem to link Elizabeth to the females represented in *Dido*.

Given Elizabeth's absolute sovereignty and her portrayal in 1580s court dramas by Peele and Lyly, one might reasonably look for signs of the queen in the realm of the gods. And indeed, one can see the logic for a specific analogy between Elizabeth and Venus. Within her culture's terms, the queen might be viewed as a female aberration akin to a belligerent Venus, having forsaken her female sexuality to become a goddess of empire and of love thoroughly sublimated and heroicized, in the process interfering with the sensual delights and power of her subjects. As such she functions, in Marlowe's narrative, as a figure of repression rather than sublimation, a counterimage deflating the Petrarchan and Neoplatonic elevation of romantic love in court drama. In this scenario, because Elizabeth (like Venus) is not the direct object of desire, her sex is not important except insofar as it makes her antagonism particularly stark (contradicting standard associations of women with the erotic).

The courtly works of Lyly, Ralegh, and Gascoigne (on behalf of Dudley) intersperse pleas for sexual release or license with devotion to the queen as an unattainable erotic ideal; Spenser links desire for his wife and duty to the queen through their shared name. By contrast, in Marlowe's play the authority figures are completely separate from the desired love objects (and all the beloveds, the "wooees," are male). Thus, while *Dido* in one sense shares the courtiers' discontent with constraint, it does not elide the beloved's withholding or inaccessibility with the sovereign's inhibiting power directly, nor gender these two dimensions of power as essentially feminine. Moreover, the graphic sensuality of Marlowe's poetry indicates that eros is at issue quite literally, not predominantly a metaphor for political desire.

The associations between Elizabeth and the gods merit contemplation. But more overt and problematic is the resemblance between Dido and the queen, reinforced verbally in Marlowe's script. In analysis of the queen's Siena portrait, Constance Jordan stresses the imperial analogies between Aeneas and Elizabeth (which Roy Strong and Frances Yates earlier emphasized), but she rightly complicates that association by noting the links between Elizabeth and the Petrarchan version of Dido found in the *Trionfi della pudicizia,* which represents her as faithful to her husband. Jordan wants to emphasize the ways in which Elizabeth was invested with masculine sexuality as part of her exceptional empowerment, and thus concludes that a visual recollection of Virgil's contrasting Dido serves "to recall *and* to suppress that queen's other and antithetical figure" (169). This highly wrought interpretation may apply to the elliptical reference in the background of that royal portrait, but here, I would argue, Marlowe's dramatization of the Virgilian story does not encourage such direct linkage of the queen with Aeneas. If one were to push such a case, moreover, Marlowe's unheroic Aeneas would hardly be a more flattering association for the queen than Richard II proved to be. As we have seen, this Aeneas is far from a self-possessed lover spurning eros for empire. In Marlowe's rendering, the compelling (albeit complex) associations are indeed between Elizabeth and Dido. And while perhaps influenced by Petrarch's rendering, Marlowe's dramatic portrait, like his choice of lyric antecedents, is squarely constructed upon the Roman model. This resemblance may partially motivate the sympathetic treatment of Virgil's queen, but it also serves to highlight some of the tensions associated with Elizabeth's sovereignty from another angle.

The most obvious link derives from the Carthaginian queen's double name, Dido/Elissa. Besides the overt echo in "Elissa," "Dido" was one of the legion of complimentary pseudonyms for Queen Elizabeth (used, for example, in Ashe's *Elizabeth's Farewell to the Army*). Less than a decade earlier, Spenser had used the name Dido for "the great shepherde his daughter" elegized in the November eclogue of *The Shepheardes Calender.* While his model was Marot's song on the death of the French queen, even in that work the implications of choosing "Dido" may well signal unease, a counterstatement to Colin Clout's other major song honoring a woman, the April eclogue celebrating "Eliza queen of shepherdes all." It seems altogether consistent that, where Peele echoes April's celebration, Marlowe draws on a dirge. As Philippa Berry illustrates in tracing images of Diana from France to England, such allusions can resonate with shared worries even as they are adapted to particular cases. What's in a name may vary, but this name surely encourages gloomy association between the queens on and off stage.[32]

A more elaborate connection with Spenser may also be more revealing. H. J. Oliver (Marlowe, *Dido* 60) cites an echo of Spenser's "Epithalamion" (with its varying refrain "That all the woods may answer and your eccho ring") which has been interpreted as a passing compliment to the queen: "And all the woods 'Eliza' to resound!" (4.2.10). But this can only be seen as a case of Marlowe emulating "his master Spenser" (as Harry Morris puts it), or indeed as any sort of compliment, if one disregards poetic and dramatic context entirely. The line is spoken by Iarbus when at prayer—but rather than asking the gods to sanctify a love affair through marriage, as Spenser does, Iarbus asks them to destroy one (and so destroy Eliza herself). As in the case of those passages in *Tamburlaine* famously cited by T. S. Eliot as borrowings from *The Faerie Queene,* the meaning of this verse is radically altered by its dramatic situation.[33] This becomes even clearer if we look at the preceding lines, ones that surely temper the assumption that any simple praise follows from being remembered in the orisons of Iarbus:

> Eternal Jove, great master of the clouds,
> Father of gladness and all frolic thoughts,
> That with thy gloomy hand corrects the heaven,
> When airy creatures war amongst themselves,
> Hear, hear, O hear Iarbas' plaining prayers,
> Whose hideous echoes make the welkin howl,
> And all the woods 'Eliza' to resound!
>
> (4.2.4–10).

The syntax slants toward making the name "Eliza" itself a hideous echo, while the diction resonates with the story of another queen's echo: Hecuba's. She, according to Aeneas's earlier account of the fall of Troy, was swung by her heels "howling in the empty air, / Which sent an echo to the wounded King" (2.1.248–49). Invoking the god whose "frolic thoughts," "hand," and indifference we have seen, Iarbus's prayer also recalls the limits of human efficacy. Surely all this does not echo the "spirit" of Spenser's "Epithalamion," as Oliver would have it. Marlowe's allusion here mocks rather than emulates the court poet's manner of compliment.

Iarbus's wrath at the current favorite and his frustration at his unrewarded service to the queen echo many a Tudor courtier's complaint. The uncomfortable analogy between Elizabeth's and Dido's dangerous treatment of wooing princes may have motivated the general shift away from public issues in this play.[34] Elizabeth had, after all, "strung along" various Iarbus-like suitors for years. If this scene contains an extrafictional allusion, then, it could hardly have flattered the queen.

Ironically, in backing away from the public consequences of a queen's wooing, Marlowe's play also limits Dido to the stereotypically feminine concerns of love and relationships. Focusing almost exclusively on the "private" story of Dido's love, Marlowe reverses the Christian positions of god and man as regards ethical (ir)responsibility, implying a dark future for human aspirations—a reading that fits with the playwright's tendency to expose the harsh workings of fate and God in other works. But it also places the queen in an erotic realm, closer to the location of Ovid's complainer than Virgil's reproachful rival. That is, even as Dido gets the most powerful speeches, the most seductive rhetoric, and the more active position within her courtship, her placement in the larger world order keeps her politically passive, distant from the public priorities of civic duty and military heroism. As I have shown, that public world is not valorized, and Marlowe's opening scene conspires against reification of the erotic as naturally a "woman's place." Nevertheless, despite its radical potential to challenge the *theory* of sexual difference undergirding the Elizabethan sex-gender system, Marlowe's retelling of the Dido story in *practice* ends up reinforcing the oppositions of public and private, male and female, political and erotic—not as good or desirable but as tragically inevitable. He makes no place for truly political queens or effective sovereignty based on love.

Indeed, the one episode in which Dido is overtly parodied may glance not only at lyric's temporal limits but at Elizabeth's own such limits to inspire love in the younger generation of courtiers—the breakdown of her public-erotic fiction. In 4.5, an old nurse dotes on Cupid-as-Ascanius: she offers him a luscious pastoral landscape if "thou shalt go with me unto my house" (3), and then vacillates between infatuation and recognition of her folly, just as Dido did (at length) earlier.[35] Coming directly on the heels of Dido's successful persuasion of Aeneas to stay in Carthage (4.4), this scene qualifies Dido's personal power even at its height; it compares her to an old crone, recalls that the gods are the true agents creating human desire, and reminds the audience that human control through words is an illusion. And despite the nurse's lower social status, there is the potential for oblique comparison with the aging Elizabeth, continuing to use her supposed beauty and sensual charms as a source for authority over courtiers (and servants, like Marlowe) half her age.

Most directly, the play's ending invites speculation on the relationship between the dramatic image and the audience, the play's possible commentary on the actual queen via the player-queen. Brian Gibbons sees *Dido*'s conclusion as a challenge to court mythology, with Dido turning "tragedy into triumph" through her "apotheosis" in flames. If true, the play would be "almost revolutionary" in its challenge to the queen's cult of virginity, setting up an opposing cult of passion and glorified love. It would then prefigure the praise of romantic love so familiar from Shakespeare's comedies, and match the growing emphasis on the sanctity of companionate marriage in Protestant culture, beyond the court's inner sanctum. However, even Gibbons notes that Dido's last scene "might imply hysteria," raising another problem with his heroic reading of Dido as Elizabeth's foil ("Unstable" 29, 44–46).

To the extent that the ending is sympathetic to Dido's plight, one can argue that it plays against Elizabeth's court ideology—an ideology which included frustration of male desire for the distant queen as beneficial in a way Petrarchism could articulate, and which courtiers often lamented but accepted (or they were rusticated). Yet the reading presented here, which attends to the failure of Dido's rhetoric as well as to the framing power of deities, better substantiates Marjorie Garber's perspective. She sees Dido "enclosed" and limited by flames, not triumphing in them (8). Indeed, one needs to be awfully inured to bodily suffering to regard self-immolation after rejection as a form of triumph (the auto-da-fé notwithstanding); in a play, and given a speaker, so acutely aware of the sensual, a purely symbolic interpretation of burning seems especially inappropriate. To recognize Dido's defeat, of course, in no way diminishes sympathy for the victim, nor is it to dismiss Gibbons's sense that Marlowe rejects the party line. Rather, the play challenges courtly mythology not by setting up an alternative goddess but by linking the failure of Dido's vision with the Elizabethan courtier's world and abandoning such inefficacious worship altogether.

In *Renaissance Self-Fashioning,* Stephen Greenblatt sets up a dialectic in which Marlowe's worldview becomes the antithesis of Spenser's, both being synthesized in the work of Shakespeare. While this model seems overly schematic and subsequent critics have rightly emphasized the uneasiness in Spenser's work, it remains true that these two rising middle-class poets found alternative methods for working with lyric traditions. Spenser characteristically venerates and tries to surpass his poetic predecessors, whereas Marlowe openly toys with dominant traditions and morals, creating an explosively dramatic field of play. For all his anxiety about gender roles and temporality, Spenser perpetuates (one might even say, given the English turn toward satire, rehabilitates) the use of Neoplatonic and Petrarchan rhetoric. Employing familiar tropes in the service of married love, he transmutes aristocratic conventions to exalt emergent Protestant, bourgeois values.

Marlowe, on the other hand, rejects Petrarchism entirely. It is doubtful that he thought overt homosexuality too much a transgression of the norm to fit the sonnet tradition; his tendency to violate and expose, as well as the privileging of homosexuality in one of Neoplatonism's originary texts, the *Symposium,* argues against it (not to mention the homoerotic sonnets of Richard Barnfield and, to some extent, Shakespeare). More likely Marlowe dismissed a tradition he found overworked, false, and, like Dido's pleas, unpersuasive on earth. Certainly it did not serve the interests of a freethinking, bloody-minded, man on the make; but one need not indulge in speculation about Marlowe's personality (fun though it be) to observe that the extant texts he is credited with authoring — even a courtly drama like *Dido* — chafe against comforting interpretation. They also refuse to credit any uplifting female power as socially efficacious.

Such a rejection, of both Petrarchan lyricism and a specifically female power, is more notable for its extremity than its spirit of discontent. By the late 1580s the queen's longevity was straining the fictions of her court. Stephen Orgel has analyzed this strain in attitudes toward chivalry, "part of a larger attitude toward poetry as a whole, toward the relation of symbolic fictions to effective action — that is, to real life" ("Making" 42–43). He notes that "a strong sense of impatience and disillusion with the royal mythology was being felt. The mythology had become increasingly private, a way for Elizabeth to see herself, and its rhetoric was adopted only by those who had a vested interest in mirroring her self-image" — that is, by the court.

This description in some ways oversimplifies the change: I doubt anyone expected a precise correspondence between the queen's two images, or was startled by the fact of her physical decay in itself. Even given a society remarkably harsh in its imaging of older women, Elizabeth's perceived virtues other than beauty remained intact, contributing to her symbolic power and complementing her continued, very real control over "real life." And of course, the cult of Elizabeth had always been a mirror for her own self-image, even when courtiers used it to present their own political cases. The focus for feelings of discontent may have been the queen's aging face, but clearly its sources resided in the minds of the male subjects assumed in Orgel's passive construction, the men who "felt" impatient for many reasons.

Nonetheless, Marlowe's lyric strains are indicative of a contemporary shift at court, and withering mortality did indeed take a special toll on the ambitious courtly love lyricist. Desire for a unified state and personal gain must needs have been great for men to overcome the ironies implicit in wooing a woman resembling one's mother more than one's lover. Although women had ruled England throughout the entire lifetimes of many, men were still raised to regard themselves as the unequivocally superior sex.

Even courteous Spenser shows the signs of strain. No wonder, then, that Marlowe's drama unmasks Tudor court mythologies by showing the temporal and worldly limits of lyric, and by exposing (if not espousing) the power of manipulation and sheer de facto force.

Although his contemporaries and many recent critics cast Marlowe simply as a reactive figure (making Renaissance evil his good), *Dido* attests to a more complex attempt to break away from a single moral perspective in order to create a dramatic world of tensions, not pronouncements. Unlike those rituals which allow disorder only to be included in and thus reaffirm the old order, Marlowe's theatrical method suggests a profound break with the drama and mythology of the 1580s court, even as he writes for that court audience. Steane avers that "Dido and her court are escapist enticements" (39), which perhaps seems true if one unthinkingly identifies with Aeneas. Certainly the history of empires goes on outside the Carthaginian queen's realm of love poetry. Yet when performed for another queen whose self-fashioning blurred such boundaries—indeed, whose New World colony would be named, uniquely, after her cult image (Virginia) rather than her Christian or dynastic name—this escapism looks more like No Exit. Elizabeth could choose to see herself allied with the repressive, manipulative order of the gods or with the constrained, deluded Dido; the queen, I suspect, was not amused.

Dido herself remains the instrument of history, working toward an idealized vision of the future that instead leads to her demise. Judith Weil states that in Marlowe's plays "history apocalyptically overwhelms those who have tried to ignore or suspend its necessities" (171). In one sense, the words "dramatic narrative" could be substituted here for "history": Marlowe's linear narrative is as irrevocable and inevitable as history, destroying those who attempt escape through lyric poetry, ritual, and fictive futures. He shapes the tale of Dido to emphasize temporal struggles within the fiction, between present imaginings and future desires, present powers and future fears.

Working in a multivoiced medium that can, as Douglas Bruster effectively argues, be regarded as dialogic, *Dido* goes beyond the single perspective of a lyrical speaker such as Dido; the playwright can de-moralize a tale without becoming demoralized. As Marjorie Garber says of *Doctor Faustus,* the protagonist is trapped, but the author manages to enclose infinite riches in the little room of the public stage. Marlowe thus defuses the problem of the first-person satirist whose own voice becomes as questionable, formally, as those of his satiric objects: he lets actions, history (very much *his* story) itself, "speak" for him. While such a move may be more of a strategic than an explicitly ideological victory, its success is born out by the satiric drama of the subsequent decades (far superior to the nondramatic satires of those years, and not entirely because of different censors).[36] Moreover, because the move to history, at least during the Renaissance, is a move into the world of patriarchy, a "big picture" in which exceptional queens can be surrounded and put in their place, this privileging of narrative drama over lyric and myth is in practice a reassertion of masculine control. Where Peele turned to mythology and rewrote it in the service a female sovereignty, Marlowe turns to the chief secondary epic of his culture, the master-artist's story written in the service of the Roman empire, and reorients the story without overturning its historical necessity. Who painted the lion? asks Chaucer's Wife of Bath; who told the tale of Troy? Queen Elizabeth might well have echoed.

To some extent Marlowe uses dramatic structure to avoid endorsing hierarchies, *including* the patriarchal, while breaking out of the Petrarchan/anti-Petrarchan debate. Hence he creates a space where gender roles are dissociated from the fascinating dynamics of erotics and societal power. Less romantic than Shakespeare, less sympathetic to his characters, and far less interested in the variations of female personality, Marlowe at the same time appears less invested in the sex-gender system that assigns women (or men) to a proper sphere. But in his extant plays, that realistic, caustic sensibility seldom allows consideration of alternative social or narrative possibilities; tragedy results from inability to evade the arbitrary structures of power that subject mortal men and, in *Dido, Queen of Carthage,* a royal woman as well.

Looking beyond Dido: Marlowe's Drama of Public Defiance

In *Dido,* to a greater extent than in his later plays for the public stage, Marlowe sets up the lyric future of sensual love as an alternative, rather than just another path to destruction. But, as in those later works, the end is death. The offers of lyric are too weak to sustain human beings on a stage of changing tenses, competing forces, and matter. Marlowe's anatomy of lyric's social inefficacy calls into question some central assumptions about both literary models and his courtly Elizabethan audience. At the same time, by replacing discrete formal lyrics with lyricism integrated into dramatic dialogue, Marlowe finds an artistic if not a philosophical resolution to the problem of courtly lyric's limited persuasiveness and power as stage speech, transforming a negative cultural critique into lively art.

By countering the variation among verse forms common in poetic drama of the 1580s, Marlowe found an aesthetic route out of what must have seemed a stale world of courtly lyricism. *Dido* contains its colliding rhetorical voices within the single metrical frame of blank verse, the new poetic norm for the drama. Almost thirty years after *Gorboduc* and *Jocasta,* Greene and other contemporaries would still emphasize the connection between blank verse and a single rhetorical stance, that of Tamburlainian "bumbast"; that link, derived from a half-century's association with epic poetry and mighty themes, was of course amplified by Marlowe's own practice on the public stage. But in fact blank verse became the dominant metrical form for the subsequent forty years not because of its booming bass but because of its flexibility, its ability to provide sufficient variety and interest for two hour's traffic on the stage. An inkling of such diversity of tone appears in *Dido,* in a court play where song and lyricism counterpoint epic and bombast, and where the gender associations of those rhetorical modes become the stuff of unsettling drama.

Marlowe pushes court drama away from the presentation of discrete, formally differentiated speeches or scenes into a dynamically varied but not obviously divided narrative, one which refuses to privilege the lyric moment over dramatic movement. Nor does he privilege one poetic form over another by distinguishing the ethical or social status of his characters through a metrical hierarchy, as Peele did. Removing social and moral decorum as the basis for poetic choice, Marlowe undermines the poetic as well as ethical hierarchies that divide gods and humans, queens and commoners; *Dido* contains no easy signals for judging the morality of its characters. It pulls the red carpet out from under courtly aesthetics.

The extent and nature of the playwright's challenge may have been more obviously constrained, but it was not silenced, by occasion.[37] When dangerous questions had been raised in earlier court interludes, a final synthesizing speech reestablished "proper" perspective from the monarch's singular point of view. The realm of entertaining uncertainty was thus delimited. But in *Dido,* the more sustained guise of fiction allowed by using a canonical narrative, and the fuller exploitation of competing poetic voices available in drama, challenges those limits; drama launches an assault against mythological, conventional bases of power.

After *Dido,* when Marlowe wrote for the public stage, the place of lyric was further undermined by the "historical reality" of its narrative frame. Marlowe's most obvious and cynical representation of lyric onstage occurs in *The Jew of Malta* (written between 1588 and 1591, and frequently produced from 1591 through 1596 under Henslowe's management). The poet's "Passionate Shepherd" echoes once more in the method and refrain of Ithamore's love scene:

> *Bellamira.* I have no husband, sweet; I'll marry thee.
> *Ithamore.* Content, but we will leave this paltry land
>   And sail from hence to Greece, to lovely Greece.
>   I'll be thy Jason, thou my golden fleece.
>   Where painted carpets o'er the meads are hurled,
>   And Bacchus' vineyards overspread the world,
>   Where woods and forests go in goodly green,
>   I'll be Adonis; thou shalt be Love's queen.
>   The meads, the orchards, and the primrose lanes,
>   Instead of sedge and reed, bear sugar canes.
>   Thou in those groves, by Dis above,
>   Shalt live with me, and be my love.
>
> (4.4.83–94; in Ribner, 224)

More than mythic geography is inverted here. Ithamore's diabolical wit places hell (Dis) in heaven, but his creator Marlowe also metamorphoses Ovidian erotic poetry into a means of satirizing its speaker. The classical allusions work ironically, to tell us more than the character means—Jason and Adonis being particularly unattractive prospects for a maid in search of lasting love. But of course Bellamira is no pastoral maid: she is a whore and Ithamore a slave (not to love but to Barabas). In addition to the internal slips in Ithamore's speech, Marlowe signals his parodic intent through this ironic situation. That such characters should mouth "sugared" (literally) poetry on the public stage says quite a lot. As Nashe and other commentators lamented, it seems that absolutely *everyone* could now babble a sonnet or a love song—albeit ineptly and at their own expense. Moreover, in contrast to Shakespeare's dominant practice, Marlowe's parody in *The Jew of Malta* is not followed by a "sincere" counterscene with noble lovers to elevate and distinguish proper use of love poetry from improper. The dramatic setting serves to satirize, exclusively and malevolently.

In Marlowe's later plays, lyricism and love are subordinated to a struggle between the stronger heroic voice of masculine self-assertion and the dramatic landscape of self-destruction. In *The Jew of Malta,* lyrical pretensions are shattered by dramatic context. Marlowe's last word, however, is never single. Another endpoint of lyric appears in the pathetic speeches of Edward II, when the humiliated king thinks back to his lost courtier youth, itself based upon illusion and artistic masking: "Tell Isabel, the queen, I looked not thus, / When for her sake I ran at tilt in France / And there unhorsed the Duke of Cleremont" (in Ribner 5.5.67–69). Here the personation of an actor combines with the fake fighting of the tournament jouster, both temporary attempts to keep an ugly reality at bay. The distance between Dido's vaunting and Edward's pitiable desire to be remembered and beloved as something other than what he is reflects the increasing nostalgia and lack of social power given to lyric speech; it also captures the sadness and pity Marlowe imparts to duped believers, the wistfulness for what might have been (though not in this universe). The pull of an unrealizable other time, conveyed by lyric's deferral, even overtakes the galloping Tamburlaine, before he harnesses it in the service of masculine action:

> What is beauty, saith my sufferings, then?
> If all the pens that ever poets held
> Had fed the feeling of their masters' thoughts,
> And every sweetness that inspired their hearts,
> Their minds, and muses on admirèd themes;
> If all the heavenly quintessence they still
> From their immortal flowers of poesy,
> Wherein, as in a mirror, we perceive
> The highest reaches of a human wit;
> If these had made one poem's period
> And all combined in beauty's worthiness,
> Yet should there hover in their restless heads
> One thought, one grace, one wonder, at the least,
> Which into words no virtue can digest.
> But how unseemly is it for my sex,
> My discipline of arms and chivalry,
> My nature, and the terror of my name,
> To harbor thoughts effeminate and faint!
> Save only that in beauty's just applause,
> With whose instinct the soul of man is touched;
> And every warrior that is rapt with love
> Of fame, of valor, and of victory,
> Must needs have beauty beat on his conceits.
>
> (5.2.97–119; in Ribner)

Here, on the public stage, the association of lyricism and femininity that was problematized in *Dido* is reified by Marlowe's icon of masculinity. The line break in Tamburlaine's final sentence allows us to hover only for a moment on "love"—the love of Zenocrate that troubles him and initiates this speech immediately after he has had the virgins of Damascus skewered. For this warrior, the appeals of virgins, beloved queens, beauty, and poetry intermingle as things of a baffling "effeminate" sphere, only to be supplanted by artfully redefining the love object; he quickly redirects his rapture toward the killing fields of heroic slaughter ("Of fame, of valor, and of victory"). He pursues beauty no longer, even though it "beat[s]" at his brain—here conceptualized like a headache, as an external agent of torture, rather than like a heartbeat, as a sign of one's own life and desire. Tamburlaine instead seeks Italianate *virtù* ("virtue") which "fashions men with true nobility" (125–26). The growing ugliness and brutality of *Tamburlaine, Part 2* illustrate the cost of this odd form of sublimation, this model of male "maturation." Alternatively, for those less "manly" such as Edward II, failure to sustain a lyric vision brings no consolation prize. With the feminine position of powerlessness comes greater pathos, a realization developed into the tragic loss represented in Shakespeare's two lyrical tragedies, *Romeo and Juliet* and *Richard II*.

Nevertheless, for the space of time that Marlowe's characters can sustain their "working words," they possess a poetic power that defies the standards of worldly efficacy his narrative ultimately reinstates. Through an artistic method which dramatically conceives and subdues poetry, Marlowe recognizes the power of those rhetorics from which he, as the invisible playwright, detaches or shields himself. His use of lyricism signals a new consciousness of both the power and limits of poetry within the drama.

Other playwrights were quick to learn his new method along with his meter. As *Dido* revises the courtly script of Peele's *Arraignment,* so Shakespeare's lyrical plays would soon revise Marlowe's work. *Love's Labour's Lost* further complicates the issue of lyrical power and efficacy, mocks Marlowe (and probably Sidney), and comes to different conclusions than *Dido*. In his plays of the mid-1590s, even as he frames Petrarchan lyric in an ultimately more devastating way, Shakespeare reasserts the potential of a "chastened," more "natural" lyricism. But in his reexamination, Shakespeare did not reject the dramaturgy of his satiric predecessor. For him as for us, Marlowe remained a pivotal playwright. He was the destructive thinker who cleared away idols, allowing what no doubt seemed truer representations for a new theatrical world of secularized space; no less, he was the creative artist who found a way for the "new men" of the theater to use poetry in that space. Shakespeare learned his lesson well.

Notes

1. My use of the term "new men" refers to a wider group than the "new aristocracy" noted by MacCaffrey and others (see P. Berry 176–77n44) though both describe part of the same Tudor phenomenon, the increasing fluidity of social status and the broadening access to power based on reasons other than birth. On Marlowe's life, see Bakeless; Boas, *Christopher Marlowe;* Nicholl; and Archer.

2. Martin gives the production date as 1587, following a suggestion in Chambers (45); the place of performance would be either at Blackfriars or at court. The 1594 title page identifies the players and Marlowe's authorship, with assistance from "Thomas Nash. Gent." Oliver discusses the possible signs of Nashe's hand, concluding nevertheless that they remain "straws in the wind" (Marlowe, *Dido* xxv). Except for Dido's seduction speech and a few other passages, which clearly are in Marlowe's style, the complications of authorship are not crucial to my discussion. Both Nashe and Marlowe were "new men" with complex relationships to the court and its traditions, and the play reflects such complexity. The continuities between *Dido* and Marlowe's later plays in representing the fate of the lyricist also support his major role in composition. Bono (*Literary*), Cope, Gibbons ("Unstable"), and Oliver consider the impact of *Dido*'s having been written for a boy's court production.

3. Ribner repeatedly equates Aeneas and Tamburlaine as "supermen" (xxviii–xxix), a claim Oliver (Marlowe, *Dido* xxxvi) accurately calls "incredible." Aeneas's weakness undermines readings heavily reliant upon an unironic link between Aeneas and Elizabeth (through the mythical Brute lineage of empire).

4. The continental use of Dido and Aeneas for a love versus honor allegory was commonplace (see Horne's account of Cinthio's version, and Stone). Marlowe removes the moral problems regarding Sychaeus from Dido's love, and reduces the role of Aeneas's heroic honor drastically; thus he can concentrate on the amoral, external foils to desire.

5. See Colie, Rosmarin, and Hosek and Parker on genre theory. Bruster shows the impact of Marlowe's lyric on later drama, and similarly discusses the rhetorical implications of Marlowe's lyric. His application of the Bakhtinian categories of the monologic and dialogic to the lyric and drama, respectively, leads him to impute a negativity to the lyric voice, a "lack," which is only addressed fully onstage. While drama certainly allows another level of commentary on this lyric voice, Marlowe's rhetoric is in itself subtle and supple enough to defy schematization. Barish's account of antitheatricalism examines some of the consequences of this notion of generic essentialism from a different angle. There is some gendered irony in countering the valorization of lyric with an attack on its implied "lack," given the association of the courtly lyric with the world in which women factor most obviously. On revised ideas about source study, see Greenblatt's "Shakespeare and the Exorcists" (in *Shakespearean Negotiations*).

6. Citations of Marlowe's poem refer to Orgel's edition (*Complete Poems* 211) throughout. Even if one discredits the title as Marlowe's the poem is obviously a pastoral piece, a familiar genre in which the sophistication of the courtier becomes all the clearer in his guise as shepherd.

7. Sylvester, *English Sixteenth-Century Verse* (331); subsequent citations refer to this edition. The most famous parody is Donne's "The Bait." *Prosopopoeia* is a rhetorical trope that was given renewed currency by the Yale critics; it signifies the adoption of another's voice, and correlates with the term for "acting" in vogue around 1600, "personation"—taking on the identity, the person, of one's character.

8. The two senses of *phantasia,* fantasy and sense impression, have a complex history. According to Harvey, Aquinas distinguished *phantasmata* (sense impressions) and *phantasia* (fantasy), but avoided the total split between the terms found in Avicenna by considering the body as necessarily linking them (53–58). Marlowe, ever aware of bodies, exploits the tenuous but obvious connection between these two senses of fantasy, as do many of his contemporaries (cf. Spenser's House of Alma episode in book 2 of *The Faerie Queene*).

9. As in many earlier Elizabethan plays, the songs seem to be part of the theatrical display, important as moments of virtuosity, as mood-setting, melodious interludes rather than verbal commentary. See my comments in the introductory section of chap. 2.

10. See Gibbons ("Unstable" 30, 34–35) who links Marlowe's stress on clothing with courtly sumptuousness, but does not investigate his specific changes from their representation in Virgil. (One can safely assume that many in the court audience would recognize divergences from the *Aeneid*.) As in his use of poetry, Marlowe exploits staging as display and also as a sign of a very different fictive world than Virgil's, one in which clothes do indeed make the man. Steane, who sees Marlowe's Aeneas as a great man, tellingly ignores the role of clothes (31); Cutts and Oliver counter his interpretation (Marlowe, *Dido*). See also Hendricks's more recent discussion of Aeneas's garb and other variations from source-narratives.

11. Allen thinks the courtly audience meant Marlowe could have a less obvious "dramatic" purpose, disregard characterization through style, and thus play the *rhétoriqueur* instead (65). Most critics have dismissed the play as apprentice work, in part because the plot is derivative and the poetry not "dramatic" enough; notable exceptions include Cutts, Martin, Turner, Bono [*Literary*], Bruster, Bartels and Hendricks).

12. Despite passing notice of a "gendered claim upon the construction of literary subjectivity" (50), Bruster does not explore the variations that create different subjects. The claim that Marlovian lyric invitation "asserts primacy of force (physical and linguistic alike) over sexual identity" (68) also seems inconsistent with Marlowe's playful (albeit satiric) tone. Bruster concludes that it is in the *power* of "drama's more social dialogue to *force* the lyric vision into a confession of its motivation" (68; emphasis added), thus investing drama, putatively the superior form redressing

the lyric's rhetorical violence, with similarly violent agency, and undermining the critical privileging of generic opposition.

13. I cite Oliver's edition of *Dido* throughout. B. Morris ignores this speech, claiming Dido and Aeneas's love is "cold and unevocative" compared to Jupiter and Ganymede's (128–29). Calling heterosexual love "hard, jeweled, and cold" because Dido offers Aeneas jewelry, he ignores a similar gift-giving on Olympus; thus his distinction between the sensuality of heterosexual and homosexual love in *Dido* is severely weakened.

14. This case of self-abandonment is certainly a power play but it does not imply violence toward the beloved; as opposed to rape, Dido's attempts to gain Aeneas's love require his consent. For parallels with *Antony and Cleopatra,* see Gibbons ("Unstable" 43) and Steane passim. The passage combines poetic beauty and humor in a way Kocher found among Marlowe's corpus only in "Hero and Leander"—the work with its own comically erotic sea voyage, and similar wryness about its own sensuality (296).

15. Martin passim. H. Levin (*Overreacher* 190) and Bruster also cite Ovid as the source for Marlovian lyric.

16. Ovid's original reads "mollior et cycni plumis et lacta coacto, / et, si non fugias, riguo formosior horto" (284; ll. 796–97). Golding beautifies "lacta coacto" to "butter newly made," while Humphries' modern verse translation tries to capture the humor: "softer even / Than swan's down ever, or cottage cheese, more lovely / (On one condition: that you do not flee me) / Than a well-watered garden" (332; ll. 796–99). In addition to highlighting the verbal echo from this passage in Jonson's "Celebration of Charis," Humphries makes the conditional overt. My subsequent quotations cite Golding's near-contemporary verse translation; obviously Marlowe read the original.

17. The same distinction applies regarding the locus of sensual poetry in the Judeo-Christian tradition, the Song of Solomon. Marlowe quite carefully makes nature into art, as Renaissance court pastoral tended to do. By contrast, *Mucedorus* (the extremely popular play derived from Sidney's *Arcadia*) shows how less crafty borrowing can reinstate "natural"—that is, conventional—morality onstage, in its scene of Amadine's wooing by the wild man Bremo (scene xv.23–56 in Baskervill et al.). In a context similar to the Polyphemus and Galatea story, the anonymous author mixes mundane and Marlovian gifts; the result is undirected parody. Decorum is reinforced by the return of a "proper" lover/speaker, who kills Bremo.

18. By calling this discourse "heroic," I am not linking it with the epic hero of the *Aeneid;* besides Hermes, Venus and Dido get more heroic speeches than Aeneas (thus in speech, as in action, Bono's contention in *Literary Transvaluation* that the play replaces love and Dido with "the glorification of heroism" is not borne out). The distinction at issue is not only what topic people discuss (as in love/honor debates) but how they speak; nor is this simply divisible into public versus private categories, for in *Dido* both lyric and heroic rhetoric can refer to personal relationships.

Martin cites Aeneas's account of the fall of Troy as Marlowe's epic voice, characterized by narrative economy and violent action (46–47). But that set piece (resembling Marlowe's translation of Lucan) is not, as he would have it, placed in dialectical struggle with lyric; instead, it serves an expository function, as does Venus's similar speech in the opening scene. Rather than reinforce Aeneas's role as hero, his account undercuts him (see Cutts). Dido encourages Aeneas to talk about Troy as an exorcism, to move his mind *out* of Troy, after his hallucinations; she chastises him to "Remember who thou art: Speak like thyself" (2.1.100). Marlowe alters Virgil's story by placing this encounter before Dido is smitten with love; hence it does not, in terms of theatrical dialogue, oppose her lyricism at all.

19. Jupiter mentions Rome's bright future to Venus in 1.1, and of course the Elizabethan audience would know that this future leads to London, but the human characters have little access to this vision in Marlowe's play; except for Hermes' passing reference to Ascanius's future, the god's-eye perspective remains separate. This Aeneas receives no omens about empire from Hector's ghost, sees no flames around Ascanius's head, and shows no desire for conquest; thus empire is reduced as a motivation for human action. Nor does the play stress patriotism, as English history plays tend to (and could easily have been done through explicit mention of Ascanius's descendant, England's mythical founder). Instead, Aeneas *under*reaches even in the cave scene: "Aeneas' thoughts dare not ascend so high / As Dido's heart, which monarchs might not scale" (3.4.32–33). He denies his potential as king, the epic epitome of his people, preferring his solitary role as warrior: "A burgonet of steel and not a crown, / A sword and not a sceptre fits Aeneas" (4.4.42–43). In the amoral scales of sociopolitical power, Aeneas carries less weight than his epic original.

20. See Patricia Parker's similar argument about narrative movement versus lyric rest in Spenser's Bowre of Blisse ("Suspended Instruments" in *Literary Fat Ladies,* which also shares the project of complicating some of Greenblatt's claims in *Renaissance Self-Fashioning*).

21. We could interpret this as another version of Rome's future, prefiguring the destruction of Carthage in the Punic Wars; but it is represented as utter obliteration, showing the cost rather than the glory (not to mention the blindness to the body such allegory requires, and against which Marlowe's sensual rhetoric conspires).

22. See Kocher (176). While Elizabeth aspired to absolute sovereignty, this scene hardly presents a context in which she would be flattered by such claims; she carefully avoided subordination to, or even collaboration with, a consort. Gill thinks that by convention Aeneas should "grow" into Sychaeus's clothes, but instead he is a "prisoner or pet for Dido to show off" (151). He does not grow because Marlowe is not fully endorsing his epic stature; yet Dido's poetry does not sound like pet-talk either. Brodwin, having adopted a Neoplatonic classification of earthly and transcendent (her view of courtly) love, blames Dido for selfishly asserting herself and hence being earthly (186–89). I would counter that the drama's power lies in

the tension between Dido's desire and the way of the world, between her project and that of the gods. Oliver notes more generally that much criticism of Marlowe evaluates him as if he were a polemicist rather than a dramatist (Marlowe, *Dido*); the scholarship about this passage provides a good example.

23. Mizener observes that Faustus's words have the irony of the whole play behind them; he sees in *Dido* "little more than a version of the Elizabethan convention in which the lover, by ascribing to the beloved the attributes of divinity, at once finds for him the maximum glory and ironically suggests the tragic limitations of all those marvelous earthly things, such as human and physical love, which remain forever at the mercy of time" (84). But contextual irony complicates this very convention, for it is the stronger, literal reading of Dido's lines that become true for her (as for Faustus) in an unintended way. For Faustus, desire for Helen (a demonic succubus) is only an alternate route to damnation; Dido's desire for the worthy Aeneas is not similarly dooming in itself, though it is supernaturally induced.

24. Powell attends to the distancing irony of Dido calling Aeneas "Jove" (202); this corresponds with what Hattaway, following Harry Levin's lead, calls an "alienation effect" akin to Brecht's. In neither playwright's actual practice, however, does irony preclude sympathy. Gibbons's emphasis on the "almost pathological quality" of passivity in Aeneas's "impotent retreat" from Dido's arms ("Unstable" 44) deflects attention from the pathos of the drama's more general comment on love, which extends beyond Aeneas's particular neuroses (or variance from gender and sexual stereotypes).

25. Jodelle's play adds the death of Anna (not in Virgil). When the social self is no longer empowered in Marlowe, it is dead and the play ends. In contrast to Ben Jonson's attempts to constitute a self outside the dramatic realm of action (see Danson), Marlowe treats the self in almost exclusively social terms, which is one of the reasons it matters that Dido speaks well. See Rousseau for identification of the rhetorical figures employed, although he, like Steane (48), decides Marlowe was "uninterested" and hasty in concluding *Dido* (47).

26. Art historian James M. Saslow notes the Renaissance popularity of representations of Juno strung up in the heavens (117–18). Steane observes that "Jove has the power to do what all lovers have wanted to do"; he can indeed slow the horses of night (33).

27. In Ovid, Dido cries out "Exige, laese pudor, poenas! violate Sychaei . . . !" (*Heroides 7;* Loeb translation: "Exact the penalty of me, O purity undone!—the penalty due Sychaeus" [90–91]). Dolce's and Pazzi's plays include the ghost of Sychaeus à la Seneca, returning to haunt the wife who betrayed his memory. In Pazzi, Iarbus presents the head of Pygmalion, and Dido plans to chop up Ascanius (Horne 79, 87–88). In contrast, Marlowe does not even have Venus tell the Virgilian story of Dido's first marriage, and Dido only mentions her husband's clothes as more apt for Aeneas than his own rags; Dido's vow not to remarry in honor of Sychaeus's memory is removed. Hence the dead Sychaeus does not come to sym-

bolize "widow Dido"'s moral violation or lack of responsibility as in Virgil, nor her fidelity, as in Petrarch's *Trionfi*—once again, removing traditional issues of sexual morality from the play. (The reduction of Sychaeus's importance also increases the resemblance between Dido and and Queen Elizabeth.)

28. While Jupiter's philandering is traditional, Marlowe's original juxtaposition of this material with the Dido story gives it new meaning. It is obviously *not* his sexual orientation, but the violent and casual use of unlimited power, that makes Jupiter a less attractive lyric speaker than Dido. Those, such as Turner, who regard all love in *Dido* as irrational and the character's crucial mistake, emphasize parallels between Ganymede and Aeneas.

29. Gill recognizes the scene as functional, including Marlowe's "peculiar sardonic gaze" at the gods (143–44). Earlier critics tended to dismiss the scene altogether; see Bredbeck and Bruce Smith (*Homosexual*) on homosexuality and the interpretation of Marlowe's plays.

30. Aeneas will add violent and vivid imagery to his mother's meter. See *Hamlet* 2.2 (discussed by Steane [56] and Oliver [Marlowe, *Dido* xxxi-xxxii]). It seems most likely, as Boas (*Queen Elizabeth* 85) noted long ago, that it is Marlowe's version which is imitated in the Player's speech. A Dido play was revived in 1598 by the Lord Admiral's Men; if Marlowe's, no doubt this piece would have sounded dated, its elegance and classicism seeming "caviare to the general" (details of the *Dido* revival are recorded in Foakes and Rickert, *Henslowe's Diary* 319ff.). An adult troupe's failure to capture the public with this boy's company script might, moreover, aggravate the players' resentment toward the "little eyases." See Howard Baker on Sackville's style. Marlowe's use of Sackvillean passages to evoke traditional ideas of epic heroism, then shifting to a less grand voice of force in his main story, befits his "modern" critique; as he finds new reasons for discontent with conventional lyric, so he replaces the epic voice with a less romantic voice of power, of realpolitik. The old style displays rhetorical skill but fails to gain a major place in the ensuing earthly narrative—emphasizing the distance of old heroic motives from Marlowe's representation of the world.

31. Venus's reference to Ganymede as a "female," an insult from her, indicates the use of gender labels as a way of identifying positionality in social relations, not necessarily correlating with a person's biological sex. (Constance Jordan and Jean Howard engaged this distinction at the Newberry Library's conference on women in medieval and early modern studies, spring 1991; but see C. Brown Kuriyama for a quite different reading of *Dido*.) To see the constructedness of the sex-gender system, and this potential fissure between theory and performance, obviously has radical implications.

32. See P. Berry chap. 3 (61–82). Ashe's use of Dido is cited by Clark, who gives many examples of complimentary titles used for Elizabeth (92). My reading thus departs from Margo Hendricks's, which relies on hypothesized links within *Dido* between Aeneas and Elizabeth as well as between Carthage and Spain; she posits

an intriguing allegorical reading of the English/Spanish conflict that would make Marlowe's work more conventionally nationalistic and politically focused. Analysis of the play's lyricism and erotic emphasis, as well as Marlowe's subtle variations and inversions of tradition, lead me to think otherwise.

33. Eliot quotes the echoes he learned from J. M. Robertson's book, but doesn't consider their effects ("Christopher Marlowe" 24). H. Morris aptly perceives Spenserian melody here and in "The Passionate Shepherd" (137), but Spenser is not so much followed as turned upside down. These arguments all presume (as do I) that Marlowe's writing reacted to Spenser, although the publication dates make it at least conceivable that the "Epithalamion" partially "rehabilitates" Marlowe's lines.

34. Only when Aeneas is leaving does Dido mention that other princes are angry; unlike Cinthio, Marlowe makes the rejection of those suitors primarily a personal matter. Iarbus is no longer a threatening neighbor whose rejection may cause war, but rather the scorned corner of a love triangle, in turn rejecting another suit from Anna—all the human players being motivated by erotic desire rather than public policy. While Jodelle may have provided the suggestion for the Anna-Iarbus affair (and Nashe may have written it), I suspect the shift from public struggle was in part a matter of safety; advising the queen about foreign suitor-princes had proven unwise for writers of much higher status than Marlowe. Portrayal of a queen rejecting princes in favor of a gallant commoner might have reminded the audience of the old Dudley scandal (or might have suggested a parallel with the contemporary favorite, Ralegh, as Bakeless and Clark argue).

35. While the nurse's earthbound speech does in fact resemble the rhetoric of Ovid's Polyphemus more than do Marlowe's other lyric offers (matching her lower social position), it still comments on Dido's desire as well as her own absurdity. It complicates the reading of Marlowe's lyric as implied force, for the nurse is the dupe of her would-be "victim," the baby god who is inducing her passion.

36. As Greenblatt notes in the first chapter of *Shakespearean Negotiations,* his earlier work tends to view "orthodoxy" as a monolithic system based on the pursuit and preservation of power, rather than as competing strains of tradition and sources of power. Greenblatt's discussion of Marlowe's repetition compulsion in *Renaissance Self-Fashioning* (chap. 5) is a case in point, as it equates neglecting or ignoring certain values with hating or doing violence to them (for example, see his comments on the family [212] and the general discussion preceding it, in which he collapses power and violence). Thus Marlowe becomes trapped by the orthodoxy against which he rebels, just as his protagonists do. But aesthetic creation in the dramatic mode provides a partial "out" for Marlowe, allowing him to do more than blaspheme. Goldman discusses (in different terms) the constant need of Marlowe's protagonists to get beyond this world, which makes their aspirations self-defeating (39).

37. Discussing the dramatization of blasphemy in *Doctor Faustus,* C. L. Barber comments that the London theater was a "place apart" where drama was presented not as a servant to occasion but in its own right; thus it had a "special vantage on

experience" ("Form" 92). Kastan believes that the public playhouse and its stage devices did not need to, and therefore did not, keep a respectful distance between audience and the dramatic "subject": "The mode of representation in the Elizabethan popular theatre refuses to privilege what is represented" (467). Subsequently, numerous critics have explored this notion as it affected the representation of royalty, while others have begun to complicate the picture of the public stage as exempt from sociopolitical pressures (see Weimann, Mullaney, Cohen, Tennenhouse, Yachnin). While Barber is probably right to credit the playing space as an aid in Marlowe's avoidance of a single (religious) perspective in *Doctor Faustus,* the beginnings of such perspective play clearly appear in his court drama as well.

FOUR

Shakespeare's Laboring Lovers

Lyric and Its Discontents

> Now, sir, for the manner,—it is the manner of a man to speak
> to a woman; for the form,—in some form.
> Costard

> Assist me, some extemporal god of rhyme, for I am sure I shall
> turn sonnet.
> Don Adriano de Armado (Love's
Labour's Lost, 1.1.206–8; 1.2.172–74)

Like *Dido* amidst Marlowe's dramatic corpus, *Love's Labour's Lost* has often been regarded, and sometimes dismissed, as among the most "courtly" and hence self-enclosed of Shakespeare's Elizabethan works. Shakespeare's interest in the fashionable literary scene appears in the many allusions to his predecessors in both pageant and poetic composition, including Sidney and Marlowe—not to mention the explicit links with his own lyric sequence, the *Sonnets*.[1] Yet for all its echoes, allusion, and borrowing, this lyrical play reflects a very different artistic and political occasion from the courtly art of earlier years. Satirizing aristocratic poetasters, the play is unrelentingly critical of its four lords' notion of courtliness, especially as they render it in verse. Moreover, *Love's Labour's Lost* represents women as most skeptical and antagonistic to Petrarchist indulgence, thus fusing the censorious possibilities of female sovereignty with a position opposed to feminine idealization. At the same time the comical lords, whose lyricism works mostly to undermine their own desires, remain the protagonists, the subjects of the central dramatic action—and of course in representing such courtly "play" Shakespeare finds it worth considering with amusement. Thus *Love's Labour's Lost,* with its poetic love, satiric edge, and ambiguous ending, provides a congenial landscape for the study of distinctive intersections between lyricism and social performance in Shakespeare's Elizabethan plays. Performed both at court and on the public stage, not relying on a specific audience for its success, *Love's Labour's Lost* demonstrates one way in which a playwright of the 1590s could rework courtly lyricism for the public repertory. Shakespeare typically has it both ways, distancing lyric artifice as a facet of flawed characters, but displaying his poetic skills and their power to please as well.

Love's Labour's Lost is indeed courtly in the crucial sense that it borrows and plays with the conventions of courtly aesthetics. One could even say that the Elizabethan entertainments and progresses are the source material for this, the rare play by Shakespeare without any known literary narrative source.[2] The play shares affinities with Sidney's 1578 court pageant *The Lady of May,* updating its version of the pedantic local schoolmaster, Master Rombus, to produce Holofernes; the words of Shakespeare's title had been used by Sidney's Dorcas in describing courtiers frustrated by love, who retreat into his pastoral world lamenting (much like these Navarrese lords) their mistresses' "beautie cupled wyth extreme creweltie some of to much witte which mad all these theire Lovinge Labors folly . . . so that with longe loste Labor fyndinge theyre thoughte bere no other wolle but Dispaire" (Kimbrough and Murphy 115–16). Various courtly figures (including some within Sidney's and Ralegh's circles) have been posited as the originals for the fantastical characters in *Love's Labour's Lost.*[3] The play certainly mocks many of the court's linguistic fashions through the pretentiousness of Don Adriano de Armado as well as the four lords of Navarre who labor at love. Moreover, the arrival of female "majesty" for a visit, and her outdoor entertainment, provides the play's central action.

Aptly, then, the play unfolds through a pageantlike series of debates, displays, and parallel self-presentations rather than a dominantly linear plot. Division into five acts is particularly misleading in this case, since the first three acts make up little more than a third of the play, setting the stage for a variety of courtly "performances": a deer-shoot, sonnetizing, masquing, and a pageant capped with song.[4] Given these links with courtly love and more particularly the royal entertainments, it is fitting that Shakespeare's play benefits from, and toys with, their heritage of generic interaction. It blurs the boundaries of genre and plays with the meanings of gender, especially as they relate to female authority and the defeat of fertile community. In so doing, the play comments on its contemporary culture in ways hardly laudatory to a virginal queen, though no doubt pleasing to the married ear of a middle-class male playwright and his like-minded listeners.

Love's Labour's Lost fully exemplifies Shakespeare's particular twists on stage lyricism. Predictably, the many interpretations that view lyric and dramatic impulses here as antagonists discount the play's dramaturgical aesthetics—and much of its energy as well. Even so fine a reader as James Calderwood acknowledges that he deals "a bit roughly with the lyric" when "it gets imported, or more likely smuggled, into the domain of drama"; he generalizes that "it is associated with the insular, private, and indwelling, with the static and retarding, and with verbal purity" (72n). Having thus reduced the various lyric voices of the play to inferior Petrarchism, he is forced to the conclusion that the play is similarly "reduced to . . . verbal events," making it seem "almost an experiment in seeing how well language spun into intricate, ornate, but static patterns can substitute for the kinetic thrust of action in drama" (72). Discounting the reverberations of gendered dismissal in this dichotomy between the desired "kinetic thrust" and passive Petrarchism, this interpretation still misses the potential of lyric as the playwright's subject as well as style, and hence its ability to represent conflicts and social issues.[5] As the courtly works of Gascoigne and Peele have demonstrated, lyric, while suggestive of alternative times and visions, in performance attained resonances far from "static" or insulated from social and political drama (in all senses of that word). Similarly, Shakespeare's play is very much about lyricism as a social act, be it in the form of those "abortive births" of stale Petrarchism, the botched verse of pageant performance, or the rhetorically and dramatically endorsed songs of the seasons.

Like Marlowe's *Dido, Love's Labour's Lost* uses lyricism to qualify the reality and results of courtly wooing—but its tone is utterly different. Its mockery is kinder, its consequences more benign. The attempt to reject all courtship, linguistic and romantic, appears as silly as idolizing its artifices, as much a futile defiance of necessity as was Dido's attempt to keep Aeneas in her lyrical fantasy world. Rather than emphasizing the claustrophobic collapse of erotic fantasy, this drama generates energy through wordplay and the performance of lyric; competing voices create tension, often overtly sexual, leading to more "potent" exchange even at the expense of the prince's decrees and the lovers' fantasies. As in the other plays often grouped with *Love's Labour's Lost* as the lyrical phase of Shakespeare's career (*A Midsummer Night's Dream, Richard II, Romeo and Juliet,* and *The Merchant of Venice*), styles of poetry signify varying degrees of sincerity and efficacy in the mouths of protean characters.[6] Moreover, even in this satiric comedy, a "mature" lyricism is vindicated in its claims to imaginative power. Thus by revising the functions of lyric as well as of courtship, Shakespeare posits a "worthier" courtly art, encompassing and surrounding his pageant of the Nine Worthies and his lyrical lords, and complicating any simple judgments of language or lovers.

The Framing of Astrophil, Or Lyric Implosion

Shakespeare happily transforms the devices of courtly culture to serve his artistic ends, making poetic style a functional part of his narrative fiction as well as a delight to the ear. *Love's Labour's Lost,* like *Romeo and Juliet,* makes special use of the sonnet form in this endeavor. With the works of Gascoigne, Peele, and Marlowe in mind, we can see this and other lyric forms in their broader cultural as well as dramatic context, considering what it means for this play to be, as Anne Barton rightly notes, both "lyrical and ornate, various and highly patterned in [its] verse forms" and "quintessentially Elizabethan" (Shakespeare, *Riverside* 174). Indeed, we can see the clear *intersection* between these two comments, not only in Barton's stylistic sense of "Elizabethan" but in terms of the cultural relationship of lyric poetry to female sovereignty exploited variously by Spenser, Peele, and Marlowe.

It might seem retrograde after Marlowe not to submerge lyric entirely within the drama as a style, dismissing rhyme or use of lyric forms such as the sonnet; yet Shakespeare modulates between forms as well as styles and situations, conserving the lyric in a way that signifies his double attitude toward the courtly tradition as well as allowing the game to be revised for the public audience. Nor was this a simply conservative choice, for the sonnet as a form was newly popularized and current, thus invested with special appeal for an author addressing a wide spectrum of society. With the unauthorized publication of Sidney's *Astrophil and Stella* in 1591 (literary remains of the safely dead paragon of Elizabethan culture), the sonnet became more widely hailed as the premier symbolic form for courtly lyricism. Ironically, its cachet led to the sonneteering craze of the 1590s, so distasteful to admirers of Sidney such as Nashe, in which less-than-aristocratic poets and poetasters produced a massive number of mediocre sequences for the reading public. J. W. Lever observes that in the four years following the appearance of Sidney's poems, "more sonnets saw the light than in all the decades since Wyatt made his first renderings of Petrarch" (*Elizabethan* 92). Shakespeare was one of the most successful heirs of Sidney in making the sonnet sequence his own—although in keeping with his genteel pretensions he had them circulated in manuscript rather than published.

In *Love's Labour's Lost,* Shakespeare makes a favorite form into an occasion for laughter, by having amorous courtiers compose and recite their lyrics in unseemly circumstances—most notably in act 4 scene 3. Ironically, while Shakespeare's own sequence was not printed until 1609 (and even then without authorization), three of the lords' lyrics from this play, often dismissed as mere parodies of trite sonneteering, appeared almost immediately in literary miscellanies: Berowne's and Longaville's sonnets were included in *The Passionate Pilgrim* (1599), while Dumain's lyric in tetrameter couplets appears both there and in the pastoral collection, *England's Helicon* (1600). While Petrarchism might be an exhausted tradition in the eyes of a master poet, as Joel Fineman asserts in discussing Shakespeare's sonnets, it was commercially viable for a man making his livelihood from box office receipts. If nothing else, these lyrics' removal from their theatrical context for popular publication suggests the new delight in poetic display that was a factor in the public Elizabethan audience's enjoyment of lyrical drama during the 1590s; this faddish pleasure was not confined to a tiny coterie audience, as is often casually asserted. The verses were enjoyed for their "rhyme" if not "reason"—a social tendency that provides a source of dramatic amusement, as Shakespeare makes the sometimes tenuous relationship between these two words a major concern of his play. The publication of such poems indicates the temporal and also financial currency of sonneteering, its nonaesthetic value noted in Shakespeare's own lyric metaphors.[7] But in his play, Shakespeare does more than merely insert or comment upon faddish poetry; he also makes the location or source of aesthetic value part of the drama's subject of investigation. None of this implies that the humor of these portable sonnets as presented onstage was missed, or that their interest is entirely reliant on cultural context. The scene in which the lords labor at lyric composition remains a hilarious as well as ironic reflection upon poetasting and human vanity. Nevertheless, its interest is compounded when one recognizes how Shakespeare exploits the play of perspective afforded by the Elizabethan theater and by a culture in which lyric poetry was multiply significant, rendering formal, courtly, and political messages through verse "play."

While act 4 scene 3 most obviously reflects on its media of lyric poetry and stage performance, its context includes not only the Elizabethan world of art and the character of its speakers in the fiction but also the theatrical scenes which lead to it and condition our "reading" of its performance. To view the scene in its dramatic sequence first requires a glance backwards. As in the case of Romeo and Juliet's shared sonnet at Capulet's ball, some of the verse that reveals most about the playwright's subtle use of stage lyricism is semisubmerged rather than set off explicitly from the surrounding verse. Thus Shakespeare quite literally plays off an awareness shaped by Marlowe's experiments, now precedents incorporated into a larger dramaturgical vocabulary. Even more significantly, Shakespeare echoes Marlowe's use of tensions between lyrical discourse and its theatrical framing to investigate the social functions of this poetry within a gendered political landscape.

This interest appears in the very first words of *Love's Labour's Lost*. Scene one begins with something very like a sonnet, the prince of Navarre's fourteen-line, heavily end-stopped, blank verse announcement of his intention to transform his court:

> Let fame, that all hunt after in their lives,
> Live register'd upon our brazen tombs,
> And then grace us in the disgrace of death;
> When, spite of cormorant devouring Time,
> Th'endeavor of this present breath may buy
> That honour which shall bate his scythe's keen edge,
> And make us heirs of all eternity.
> Therefore, brave conquerors—for so you are,
> That war against your own affections
> And the huge army of the world's desires—
> Our late edict shall strongly stand in force:
> Navarre shall be the wonder of the world;
> Our court shall be a little academe,
> Still and contemplative in living art.
>
> (1.1.1–14)

This last line may again recall Sidney's *Lady of May*, in which Dorcas applauds the retreats that courtiers make into the pastoral world of shepherds for "templation," as opposed to the more "lively" endeavors of the forester Therion. Surpassing his theatrical predecessor along with the traditional debate over the active versus contemplative life, Shakespeare's prince tries to condense the two ways of life into a single ideal and a single line of verse, at first seeming to defy conventional antagonisms. But as far as convincing those whom he addresses of the desirability or indeed the possibility of such a life as he envisions, Navarre will be no more persuasive than was Sidney's rejected forester when standing before Queen Elizabeth.

The resemblance between Navarre's verse and a formal sonnet hints at the doom of his academy even before his friend Berowne begins to mock it, immediately indicating the complex signification of poetic discourse within the narrative matter of this play. The very diction and lyrical echoes of his ascetic announcement undermine the king, for the sonnet was typically a poem of erotic desire, not public fame or renunciation.[8] In the next scene, when the fantastical Spaniard Armado falls in love, he articulates this common assumption (as well as demonstrating the self-involvement of some poet-lovers, oblivious to their putative audience). Having decided to win his beloved through a specific kind of rhyme—even though the low-born Jaquenetta unsurprisingly turns out to be illiterate—Armado discards soldiery and exits with a flourish: "Assist me, some extemporal god of rhyme, for I am sure I shall turn sonnet. Devise, wit; write, pen; for I am for whole volumes in folio" (1.2.172–75). Desire implies a search for that which one lacks; Armado's parody literalizes the king's ill-placed and premature poetic pride over his posited fame.

In the opening scene, the prince of Navarre is not consciously reciting a sonnet, of course (he will once he too falls in love). He thinks he is making an heroic call to action, in his first seven lines positing the goal ("Let fame . . . Live register'd upon our brazen tombs"), and in the next seven the means of attaining it, presented as a logical conclusion ("Therefore . . . Our late edict shall strongly stand in force"). Nevertheless, his fourteen lines clearly echo the form and endeavor of Shakespeare's own sonnets "all in war with Time for love" (*Sonnets* 15.13), implying that a more plausible means for the lords to adopt in pursuing their desired end of living stillness might be to become self-conscious lyric poets. Navarre hopes that "spite of cormorant devouring Time," his words may lead to such "honour" as will "bate his scythe's keen edge, / And make us heirs of all eternity." The grandiosity of such a claim is traditionally the province of poets, not scholars. More precisely, poets are the ones who transform "this present breath" into Navarre's desired "living art" through their inscriptions, hoping that "So long as men can breathe or eyes can see, / So long lives this, and this gives life to thee" (*Sonnets* 18.13–14). Shakespeare's sonnet 55 makes this poetic claim most strongly, diminishing the alternative vocabulary of conquest used by Navarre in the process: "Not marble nor the gilded monuments / Of princes shall outlive this pow'rful rhyme"; "Nor Mars his sword nor war's quick fire shall burn / The living record of your memory" (*Sonnets* 55.1–2, 7–8). So much for "brazen tombs" won by these hermetic "conquerors" of their own affection, hoping to make themselves the only subject of "living art." Shakespeare's sonnets provide a foil to the narcissistic Navarre, a reminder that the poet—at least in theory—makes himself eternal by memorializing not just himself but the existence of a beloved. Indeed, fleshly existence provides the only overt means for the beloved's *self*-memorializing offered within the *Sonnets,* achieved through the very actions Navarre's academe forbids: "nothing 'gainst Time's scythe can make defense / Save breed, to brave him when he takes thee hence" (*Sonnets* 12.13–14).

Even before we hear the particulars of his decrees, then, Navarre's use of a sonnetlike vocabulary and form recalls the arguments for the very "affections" his academe would "war against"; our doubt about his success will be increased if we, like Francis Meres, know Shakespeare's own "sugred Sonnets, [circulated] among his private friends" (Shakespeare, *Riverside* 1844). The execution of Navarre's vision will be fraught with difficulties, as he creates a rigid legal code to replace complex poetic language and the complex experience which it tries to shape and express. At the same time as he retreats from his political duties as sovereign—the performance of which would provide the most obvious means for him to become a memorialized "conqueror"—he fails to abandon his sovereign self or legal vocabulary entirely. Were he to search for "fame" through artful sonnetizing about nature, rather than by dismissing nature's demands, he might indeed sound like Shakespeare (or one version of that literary voice). But because he does not hear the implications of his own poetry, we are immediately signaled to look for the ironic fulfillment of his words. In contradistinction to the pageant devisers who failed to move Elizabeth as they wished, here the irony and additional distance between the playwright and his fictionally contained dramatic speaker serves to insulate Shakespeare from Navarre's poetic folly.

Moreover, the playwright also inscribes, and hence controls, the overt mockery of this speaker. It does not take long for dramatic conflict, in the figure of Berowne, to intrude on this inappropriate lyrical vision:

> *Ber.*: Why! all delights are vain, but that most vain,
> . . . to pore upon a book
> To seek the light of truth; while truth the while
> Doth falsely blind the eyesight of his look
> Light seeking light doth light of light beguile:
> So, ere you find where light in darkness lies,
> Your light grows dark by losing of your eyes.
> Study me how to please the eye indeed,
> By fixing it upon a fairer eye,
> Who dazzling so, that eye shall be his heed,
> And give him light that it was blinded by.
> (1.1.72, 74–83)

Berowne's desires will soon be ironically literalized, as he fixes his eye on the dark eyes of fair Rosaline, overgoing his own dazzling pun by showing his "I" to be ethically "light" in his oath-taking. Berowne concludes that "Small have continual plodders ever won, / Save base authority from others' books" (86–87), thus resembling Sidney's Astrophil, whose inventiveness flees from "step-dame Studies blowes" in favor of a lady's eye and self-perjuring desire (*Astrophil and Stella* 1). Shakespeare uses the arguments and wit of his poetic predecessors to outdo them in a dramatic form that, unlike the court pageants, is not directly subjected to royal authority; he thereby retains verbal authority over both sides of a debate. Whereas Queen Elizabeth as judging audience mocked the lively desire of Sidney's Therion (and hence, because of his clear partisanship, indirectly mocked Sidney himself) in *The Lady of May,* it is Shakespeare's own Berowne who (Sidney-like) mocks the contemplative retirement from sensory experience of Shakespeare's Navarre:

> *King.* Berowne is like an envious sneaping frost
>   That bites the first-born infants of the spring.
> *Ber.* Well, say I am; why should proud summer boast
>   Before the birds have any cause to sing?
>   Why should I joy in any abortive birth?
>   At Christmas I no more desire a rose
>   Than wish a snow in May's new-fangled shows;
>   But like of each thing that in season grows.
>   So you, to study now it is too late,
>   Climb o'er the house to unlock the little gate.
> *King.* Well, sit you out: go home, Berowne: adieu!
> *Ber.* No, my good lord; I have sworn to stay with you:
>   And though I have for barbarism spoke more
>   Than for that angel knowledge you can say,
>   Yet confident I'll keep what I have sworn,
>   And bide the penance of each three years' day.
>
>   (1.1.100–115)

Berowne's attack on what he perceives as Navarre's untimely, unnatural retreat foreshadows Shakespeare's own dialectical appeal to nature in the play's last words, its song lyrics about spring and winter. Berowne also echoes the opinion of the *Sonnets* narrator when he attacks Navarre's unnecessary exclusion of the "living" world of the body from their study, leaving them "quick" only in language. This latter field of performance being Berowne's forte, however, it is not surprising that he eventually submits to the king's rules, though he believes them impossible to follow. The sounding and significance of Berowne's skeptical words nevertheless remain, temporally impossible — despite our common figures of speech — to erase or retract. Forestalling criticism by including several perspectives within his fiction, yet denying any character full cogency or consistency, Shakespeare will reserve the greatest authority for himself alone.

Within the first scene, then, Berowne reveals his own arguments against the academy to be sophistry, in what becomes only the first case of his "lightness" in and toward language, regarding words as ethically inconsequential displays. In Shakespeare's version of the age-old antagonism between seekers of absolute truth and persuaders to contingent opinion, Berowne becomes not only *homo rhetoricus* to Navarre's *homo seriosus*, but also the symbol of the ethical fears such an orator inspires.[9] By undermining Berowne even as he voices positions upheld elsewhere in the play and in Shakespeare's lyrics, the playwright complicates his examination, introduced with Navarre, of the relationships between language and its speaker. At the same time he denies the audience any simple identification with a superior character, provoking (to quote Feste) "misprision in the highest degree" by many a frustrated scholar in search of Shakespeare's own positionality. Like the Vice Ambidexter of *Cambises* who "plays with both hands," this drama plays with both sides — not only of this philosophical debate over the ability of language to express truths but also of the social split between the world of courtly lyric and its critics. From what is perhaps a safer distance as narrative playwright, especially given the topical satire in *Love's Labour's Lost,* Shakespeare can represent court culture without being easily located (and hence dismissed), either by courtly insiders or critical outsiders.

Shakespeare usually hints at his dramatic ending in his opening scenes, but without revealing the intervening narrative twists that will modify its meaning; here Navarre's opening poetry hints at his later language and the dramatic conflicts it will induce. While the ascetic academe will only be realized ironically by the ladies' assignment of penitential tasks for the lords in the play's final scene, the fulfillment of the stylistic signals encoded in Navarre's sonnetlike decree arrives earlier, when the men become lyricists. His verse resounds when the men turn to more conventional sonnets of erotic desire in act 4. Forsworn because of "necessity," state policy, and now their desire for the ladies, each nobleman begins secretly to woo his beloved through verse. What better medium for the task than the sonnet, used with the same putative aim (as well as the same subtext of actual male competition) by Petrarch, the Pléiade, Gascoigne, Sidney and, in the 1590s, a myriad of lesser talents? The attempt becomes a predictably comical satire on Elizabethan courtliness.

The scene immediately preceding the group poetasting (4.2) reveals the ill-fated reception of Berowne's first try at love poetry, foreshadowing the other lords' fortunes and increasing the audience's ironic distance from the lyricists. Like Longaville's sonnet to come, Berowne's poem is misguided in trying to justify its betrayal of their "academe" through conventional praise of a lady too discriminating to be moved by sophistical wordplay. But Berowne's poem has also been literally misguided, by his hired hand Costard; not altogether clownishly, he confuses it with Armado's absurdly inappropriate love letter to Jaquenetta. Armado, a step ahead in his suit, is the comic foil and even the unwitting model for the loving lords. Just as his love gestures forecast Berowne's, with a difference in wit but not in kind, so will Berowne's inability to properly "deliver" his poem echo after. Because the difficulties of communication are literalized, several of the courtly lyrics within *Love's Labour's Lost* come to resemble personal letters more than social performances; these poems are susceptible to all the difficulties of reading and interpretation by, as well as indirect delivery to, their "proper" audience. The awkwardness of this mediation, as sonnets are sent by indifferent messengers and read apart from the goodwill (or at least passionate energy) of their composers, accentuates the poetry's conventional staleness. We first hear Berowne's sonnet, therefore, as it is translated into speech for Armado's illiterate beloved and subjected to the ludicrous yet surprisingly accurate appraisal of Holofernes: "let me supervise the canzonet. Here are only numbers ratified; but for the elegancy, facility, and golden cadence of poesy, *caret*" (4.2.116–18). The grandiloquent schoolmaster is the wrong audience, of course, but later sharp-witted Rosaline will voice an almost identical criticism of another of Berowne's verse attempts:

> The numbers true; and, were the numbering too,
> I were the fairest goddess on the ground:
> I am compar'd to twenty thousand fairs.
> O! he hath drawn my picture in his letter.
> *Princess.* Any thing like?
> *Ros.* Much in the letters, nothing in the praise.
>
> (5.2.35–40)

Reminiscent of the primary Elizabethan definition of "character" as a letter rather than a personality, her comment adds to Holofernes' formalist criticism another reason for dismissing the poem: its obvious lack of plausible correspondence to its subject, in sensory terms. Her (supposedly) inky complexion belies his conventional praise of her as the idealized Petrarchan fair lady, indicting his "perjured eye" on the most literal level—raising in a far simpler manner the issues of subjectivity and its derivation in distance from sensory experience so artfully played upon in *The Sonnets* (152; see Fineman). The lords' own sonnets, then, are surrounded and framed by these other signs of less-than-enthusiastic reception. As we shall see below, the French ladies' perspective is a forceful one; and even before act 5 we have been given adequate clues that these women are as unlikely to be moved by reading stale sonnets as is the illiterate Jaquenetta.

Enter the lovers. With Berowne's folly in mind, we watch the noblemen arrive to compose and be observed in turn by one another, like a set of Chinese boxes. As if to substantiate modern criticisms of the idolatrous narcissism (if not misogyny) implicit in Petrarchan poetics, Shakespeare's staging artfully uses the potential of theater to expose the limits of the single voice. For the young men are not only exposed by their compatriots and by the blatancy of their self-involvement but ultimately by the medium in which they are fictional characters, the medium that displaces the sonneteer's words from a page. Rather than hearing experience filtered through the male sonneteer's point of view, as in Sidney's and Shakespeare's collections, we are allowed to see the whole situation—rather like watching Astrophil onstage.[10] And as in the opening scene, the playwright exploits his unique authority to remain safely unseen, unlocated in body while potent in "voice."

The implied audience of the standard Elizabethan sonnet collection is undermined here (or perhaps more truly revealed as masculine) by having the lords recite to themselves in supposed solitude, rather than to the ladies—and then having them discover, to their discomfiture, that they have been overheard by men. The women are excluded from the scene of poetic composition aimed at them; no more than in Armado's case does the "extemporal god of rhyme" lurk here. Indeed, even when the would-be lovers finally confer in act 5, we never directly hear the lords' poetic courting: they will be foiled as Muscovite masquers, first by the craft of the ladies, who turn away from Moth's prepared compliments and mock the men, and then by Shakespeare's art, which has them "converse apart" (*Love's* 140) when they press their suits to the (wrong) "sign" of the woman they profess to love (cf. 5.2.160–309, a scene echoed in *Much Ado about Nothing*). Thus, as courtly lyric poets, these men are repeatedly presented at their worst: unaware, self-absorbed and isolated.

Later, we will see just how unappreciative their intended audience is.

Here, the mere logistics of communication are so tenuous that the prince would "drop the paper" on the ground, in a desperate hope that the right lady will pick up his poem (4.3.40)—a neat reversal on the convention of the silent lady dropping her glove as an opportunity for her would-be lover. (The lady must needs be silent to avoid being "cheap," which is the reputation ascribed to Rosaline, the loose-tongued dark lady of this play who later foils the prince's masqued wooing; by contrast, the male lover's loose tongue does not shame his body but his mind, the incorporeal location of male honor.)[11] This tangible problem of relaying the lyric message is not created but importantly compounded by bad practitioners.

And indeed, the sonnets themselves do not help the situation, being derivative and pedestrian verse. The king's verse, "So sweet a kiss the golden sun gives not," may resemble Shakespeare's sonnet 33 ("Full many a glorious morning have I seen") in its opening phrases, as Richard David suggests (Shakespeare, *Love's* 89n), but it does not develop the imagery in the same way. Rather than follow Shakespeare in recognizing the "ugly rack" of "basest clouds," or any other worldly intrusion that would complicate (and moralize) the scene, Navarre shifts associatively from dew to other tear-related images—and thus to self-display.

> So sweet a kiss the golden sun gives not
> To those fresh morning drops upon the rose,
> As thy eye-beams when their fresh rays have smote
> The night of dew that on my cheeks down flows:
> Nor shines the silver moon one half so bright
> Through the transparent bosom of the deep,
> As doth thy face through tears of mine give light
> Thou shin'st in every tear that I do weep:
> No drop but as a coach doth carry thee;
> So ridest thou triumphing in my woe.
> Do but behold the tears that swell in me,
> And they thy glory through my grief will show:
> But do not love thyself; then thou will keep
> My tears for glasses, and still make me weep.
> O queen of queens! how far dost thou excel,
> No thought can think, nor tongue of mortal tell.
>
> (4.3.24–39)

This extended sonnet is more like "A Valediction: On Weeping" without Donne's ironic ingenuity. When the king pleads "But do not love thyself," he does not suggest that the beloved would deprive the world of offspring, but merely that she would "keep / My tears for glasses, and still make me weep" (36–37). The lyric itself reinforces the poet's self-absorption as well as overflow of emotion, neatly matching the effect of its dramatic context. Moreover, the poem exaggerates the most predictable formal tics of Shakespearean sonnetizing—the division between segments, the disconnected final couplet (here doubled).

Nor do the sophistical poetic attempts of Berowne (in 4.2) and Longaville, seeking to legitimate their own oath-breaking, show remarkable invention or winning self-deflation in their rhetoric. Sadly, the ironic disregard for his own immorality that makes Berowne's discourse so intriguing disappears in his lyric. As a group, then, the lords can claim the formal correctness of numbers so disdainfully received in Berowne's earlier sally, but little more to their credit—and, as even Holofernes can discern, "Imitari is nothing" without the "jerks of invention" (4.2.120–21).

Holofernes' sixteenth-century prototypes theorized that true invention sprang from within the poet's imagination, negotiating between reason and perception. Sidney plays with this notion at the beginning of his sonnet sequence when Invention flees as Astrophil looks through others' "leaves" for his words, the muse appearing only when he finally looks in his own heart (presumably to find Stella's image) and writes. This does not necessarily mean the poet discards his literary models any more than his perception and reason, but it does imply that he at least filters language through his own mental faculties rather than being an "ape of fashion." In contrast to Sidney's rich and ironic use of the metaphor, when the king says "sweet leaves, shade folly" (41), he speaks quite literally, placing his sonnet among tree leaves. The audience hears more: the doomed attempt these lords make to "shade" or hide their own oath-breaking, self-display, and giddiness beneath the language of courtly love, creating a subtext all too apparent to the ladies. The mockery in the presentation of the lords' sonnets is manifold, in part illustrating the insufficiency of Petrarchan formulae alone, but also more ingeniously playing with various ironies and gaps in the relationship between the courtly speaker and his use of poetic discourse.

The lyrics are indeed uncomfortably far removed from the lords' usual style of communication, inadequate though that may be. Berowne agonizedly recognizes this and is disgusted by his "fall" into love language (although not by his equally hackneyed raillery against love): "I am toiling in a pitch—pitch that defiles . . . I do nothing in the world but lie, and lie in my throat" (2–3, 9–10).[12] Nor need one rely on Berowne's jaundiced testimony to recognize how far the lords have strayed from their conversational voices; even when they first addressed the ladies in 2.1, they did not speak in courtly compliments, instead becoming enamored (like other "naturally matched" lovers in Shakespeare's comedies) during battles of wit and skirmishes over state affairs. The poems do not indicate any obvious correspondence between other verbal skills and amateur poetasting. Indeed, as in the cases of Benedick in *Much Ado about Nothing* and bluff King Hal in *Henry V*, the inability to sonnetize seems oblique testimony to a more frank and "manly" affection. The contrast between courtly poetizing and the lords' usual style of communication among themselves is repeatedly remarked upon in 4.3, especially by the self-conscious Berowne. He does not believe in the claims of his own metaphors, as he makes explicit in criticizing Longaville's "defense" of perjury, so like his own: "This is the liver vein, which makes flesh a deity; / A green goose a goddess; pure, pure idolatry. / God amend us, God amend! we are much out of the way" (71–73). Unlike John Freccero's modern critique of Petrarchist substitution of self-inclosed language for referential signs, Berowne's complaint stresses the force of fleshly desire in creating this "pure" idolatry. Nevertheless the consequence of these critiques is similar: erotic poetry is discredited as a location for valid and sincerely believed praise of women. The pure is impure, an inversion with no middle term between goddess and green goose; the complex web of linguistic relationship and difference becomes simple comic antithesis, the speaker moreover imputing greater referential truth value to the debasing term than to the inflating. Berowne's voice remains only the wittiest of these lords, of course, and does not necessarily match the playwright's perspective—but the scene certainly supports Berowne's sense of courtly lyrical discourse, if not the lords' love, as "unreal." Their language of solitary lyric composition, as juxtaposed with their dialogues, appears nearly as formulaic, their sincerity as insincere, as that of the immature Romeo wooing *his* Rosaline.

Shakespeare keeps us comically detached from all four lords by allowing the "simple" rather than the witty ones to admit their own amateurishness and poetic inadequacy openly.[13] Despite Berowne's wry skepticism, he does not apply his critical awareness directly to his own sonnets, or show doubts as to their efficacy with Rosaline. He is working on a second poem in this scene, and in act 5 Rosaline testifies to having received still more verse from him. Berowne mocks being in love, but not his ability to move others with words. By contrast, Longaville laments, "I fear these stubborn lines lack power to move . . . These numbers will I tear, and write in prose" (4.3.52, 54). Dumain distinguishes his courtly gesture from his "true" experience, choosing to send a supplement to his poem: "This will I send, and something else more plain, / That shall express my true love's fasting pain" (4.3.118–19). (The irony of his aspiration to "true love" when forsworn seems lost on him.) Meanwhile the generally wittier king and Berowne neither question their own poetry's persuasiveness nor admit their guilt until exposed by events, having lectured their fellows at length. This converse relationship between verbal wit and morality is a familiar yet hardly comforting connection in many of Shakespeare's works. It is the biggest hypocrite, Berowne, who will "step . . . forth to whip hypocrisy" (148) and who has the rhetorical ability to rally their perjured spirits.[14]

Berowne accurately mocks "all three of you" lovers for similarly falling into clichés (4.3.157), although we do hear slightly different approaches to the lyric among the lords (three here, Berowne's previously). The distinctions reinforce the need to consider not just poetic form but the relationship between the two meanings of "character" when examining lyricism in drama. Berowne's poem is most like Longaville's, a defense of the indefensible oath-breaking, in neither case persuasive. To recognize and then inadequately color over immoral desire makes a more interesting character, perhaps, but a less persuasive lyricist. Longaville's poem is more fatuous and obvious in its misuse of metaphor to get free of the legal language that has made him untrue (the struggle between two types of discourse introduced in the play's opening now returning to haunt this failed sonnet). He claims she "being a goddess, I forswore not thee: / My vow was earthly, thou a heavenly love" (62–63). Moreover, the "heavenly rhetoric of [her] eye" is responsible for his action, not he (57). Berowne's sonnet, had it come after this, might seem an improvement on the same theme. But because we have already heard it deflated by its unintended audience, and know that Berowne has always known the better (his argument in act 1 that love is the truest teacher), and yet done the worse (swearing against it), his sonnet seems just as shallow and false. Even were it internally compelling, our awareness that its putative author regards such poetry as silly idolatry undermines its power to persuade. The distinction between the speaker and the lyric style he relies on to hide his personal guilt has been dramatized, so that neither of these poems can stand "on its own." Instead, the play's wit is premised upon the gaping gulf between lyric statement and its dramatic frame.

By comparison, the king's poetic imagery, equating tears with mirrors, the sea, and so forth, is merely self-indulgent, and Dumain's story of the wind and the rose seems almost charming.

Dum. [*reads his sonnet*].
    On a day, alack the day!
    Love, whose month is ever May,
    Spied a blossom passing fair
    Playing in the wanton air:
    Through the velvet leaves the wind,
    All unseen can passage find;
    That the lover, sick to death,
    Wish'd himself the heaven's breath.
    Air, quoth he, thy cheeks may blow;
    Air, would I might triumph so!
    But alack! my hand is sworn
    Ne'er to pluck thee from thy thorn:
    Vow, alack! for youth unmeet,
    Youth so apt to pluck a sweet.
    Do not call it sin in me,
    That I am forsworn for thee;
    Thou for whom Jove would swear
    Juno but an Ethiop were;
    And deny himself for Jove,
    Turning mortal for thy love.
                (4.3.98–117)

Dumain's tetrameter hearkens to a seemingly simpler song tradition and his use of the pathetic fallacy links the poet-lover's sensory experience with nature as well as art, as the wind finds "passage" through these "velvet leaves." Dumain's performance differs notably, not in the wit displayed but in the rhetorical strategy chosen and its adequacy for the purpose of winning these ladies. The difference could be broadly labeled as Petrarchan versus Ovidian (or, in contemporary terms, Sidneian sonneteering versus pastoral song). But perhaps most important is the difference in what is foregrounded: the poet's own mind and psychic turmoils, as in Longaville's sonnet, or the lover as type within nature and narrative, as here; the image as mental metaphor or as the expression of a sympathetic correspondence. With the ladies as audience, as we shall see, the latter style bodes better.

    To the extent that Dumain's simpler song and greater directness look forward to Shakespeare's comparatively successful lyric conclusion of the play in pastoral song, one is tempted to see his poem as unexpectedly the "best" as well as the last. However, it would be well to remark that his poem is derived from a literary tradition allied with the seduction poetry of Marlowe, in its carpe diem imagery of plucking the rose and the descent of Jove to deflower chaste maidens. Additionally, there may be intentional echoes of language from the 1591 court progresses here—hardly signs of "natural" rather than "literary" imitation. Like his peers, Dumain includes a reference to his oath-breaking, and uses the gods to enoble his illicit passion. The style and form are simpler and the breach of oath is not shamelessly explained away but merely presented; nevertheless, the poem is clearly related to those of the other courtiers as a display of (a different school of) rhetoric, and subject to the same accusations of unethical, derivative, and often merely decorative use of metaphor and imagery.

Although its differences in part account for the contemporary anthologists' attraction to Dumain's poem, within Shakespeare's drama it clearly remains part of the courtly gang of four's guilty posturing. The drama does not stop to allow more than momentary formalist criticism—anti-Petrarchist or otherwise—without regard to character and context. Even within the scene, the order of recitation (Berowne through Holofernes, the king, Longaville, Dumain) does not reveal any obvious pattern for assessment based on style alone. The poems always function as part of the fiction, and judged by their efficacy therein are equivalent failures. The slight variations between the poems and their speakers remain suggestive, but in its narrative "plot" of discovery, the scene highlights difference only in the level of rhetorical insincerity; Berowne has the most protracted comeuppance because he is the most complex character making the biggest false claim.

Careful reading of this scene reveals the countertendencies of formal and ethical evaluation, perpetuating the tension between character and discourse. In one sense, poetry seems to be presented as a specific *kind* of language skill, hence a craft, reserved for gifted practitioners—like Shakespeare. Good poets might be idiots savants (Dumain to an extent, or Holofernes at the end of the play) with a detachable skill; or (since even Dumain's poem is not very memorable or effective within the narrative, and the songs don't sound at all like the products of the pedant Holofernes' *inventio*), the relationship between a successful poet and his art may not be represented at all. Instead, the negative examples here make us wary and suggest an alternative: that the good poet incorporates linguistic awareness without trying to make rhetoric cover up a lack of ethics or a sensory lie, producing a lyricism correspondent to earthly experience and perception which could escape these courtly dead ends of vacuous prettiness and immoral sophistry.

Such artistry demands a poetic awareness beyond the lords' (or, as we shall see, the ladies'), and does not occur until—if indeed it occurs in *any* single passage—the poems at the end of the play, outside the courtly vocabulary. In other words, Shakespeare reserves unmocked poetic achievement for himself.

As in *A Midsummer Night's Dream,* where the playwright inserts the mechanicals' idea of theater to illuminate his own wittier imagination, Shakespeare's practice outshines that of his characters. The lords' sonnets make obvious the status of florid figurative language and ingenious conceits for these lovers: their words are not the means to express an experience or idea that a plainer style can't. Rather, they paint an elaborate veneer over weak ethical positions, in stanzas of whirling words only tenuously linked to their emotion of love. In context, then, the lords' travesties mock their immoral use of poetic language even more than the particular variety of lyrical discourse. Especially for twentieth-century readers influenced by a hearty tradition of ethical evaluations on the basis of style, this distinction deserves reiteration.[15] William Carroll observes that "there neither is nor can be any such thing as unadorned verse" (179). And although scholars recognize this play's complex ironies, the impossible dream of resolution through a formally identifiable plain style (unadorned, un-Petrarchan) and unmediated experience in some unrepresented offstage fictive future still haunts critical commentary, as when Mary Beth Rose concludes that in *Love's Labour's Lost* "the exchange of overblown rhetoric and narcissistic posturing for a plain style and shared experience *has not yet* come to pass" ("Sexual Love" 23; emphasis added). Regarding style, we had best not hold our collective breath.

Instead, we can attend to the complex play and dramatic function of the poems within the world actually represented onstage. The aristocrats' sonnetizing does mark a turning point in the play, displacing solitary lyric and its judgment by style alone with a scene that contains dialogue, an inevitable and uncontrollable audience, and the necessary address of that audience's response. Lyric as sonnet-writing is replaced at the end of the play by lyric as performed song, the way being paved by the intervening scenes. In the second part of 4.3, the lords begin to consider the larger social context in which lyric poetry appears as they banter and then rally to face "love" together. The complex relationship of style to speaker, a matter of epistemological and moral concern, is represented most richly in the discourse of Berowne.

Theatrically positioned closest to the audience's perspective in this "poet-within-a-poet" presentation, Berowne regards himself as the anti-Petrarchan in love, a reluctant Astrophil. Despite his lack of self-mastery and consistency, he repeatedly pretends to moral superiority over the other lords on the basis of his greater knowledge. Here, as at the play's start, he wishes (like the audience) to be the removed satirist, the voyeuristic "demigod" who watches and can therefore judge others without judging himself (76). But his words undo him:

> All three of you, to be thus much o'ershot?
> You found his mote; the king your mote did see;
> But I a beam do find in each of three.
> O! what a scene of foolery have I seen,
> Of sighs, of groans, of sorrow, and of teen;
> O! me with what strict patience have I sat . . .
> (157–62)

He would enlarge his importance by finding "a beam" in the eyes of *others* whereas the king saw merely "your mote"; Berowne's obvious perversion of Christ's parable, as well as our knowledge of his own unrevealed poetasting, deflates his presumed superiority. The dramatist thus uses his own superior position, his particular shaping of the character's language (and soon his narrative fate), to expose Berowne as one of the courtly party, implicated alongside his three companions before the theatrical audience. Similarly, by having Berowne adopt lyric discourse against his own judgment and then invoke his satiric removal from romance with equal bad faith, Shakespeare's satire glances at those who would posit stylistic superiority for either Mercutios or Romeos without attending to the spirit behind their letters, be they fashionably florid courtiers or "plain speaking" men who leave no place for the figurative, woman-worshipping world of the Elizabethan love lyric. Indeed, act 4 scene 3 discredits any simple distinction between these oft-opposed positionalities as it proceeds, as the conventions of courtly poetizing blur with the witty flytings of satiric banter.

Throughout the sonneteering scene, Berowne provides the testing ground that mocks but defines the courtly. He began the scene alone, sounding like Don Armado with his oath "By the world" and his mannered (and referentially inaccurate) comparisons: "Well, she hath one o' my sonnets already: the clown bore it, the fool sent it, and the lady hath it: sweet clown, sweeter fool, sweetest lady!" (114–15). In fact it is Jaquenetta who has Berowne's poem, and while she *may* be no "wench" or "damsel," as serves Costard's evasive linguistic turn, she is assuredly no "lady." Without his knowledge, Berowne has become confused with Don Adriano de Armado. And indeed, during the first three acts (before the appearance of Holofernes as the Spaniard's match) Berowne is closely aligned with Armado not only in the confusion of their missives but also in their mixed attitude toward rhyme: Armado turns to rhyme because he knows his passion is "unreasonable" and hypocritical, "And how can that be true love which is falsely attempted?" (1.2.160–61). In their reaction to love and their use of rhyme, significant difference between the pseudo-Petrarchan Spaniard and anti-Petrarchan satirist disappears. Armado's question remains unresolved, demanding more than a choice of plain or fancy poetic techniques.[16]

Nor does the force of this question disappear when the lords stop their conscious composition. After being exposed by the unexpected return of the "sweet clown" Costard with that very different "lady," Jaquenetta, Berowne's banter with Navarre will shift about for the remainder of the scene, leaping from his casually sardonic wit, to romantic hyperboles, to anti-Petrarchan disdain. The humor resides in his blatant self-contradiction, and privileges no stylistic stance; indeed, we are forced to meditate upon the fluid boundaries between styles. To look for the single "true" perspective of Berowne in all this (as has many an eminent critic since Pater) is to miss the fracturing of such a concept that Shakespeare dramatizes through his creation. Indeed, the playwright exploits the volatility of this lord's representation, its potential for dynamic variation during the time of performance, to highlight style both as a facet of and separable from character (an especially duplicitous word for an actor).

Berowne has several moments in the latter part of 4.3 which exemplify the increasing complexity of the play's analysis of rhetoric, but also reveal the lords' courtly limitations ever more clearly. The first occurs when he invokes the metaphor of painting. Finally recognizing the inadequacy of his words to describe Rosaline, Berowne implies that poetic praise, like cosmetics, debases rather than exalts the naturally beautiful:

> Lend me the flourish of all gentle tongues,—
> Fie, painted rhetoric! O! she needs it not:
> To things of sale a seller's praise belongs;
> She passes praise; then praise too short doth blot.
>
> (234–37)

Dismissal of such "selling" may glance at the extravagant offers of Marlowe's lyrical seductions (especially apt if the Ralegh "school of night" is being satirized by this "academe"),[17] but it more immediately undermines the lords' courtly sonneteering. Rather than associate hyperbolic versions of love and romance with the aristocratic speakers we have just heard and the court in which they developed, Berowne tries to discredit "painted rhetoric" as part of the crass mercantile world. Purity nevertheless has its cost, the logic of this speech leading to silence. The link between inflated Petrarchism and money is reminiscent of Bassanio searching for his "golden fleece" (Portia) in act 1 of *The Merchant of Venice,* another play of the lyrical period in which commerce traffics perilously near the landscape of moonlit romance; Bassanio's financial needs induce the explicit admission of what Berowne's courtly purity would deny, the insertion of emergent capitalism and entrepreneurial venturing into the erotic narrative of aristocratic purity and blood ties. In *Love's Labour's Lost,* no one can keep track of numbers or money yet they intrude everywhere, making obvious what is usually suppressed in romantic versions of aristocratic courtship, that the relationship has an economic as well as erotic value for the speaker.

Despite Berowne's vehement protest, then, which echoes the princess of France's opening speech (as well as, more ironically, sonnets by Sidney and Shakespeare), love may blossom and supersede pragmatic concerns within Shakespeare's dramatic world—but *not* by simply denying mercantilism and exchange, be it of money or women. Indeed, the discussion of money in act 2 spurred these love suits. Similarly, Berowne soon will regroup and argue that painting has become "nature's" province, incorporating potentially satiric realities into the discourse of desire. Yet as we shall see in the last act's courtly sparring, this vexatious vocabulary of selling will continue to intrude as a perceived insult among the aristocrats, allowing the ladies (who have their own rigorous—and "unproductive"—standards of courtly purity) to chastise their lovers thoroughly.

Even in this single speech of Berowne's, no single perspective toward love rhetoric provides conclusory rest, a technique expanded in subsequent dialogue between the lover and his mocking friends. His rejection of rhetorical praise remains inscribed in quatrain form, a sign of "infection" either by love or by the seemingly inescapable artifice of courtly discourse among the aristocrats, despite the speaker's own intentions. For the lords, some manner of rhetorical painting or flourish remains unavoidable if they wish to be heard. Nevertheless, this speech does signal a new, albeit fleeting, recognition on Berowne's part that his beloved could in fact be worthy without his rhetoric. This is quite a shift from the man who began the scene "toiling in pitch" that "defiles" (the dark eyes of Rosaline, as well as his passion and verse). He is seeing value outside himself, for a moment. Thus he temporarily moves beyond the earlier Petrarchan/anti-Petrarchan dichotomy of idealized beauty/imperfect woman, having recognized an alternative third term: that the woman might be earthly and yet worthy, her value created not so much by his words in an effort to justify his desire as by her qualities. Given that the men's subsequent quest to win the ladies as marriage partners matches the emergent Protestant ideology that regarded the wife as a necessary earthly "help-meet," this narrative and verbal shift may reflect the middle-class playwright's more than the character's social perspective (which may also be why it appears to us a move toward "common sense").

But even if we confine our view to the fictional landscape, a new poetic attitude clearly accompanies Berowne's altered state. A second key moment occurs as he reevaluates the beloved as poetic topic, extemporizing upon his "black beauty" without simply writing an anti-Petrarchan exposé of "false compare" (even one so artful as Shakespeare's sonnet 130). His claims are not just denials of the existence of traditional beauty but positive assertions of her "new" and paradoxically more beautiful "black fair." The antitheses supersede simple dichotomies of nature and art, and of plain versus Petrarchan style, while holding on to the rhetorical power of Petrarchist techniques such as paradox and the oxymoron—since these devices of differentiation can be used to distinguish this lady from others. Coming after Moth's song of colors ("If she be made of white and red" at 1.2.92–99) as a dialogue between two would-be sonneteers en route to the play's own paradoxical ending, such love poetry becomes particularly significant in dramatizing what was previously the lyricist's internal struggle:

> O! who can give an oath? where is a book?
> That I may swear beauty doth beauty lack,
> If that she learn not of her eye to look:
> No face is fair that is not full so black.
> *King.* O paradox! Black is the badge of hell,
> The hue of dungeons and the school of night;
> And beauty's crest becomes the heavens well.
> *Ber.* Devils soonest tempt, resembling spirits of light.
> O! if in black my lady's brows be deck'd,
> It mourns that painting and usurping hair
> Should ravish doters with a false aspect;
> And therefore is she born to make black fair.
> Her favour turns the fashion of the days,
> For native blood is counted painting now:

> And therefore red, that would avoid dispraise,
> Paints itself black to imitate her brow.
>
> (4.3.246–61)

The obvious self-parody in wishing to swear another oath makes the banter more amusing, if not any more legitimating for Berowne's own worthiness as a lover. Using a word such as "beauty" doubly (in the second line cited above) characterizes courtly wit; some have seen it as a vestigial mannerism that Shakespeare needed to get out of his system before he could write his "mature" verse. Yet this judgment also may imply that getting beyond one's attentiveness to the indeterminacy of the word (if possible) is mature, an aesthetic dismissive not only of puns and setting "the word against the word." It dismisses Shakespeare's sonnets as well as Sidney's, a dominant lyric style within Elizabethan culture. Here, such wordplay clearly signals Shakespeare's engagement with Sidneian rhetoric and the problems of lyric praise, and serves as a prelude to Berowne's unsettling of simple terms of aesthetic judgment based on vision alone.

Amusingly, Berowne's praise of blackness incorporates one of very few particular facts we learn about the looks of these much-praised ladies. Unlike the poem Rosaline criticizes, this passage at least attempts to represent her, momentarily acknowledging "this thing of darkness" before relying on paradox to incorporate her back into the Petrarchan schema. As in most Elizabethan lyrics, the attributes of the supposed inspiration remain for the most part amorphous or unspecified. Only when sensory perception of one body part or quality actively counters a conventional phrase of praise, as in the case of Stella's black eyes in *Astrophil and Stella*, must the lady's idiosyncrasies be considered. This moment of poetic emphasis on the particularity of Rosaline furthermore befits its theatrical context, which demands attention to the world of nonlinguistic, unidealized signs as well. Unlike Moth's lyric, which initiated the poetic inquiry into colors, nature, and art by questioning the accuracy of the "signs" women give in blushing and blanching, here the easy distinction between colors is dismissed in order to praise rather than satirize the lady.[18] Berowne articulates the problem with earlier rejections of "art" or "painting" made by the princess, and as such is not deflating figurative rhetoric at all; he is merely adapting it to an altered object. In the end, darkness does not explode the rhetoric or terms of praise but instead calls attention to *all* styles as conventional and strategic.

The complexity of such a lyric vision appears in Berowne's protestation that if Rosaline is not brightness, "My eyes are then no eyes, nor I Berowne" (228). Certainly the punning on the poetic I and his viewing eye is among the devices Shakespeare employs in his own sonnets to create his distinctive lyric subjectivity, as Joel Fineman has so thoroughly explored. Even while immersed in courtly schemes, then, this move toward the particularized and toward sensory complexity both seems more akin to Shakespeare's sonneteering and matches the play's narrative trajectory toward modern love. This love speech also addresses that crucial third basic element of rhetoric, an audience, whose role increases as the lovers attempt to act on their passions.

Although Shakespeare is clearly directing the theatrical audience to notice how style shapes and varies with perception, it is not clear that Berowne (any more than Astrophil) actually recognizes greater value or truth in his less conventional praise; he is simply on the defensive, faced with a "hostile" audience. Berowne remains *homo rhetoricus*. Yates (*Study*) felt this was the unironic core of Shakespeare's thought, and William Carroll regards Berowne's "Promethean fire" speech as a "genuinely poetic transformation through language" of his sonneteering impulse, praising it as a sign of "private intensification" (150–51). Perhaps this is instead the most complex Sidneian echo of all, invoking his theories from the *Apology*. Whether Berowne believes his rousing defense of love remains highly questionable. It may just be one more *débat* position, though creating images of sufficient *energeia* to hearten his peers. In the latter part of 4.3, Berowne parodies Sidney's defense of poetry as praxis, calling his friends "to arms" as suitors; he trivializes the equally serious issue of oaths and the spirit of charity investigated in several of Shakespeare's lyrical plays (*The Merchant of Venice* is again especially relevant). In the end, Berowne disconcertingly implies that his eloquence is all a ploy to distract attention from their guilt and immoral desire. After his praise and suggestion that they find "some strange pastime" to please the ladies ("For revels, dances, masks, and merry hours, / Forerun fair Love, strewing her way with flowers" [4.3.375–76]), he recognizes their own guilt and discredits the ladies, too. He does so in the conventional anti-Petrarchan fashion, opposing idealized goddesses with cheap unworthy "wenches" (once more presented as the reality). No idealizing climb up a Neoplatonic ladder here; his aim is to "beat the time," to purchase the goods before the punishment:

> Allons! allons! Sow'd cockle reap'd no corn;
> And justice always whirls in equal measure:

> Light wenches may prove plagues to men forsworn;
> If so, our copper buys no better treasure.
>
> (4. 3.379–82)

By the end of this scene, despite the repeated cues and emphasis on whirling words, disarmed by (or choosing to hear only) the oft-quoted Promethean fire speech, many auditors discount the distance between the lords' use of language as display and as a means to truth. Hence these closing lines become a contradiction, a puzzle to be explained away. But it seems more to the point that Berowne, like the play itself, concludes by displacing easy resolution. Being a smart immoral wit, he has chosen to make his oaths light and knows it, even before the ladies "unmask" them in act 5, making them "again forsworn in will and error" (5.2.471).

Thus he comes closest to our own perspective—and not merely by sitting in a tree observing, the passive role of the audience he shared in the sonneteering segment. Rather, through his awareness, knowledge, and wit, and his somewhat jarring mix between satiric and romantic love speech, Berowne assumes an active, critical role which calls attention to the theater audience's equivalently various possible responses to different strategies of lyric discourse and desire.

As did Sidney in *The Lady of May,* Berowne tries to discard what is putatively the corrupt version of courtliness only to be co-opted by its greater power and the inability to articulate a position outside its terms. Berowne fails to translate his satiric abilities into effective courtly art when the ladies appear. But for Shakespeare and his audience in the theater, the stylistic complexity of the last two acts provides an opportunity to look beyond opposition. Using the resources of drama, the playwright can allude to his own and others' sonnets without just re-presenting their rhetorical struggles; rather, he frames the lyricist with other styles of speech, the "great feast of languages" which not only mocks excesses but shows all styles to be partial.[19] Long before the idea of *heteroglossia* was articulated by Mikhail Bakhtin, *Love's Labour's Lost* deflates the pretensions to authority on formal grounds of any single voice, be it Petrarchist or satiric, within its narrative.

Dissension in the Ranks:
Lords, Ladies, and a Worthier Lyricism

The most compelling contrast regarding love language within the play is not ultimately between Berowne and the other lords, but between the lords and ladies. The female countervoice, although most fully rendered and topically suggestive in the play's conclusion, parallels the men's in being announced from the start. When the women first appear, the princess chastises Boyet's conventional courtly compliments in words that introduce the criticism of poetic praise as basely mercantile and inform our reception of the sonnets to come:

> Good Lord Boyet, my beauty, though but mean,
> Needs not the painted flourish of your praise:
> Beauty is bought by judgment of the eye,
> Not utter'd by base sale of chapmen's tongues.
> I am less proud to hear you tell my worth
> Than you much willing to be counted wise
> In spending your wit in the praise of mine.
>
> (2.1.13–19)

Worth is based in sensory experience for the pragmatic ladies, a realm displaced by rhetoric in Navarre's academe. Rosaline thus would hardly value Berowne's sophistical excuse for oath-breaking ("Ah! never faith could hold, if not to beauty vow'd; / Though to myself forsworn, to thee I'll faithful prove" [4.2.102–3]) or his idolatrous closing antithesis ("Celestial as thou art, O! pardon love this wrong, / That sings heaven's praise with such an earthly tongue" [113–14]). The princess's perspective encourages a critical reading of the lords' sonnets, as we know in advance the demanding standards of their intended audience. The juxtaposition makes the men appear all the sillier.

Which is not to say that the ladies' view is the correct one, nor that Shakespeare agrees with their simple appeal to sense perception—clearly problematic for a professional writer, both aesthetically and materially. Indeed, the princess's opposition between "painted" words and visual perception is undermined by her own use of metaphor (one blurring vision and discourse, at that), and can lead only to silent appreciation. Her notion taken literally would destroy communication just as surely as her final test of the king's love will isolate him from all community. The ladies, then, present a commonsense view that deflates overt forms of verbal pretension, but they do not resolve the stylistic problems inherent in language and especially poetizing. Nevertheless, Shakespeare does allow the ladies (unlike the lords) to state their views without overt and direct mockery, and their perspective shapes the dramatic reception of the lords' courtly performances to their detriment and discomfiture.

In the final act, courtly lyricism is set in a more complicated relationship to its gendered audiences. When the men visit as Muscovite masquers, the women refuse to play along with courtly conventions, and mock both the men's lyrical discourse and their masquing. While the men pretend to be strangers, the women more subtly pretend to be one another—a harder trick to expose. As in *Much Ado about Nothing*'s scene of masked dancing, the ladies deflate the men's presumptions of superiority; they both see through the men's disguises and show their greater skill in using masks. This gendered reversal of the knowledge gap leads to the lords' most thorough comeuppance. The women similarly hide their vulnerability behind a false front, but here (in contrast to the sonneteering scene, where the critical lords were hypocritically denying their equal guilt) they do so only in reaction to the men's attempt at an unfair advantage, and without violating any oaths. Thus as in Shakespeare's later comedies, the ladies are presented as more shrewd and intelligent than their mates, even as they are being employed by the playwright to displace the courtly ethos of idealizing femininity. Ironically, they serve as the tools for his romanticization of companionate marriage, an ideology arguably working against the power awarded aristocratic women by elite privilege.

The French ladies' exchange of identity dramatizes the courtly lovers' shallowness in wooing, for none discerns his beloved without seeing her face. But the ladies are not content to use appearances alone to outwit the men; they also use their skill with words, exemplified earlier in their critical reception of poetry, to debilitate the laboring lovers. Rosaline, playing the princess, is especially sharp in detecting any inflated or obviously poetic expression and making it a reason to discredit the speaker's emotional authenticity. When the Muscovites speak of having "measur'd many miles / To tread a measure," she deflates their loosely figurative punning with a request for arithmetical calculation of the distance (5.2.184–85). She undermines the king's wooing by demanding a sensory correspondence between his compliments and her appearance, and then turns the now-familiar metaphors of tears and planetary orbs against him (with the same reference to the moon's fickleness used against Romeo by a skeptical Juliet). The king pleads for her to unmask:

> Vouchsafe to show the sunshine of your face,
> That we, like savages, may worship it.
> *Ros.* My face is but a moon, and clouded too.
> *King.* Blessed are clouds, to do as such clouds do!
> Vouchsafe, bright moon, and these thy stars, to shine,

> Those clouds remov'd, upon our watery eyne.
> *Ros.* O vain petitioner! beg a greater matter;
> Thou now requests but moonshine in the water.
>
> (5.2.201–8)

She obviously finds him "vain" in both senses, and thus will continue to toy with him. Beginning to dance and then stopping, she retorts "thus change I like the moon" (212). Her wit exemplifies the difficulty for the poet-lover in controlling interpretation, even when speaking his own words. Rather than allowing the king to delimit his metaphor's particular applicability, she exploits the possibility for other analogies between her symbolic representation and herself. Like the "moon goddess" Queen Elizabeth presiding over the courtly progresses, this player-queen preempts authorial desire, making her suitor's text the locus of her play.

Moreover, as she catches the king in his own web of metaphors, Rosaline reiterates the conflict between mercantile and courtly romance vocabularies:

> *King.* More measure of this measure: be not nice.
> *Ros.* We can afford no more at such a price.
> *King.* Price you yourselves: what buys your company?
> *Ros.* Your absence only.
> *King.*   That can never be.
>
> (5.2.222–25)

Since it is only the lords' absence that buys the ladies' company (not a Petrarchan paradox but an extralinguistic impossibility), she can retort, "Then cannot we be bought" (226). She extends his figurative language to expose the mercenary motive of possession metaphorically associated with it, as well as glancing at many a Petrarchan sonneteer's tendency to delight more in the verbal fiction of his absent lady (her "sign") than he does in the living woman.[20] Thus Rosaline uses the free play of words as a strategy to call greater attention to herself as the putative but not actual subject of his speech, and therefore reclaim her place as more than a poetic topic.

Of course, how seriously or sincerely we, as the actual audience, take her criticism depends on our own interpretive choices: because exact bodily representation is precisely what the Elizabethan use of boy actors prevented, attention to this scene's theatricality counters the reading of her words as a protofeminist objection to Petrarchism. Similarly, we may or may not credit the parallelism in temperament between this boy-imitating-female-prince-imitating-moon onstage and the imperiously sardonic female prince of England who played the moon goddess at court. But whichever interpretation one stresses, the men are temporarily humbled. Even Berowne, again put down by Rosaline, gives up in his attempt to speak for the group. And yet the problem of desire and its discourse will not die, and so Berowne keeps talking despite himself, like a Mercutio in love. He continues his pattern of rhetorical implosion, perhaps inevitably, for one cannot woo without choosing some style and the ladies' sense of decorum, as becomes progressively more apparent, is so rigorous that it leads logically to silence. Their purity cannot be satisfied and instead induces contradictory responses from their wooers. Berowne's famous avowal to exchange "three-pil'd hyperbole" for "russet yeas and honest kersey noes" is nevertheless expressed in sonnet form, this time forswearing figurative speech rather than oaths:

> O! never will I trust to speeches penn'd,
> Nor to the motion of a school-boy's tongue,
> Nor never come in visor to my friend,
> Nor woo in rhyme, like a blind harper's song,
> Taffeta phrases, silken terms precise,
> Three-pil'd hyperboles, spruce affection,
> Figures pedantical; these summer flies
> Have blown me full of maggot ostentation:
> I do forswear them; and I here protest,
> By this white glove (how white the hand, God knows),
> Henceforth my wooing mind shall be express'd
> In russet yeas and honest kersey noes:
> And, to begin: Wench,—so God help me, law!—
> My love to thee is sound, sans crack or flaw.
> (5.2. 402–15)

This comical sonnet may show more self-awareness than the earlier attempts, but it is hardly the unambivalent renunciation of wooing in rhyme he professes. It exemplifies the desire, if not the need, to use lyric form even as its stated message chastises fashionable lyric style, signaling the enduring power of the courtly world in shaping language and emotion. Berowne's mockery is more specifically aimed at verbal style than at the aristocratic ideology framing it, for unless one believes these lords intend to abandon their positions permanently, the prediction of sartorial simplicity remains entirely metaphoric. Rosaline's rejoinder "Sans 'sans'" (416) echoes the ladies' earlier demands for directness but also glances beyond his fashionable diction to embrace her own expression of that objection; the playwright thus implies the impossibility of attaining absolute purity and exact referentiality within, or conversely escaping from, the symbolic order. With exquisite irony, the word dismissed for its pretentiousness is the only one in the native tongue of these fictionally French characters. Thus despite numerous scholarly attempts to interpret this speech as a rejection of "the courtly-love syndrome as sterile, shallow, and static" (Rose, *Expense* 35), Berowne's lapse here signifies more than "a trick / Of the old rage" (416–17).

These dramatic interchanges demand attention to context and intent, defying a formalist aesthetic based on the word alone. But they also illustrate the difficulties of extrapolating from the word to the larger sense of "character" or that amorphous concept, the "spirit" behind the letter. Similarly, one easily discerns the critical wit and power of the ladies in *Love's Labour's Lost,* but has a harder task in articulating the functions of the play's representation of female power. The women's ability to outwit and educate the men in the matter of manners befits an Elizabethan courtly show, as when the queen tamed the Savage Man at Kenilworth or toyed with her princely suitors. But does the representation of these ladies serve Elizabeth's courtly terms of female sovereignty, or undermine them? Does the Frenchwomen's mockery simply delay and hence increase the men's erotic satisfaction, or does it preserve female invulnerability as requisite to power, hence implying the lords' labors will indeed be "lost"? To hypothesize answers, we need first to consider the impact of one more comical courtly event involving more than the lords and ladies, one which broadens and complicates the societal representation by positing a sympathetic perspective outside the aristocracy.

Up until the play's last scene, the ladies have functioned primarily as foils to the lords' wooing, but now the social picture shifts slightly. A different form of performance accents the importance of the spirit as well as the mode of speech, and it foregrounds class differences in the process. The pageant of the Nine Worthies, although again a courtly genre and performed at the lords' behest in honor of the ladies, nevertheless reinforces the gap between aristocrats and actors—and directs our attention toward the latter. The pageant re-views the issues of artistic intention, style, and audience relationship presented in the sonneteering scene, in a way that further displaces the authority of courtly aesthetics. Here too is a different kind of relationship between speaking groups. Rather than viewing a simple series of overheard speakers or even a scene of foiled romantic bantering, we now attend a more anarchic play among levels of discourse, conscious artistic display, and visual data as well.

The lords have been accused of using art deceptively, hiding their identities in a way that their female audience believes is designed to discredit them; lyrical language has been a tool in this masquing deceit. Now exposed and forced to watch another entertainment which they commissioned, the lords assume the courtly and (given their history) hypocritical role of refusing to take the humbler performers seriously. The sonneteers' language of love is for a time displaced by a self-conscious piece of artistic presentation that brings the play full circle, back to the images of heroism Navarre idealized in his opening decree. The prince watches a travesty, not only of a courtly pageant but also of the mythic fame to which he aspired. Even in the wake of love's folly, heroic "worthiness" is not presented as any more serious. Aptly, Berowne does not worry about the impact of this pageant on the ladies' opinion of them, unlike the would-be heroic king: the former has had his amorous rhetoric deflated and cannot be further shamed, whereas the king has professed ideals that can be undermined by the presence of these unworthy Worthies as his servants.

Despite their different reaction to news of the impending pageant, Berowne soon fades in with "the gentles"—including his personal foil as regards masculinity, "please-man" Boyet (whom Berowne has just insulted by accusing "a smock shall be your shroud" [463, 479]). During the pageant, wit and sex roles are displaced by class as the most significant mark of difference. The subtler factiousness and gender differentiation among courtly stylists becomes insignificant when contrasted with the Worthies; the antagonists Berowne and Boyet collapse into one (rather hollow) satiric voice, their interrupting banter all too repetitious. What ultimately turns out to be "worthy" is neither good mockery nor good performance, but charitable spirit and consciousness of one's social situation. Thus Costard the clown displaces the witty Moth (and perhaps even the witty lords) as the most knowledgeable and astute commentator, and a reforming Armado finally distinguishes himself from his linguistic double, Holofernes. And, as in the parallel masque of *A Midsummer Night's Dream,* each of these bungling hired players appears more distinct than the courtly watchers whom he serves.

The courtiers do their best to sabotage the show by making it yet another occasion to display their own wit, and they are effective in deflating the pedant and putting Sir Nathaniel "out of countenance." But they also expose themselves as quite a limited audience, easily countered by Costard, understood by Armado, and shown hollow by Holofernes. Costard points out that the man the lords mock as unworthy in art (the "o'erparted" Nathaniel) is in life "a marvellous good neighbor" and "an honest man," which is more than one could readily say of his mockers (5.2.579, 577, 576). The relative success of the Hercules "in minority" tableau (the performers get through it without interruption) confirms one solution for dealing with the absence of sensory correspondence to words, without falling into the falsehoods criticized by the ladies: Holofernes admits and explains the difference between idealized expectations about a Greek hero and what is seen onstage—the mote-like Moth. Obviously comic, this open acknowledgment still works more honestly and successfully than the lords' previous attempts to bridge a similar distance in art, especially that between the "dark lady" and the Petrarchan discourse used to praise her.

Costard and Armado break out of their roles entirely to create delightful commentary on their own fiction. Despite their naiveté and comical explanations, they display an appropriately humble awareness of their art's limits which is lacking in the wittier lords' discourse. Having heroically announced himself to be "Pompey surnam'd the Big," Costard responds to the princess's "great thanks, great Pompey": "'Tis not so much worth; but I hope I was perfect. I made a little fault in 'Great'" (554–55). Moreover, they are generous to others, including the heroes they play. Armado graciously defends his Worthy, Hector, from Dumain's copycat jabs: "The sweet warman is dead and rotten; sweet chucks, beat not the bones of the buried; when he breathed, he was a man. But I will forward with my device. Sweet royalty, bestow on me the sense of hearing" (653–57).

The pageant does not unambiguously encourage the theatrical audience to identify with the aristocrats, despite our shared position as watchers. As in the earlier sonneteering scene, we can see parallels in our positionality but also savor some ironic distance. This distance is most obvious as regards the men, but may also glance at the women, depending on how one evaluates the princess's argument for watching the show:

> Prin. . . . That sport best pleases that doth least know how.
>   Where zeal strives to content, and the contents
>   Die in the zeal of that which it presents;
>   Their form confounded makes most form in mirth,
>   When great things labouring perish in their birth.
> Ber. A right description of our sport, my lord.
>
> (5.2.512–17)

Mockery of others' inability to realize their desire, then, becomes the fundamental source of amusement. As Berowne perceives, this aesthetic finds equal fodder for fun in the lords' masquing as in the pageant, but despite this parallel the lords cannot desist from disrupting the latter show in their vain attempts at superior wit. Their rhyming and sophomoric insults are indeed, as even Holofernes discerns, "not generous, not gentle, not humble" (623)—the schoolmaster's awareness of his humiliation here investing his inevitable repetition of synonyms with poignance. This is not to say that the pageant, with its inferior verse and inept performers, would ever be "good" art; rather, its bad rhymes and confused players provide too easy a target to lend the lords' satiric mocks any distinction, any witty profundity.

The women, who desire to laugh at the show's confounded attempts and yet are kind to the performers, seem more complex. As an audience member if not in her pronouncements, the princess seems to display a more "generous" humor, one that revises what is "gentle." As cited above, she thanks Costard for his performance as Pompey; and when Armado wishes, despite the lords' quips, that royalty "bestow on me the sense of hearing," the princess graciously prompts, "Speak, brave Hector; we are much delighted" (5.2.656–58). The princess does not actively conspire to derail the well-meaning actors.

The princess's aesthetic seems one of "unnatural" mirth in watching failure, the abortive birth of great things. But the actual performance which she encourages (repeatedly, despite the male mocks) produces vital delight as well: the absurd and funny wordplay, and especially the exchanges between performers and audience which assert community even in the face of abuse. While Anne Righter [Barton] may be formally correct to blame the performers for their confusion of boundaries between art and reality, hence provoking their interruption, the charm and fitful eloquence Shakespeare accords to these bumbling, well-meaning amateurs militates against her emphasis.[21] One could even argue that the Worthies do not so much misunderstand categories as value the larger context of their art more than its discrete form. They are sensitive to their audience's hostility, and recognize that actual events may take precedence over artistic performance—as do the ladies. Their "art" does fade before "real life," the fluid line being irreparably crossed when Armado speaks of "Hector surmounted" (662). His words invoke for Costard the truly sir-mounted Jaquenetta, and a quarrel ensues. (Some argue that the stage direction six lines earlier, "Berowne steps forth," suggests his whispering to Costard the grounds for this fight; if so, it is one more instance of the lords' self-aggrandizement at their servants' expense). Foreshadowing the breakup of the comedy to come, the "confounded form" of this pageant nevertheless suggests a source of "merriment" beyond mockery, in its exuberance and the communal spirit of its performers. This too implies an aesthetic more applicable to this play (and

Shakespeare's comedies) as a whole than the courtly humor of the witty and lyrical lords can encompass.

The pageant to some extent qualifies our regard for the courtiers, both male and female. Are we to align with the ladies as more generous courtly watchers, or see their aesthetic of mockery as part of the court's limitation? This latter question arises during the pageant and remains applicable afterwards, when the women determine the play's indeterminate conclusion. Ultimately, I would argue that the play presents an artistic and social world too complicated for the ladies' simply sensible solutions. They do provide a source of resolution, just as the female monarch watching Gascoigne's or Sidney's court pageants got the last word. Certainly the courtly women exert ethical force in attempting to realize an idealistic correspondence between the lords' use of language and their "spirits" or sensory experience through punishments; critics such as Thomas Greene and William Carroll have impressively defended the ladies' superiority. As witty strong women, too, they appeal to feminist reinterpretation (Marilyn French being among the earliest and most energetic partisans), as they seem to defy the romance plot and its courtly techniques which would seduce them into being the objects of love rather than agents. All this is true, and yet simplifies the issues foregrounded by the language and performances at the end of the play.

Not only were they originally dressed-up boy actors rather than courtly ladies, thus (according to Lisa Jardine and others) blurring gender to thwart easy identification. The play also allows if not encourages a subtext for the ladies of unspoken positive reaction to the Navarrese lords, whom the women don't absolutely reject or ignore, so that their potentially subversive female power within the fiction may still be discredited or at least strongly tempered in performance today. More overtly, within the fiction they soon resume their mockery of the lords; thus the ladies embody the satiric impulse which must be qualified if it is not to become anticomedic in its universal destructiveness. Even when benefiting from the labor and advice of a "good" honest man, such as the hunter in 4.1, the ladies manage to silence men, if not by overt raillery then by their superior quickness. Only Boyet seems simply to enjoy it. To the extent we regard these as representations of women, then, their wit undermines Carroll's gendering of that trait: "Wit is 'sharp,' 'piercing,' or 'cutting' in the play; hence masculine" (137). Cutting, yes—but in its effective moments of destruction, often identified with feminine rather than masculine power. These are indeed Elizabethan ladies.

In Shakespeare's play, the feminized impulse toward satire (and the analogy with the actual female sovereign) remains incomplete, for the ladies are willing to take the men finally if they do penance in the fairy-tale form of yearlong quests. The women agree to a "world-without-end bargain" with lords they have exposed as less witty and "gracious," not matching their own terms of courtliness (781). Thus Shakespeare has the ladies go "against character" to advocate, albeit tentatively, a constructive comic vision. They will marry the men when they have learned by sensory experience. Yet this seeming victory for eros still has a dubious dimension.

The need to defer an aristocratic bond between the sexes here oddly prefigures and yet inverts the logic of E. M. Forster's deferential conclusion to *A Passage to India,* in which the divisions created by imperialism and race subsume and displace the problems of heterosexual romance, but cannot themselves be surmounted by individuals ("not yet . . . not there"). From a twentieth-century perspective, one might read the delay in *Love's Labour's Lost* as a deeply satiric comment on marriage as an inadequate comic solution, although this is most likely anachronistic and certainly runs counter to Shakespeare's own innovative practice of romantic comedy. Rather, the deferral here evades confronting the systemic problems adhering in the patriarchal institution of marriage (obliquely made the stuff of drama by Shakespeare's comic inversion of gender superiority) by turning back to the lords as individuals whose subtle differences demand slightly varying forms of penitence. Yet even if this move allows the goal of marriage after reformation to be accepted uncritically, the men appear to have limited potential for success. When Rosaline demands Berowne make the incurably ill laugh, he seems "sans" true reformation or perhaps even understanding of his year's duty. Having acknowledged that "To move wild laughter in the throat of death? / It cannot be; it is impossible: / Mirth cannot move a soul in agony" (5.2.847–49), he retreats into a typical quipping couplet: "A twelve-month! well, befall what will befall, / I'll jest a twelvemonth in an hospital" (5.2.862–63). For us at least, Rosaline's "punishment" of Berowne reinforces this entire act's emphasis on attending to one's audience, in whose ears all jests must find prosperity—although to silence Berowne's banter through hostile response bodes badly as a comic solution, echoing the abortive fate of the Nine Worthies' pageant.

As regards the lyric style that the courtly ladies attack, another double bind remains implicit. Ladies do die because of love suppressed, hidden, or rejected, as we know from the case of Katherine's sister (as well as Shakespeare's tales of Ophelia and the fictional sister of Viola/Cesario); when bantering about Cupid with Katherine, Rosaline notes "You'll ne'er be friends with him: a' kill'd your sister." Katherine agrees: "He made her melancholy, sad, and heavy; / And so she died" (5.2.13–15). By their own standard of experience, then, the ladies have good reason to avoid the dangerous passion that makes them vulnerable and sometimes dead. To the extent that courtly language can ensnare a feminine heart, it too becomes dangerous. Nevertheless, though the terms of praise may be false and potentially victimizing, if the ladies give up such praise, they may be faced not with independence but with Berownian degradation, or worse, "Armadan" force. Consider the violence lurking even in Armado's attempt at courtly verse, the "sonnet" that reads more like a threat:

> Thus dost thou hear the Nemean lion roar
> Gainst thee, thou lamb, that standest as his prey;
> Submissive fall his princely feet before,
> And he from forage will incline to play.
> But if thou strive, poor soul, what art thou then?
> Food for his rage, repasture for his den.
> (4.1.89–94)

Indecorous and absurd, Armado's poem may be the only thing in the text that makes the lords' subsequent Petrarchism look good. And as Costard tells us in the first scene, "it is the manner of a man to speak to a woman; for the form,—in some form" (1.1.206–7).

Shakespeare's ladies may appear charming because of their common sense, especially if viewed from a reasonably secure point of view (that is, from a socially empowered masculine and/or aristocratic perspective within the fiction, or from the theatrical audience's remove). But they are not necessarily any wiser than the lords in their use of language. They may present a female model that is in fact self-destructive rather than selfish. Without an alternative empowering discourse, it seems suicidal for the women to give up their courtly sources of respect and power, qualified though they be. As aristocrats, the ladies may be able to sustain their power when together, as they conspicuously remain throughout this play; but one need only look to Jaquenetta to remember what could happen to a woman alone without exceptional status. And imagining Jaquenetta without Armado's miraculously comic conversion to responsibility may move us, Costard-like, beyond the fiction to remember sixteenth-century accounts of abductions, flytings, and forced marriages, the world in which Shakespeare penned his amorous fantasy. One can imagine why a woman might, within the hierarchies of this play and this society, venerate the "worn-out" sonneteering tradition, even if it be as "perjuring" to the poet as Joel Fineman argues. For the drama is a world of represented action as well as words, and in it Jaquenetta submits to Armado's slightly masked force. This being Shakespeare's comedy she is finally "rewarded" with marriage, defusing the problem. In other plays, such as *Two Gentlemen of Verona,* the threat of sexual violence is more overt and acted upon (Sylvia is saved from rape only at the last moment and then uneasily). Even within Shakespeare's dramatic world and certainly outside of it, the less refined attitudes and behaviors of men often deemed "natural" can be more dangerous for women than is the lyrical deception these ladies battle.

The resolutions of this play, then, testify to the skill of the playwright's invisible hand but do not carry such simply progressive messages about female power as at first may appear.[22] Not only do the lovers face a questionable future but the ladies advocate dismissing the type of courtly rhetoric that Queen Elizabeth had been manipulating to such effect. Indeed, in one of Shakespeare's many ironic twists, one can discern echoes of the queen's imperious manner in the French ladies' moments of disdain. When the ladies explain their mockery of the men's lovesuits, having "rated them / At courtship, pleasant jest, and courtesy, / As bombast and as lining to the time," the men protest that their letters and looks "show'd much more than jest." To this Rosaline regally responds, "We did not quote them so" (5.2.771–72, 777–78). Many an Elizabethan courtier experienced the same mercurial mixture of cat-and-mouse meets lioness when participating in court spectacles and other forms of jestingly serious lyric "play." But Shakespeare then uses his position as dramatist to suggest that courtly ladies desire to give up the discourse which desires them, willing their removal from the landscape of Petrarchan worship—unlike Elizabeth, to become *femmes couvertes.* Those who wish to claim Shakespeare as progressive emphasize his ideal of companionate marriage as a victory of human bonding and likeness overcoming gender difference in a misogynist culture. But this may be a misplacement of enthusiasm, and a partial mislocation of (one version of) gender trouble. Not only the absence of certain resolution in marriage signaled by the play's title and ending (and the often-noted infrequency of happy marriages represented in the playwright's work as a whole) but also the cultural impact of this shift away from a powerful and vocal female community, with its bantering countervoice to male self-aggrandizement, can make one dubious about this as a happy ending.

More overtly, into the last act of *Love's Labour's Lost* the death of a monarch intrudes with its attendant fears, which were especially potent during the last years of Elizabeth's reign. When language articulates sensory experience as "reality"—the ladies' putative goal—the comedy must end:

> *Marcade.* God save you, madam!
> *Princess.* Welcome, Marcade,
>   But that thou interrupt'st our merriment.
> *Mar.* I am sorry, madam; for the news I bring
>   Is heavy in my tongue. The king your father—
> *Prin.* Dead, for my life!
> *Mar.* Even so: my tale is told.
>   (5.2.707–13)

The news, known by the princess before articulated by Marcade (presence itself becoming absolute communication), announces the death of the old king—or at least one of his two bodies. Given a monarchal theory in which "the king" can never be entirely dead, and given a political reality in which the queen of England was in declining health, this announcement must have been an even more stunning "coup de théâtre" than it remains for us. The communion of language with the world of temporal events (phenomenal "reality" from the perspective of these fictional ladies and many subsequent thinkers, but offstage nothingness in theatrical terms) brings death rather than fertility. Moreover, as the women ready themselves to return to France, their attempt to close the spaces among the lords' courtship and intentions (which they have not believed), their words, and their behavior requires of the men a temporary return to the barren world of academe with which the play began its mockery.

A community of men and women is defeated until purified, idealized. To reach this desired end would not only take "too long for a play," as Berowne laments; it would result in a finale too simple and unbelievable for this sophisticated play (870). Within the comic plot, the larger questions regarding poetry, love, and courtly culture are left, aptly, unresolved. The playwright has used theater's ability to represent multiple perspectives on language and the life surrounding and involved in it. The ladies do not get the last word after all. Instead, an alternative source of closure appears in lyric language presented as performance and less mediated by story and character: the songs of Spring and Winter. The songs are announced by Armado as "the dialogue that the two learned men have compiled in praise of the owl and cuckoo" that "should have followed in the end of our show" (887–80), restoring the artistic order disrupted by the sexual fate of Jaquenetta. As such, the humbler pageant supersedes both the narrative fate of the ladies and, yet once more, the wit of the laboring lords who consistently fail at artistic dialogues. Moreover, while these "learned men" are hardly direct surrogates for the playwright, they do come from a social background more akin to Shakespeare's than the play's other lyricists, and signal still one more shift in the location of verbal authority.

The songs ("When daisies pied and violets blue" and "When icicles hang by the wall" [5.2.886–921]) have been praised almost universally, even by critics who dismiss *Love's Labour's Lost* as the work of a—as Armado says of Moth—"tender juvenal."[23] The songs' immediate interest here lies in how they function as a concluding commentary on the drama's portrayal of courtly art and lyric poetry. Their verses relate routine and unidealized sensory experience yet exploit the harmony of sound and form to do so. They appear different from the self-conscious poetizing in the play because of their greater referentiality to nature (and many values implicitly supported by the narrative, such as attention to sensory data). Yet they derive from a traditional and common artistic topic as well, the spring versus winter *débat,* and as J. W. Lever discovered by comparing them to Gerard's 1597 *Herball,* even the flowers named may be a product of book-learning ("Three Notes"). Shakespeare seems to be extending his personal play with the fluid boundaries of life and art.

The lyrics are relatives to Dumain's poem as well as Moth's song of red and white, both of which mix courtly tropes with simpler song forms that blur the division between courtly and "folk" (as well as written and oral, authorial and communal) culture. They may be intended thus to subordinate that distinction temporarily among the audience as well, allowing the playwright special access to the strengths of both literary domains without recognizing social barriers. The songs also deny priority to one season over the other, even in pleasantness. Spring brings flowers and cuckoldry (a "word of fear / Unpleasing to a married ear!") while winter's nipped blood and foul ways also bring the owl's "merry note, / While greasy Joan doth keel the pot." The syntactic (when-then) and verse structures are quite obviously parallel without parody or preference (contrasting with Ralegh's "If . . . then" rebuttal to Marlowe's lyric). The dramatic narrative's oppositions of class and gender are now displaced by an opposition that is actually a sequence or companion relationship, presented as the truest "dialogue" of all. By placing these songs at the end of the story, without the narrative framing that has mocked earlier lyric art, Shakespeare gives them a privileged position and special resonance.

Given the play's attention to the ethical correspondence (or lack thereof) between speaker and speech, perhaps most intriguing here is the dissociation of song from character entirely. As William Carroll suggests, it seems impossible that Holofernes (much less good neighbor Nathaniel) could compose the closing songs (208ff.); if, as Armado's words suggest, they "compiled" traditional songs, this would match the fifth act's general transfer of emphasis from individual authorship to communal inheritance. In either case, the songs are "known" only by their form and function, that of ending the play. This is a move outside the narrative but not outside the concerns voiced within the fiction. By ending with these songs, Shakespeare concludes with a gesture at the immediate community between actors and audience rather than the idealized community of love's labour's won (perhaps unsurprisingly, the play so called by Francis Meres has been "lost"). The play resolves by asserting a final voice of dialogic song that can easily be understood by us as poetic communication, if not defined in relation to the "authority" of a single speaker. The songs stretch beyond discursive language without self-silencing or a doomed attempt at the unconventional. Indeed, they work because they are simple and familiar enough to be easily shared by their audience in the theater. Providing this similar basis of aural pleasure with the short courtly sonnet, these songs performed before almost the entire cast onstage also unite rather than divide the represented social groups as an audience of listeners.[24]

Ironically resembling the fight of Armado and Costard that ended the pageant of the Nine Worthies, the songs provide a means of closure that is not so much a definitive last word as a transition out of the realm of artistic fiction. Carroll emphasizes the presence of Shakespeare's "voice" in the songs as being the source of their excellence and aptness, unifying them into one whole which becomes a sign that now "the literal marriages can readily be imagined" (225). Perhaps. And yet instead of asserting himself explicitly through any single-voiced authority, any epilogue or courtier's voice wise or honest enough to make sense of the show, Shakespeare concludes with a double image and a dialogue. In contrast to the dramatically contextualized poetry within the play which mocks the insulated lyricist, we now hear the lyric "itself," filtered through singers and presented in a familiar form, given resonance by an audience (on and offstage) that made up a various part of Elizabethan society. The songs unexpectedly vindicate the promise of Navarre's opening "sonnet," being indeed "still and contemplative in living art." Thus the drama ends.

At the same time, the narrative "ending" for the lovers allows the tensions with which Shakespeare has played to remain unresolved and hence engaging. These were tensions about ethics, aesthetics and power with which Elizabethan society was struggling as well. In playing with courtly discourses, Shakespeare is mocking mannerisms, but also and more compellingly enacting a struggle, prefigured as a personal internal battle in Gascoigne's lyrics and Sidney's *Astrophil and Stella* but broadened here into a social pageant informed by intelligence, class and gender. As such, *Love's Labour's Lost* suggests questions beyond the ethical meaning of lyric conventions for the lover or poet (or madman), and ties the "problem" of lyricism with other societal issues.

These issues include the lyric's relationship, difficult to determine at best, with hierarchies and factions at the court itself. Beyond such specifics, the play's concern with feminine power remains intriguing in light of Elizabeth's regency. Shakespeare has revised Marlowe's critique in a way that is not so much reactionary as redemptive: courtly art after the fall, not a Peelian removal into myth. Like Peele's *Arraignment of Paris, Love's Labour's Lost* concludes with a lyric "solution" removed from character—but one that this time neither offers overt compliments nor supplants the world of desire, time, and sexuality that we have seen dramatized. From outside the court, Shakespeare "contains" the visions of Elizabethan courtly life, refusing to reject its matter as simply false, yet withholding endorsement of its manners. In ending with his songs as well as by making the witty court ladies advocates for companionate marriage rather than female idealization, Shakespeare obliquely posits his own social agenda: the emergent bourgeois ideology that reestablished patriarchal dominance through the "natural" family unit.

Dr. Johnson may well have been right to remark that *Love's Labour's Lost* includes passages "which ought not to have been exhibited, as we are told they were, to a maiden queen" (89). But whereas his implicit stress was on "maiden," I would reiterate his actual words: "maiden queen." In the background of this play remain the specific contemporary problems of sovereignty, not obvious enough to disturb the comic effects but jostling the audience's mind. This drama suggests how a play (subject to censorship) might reflect a culture in which the queen's choice of infertile female power had become a constant worry as she aged. How can Shakespeare celebrate the cycles of nature if the wooer's suit may always be deferred another year by his fictive princess, as it had by the woman on the English throne? How can he celebrate such a queen? Without openly satirizing her, *Love's Labour's Lost* certainly suggests Shakespeare's discontent with her courtly ideology, and obliquely seems to put her in her feminine place by framing sovereignty with death and natural change. The "weak king" plays, including *Richard II*, consider more overtly worries about a "sterile" gardener as king, and Elizabeth was surely right (not irascible, silly, or growing senile) to see herself in that play, at least as it was used by its audience—specifically, by Essex's followers on the eve of his abortive 1601 rebellion. The king of France dies in *Love's Labour's Lost;* while Navarre magically runs itself, the princess must return to France. We do not hear whether there is a brother to follow her father, and if the sixteenth-century English audience was to imagine this Navarre becoming king of France, the recent resolution of religious wars there through the conversion to Catholicism of another Navarrese prince would hardly provide a consoling nonfictional parallel. In 1593 Paris had been worth a mass for Henri IV, who thus became regarded as the great betrayer of Protestant hopes—and hence of England—on the Continent.[25] In this most "courtly" play, then, it is ironic that the putative solution lies in a celebration of nature and renewal, even as the "natural" order of Tudor succession was threatened with violent overthrow, the queen crawling toward death without a "natural" heir or a proclaimed successor.

The French Henry's grandmother, moreover, was the very famous Queen Marguerite of Navarre whose *Heptameron* (translated into English and printed in 1599) satirizes male assumptions about the gender wars. In addition to providing a witty and challenging source for female self-assertion within the erotic realm, she had also provided a model of female authorship to Lady Elizabeth Tudor during her uncertain youth as bastard princess. In 1548 Elizabeth had translated one of Marguerite's devotional works as "A godly Medytacyon of the christen Sowle," testimony to the princess's intellectual precociousness. This direct link between Marguerite and Elizabeth could reinforce the audience's uncertainty during the final scene of delayed nuptials, for unlike the Navarrese queen obviously Elizabeth had never married, but instead frustrated her royal suitors with the prospect of protracted, and ultimately unsuccessful, courtship.

All this remains outside the main dramatic representation, but informs the action of this play and its use of lyricism in a specifically Elizabethan way. Marcade may resemble Mercury, mythological guide to the underworld (as Malcolm Evans and others highlight), but he also eerily prefigures the historical messenger Sir John Harington waiting impatiently to deliver the long-expected "news" of his godmother and great patron Elizabeth's death to her successor, King James VI of Scotland. Rather than erasing the ideological imperfections of mortal female sovereignty, keeping cultural crises at bay in the manner of earlier courtly shows, *Love's Labour's Lost* uses its lyrical poetry to capture the dynamics and tensions of courtly struggles within and outside its fiction.

Shakespeare does not leave us with an individualistic voice, even in his songs, nor any simply comforting (and hence superficial) endorsement of the artist's voice or the powers of poetic language well used. Rather, we are left with a lyrical dialogue, and no single perspective even within the music. The songs, while clearly related to the courtly art of the play, are not products of an exclusive court culture but of the broader society's shared traditions and experience. Their music remains, moreover, distinct from the language and conflicts of court life as we have seen it represented. But despite the more obvious mockery of loving lords, the ultimate sacrifice in this gesture at cultural inclusiveness and harmony may well be the powerful role of royal women, and with it the incorporation of courtly lyric poetry within the representation of serious public discourse and political reality. We are left instead with greasy Joan and transcendent song. As the quarto concludes, "The words of Mercury are harsh after the songs of Apollo," and the language of Navarre, comic wonderland though it might be in part, would jar after melody (922).[26] In Shakespeare's representation, the rest is either silence or song.

Notes

1. Paul Ramsey and others have collected many of these echoes, which foreground self-consciously literary issues among the interests of this drama. Allusions include parodies of Marlowe both here and in the *Sonnets*. The honest huntsman silenced by Her Majesty's wit in 4.1 may be a reminscence of Gascoigne's performance at Kenilworth as the well-intentioned but easily dominated Savage Man and woodsman.

2. *A Midsummer Night's Dream* is another of the lyrical plays with no main narrative source, though it does (like *The Tempest*) have known literary sources for parts; on sources, see Muir (*Sources*) and Bullough. Venezky explores the connection with pageants and progresses, and Barber (*Shakespeare's* 87–118) discusses the play's relationship to holiday rituals. Grace, among others, believes "Shakespeare has not freed himself from forms that are only suitable for lyric poetry" (81–82).

3. Topical allusions have been studied extensively by Yates (*Study*), David (Shakespeare, *Love's*), Bradbrook (*School*), and Wickham, among others. Ties with Ralegh and the supposed "School of Night" (antagonists to Essex's faction at court) may connect the parody with Marlowe. Copious allusion to the prose mannerisms of Harvey, Florio, Nashe, Lyly, and Sidney also figure here.

4. *Pace* Baldwin, who found it Shakespeare's most perfect example of the five-act structure. Wilders notes the similarity of this "consort of voices" to Lyly's dramaturgy, in which irresolution is central to the artist's method. See also Heninger. Montrose's *Curious-Knotted Gardens,* which has enriched my reading, observes that the sonneteering scene (4.3) marks the play's numerical center, as measured by line count (167).

5. Calderwood's judgments have more validity if confined strictly to the use of Petrarchism (which he discusses). Though his dichotomies between "common speech" and "Baconian invisibility," words as a closed sign system versus absolute referentiality (54–55), seem too schematic to capture the play's fluidity of wit, his reading is characteristically astute and compelling.

6. See Harold Brooks (Shakespeare, *Midsummer* xliii-liii) on shared traits among these works, although he concludes with the paradoxical assertion that the lyricism "ideal" for *A Midsummer Night's Dream* is in later works "improved."

7. Stage sonnets perhaps signal a widespread voyeuristic interest in the language as well as events at court, an interest which Puttenham elevated into an aesthetic principle. Calderwood, in discussing *Romeo and Juliet,* notes that the lovers adopt "that inflationary species of linguistic currency that was flooding the poetic market in the 1590s—the Petrarchan" (Shakespeare, *Midsummer* 68). See Wendy Wall's chap. 1 ("Turning Sonnet: The Politics and Poetics of Sonnet Circulation") for more on the effects of this print marketplace on the interpretation of sonnets.

8. Desire was the norm even when sublimated into religious passion (as in Donne's "Holy Sonnets") or directed toward an intellectual abstraction as mistress (as in Chapman's "Coronet for His Mistress Philosophy"). There were occasionally other topics for sonnets, as Spenser's *Ruins of Time* (based on Marot) demonstrate, but the faddish norm in the 1590s remained the love sonnet. See Montrose on Navarre's opening "sonnet" (*Curious-Knotted* 92–94), and Bobbyann Roesen [Anne Barton] on the prince's endeavor (411–26).

9. See Lanham's first chapter and his discussion of "Superposed Poetics" in the *Sonnets* (chap. 5). These terms and the larger historical debate between them are the subject of Stanley Fish's entry ("Rhetoric") in Lentricchia and McLaughlin (203–22).

10. See Yates (*Study*) on the possible character identifications with the Sidney circle, most obvious in the association of Rosaline with the life model for Stella, Penelope Devereux Rich; she also finds signs of Sidney's Italian guest, Giordano Bruno, in Berowne. See Wickham for a direct tie between Sidney and the four lords.

11. The commonplace equation of loose female tongue and unchaste female body has been thoroughly discussed by feminist criticism; see, for example, Jardine (121), Jones, and Boose ("Scolding").

12. See Falstaff's less troubled self-presentation to Hal in *Henry IV Part I,* when he compares all Hal's other bad company to "pitch that defiles"—an ironic sign of his more consistent absence of conscience.

13. Hurston finds the sonnets indistinguishable; while not wishing to overstate

the significance of these individual differences, I find enough variation to merit consideration as comic commentary on each male lyricist's relationship to his art.

14. In Greek the actor is linked etymologically with the hypocrite, a connection always applicable to Berowne. He is a seductive character, smart, funny, and never to be taken simply at his word(s). While he may not be "on a level with the audience," as Carroll (55) asserts, his asides do bring him closer—which should not necessarily make us comfortable.

15. While decorum was a ruling principle of Renaissance aesthetics, ethical preference was not often attributed to one style—merely to the proper match between *res* and *verba,* contingent on context, audience, and art form. In sixteenth-century interludes, various forms were used depending on class, mood, and a host of other considerations, but rarely on a particular character's morality (see Bernard); such moralized style was just emerging in English stage speech at this time.

16. The collapsing of Petrarchism and anti-Petrarchist satire into one "coterie" style may seem obvious from our historical distance, but the distinction carried force at court with reference to Elizabeth and attitudes toward women's authority. This difference is reasserted later in the antagonism between disdainful Berowne and the lady-following, "honey-tongued" Boyet.

17. Yates (*Study*) sees a jest at the expense of the mathematician Thomas Harriot, Marlowe's "associate." If so, the hypothetical school's intellectual pretensions and rejection of Petrarchan woman-worship, as embodied in Berowne, is satirized alongside excessive Petrarchism (cf. Campbell 31).

18. Carroll, to whose work I am deeply indebted, believes the play moves from an opposition between art and nature to an assertion that "the distinction is simply arbitrary" (186); I think differences—albeit shifty ones—still exist. As Doran demonstrates, unconcluded debates were central to the Tudor aesthetic, and could signify even when one side wasn't clearly victorious (311).

19. The "great feast" derives from Moth's comment that Armado and Holofernes have there "stolen the scraps" (5.1.33). Scraps in the wholecloth of this play, these characters highlight the absurd end point of empty rhetoric as well as the association of verbal style with a speaker's character; but as *commedia* figures who ironically counterpoint the central romantic figures and vary their own styles in somewhat unexpected ways (cf. Holofernes at play's end), they also caution against too automatic a formalist equivalency between poetic style and moral maturity in the main characters.

20. On the relationships among lyric discourse, gender, and property, see Parker.

21. See Righter 106–12. Homan's charge that Costard's earlier comments violate "the theatrical tradition of not mingling with the audience before the show" seems anachronistic (74). At the other critical extreme, Bevington regards Costard as the "perfectly assured male" who always wins—despite the fact that it is Armado who gets the girl (the putative goal of "mutuality" which Bevington valorizes in the main plot [11]).

22. Bevington concludes that there is "misogyny implicit" in the representation of the women for different reasons (because of Shakespeare's "uncomfortable vision of the female as the attractive yet baffling prize that seemingly cannot be attained or controlled" [2]). Although thematizing male fears, his reading presumes masculine identification with the playwright in the assertions that "the women remain a mystery" and then that their "sexual denial" is "justified . . . by what the men must learn" from it (7, 10). Like Rose, he sees marriage as the sign of a less vexed gender system, noting a final movement toward "some genuine accommodation and mutuality, towards some hint of softening in the women and self-knowledge in the men" which nevertheless fails to offset its "more overt impositions of patriarchal control" (13). This "accommodation" seems precisely to reinscribe patriarchal stereotypes (softer women, smarter men), and the systemic subordination of women may remain more worrisome than is the masculine experience of anxiety about powerful women earlier implied. Bevington clearly links the strained gender relationships herein represented and Shakespeare's uneasiness with Queen Elizabeth.

23. The marvelously bombastic Armado explains to the brighter Moth that "tender juvenal" is "a congruent epitheton appertaining to thy young days, which we may nominate tender" (1.2.13–15). See McLay, R. Hunter, Barber (*Shakespeare's*), and Carroll for detailed discussion of the songs.

24. Calderwood's assertion that Shakespeare ignores or discounts the creative role of the audience in this play (136) is countered by this final union of courtiers and commoners, men and women, listening together with the "non-fictional" theatrical audience. Montrose observes that "The love sonnets and final songs embody the contrast of an emphatically secretive medium of written composition with a collective oral performance. Lyricism in the ironic context of drama is supplanted by lyrics which transcend the boundaries of the dramatic fiction" (*Curious-Knotted* 168).

25. Marcus's wise cautions (in *Puzzling*) about "local reading and its discontents" when "puzzling Shakespeare" are worth remembering. Essex's sister was Penelope Rich, and his wife Frances Walsingham was Sidney's widow (but see Richard David's introduction [Shakespeare, *Love's*] for the problems with these associations). The parallels in this play with names and events relating to Biron's French conspiracy against Henri IV (contemporary with Essex's rebellion) seem almost too apt to be, as they must be, coincidental.

26. Dover Wilson interpreted the larger type to mean this final statement is "merely" a reader's comment (Shakespeare, *Love's* 187n). Evans associates Mercury with scholarly "reason" and hence the written word, versus Apollo, "rhyme," and speech; although the difficulties with written poetry are clear in *Love's Labour's Lost,* courtly compliments spoken by the lords in act 5 thrive no better, implying stylistic and ethical distinctions beyond a "central duality" of speech and writing.

FIVE

Legacy

> This will celebrate the occasion—a curious sense rising in her, at once freakish and tender, of celebrating a festival, as if two emotions were called up in her, one profound—for what could be more serious than the love of a woman, what more commanding, what more impressive, bearing in its bosom the seeds of death; at the same time these lovers, these people entering into illusion glittering eyed, must be danced round with mockery, decorated with garlands.
> Virginia Woolf, *To The Lighthouse* (100)

> If you want to write a song about a face,
> If you want to write a song about the human race,
> Write a song about the moon.
> Paul Simon, "Write a Song about the Moon," *Hearts and Bones*

> Speak low if you speak love.
> William Shakespeare, *Much Ado about Nothing* (*Riverside* 338)

Whether the play be a tragic tale of doomed desire or a courtly comedy of sovereigns and sonnets, the resonance and appeal of staged love extend far beyond the bounds of a particular social context or scholarly articulation. Like Woolf's Mrs. Ramsay selecting a bit of *boeuf en daube* as she ruminates on love's complexity, what one offers up may best serve as a symbol, a gesture, of complex and perhaps competing discursive reflections. Without doubt the very worship and mysteriousness that accompanies love, both romantic and literary, can serve as a dangerous veil—as Woolf's Lily Briscoe, excluded and exempting herself from the romantic plot, recognizes. It may coerce women into highly constrained social roles, or expend energy that could have reformed dairies and challenged empires. Three centuries before Woolf's powerful rendering of love's mixed blessings, Sir Philip Sidney's friend and biographer Fulke Greville appears to have recognized (as did Spenser more famously in book 3 [canto 2, st. 1] of *The Faerie Queene*) that the veil which creates a culture's conventions of romance and desirability may obscure women's heroism and power. Speaking of Lady Sidney's more literal veiling after her disfigurement by smallpox, Greville proceeds with a remarkable simile that implies femininity can be a disabling performance: "she was by nature of a large ingenuous spirit: whence, as it were even racked with native strengths, she chose rather to hide herself from the curious eyes of a delicate time than come upon the stage of the world with any manner of disparagement — the mischance of sickness having cast such a kind of veil over her excellent beauty *as the modesty of that sex doth many times upon their native and heroical spirits*" (cited by Kay 18; emphasis mine). The glittering illusion of love can lead to a glossing over of the disruptions and oddities — including the trajectories for powerful women — that attend the construction of modern culture's happy ending, the gauzy fade-out with kiss. As the last chapter partially illustrated, this has often been true in the critical interpretation of Shakespeare's plays. And simply mocking all Petrarchism at first sight or reducing courtly love to a single function in drama can result in readings just as limited and skewed as those simply celebrating love and marriage. At court, lyrical discourse clearly served a range of interests, including those of the female monarch but also those of the devisers and playwrights asserting their literary mastery.

My exploration of those courtly works has tried to illuminate the various and subtle messages lyric poetry could relay, depending on its fictional and performative setting. The three plays analyzed in detail, among the most complex and fascinating examples of lyrical drama, reveal the inadequacy of interpretation based on merely identifying the presence of certain tropes, attitudes, or styles; we must also attend to whom and how they serve. In all three cases, stories that emphasize the language of love present its consequences in a world larger than the lyric speakers, belying the possibility of a "private life" detachable from its social framework. In lyrical drama, private affairs become public representations. Furthermore, the tensions therein represented extend beyond an erotic realm to a political one, in which royal women wield substantial power. Only in Shakespeare's play does the prospect of marriage as a conventional comic ending suggest an eventual restoration of a social order more comfortably in line with patriarchal theory. Even there, the solution is deferred. Elizabethan lyrical performances remain sites of drama and cultural strain. Seen in historical context, they hardly substantiate the scholarly dismissals cited earlier, that they are merely "static," vacuously sugary and disconnected from "life," or lacking in "kinetic thrust."

Shakespeare's practice has had such resonance that we may equate his vision with timeless truths about lyric's place in the world without realizing it. By historicizing Shakespeare, undeniably the Bard of English literature for many a reader, scholars consciously alienate as they strive to enrich words that have been cherished as immediate, transcendent, familiar. Yet historicism's compensatory pleasures are not confined to antiquarians or specialists, for the added critical perspective allows us to see in a clearer light not only the artwork but also our own cultural predilections and prejudices. We may begin to understand, for example, how Shakespeare's drama foreshadows and provides a powerful precedent for the subsequent privatization of lyric.

John Stevens observes that the early Tudor tradition of love lyric was "dependent . . . on social usages, [and] never pretended to self-sufficiency; it was never intended to be mere words on a page; it was part of a social 'drama'" (215). Shakespeare's representations reflect a contemporary shift in the place of lyric, with the rise of printing and the circulation of sonnet manuscripts and miscellanies; unlike the poetry of many early Tudor courtly makers, whose lyric compositions were often recited or set to lute music (as Stevens well documents), many Elizabethan lyrics were addressed primarily to a reading audience.[1] Thus despite the courtly lyric tradition, the lyric audience was becoming more frequently a solitary reader, encouraging associations of lyricism with intimacy rather than with public speech acts. The erotic subject matter of love songs and sonnets obviously accorded well with that shift. Nevertheless, Shakespeare's dramatic choices not only reflect but thematize such changes, instilling lyricism (particularly Petrarchan lyricism) with an "otherworldly" quality—for better or ill. Like Peele's *Arraignment, Love's Labour's Lost* ultimately asserts the value of political community, here more realistically including both sexes in its finale though still deferring the consummation of sexuality among the aristocrats. En route to the establishment of that community, the logic of its narrative demands the sacrifice of the lyrical poetry associated with eros—akin to the fate of its counterpart in Marlowe's *Dido, Queen of Carthage*, though in Shakespeare's comedy its rejection is neither absolute nor deemed tragic.

Shakespeare's other lyrical plays of the 1590s bear out many of the patterns and ambiguities revealed in *Love's Labour's Lost,* albeit with less overt delight at the purgation of courtly lyricism. These dramatic works remain among the playwright's most popular, indicating the widespread appeal of what might seem at first glance to be a coterie interest in court styles. Indubitably Shakespeare's verse, like that of Marlowe and Peele, retains its aural beauty. But the detailed and subtle functions of lyric poetry within these plays, especially as they involve gender, may be lost or oversimplified if we lack awareness of the courtly cultural landscape.

In both *Love's Labour's Lost* and *Romeo and Juliet,* sonnets and lyrical set pieces are to some extent set against a more cynical "real world" of death and violence, although the opposition and distinctness between these domains has often been exaggerated by those anticipating a nineteenth-century model of more impermeably separate spheres. In *Love's Labour's Lost,* the lords' amorous lyrics resemble private letters and suffer from their public recitation; the interplay of textuality and performance thus becomes a satiric tool exposing courtly narcissism. In *Romeo and Juliet,* the lovers are not separated from one another, but from the crass world of Veronese feuding, by their sonnet at the ball. Aptly, the status of lyric is more complicated here (as in Berowne's final "renunciation" sonnet). The shared sonnet appears not as a self-consciously written composition but as an improvised oral exchange, yet its perfect resemblance to a Petrarchist poem defies simple opposition of orality versus textuality, lyric versus drama, true love versus courtly infatuation. This dramatized sonnet thus undermines formalist judgments and calls attention to the paradoxes and inversions characterizing Shakespeare's lyrical-comical-tragical-drama.[2] No wonder, then, that familiar Petrarchan tropes and figures such as the blazon and the ship of love haunt the play's tragic climax, as Romeo prepares to die:

> . . . O my love, my wife,
> Death that hath suck'd the honey of thy breath
> Hath had no power yet upon thy beauty.
> Thou art not conquer'd. Beauty's ensign yet
> Is crimson in thy lips and in thy cheeks,
> And Death's pale flag is not advanced there.
> . . . Eyes, look your last.
> Arms, take your last embrace! And lips, O you
> The doors of breath, seal with a righteous kiss
> A dateless bargain to engrossing Death.
> Come, bitter conduct, come unsavoury guide,

> Thou desperate pilot now at once run on
> The dashing rocks thy seasick weary bark.
> Here's to my love!
>
> (5.3.91–96, 112–19)

The lyric vocabularies of Petrarch, Wyatt, Sidney, and Daniel echo in this burial chamber, ironically transmuted by the visual and verbal representation of death. The bravado and faith of callow Romeo's first Petrarchan speeches are now literalized as he will die for, with, and toasting his love. His rival is no second-rate poet nor stolid Paris but "unsubstantial Death," and his drink poison (103). Like the transmuted blazon honoring Elizabeth at the conclusion of Peele's *Arraignment,* Romeo's Petrarchist catalogue of body parts— *both* his own and Juliet's—does not foreground domination (as feminist revisions of Freud's reading of the sadistic gaze might lead one to assume). Instead, the list lingers on the cherished, cherishing attributes of life in the body which is about to be sacrificed, intensifying the scene's poignance and our own grieving consciousness of physical loss as heartbreaking. All the while controlled and smooth, the death speech melds love lyric and heroic action; moreover, in addressing Juliet both as his "love" and his "wife," Romeo's words serve Shakespeare's transference of honor from the unavailable moon goddess at the Tudor court to the bride of sunlight, the companion of the marriage bed. At least if viewed with an eye sympathetic to the play's location of value, Petrarchan lyricism, like Romeo, has grown up.

From one perspective, *Romeo and Juliet* thus redeems the rhetoric mocked in *Love's Labour's Lost,* yet it too emphasizes the privacy of that discourse. Although the lovers are united by lyric, and their emotions are represented with beauty and affection, as in Marlowe's *Dido* their lyrical vision cannot be integrated into the political landscape and leads quickly to death. To blame the lovers and their discourse for this societal failure as so many critics do, rather than to see it as the product of Shakespeare's social and dramatic construction, seems a bit perverse. Like the songs concluding *Love's Labour's Lost,* Romeo and Juliet's lyricism throughout the play not only strives to capture an alternative temporality, a beautiful moment of harmonic dialogue, but remains discrete from the horizontal movement of worldly events toward death. Yet this does not mean the *kairotic* yearnings of lyric are thus condemned or are antidramatic, nor that the narrative movement alone represents a truer, more mature vision which outgrows or erases the power of lyrical moments.[3] Rather, this reading recognizes that lyricism provides an essential position in the play's tragic dynamics: here the interplay between lyricism and narrative *creates* the unresolved conflict which constitutes drama.

It creates a particular social vision as well. Reading historically highlights another aspect of this dramaturgical choice: Shakespeare's drama relies on the effective removal of lyric from the public domain it had occupied within the Elizabethan court, and removes female political power along with it. This gendered aspect of the privatization of lyric is perhaps most overt in another lyrical play, *A Midsummer Night's Dream,* where both the Amazonian and fairy queens are reinscribed within patriarchal rule through male domination and marriage.[4] But in all Shakespeare's lyrical plays the pattern appears, whether the female characters blithely dismiss a lyrical domain or lovers die with it.

This movement may be read more benignly as an affirmation of a private space: an attempt to elude the social categorizations and conditions of early modern life, and to claim an internal and distinct subjectivity for dramatic characters reflective of its audience's desires. Surely the drama has served these purposes and needs, both intellectually and viscerally; the rich characterization of late Elizabethan and Jacobean drama continues to delight theatrical audiences and readers alike, as does its intricately textured poetry. Nevertheless, interwoven with a narrative of increasing psychological "depth" and the representation of subjectivity (whether regarded with scorn or celebration) is another movement, one with profound and varied consequences depending on one's particular social location. In Shakespeare's lyrical plays, as a quick survey will indicate, dramatic conflict emerges between the representation of lyricism as a voice of glimmering beauty and its active expulsion or distancing from the world of politics and statecraft; and this conflict intersects with tensions in gendered representation.

For example, in the last act of *Richard II,* the courtly artifice of word-weaving Richard's farewell to his queen is rudely interrupted by Northumberland, the hatchet man and gruff voice of the new Machiavellian regime. The only woman in the play's last scenes is the inelegant duchess of York, whose comical pleadings and ignoble kneeling exasperate a queen-less Bolingbroke to appease and hence silence her by granting the life of her traitorous son Aumerle.[5] Thus the ineffectual courtly lamentations of the duchess of Gloucester and Richard's queen are supplanted by the thoroughly *un*lyrical domestic desperation of a mother who successfully intervenes (behind closed doors) in a treacherous male sphere. The public "new world order" is bloody, prosaic, and thoroughly male-dominated (a movement confirmed in the *Henry IV* plays). Within it—inverting the courtly love scenario—it is the woman who must literally stoop to conquer.

In *The Merchant of Venice,* the lady who was sad when ruling her own estate exercises power on her husband's behalf by becoming a male clerk, using the sort of legal discourse Navarre invoked in decreeing an all-male academy rather than the lyrical moonlight discourse of her native Belmont. Indeed, the play's most thoroughly and self-consciously lyrical interlude in Belmont (5.1.1–109) is dominated by the Venetian escapees Lorenzo and Jessica, not by Portia, and its meditations on music, moonlight, and lovers have no direct impact upon or consequence for the plot.

> *Lor.* The moon shines bright. In such a night as this,
> When the sweet wind did gently kiss the trees,
> And they did make no noise, in such a night
> Troilus methinks mounted the Troyan walls,
> And sigh'd his soul towards the Grecian tents,
> Where Cressid lay that night. . . .
> . . . In such a night
> Stood Dido with a willow in her hand . . .
> *Jes.* In such a night
> Medea gathered the enchanted herbs
> That did renew old Aeson.
> *Lor.* In such a night
> Did Jessica steal from the wealthy Jew,
> And with an unthrift love did run from Venice,
> As far as Belmont.
>
> (1–6, 9–17)

Troilus and Cressida, Pyramus and Thisbe, Dido and Aeneas, Medea and Jason, Jessica and Lorenzo—hardly a comforting Ovidean lineage. All these mythic lovers are doomed or unfaithful, recalling not only the *Heroides* but Marlowe's parody of his own Ovidean lyric in *The Jew of Malta* (Ithamore's speech, cited in chapter 4 above). In a play so obviously based on Marlowe's as is *The Merchant of Venice,* Shakespeare again illustrates his ability to have his lyric cake and satirize it too. His moments of lyricism are more sentimental than Marlowe's, the satire kinder and gentler, but the dramatic method is familiar. And as in *Romeo and Juliet,* lyrical imagery and refrains are employed to create a private moment between lovers, in this case providing an alternative to the commercial discourse of Venice, but one lacking its material consequences.

Yet Lorenzo's financial concern encroaches even here, and signals the dominance of a mercenary stage "reality" represented as unlyrical, male, and Venetian. Moreover, Belmont by day remains a patriarchal territory successfully ruled by the dead father's law, in which Portia does indeed become Bassanio's desired "golden fleece" and male suitors reinscribe property laws by gaining the women's fortunes as well as their rings. Lyricism may be viewed cynically as the poetic cover-up, the cosmetic coloring that decorates the merchants' pursuit of social position. At the least, a pragmatic sense of poetry as a means to erotic ends intrudes. Here again Shakespeare's dramatic lyricism functions somewhat similarly to Marlowe's, calling to mind an early scene in *Tamburlaine Part I*. After Tamburlaine's impressive lyrical (and typically egotistical) speech of future offers to Zenocrate, having praised her brightness and whiteness and having imagined "milk-white harts" to draw her ivory sled "amidst the frozen pools . . . Which with thy beauty will be soon resolv'd," the warrior shifts his tone abruptly to explain his extravagant speech to a male follower:

> *Tamburlaine.* . . . My martial prizes, with five hundred men,
>   Won on the fifty-headed Volga's waves,
>   Shall we all offer to Zenocrate,
>   And then myself to fair Zenocrate.
> *Techelles.* What now! in love?
> *Tamburlaine.* Techelles, women must be flattered:
>   But this is she with whom I am in love.
>   (*Tamburlaine, Part One* 1.2.102–8)

The emotion is real, but the style is exposed as a male display of "flattery" to woo a lady, rather than vaunted as the means to express a higher, truer vision. In Zenocrate's case the flattery works, but in Shakespeare's drama the women sometimes seem to desire only the marital ends without the poetic means; not only was this evident in *Love's Labour's Lost* but it may help explain Jessica's doubts and skepticism in reaction to lyrical Lorenzo in *Merchant,* even on their "honeymoon."

Garbed as a woman, Portia follows the law and gives away her personal power for the sake of what Shakespeare presents as a single concept, love-and-marriage. Instead of courtly love language, then, this play (like *Love's Labour's Lost*) has its courtly lady endorse marriage and male acquisition as the route to a "romantic" happy ending. Even Jessica's inheritance, sacrificed through her elopement with Lorenzo, is passed from her unacceptably Jewish father to her Christian husband through the legal machinations of the female-as-male collaborator, Portia. In act 5 scene 1, Portia invokes the moon to end the music and the lyricism begun by Lorenzo's attention to the moon, structurally reinforcing the sense that this lyrical scene is an ethereal night interlude: "Peace ho! the Moon sleeps with Endymion, / And would not be awak'd. [Music ceases.]" (108–9). Having just honored the aptness of nightingale music by night but not day, noting that "things by season season'd are / To their right praise and true perfection," Portia's speech confirms Shakespeare's active participation in the division of the spheres, astrological and social, as part of a "natural" order: lyricism occurs in an alternative landscape of night, dreams, and lovers, not in the province — despite the nonfictional context of Elizabeth's court where Lyly's *Endimion* represented the myth quite differently — in which earthly female power or political sovereignty is affirmed.[6] Instead, talk of moonlight defines the territory where the playwright confirms his mastery of the literary landscape, his sure sense of order and beauty, before returning to the daylight "reality" of plots and politics.

In *A Midsummer Night's Dream*, Shakespeare's evocation of the moon similarly demonstrates his own ability to represent a world through sophisticated command of both dramaturgy and verse, in contrast to the "rude mechanicals" who worry too much about the deceptive power of spectacle but insufficiently credit the metaphoric power of poetry to create an illusion. They would present moonshine by opening a window or represent it allegorically in the person of an actor, whereas Shakespeare gracefully and obliquely introduces his lyrical landscape with Oberon's first line: "Ill met by moonlight, proud Titania" (2.1.60). Ironically, moonlight here becomes the realm in which male mastery is reasserted, as Oberon humiliates his Fairy Queen, only to gain her gratitude as well as her changeling boy on the morning after. Moreover, lyrical passages are neither addressed exclusively to women nor focused on their beauties; Oberon speaks lushly of "love-in-idleness" and the "bank where the wild thyme grows," praising nature more than his consort and speaking not to his queen but to his henchman Puck. Daylight brings marriage and happy reintegration of women as domestic partners rather than political threats. Instead of consigning his unruly queen to the flames, as Marlowe did in *Dido,* Shakespeare tames his into erotic submission. By making this comic conclusion acceptable to the play's female as well as its male characters, the drama encourages us to discount the cost of autonomy and social power sacrificed or discarded by the women for the sake of a happy marriage. Whereas Gascoigne (like so many other male poets) turns to the myth of a doomed queen to remind us of his own woe, adopting the voice of the nightingale Philomel, Shakespeare reverses the logic and turns a conquered Amazon and a surrogate for his Tudor Fairy Queen into willing advocates for his own fantasy of a benign, male-ruled patriarchal state.[7]

Shakespeare's skill in ventriloquizing female desire matches his artistic achievement in overgoing courtly aesthetics to become our culture's master playwright. In his comedies and lyrical plays, female characters are often portrayed as rejecting lyricism and courtly love as untrue or victimizing, in favor of self-domestication. (Cordelia in *King Lear* goes further in her attempt at authentic speech, coming close to absolute self-silencing, akin to the failure of all poetic styles to redeem the speaker in Marlowe's later plays.) By contrast, when Benedick and Hotspur and Hal assert as men that they can't compose sonnets and don't want to become feminized, the reasoning seems reassuringly straightforward. To recognize Shakespeare's artful role in constructing the woman's part is not, of course, to deny the basis for such a representation in his social world. Nor is it to say that sixteenth-century women should not have distrusted men's poetic affection and affectation, or that these had no debilitating consequences. Indeed, the wisdom of such female skepticism is not confined to plays in which male public sovereignty and female domestication are celebrated; witness Peele's Oenone, whose plight is but one instance in the long and tenacious history of representing male desire as erratic and uncontrollable. The notion that marriage will somehow solve such instability and reasonable doubts, however, remains one of Shakespeare's most enduring legacies, not because he created (or even believed) the idea but because he dramatized it as the perfect comic conclusion with such stunning success. While courtly ladies, then, may often have doubted or rejected their lyrical suitors, in Shakespeare's plays by and large their disbelief in such rhetoric does not serve to perpetuate their own power through rejection of a system that makes them legally invisible *femmes couvertes* but rather leads them only to reject the means to that end, lyrical courtship.[8] And traditionally courtship, as Carolyn Heilbrun points out, is the moment when women become important in narrative.

To recognize Shakespeare's powerful role in "re-placing" lyric as an assumed, artificial masculine voice to gain women who are usually skeptical and prefer a more "natural" dialogue is not to dismiss his drama nor presume his intentional delimitation of female possibility. Indeed, excellent arguments can be made for interpreting his plays as culturally subversive and exceptionally affectionate in the treatment of particular female characters, such as Portia, Rosaline, and Juliet. It is precisely because these portraits are so enchanting, nonetheless, that the narrative trajectory and social vision they serve may remain unexamined. By contrast, Marlowe's rendering of women in his plays for the public theater is sketchy at best, at times monstrous (as in the case of Queen Isabella late in *Edward II*), obviating the desire to justify both the character and its social positioning. Whereas Marlowe's plays vividly render the conflict between a heroic voice of power and a lyrical voice of desire, such oppositions are more subtly dramatized in Shakespeare, and often obscured by the unexpected advocacy of women outside the province of lyrical discourse (especially but not exclusively when they are dressed as men). The woman's part is not at all moments eroticized, any more than in Peele's *Arraignment,* which of course gives it a greater sense of range and possibility. But the one possibility that effectively disappears in Shakespeare's plays is the one that Gascoigne and Peele employed in their courtly entertainments: emphasis on a rhetorical situation in which the woman as a powerful public figure welcomes courtly lyricism as a social discourse capable of signifying veneration and respect as well as desire. A different social fiction, and with it a different use of rhetoric, takes precedence. Like his fairy king Oberon, Shakespeare does not woo his Fairy Queen but rather claims lyricism for himself, for his poetic property, while he leads his earth-treading female characters to the marriage bed.

The contrast between Shakespeare's lyrical placement and Peele's, like the functional affinities between lyricism in *The Merchant of Venice* and in Marlowe's practice (despite very different tonalities and emphases in the lyrical passages themselves), reinforces awareness that the intersections of lyric and drama led to a range of cultural possibilities and messages. The choices of playwrights (and the patrons or auditors they addressed) in representing lyricism carried ideological weight given the context of Elizabeth's sovereignty, and in other, unforeseeable ways may continue to influence audience conceptions of gender and genre. Recognizing Shakespeare's careful creation of lyrical moments that function within his dramatic narratives as representative of a distinctly "other" world can help us avoid the trap of replicating uncritically the playwright's definition of reality and dreamworld, his association of lyric with the private and of drama with the public domain, as even brilliant scholarly critics often do.

Such elisions are legion. For example, speaking of *Love's Labour's Lost,* Montrose (*Curious-Knotted* 34) remarks that "The immediate concerns and preoccupations of earthly life—the play's 'first world'—are not realized in dramatic action but are rather presented obliquely through the resources of imagery and techniques of parody." This seems to presume that lyrically expressed desire and the constellation of concerns associated with that rhetoric were not immediate preoccupations of "earthly life." Yet the practice of Elizabethan courtly art and pageantry belies such a claim. Montrose explicitly equates Shakespeare's vision with reality when he further claims that Lyly's *Endimion* and other plays "mirror the Court's ideal self-image; critique remains latent in the discrepancy between ideal and actuality. [By contrast] Shakespeare's artistic integrity remains uncompromised even in his most explicitly courtly comedy" (39). If one substitutes the word "Elizabeth" for "Court," and "authority" for "integrity," the buried issue of gender and power becomes apparent, and undermines this easy praise of the masculine perspective as more real, authentic, and (not coincidentally) more critical.[9] Without denying courtly idealization, one can certainly recognize that those who criticized this aesthetic were no less involved in their own idealizations. Shakespeare's choices may have been motivated less by "integrity" and disinterestedness than by an active desire to advance a different social and aesthetic position from his sovereign's. Whereas Lyly's epilogue offered his play to his "Dread Sovereign," Montrose adds, "Shakespeare's epilogue, the songs which were probably added about 1597, was an offering to anyone who would listen. The difference exemplifies the movement towards a more autonomous class of writers." To the extent this account is true, and Shakespeare is not merely serving a *different* audience, the movement more than happens to serve male as well as authorial autonomy.

Laudable feminist attempts to find the good in Shakespeare often lead to a similar adoption of the male playwright's perspective as if it were disinterested and transcended its historical placement. Thus Marianne Novy, aptly stressing the mutuality and individuality of love as represented in Shakespeare's conclusions, argues that especially in the later comedies "women's gestures of submission are often balanced by similar gestures from the men." But even so, it is hard to see how such personal "gestures" of humility upon entering into the social contract of marriage can be equated given its obviously hierarchical structure in early modern England, unless one keeps one's eyes firmly fixed only on the particular characters as if they were individuals with private lives utterly unconstrained by the political and theoretical contexts in which they were created. Novy argues that Elizabethan marriage was not an unvarying monolithic structure in practice and rightly wishes "to note variations in practice and in presentation," yet this attempt to erase Shakespeare's less pleasant social messages by narrowing the focus and dismissing patterns of male dominance as mere "conventions" seems self-defeating for both women and men; it exempts the very social structures which perpetuate such dominance from critical analysis, and undermines her attempt to distinguish a valuable "woman's part" obliquely related to women's lives offstage (43).[10] If the comic endings are then venerated as a positive legacy, one ends up replicating Shakespeare's creation of a private sphere for love and lyricism within a patriarchal social order.

Leonard Tennenhouse, although remarking on the dangers of reinscribed patriarchy, also stresses what he sees as a "society that is rigidly hierarchical and more inclusionary at once" created at the end of Shakespeare's *Taming of the Shrew* (52). He proposes that this renewed social order relies upon the aristocratic woman's "power," but hardly in a sense that would please a woman suspicious of bourgeois patriarchy. It is her speech of wifely submission that "gives Kate real political power for the first time in the play. If she is no longer the Petrarchan ideal, neither is Kate the fishwife and bawd. In remaking her language, Petruchio appears to have invalidated the opposition that initiated the action of the play and prevented the inclusion of various women in the system of sexual exchange" (51). Tellingly, "her" speech with "real" power turns out to be Petruchio's "remaking," Tennenhouse's last sentence transferring her subjectivity to her husband just as the play does, and moreover arguing that the transfer is good for her. The desire to displace a theoretical problem associated with Petrarchism (the chasm between the idealized aristocrat and the sexual woman) here vindicates the effacement of Kate as a shrewd character with a distinctive voice in favor of "her" "power" to be fit into the patriarchal system of sexual exchange as a male creation. For Tennenhouse, Kate's only act approved by the men becomes the only consequential one, obliterating her earlier uncoerced identity as "the Shrew." Whether this constitutes a more "inclusive" vision for women seems questionable. Indeed, within this particular fiction, harmonic society is created by denying differences among women, by rejecting the legitimacy of female rebellion and indeed of women's very existence outside marriage. Debunking Petrarchan ideals doesn't necessarily empower women, and making Kate sexual as well as subservient serves a bourgeois Protestant rather than a courtly aristocratic male idealization of woman—one arguably *less* empowering. Although I empathize with the desire to laud the incorporation of sexuality into the positive portrayal of women, praise for public theatrical representations such as Shakespeare's *Taming of the Shrew* over court idealizations such as Peele's *Arraignment of Paris* on that basis seems to refetishize sexuality at the woman's expense.[11]

More is at stake than the understandable and recurrent desire to make Kate's fate seem less discomfiting. As Lynda Boose concludes in her discussion of the critical history of *The Taming of the Shrew,* "Ultimately, what is under covert recuperation and imagined as tacitly at stake is the institution of heterosexual marriage."[12] The ideal that love and marriage must coincide informs not only Shakespeare's plays but also Tennenhouse's argument about their distinction from narrative romances, as when he asserts that "To remain pure, the aristocratic woman [in romances] refuses desires, and when desiring, she never marries happily. By contrast, Shakespeare's romantic comic heroines are both pure and capable of desire" (40). (One may note that Marlowe's Zenocrate is also both, and that this categorical assertion relies on the comparison of aristocratic romances with public plays, thus discounting generic differences as well as the possible representational license encouraged by the use of boy actors.) Tennenhouse also observes that Shakespeare's comic women, unlike male overreachers, do not "threaten to seize control of the state—or its icon—the body of the aristocratic female" (41). The heroines, being aristocratic ladies, are hardly likely to "seize" themselves—unless of course one considers their self-rule and withholding as a means of challenging exchange, as the ladies in *Love's Labour's Lost* themselves do. Remembering court performances, one might argue that it was in this application of chastity or sexual unavailability to men that greater potential power for a woman—and perhaps not only Queen Elizabeth—once resided; this undermines the claim that the representation of female protagonists as sexual is perforce more subversive or salutary.[13] Unless one discounts such courtly power as illusory, and ignores the equation of female power with self-sacrifice implicit in Tennenhouse's reading of *The Taming of the Shrew,* it is hard to feel comfortable with the positive rhetorical construction of his conclusion that "Central to the special status Shakespeare claims for his drama is the manner in which the wellborn lady, and only the wellborn lady, becomes invested with certain powers to make a more flexible and inclusive political world" (45). The three lyrical plays analyzed in this book point in the opposite direction, even investing some female characters with political and personal power when they *avoid* the "one-and-only" trajectory of marital love. One need not favor utopian plots nor ignore the tensions played out through the subtle interweaving of lyric and narrative to note the presence in these courtly works of a more public, and perhaps ultimately less masochistic, version of female power.

Shakespeare's complex vision is often invoked to criticize or belittle aristocratic court culture. More subtly, David Bevington's comparison of Lyly and Shakespeare posits that the "misogyny implicit" in their plays is attributable to their courtly context. Ironically, the dissatisfactions with female sexual unavailability found in Shakespeare reappear when Bevington remarks that even if Lyly's *Sappho and Phao* "*seems* to insist instead on the glories of chaste matriarchal rule, it does so at the tremendous expense of banishing the erotic from noble human relationships—an *impossible* condition at the end of a romantic comedy" (12; emphasis added). But given Peele's *Arraignment,* the notion of eros banished does not seem so impossible, be it in Lyly's romantic comedies, Peele's court drama, or even, arguably, *Love's Labour's Lost.* Seen from the male characters' perspective, unavailable women may indeed be a problem. But is this in fact the only perspective at play, the only viewpoint an audience—especially one including Elizabeth Tudor—can conceive? For whom is the author creating a happy ending?

A tension exists here between (at least) two audiences, two perspectives, and two strains of Tudor ideology. The "cult" of Elizabeth with which courtly lyric was associated valorized the sublimation of eros, whereas a burgeoning bourgeoisie idealized the love match culminating in marriage. Despite the absence of happy married couples within his plays, Shakespeare's narrative line in his lyrical plays emphasizes and rewards the latter vision. Some argue forcefully that the ideal of companionate marriage more than compensates for the eradication of a few powerful aristocratic women along with the courtly love scenario.[14] The Protestant ideal of the domestic "helpmeet" certainly held wider applicability for nonaristocratic women. Furthermore, there seems a positive shift in the grounds upon which a woman is valued, in the change of emphasis from woman-as-Other, distanced and fetishized, to woman-as-same (or similar, even if lesser). These observations have merit, especially if they accurately match actual changes in the material conditions of and attitudes toward women. But the historical upheavals of the early modern period (not to mention such formidable literary achievements as *Paradise Lost*) do not unambiguously support such an optimistic reading of this cultural shift; moreover, the latter claim about the way women were perceived hinges on an assumed change in the male perspective rather than an expansion of women's actual roles.[15] As noted by many historians following in the wake of Joan Kelly, it is not obvious that women had a renaissance, nor that the seventeenth century signalled a time of unambiguous progress for women.

Sara Heller Mendelson observes that of the three stages into which female life was divided by seventeenth-century thinkers (virginity, marriage, and widowhood), Stuart women's diaries make clear that "despite continual subordination to parents or guardians, maidenhood represented the most carefree and enjoyable of the three female conditions. Indeed, most of the anxieties expressed by the youngest writers in the group stemmed from their guilt at taking too much pleasure in life. . . . Once marriage was in prospect, however, young women often entered a tense and anxious period" (191). She quotes Alice Thornton, who wrote "For my owne perticuler, I was not hastie to change my free estate without much consideration . . . wherein none could be more satisfied," and Mary Boyle, who "still continued to have an aversion to maridge, liveing so much at my ease that I was unwilling to change my condition" (192–93). Remarking that two diarists who remained unmarried apparently "were perfectly happy in their maiden state," Mendelson also notes that "one pattern exhibited in both happy and unhappy marriages is the role played by contemporary religious teaching in reinforcing wifely obedience" (193, 194). Along with the teachings often came the physical devices of constraint, including the horrific scold's bridle. Without in any way presuming that single life was generally preferable, one can still observe that marriage was seldom a state to be idealized from the woman's perspective. Even if one wishes to emphasize the existence of individual companionate arrangements that avoided such problems and restraints, the marriage itself remains more than a "private" pact, and involves both parties in the legal and social inequalities of that institution. Writing in the early eighteenth century about "the forlorn state of matrimony," Lady Mary Wortley Montagu sardonically concluded, "we have nothing to excuse ourselves but that it was done a great while ago and we were very young when we did it" (Moira Ferguson 7).

Obviously the aristocratic emphasis on courtly love did not prevent the marital traffic in women from being a means of restricting social power and access. Tennenhouse emphasizes this economic and social collusion of marriage: "Strict regulation of marriage insured the power of those inside the empowered community, which in turn enhanced the value of their bloodline and the desirability of marrying into it. In short, strict regulation of marriage insured the value of aristocratic women" (26). Even if the "empowered community" and the equation of aristocratic women's value with their role as breeders remain problematic, Tennenhouse's comments usefully counter any reading that would romanticize the aristocratic representation of women as simply superior or liberating. But they also remind us that even for wealthy, privileged women, marriage as happy ending implies not just a place for the expression of female sexuality but also a policing of desire in the service of the patriarchal order.

For many reasons, structural as well as political, marriage can serve as an exquisite narrative conclusion: in theory, it unites erotic passion with legal restraint in a social contract, brings the "opposite" sexes together, and licenses procreation. Yet its symbolic power, like that of an elegant causal narrative, may obscure its cost, that which is subordinated or sacrificed en route—be it socially efficacious lyricism, female self-assertion, or "feminine" values. Viewing in hindsight, knowing the subsequent literature and history which increasingly made matrimony appear to be the *only* proper place for women, one may decide that the courtly romance plot is not as problematic for women's representation as is the marital conclusion. Although the focus was limited and self-involved, within that world of courtship women could wield power and claim status as beings, whereas the movement toward marriage coincident with the love of a "one-and-only" shifts the emphasis within the romance to a woman's lack, her sense of inadequacy or dissatisfaction.[16] That is, the woman's plot begins with a not-being who only "becomes" by acceding to another form of not-being, taking the role of silent partner in the unrepresented happy-ever-after-marriage (from which the male may sally forth on quest after quest). One can observe these tensions made absurdly overt in the draft of a seventeenth-century closet drama entitled "The Convent of Pleasure," written by Margaret Cavendish, the "mad" duchess of Newcastle. Because

> Marriage is a Curse we find
> Especially to Women kind:
> From the Cobler's Wife we see,
> To Ladies, they unhappie be,

Lady Happy retires to a virginal cloister to enjoy the single life with her dear female friends, including a cross-dressing shepherdess who pretends to be a courtly "servant" (Moira Ferguson 89). The tyranny of marriage as the standard happy ending nevertheless intrudes, leading to the perfunctory revelation that the "servant" is a prince, who marries Lady Happy and takes her away from the pleasurable convent. As exemplified here, the dramatic movement toward plots resolving in happy marriage, in concert with social changes begun with the Protestant Reformation, may have created a more monolithic and socially limiting representation of women's fortunes than did the lyrical strains of courtly love.

Of course courtly love (as an alternative or supplement to marriage) was an elitist phenomenon, and need not be glorified in order to acknowledge moments of enabling female representation within its rhetoric.[17] Marriage, no more than courtly love, need be villified. Rather, by noting these historical complications as well as those moments where commentary about Shakespeare seems to replicate the values his drama upholds, we may better understand how his legacy endures to shape our reading of alternative Elizabethan perspectives on lyricism and female power. The lyrical plays examined here, like the cult of Elizabeth itself, interrogate and qualify the images of private, romantic love-and-marriage that dominate the thinking of subsequent centuries. There remain huge differences, obviously, between charting historical trends and statistical evidence about women's conditions, and speculating about the impact or influence of stories, the role of fictions in shaping and inscribing experience. But if the romantic possibilities of illicit or sublimated courtly love narratives were in some ways an "escape valve" for those feeling restrained and in need of fantasy, the fantasy itself was surely not the root of the problem. Nor did the replacement of courtly love by companionate marriage set the stage for a consideration of novel alternatives for female characters to evade societal restriction—even when plays represent the miseries of enforced marriage, for example, or the fate of a woman who rejects social control (as in *The Duchess of Malfi*). The public drama of the seventeenth century relentlessly guides females toward marriage, death, or both. Moreover, in subsequent scholarly writing about the place of courtly lyricism, the emphasis on marriage as resolution gives undue primacy to narrative over lyric performance in drama. It has encouraged readings that evaluate the characters according to a normative biographical plot and label alternative discourses and moments of representation dismissively (the "courtly love syndrome" syndrome).

Poetic images and myths of "private" relations do not evade the "public" social orders in which they are created. Sue-Ellen Case, in speaking of the shift from one kind of female impersonator to another, rightly acknowledges that neither form of masquerade evades systemic male domination: "When female actors appeared on the stage [during the Restoration], the fiction of the female gender had been securely inscribed on real women. This age marked a transition from the virgin goddess Athena (and the virgin queen Elizabeth) to the sex goddess of the twentieth century. Either way, women did not escape the role of merchandise in the world of male exchange" (*Feminism* 27). But to the extent that the Virgin Queen also prompted consideration of women's power and roles *other than* those directly correlated to erotic male exchange and control, perhaps we should not be overhasty to equate all renderings, to see only virginity or chastity where (as in Peele's *Arraignment*) other qualities are set in play. Moreover, Elizabeth saw an alternative way of wielding power by manipulating the marital system rather than taking a position (that is, being placed) within it. Speaking of Sir John Harington's response to Elizabeth's adamant opposition to marriages, Tennenhouse observes that "Far from criticizing the queen's uncompromising regulation of marriage among the nobility, he understands it as a crucial feature of her domestic statecraft, a sovereign right, and thus as a source of state power" (29). Her repeated discouragement of marriage implied worries about more than specific dynastic threats and personal vanity, as did her expressions of concern for her ladies-in-waiting. Following Carol Neeley's advice to attend to possibilities of female subjectivity, we need not reduce all the queen's actions and artistic representation (of her or indeed of the female gender) to mere commodification of herself and others as "merchandise," even though that was inevitably one aspect of her exceptional status.

Mihoko Suzuki, discussing Olivia's role in *Twelfth Night* and drawing on earlier work by feminist scholars, sums up the case for Queen Elizabeth's impact as a literary model:

> In this case, the comic convention of 'woman on top' cannot be dismissed as merely a carnivalesque inversion, because a woman actually occupies the throne. Although Allison Heisch has cautioned that Elizabeth's rule did not improve the general lot of women in England, it is nevertheless true that Elizabeth served as a model for those of her countrywomen who aspired to assert themselves against men. 1589 saw the publication of *Jane Anger, her Protection for Women*, the first English defense of women written by a woman, and addressed to a female audience; Jane Anger was followed by other female writers such as Constantia Munda and Esther Sowernam, who cites the example of Elizabeth as 'not only the glory of our sex, but a pattern for the best men to imitate.' Lady Anne Clifford began her diary upon the death of Elizabeth and chronicled her determination to defend herself against her husband's claim to her property, even though he had James I as a supporter against her. (44–45)

Both the happily married Anne Bradstreet and the twice unhappily wed Lady Anne Clifford explicitly claimed Elizabeth as a model and authority for their literary efforts; the aristocratic ladyloves of Elizabethan fiction, resisting the plot-ending solution of marriage, may similarly have held an attraction for women seeking stories of female self-assertion.[18] Such models and representations certainly provided fodder for later women's interpretation, even if many of the authors who constructed the venerable images were themselves skeptical.

This acknowledged, it ultimately does not get us far to endorse or enshrine one strain of Elizabethan ideology over another categorically, any more than favoring only one axis of drama's interplay between lyric and narrative suffices to explain its rich representations. Instead, we need to recognize the competition and conflict between dominant and emergent cultural ideals about gender relations as another intersection, another source for complex art and debate about values and social possibilities. Clearly, the division of reality into two spheres of public and private, with love and lyricism confined to the latter, is a compelling artistic fantasy rather than an historically accurate representation of Elizabethan culture. Being conscious of this distinction, we may acknowledge the power and dangers of such aesthetic patterning. As a result, we may gain a clearer sense of the aesthetically productive aspects of the ideological tensions conveyed within lyrical drama. We may be more alert to the complex interplay between the lyrical moments within a romance plot, often associated with things feminine (although complicated by Shakespeare), and the narrative movement toward the sense of an adequate ending. In the lyrical dramas explored here, the ironies and fissures within Elizabethan representations of courtliness appear, alongside courtly love's potential for empowerment and restriction from a variety of perspectives. Thus we need not reromanticize the woman on the pedestal, as if she provided an unproblematic source of female power or was positioned outside the realm of patriarchal consent, in order to counter the converse narrative which rejects courtly love in favor of companionate marriage, as if the latter were intrinsically better and somehow avoided similar (or even greater) problems of social positioning for women.

A wildly inexact but memorable analogy may reinforce this point. During the sixties' "sexual revolution," many women found that the new compulsion to be sexually active (in a certain culturally prescribed way) was just as constraining as, and sometimes more physically dangerous than, traditional sexual prohibitions; what nevertheless *did* become significant and sometimes even liberating was the possibility of upheaval and different options, of sexuality as a mutable social construct rather than a narrow code presented under the guise of nature (although inevitably situated within an ideological frame). What remains fascinating about Elizabethan court culture and the performances that responded to it is the variety of representations and contexts in which similar lyric patterns and situations were dramatized, and the range of signification about lyric's place *and* women's place which emerged from a coincidence of concerns—perhaps foregrounded in artistic performance more than at any time in English culture, before or since.

⌘

> I shoved over a twenty for the stockings and spotted Old Bill on the back. That gave me a start, to see how Shakespeare, to whom our family owed so much, had turned into actual currency, not just on any old bank note but on a high denomination one, to boot. Though not as high as Florence Nightingale, which gives me satisfaction as a woman.
>
> Dora Chance, in Angela Carter's
> *Wise Children* (191)

In all the lyric performances examined in *Passion Made Public,* fruitful tensions emerge from perceived differences between lyric and narrative, the values of romance and of political power, and female and male. Sometimes familiar dichotomies are overturned, other times confirmed, but within the dynamic flexibility of drama these polarities contribute to capacious art, open to a multiplicity of interpretations each with cultural consequences. That multiplicity and complexity is too often discounted, and sometimes disappears entirely, in subsequent critical history. The interplay of positions becomes embalmed into categories and antitheses, rigid rules and separate spheres. Not only was lyric gradually "privatized" but the lyrical discourse that did not fit newer theoretical models was demeaned. The ever-amusing Dr. Johnson may have been the most powerful force in creating blanket criticisms on the basis of rhetorical style or form. His definitions: "sonnet"—not very suitable to the English language; "sonneteer"—a small poet, in contempt.

Dr. Johnson has many twentieth-century descendants in criticism of sonnetizing, albeit with less obvious scorn and wit. More helpfully, speaking of the linguistic energy in *Love's Labour's Lost,* William Carroll reminds us that "poetry is almost always language used for its own sake as well as language used referentially; not an absolute polarity, but a kind of double exposure" (63). The poetic functions of display and representation are neither separable nor the same, and hence cannot be equated nor judged independently of one another. At stake are aesthetic and social judgments alike.

Douglas Bruster has remarked that "As lyric and drama argue over the power of poetry and the importance of time, the definition of these two concepts becomes inextricably linked in the debate. Also contested, of course, is the concept of domination itself" (68). While it is true that a contest about domination is played out between lyric and (narrative) "drama" onstage, it involves historical investments and changes as well as two generic concepts. Before being mocked, Elizabethan courtly art managed to unite poetry and drama in a uniquely rich and close relationship, and provided a vocabulary for refinement and commentary on the public stage. The discrediting of lyric on the theatrical stage is not so much a formal necessity as it is the product of a changing social landscape, and it involved the dramaturgical choices of middle-class male playwrights. Courtly lyricism collides with different ideological agendas, as well as an ironic and compelling awareness of narrative, in the works of seventeenth-century dramatists.

During Elizabeth Tudor's reign, the tensions induced by female sovereignty helped to create the competing perspectives dramatized in lyrical plays; surprised adulation and uneasiness continued to permeate the portrayal of her in sequent centuries. Even those employed to praise Elizabeth created ambiguous images, hardly surprising given the negative stereotypes against which she contended. Although John Knox had intended that his railing against the "monstrous regiment of women" would discredit a Catholic queen, its ill-timed publication in 1558 gave powerful voice to a misogyny that knew no religious bounds. Early in Elizabeth's reign when Pope Pius V wrote to encourage the earls in the Northern Rebellion, he praised the attempt "to deliver yourselves and the kingdom from the basest servitude of a woman's lust [ex turpissimma muliebris libidinis servitute]," adding "far better is it, for the confession of God, to fly by a compendious and glorious death, to eternal life, than, living basely and ignominiously, to serve the will of an impotent woman [impotentis foeminae cupiditati], with the injury of your souls."[19]

The undercurrent of resentment and contempt for the unmarried sovereign was not confined to political enemies. In his comic conversations with William Drummond, Ben Jonson (author of the laudatory *Cynthia's Revels* only a few years before the queen's death) remarked that Elizabeth was so vain as not to look at herself in a glass when old, that she painted vermilion on her nose, and furthermore—stretching his credibility as a courtly insider—that "she had a Membrana on her which made her uncapable of man" (Herford and Simpson 1: 142–43). Like his stage debunking of the fairy queen mythology in the disguise of *The Alchemist*'s Dol Common, and his contextual mockery of lyric invitation in lewd and corrupt Volpone's "Come my Celia" (the ineffectual prelude to an abortive attempt at rape), Ben Jonson's jokes testify to backstage skepticism about the pageant of courtly praise. And like the overt satire of these plays, they illustrate the shift away from courtly comedy and potent lyricism in narrative drama during the reign of James Stuart.

Because lyric was increasingly associated with alternatives to the "manly" "public" "real world" represented onstage, especially in the complicated maneuvering achieved by Shakespeare, the late Elizabethan playwrights provide a source and authority for subsequent aesthetics that identified lyric as unworldly, private, transcendent, and apolitical. Tellingly, in courtly works written for performance before the queen, dismissiveness of lyric's social voice is masked or openly denied, whereas in works performed in public theaters, lyric forms become obviously "otherworldly" and are often satirized.[20] After Elizabeth's death, little political incentive countered the tendency toward privatizing lyric, and indeed the Cavalier poets found refuge from public hostility and defeat, as mystics found escape from the encroaching authority of empirical science, in lyric's privacy.

The growing privatization and mockery of courtly lyricism onstage was not simply a consequence of the queen's life or death, of course. The happenstance of royal inheritance by the Stuarts coincided with major social, economic, and political changes to alter the setting for staged lyricism, and indeed for poetry and theater themselves. The Civil War and epistemelogical revolution in the seventeenth century contributed variously to the reduced social place of lyric. Illustrative of this change is E. W. Tayler's account in *Literary Criticism of Seventeenth-Century England* of the narrowing definition of "wit" during that century. As a corollary, one may note the gradual separation and subordination of verse (of all sorts) from social representation onstage in Restoration comedy, even in works by, for, and about the "wits" and courtiers. The trajectory of retreat from the true political landscape in seventeenth-century country house poems, traced by Raymond Williams in *The Country and the City,* parallels the fate of courtly lyricism. Over time, some of the reasons that lyric was functional in public discourse and political representations disappeared.

Changes in the form and practice of reading also worked to erase Elizabethan contexts for lyrical drama. As in the case of the songs from *Love's Labour's Lost,* lyrics were already being published in miscellanies when enacted onstage, and so the detachment of songs and lyrics from a performance context was not entirely subsequent to Elizabeth's reign, nor entirely new. But whereas the miscellanies had been only one of several contexts for lyric, in an increasingly textual rather than oral culture (especially after the closing of the public theaters in 1642) the sense of generic distance between lyric poetry and narrative drama once again widened. Fluidity of occasion and setting for lyric poetry gradually diminished, and in the wake of Romanticism the "otherworldliness" of lyric gained a radically new value—but not as part of an alternative social or dramatic world. Instead, the insularity and sublimity of poetic odes created an idealized masculine province transforming feminized nature and mortal desire; contemporaneously, "feminine" love lyrics—such as the highly popular sonnets of Elizabeth Barrett Browning—became the poetic correlate to the sentimental novel, notoriously disdained by the likes of Coleridge, Wollstonecraft, and Hawthorne.[21] When Elizabethan lyric passages were defended, it was often for their luster and self-contained beauty, like exquisite jewels. Removed from its social landscape, such poetry also became the occasion for royalist nostalgia and the mythology of merrie olde England, sparkling into the exclusively "golden" aestheticism of the twentieth century when lauded by C. S. Lewis.

Not surprisingly, the scholarship romanticizing Elizabeth's reign as a golden age for England amassed during Queen Victoria's later years. It resurrected the powerful mythology of female rule at a time when constitutional government had superseded monarchism. Obviously less contingent on the monarch, the mystique of empire was nevertheless essential to nineteenth-century nationalist policies, and could be bolstered by appeals to royal sovereignty. Thus the image of Elizabeth's reign was codified to elicit emotion rather than complicated analysis, and has often been reinvoked in the service of Tory and nationalist agendas. Indeed, the virgin-virago Elizabeth was popularly invoked as the imperfect type prefiguring Victoria, the truly womanly sovereign. This even occurred in the United States, among those claiming their inheritance of language, culture, and gender roles from Britain. One example of such overt mythologizing may suffice to capture its mood, and substantiate critical fears about remystifying Elizabeth even from this great distance of time and place.

In Charles Morris's turn-of-the-century U.S. biography, *The Life of Queen Victoria and the Story of Her Reign: A Beautiful Tribute to England's Greatest Queen in Her Domestic and Official Life,* he praises his subject as "at once a great Queen and a noble woman," unlike her famous predecessors: "The Sovereign was not lost in the woman, as was unworthily the case in the reign of Anne. Neither was the woman lost in the Sovereign, as was too often the case amid the splendors of the Elizabethan era" (27). Morris supports his judgment with unspecified "journalistic summaries" (544) upon the death of

Victoria which at times associate Elizabeth's political power and variance from nineteenth-century gender roles with savagery, and Victoria's domesticity and less direct rule with national progress:

> Splendid as are the memorials of English power recorded by the historians of the Elizabethan era, the Victorian surpassed them in the substantial achievements of modern progress. While Elizabeth, with her masculine force and imperious disposition, exerted a more pronounced personal influence on the course of national history, Victoria was not less admirably adapted to the requirements and necessities of her own age. When her reign began personal government in England came to an end. . . . but she also exerted her influence with true womanliness, innate gentleness and marked individuality [thus advancing her subjects' prosperity and] ennobling the virtues and purity of home life. . . . Brilliant as was the reign of Elizabeth, alike in intellectual and material progress, it came in an age of mediaevalism . . . and its lustre pales before that of the reign of Victoria, when a high civilization was gathering the richest fruits. (547)

The shift to (male) parliamentary power underwrites this feminization of monarchy, enshrining a model of indirect moral influence as "true womanliness" (at the same historical moment when women's suffragists were fighting to gain access to the modern system of sovereignty, the locus of direct political power, through their campaign for the vote). In those passages where Morris wishes to compare rather than contrast the splendors of two great English "eras," he twice invokes the dashing male figure of Sir Walter Ralegh helping his queen as prefiguring Prince Albert (101, 156) and redirects attention to the true sources of greatness, the men attending the queens: "Shall we conclude that these two women shed a lustre upon their respective reigns which no man could equal? Scarcely this; but they had the happy fortune to be born into the most remarkable periods of the history of the British realm. Around the throne of Elizabeth gathered the noblest cluster of authors of modern times, at their head the prince of the authors of all time, Shakespeare the sublime" (543). In a wondrous inversion of sovereignty reminiscent of Shakespeare's own dramatic sleight-of-hand, the author becomes a timeless "prince" and the queen a historical witness legitimized by his presence. In such discussions, the complex politics of gender as they had actually been performed disappear, and history is reformulated to fit romantic assumptions and nineteenth-century notions of sexual difference.[22]

Nor did this romanticization fade away with Victoria. As Britain was threatened by invasion in World War II and then by economic and political decline as a world power, nostalgic images in scholarship served to buoy cultural spirits. F. S. Boas's "Queen Elizabeth in Drama," the published version of a 1948 address commemorating her accession date, exemplifies such nationalism only thinly veiled as literary criticism (though it does provide an introduction to many of the romanticized nineteenth-century representations such as Tom Taylor's *Twixt Axe and Crown,* Tennyson's *Queen Mary,* and Swinburne's *Mary Stuart*). Boas quotes Elizabeth's Tilbury speech as filtered through Thomas Heywood's representation in *If You Know Not Me, You Know Nobody* as "words applicable to this country's situation to-day" (19), recalling only positive contemporary allusions to the queen (hence he notes the imperial votress speech but not the mocked Titania in *A Midsummer Night's Dream,* even though he goes on to cite Dekker's Titania in *The Whore of Babylon* as a figure of Elizabeth). After describing plays in which Elizabeth denies lovers or takes them, hates Mary Stuart or laments her, he casts off his scholarly pose (and even echoes her motto "semper eadem") when he concludes that "Whether viewed by playwrights of Tudor and Stuart, or of Victorian and Georgian days, she is still the same. They and we see her proudly confronting every threat and peril; loyal to her ideals . . . even when in conflict with her womanly instincts"; no wonder when he states in a related essay that "I am still a believer in the spacious times of great Elizabeth" (35, 37).

The twentieth-century plays Boas cites share his veneration, and moreover replicate Morris's movement to crown Shakespeare as true sovereign. The wittiest and most ironic is Shaw's 1910 *The Dark Lady of the Sonnets,* in which Mary Fitton laments having struck the cloaked Elizabeth as she kissed Shakespeare: "Will, I am lost: I have struck the Queen"; to which Will rejoinds, "Woman: you have struck William Shakespeare" (32). Given Shaw's stagecraft and his sense of rivalrous superiority to Shakespeare, it is not surprising that the mockery embraces all the figures here, albeit still with the end of elevating the playwright (and more pragmatically raising money for a national theater). Clemence Dane's 1921 *Will Shakespeare* replicates this dynamic unironically, making Shakespeare the confidant of an unlikely Elizabeth who "knows the flesh is sweetest" and envies Mary Stuart's fate: "Think you I'd not have changed, / . . . To have her story?" Elizabeth herself pronounces her sovereign displacement here, welcoming Shakespeare to "Take you the kingship on you" (31). In the most bizarrely courtly anecdote, Boas unironically recalls a *Masque of Hope* performed before Princess Elizabeth (now Queen Elizabeth II) at Oxford in May 1945 and authored by the drama scholar Nevill Coghill. In it Clio, the muse of history, speaks of Elizabeth I:

>She made England one.
>Under her rule this island was secure,
>Her honour bright and her religion pure. . . .
>What more is there to say in this recital?
>This, she was *Shakespeare's friend.* Her proudest title.
>
>(34)

Given such extravagant and cautionary queenly images and the oppressive legacy of empire and monarchism, scholars may well desire to shy away from any continued emphasis on aristocratic culture and Elizabeth. Obviously many historical forces were at work in creating great poetic drama, and not all late Tudor artistic trends are attributable or even related to female sovereignty; modern historians rightly work to correct the traditional overemphasis on monarchs and "great men" as the causes of change. Nevertheless, given the close, conscious associations of Petrarchism and courtly lyricism with Elizabeth's court, in this particular and exceptional case of lyrical drama's creation and brief predominance, the queen's influence remains undeniably important. It constitutes one small yet crucial part of the answer to my initiatory question of why the Elizabethan was the great age of poet-playwrights and lyrical drama. We can surely acknowledge the fruitful intersection of interests in the specific arena of lyrical performance during Elizabeth's reign, and credit her presence as crucial in their creation, without echoing such anachronistic hagiography as Morris's and Boas's.

Especially in the United States, in place as well as time farther removed from the particular class structure and economy of British imperialism, Morris's usurpation of the throne for Shakespeare may resonate more powerfully and familiarly than do images of the queen. The gendered politics of our own fin-de-siècle decade began with the remarkable string of botched and decontextualized quotations from Shakespeare dragged out along with Anita Hill during Judge Clarence Thomas's nomination hearings before the Senate Judiciary Committee. Marjorie Garber (along with many journalists) has called attention to the absurd ironies in these allusions, as well as the equally thick referentiality to Shakespeare in Oliver Stone's *J.F.K.* —the Bard haunting two rare moments of direct intersection between the national political process and popular media in the United States.[23] Shakespeare's ghostly presence has been invoked to provide requisite weight and stature to political discourse at those moments when even the most seasoned public speakers seem to be conscious of their potential absurdity.

A related case of recent popular borrowing, this time from the lyrical play *Richard II,* is equally rife with irony. It provides a parallel to the scholarly decontextualization of Elizabethan love lyrics that I have remarked upon; it also displays the humorous consequences of separating lyrical language from its dramatic location unwittingly. The famous passage begins:

> This royal throne of kings, this sceptred isle,
> This earth of majesty, this seat of Mars,
> This other Eden, demi-paradise,
> This fortress built by Nature for herself
> Against infection and the hand of war,
> This happy breed of men, this little world,
> This precious stone set in the silver sea
> Which serves it in the office of a wall
> Or as a moat defensive to a house
> Against the envy of less happier lands,
> This blessèd plot, this earth, this realm, this England.
> (2.1.40–50)

In the "free market" era when capitalism seems to have displaced religion as the bedrock of faith and when a global economy shakes the sovereignty of nations, a few of the words of Shakespeare's John of Gaunt reappear, to console and give direction—in an advertisement for United Airlines. Having taken over the European routes of failing Pan American Airlines (one of many casualties of 1980s government deregulation and a deficit economy), United found a genius of the soundbite to choose lines that had earlier stirred patriotism in the breast of Samuel Taylor Coleridge. And as in Coleridge's quotation of this speech, the airline ad relies on the audience's contextual amnesia.

According to Collier's transcript of Coleridge's twelfth lecture (1811), "When Coleridge felt that upon the morality of England depended her safety, and that her morality was supported by our national feelings, he could not read these lines without triumph." The triumph is one of selective quotation, for Coleridge cites the words beginning "This royal throne of kings" and ending with the words "Of Watery Neptune" (despite Shakespeare's syntax, Collier inserts a period after them; see Foakes 117). What he omits from direct quotation (or even mention) is the historical action being lamented amidst the eponyms, the action motivating John of Gaunt's speech and inciting the subsequent tragedy: that the land of England "Is now leased out, I die pronouncing it, / Like to a tenement or pelting farm" (2.1.59–60). The speech, that is, laments a paradise already lost, a debtor government rather than an empire triumphant. By proceeding until "Neptune," Coleridge seems to signal his own delight in misprision, for that requires him to ignore the grammar of not one but two parallel sentences, twice deleting the less glorious predicates that would undermine his nominal praise.

> England, bound in with the triumphant sea
> Whose rocky shores beats back the envious siege
> Of watery Neptune, *is now bound in with shame,*
> *With inky blots and rotten parchment bonds,*
> *That England that was wont to conquer others*
> *Hath made a shameful conquest of itself.*
> (2.1.61–66; emphasis added)

Erasing Gaunt's angry conclusions, Coleridge disrupts the periodic syntax and the careful balance between two images of England—past and present, glory and shame, power and impoverishment, shining poetic ideal and inky historical reality—that allowed the speech to epitomize the dramatic structure and thematic conflict of *Richard II*. His is the truly sentimental reading, for all his professions of manliness and triumph.

What for Coleridge swelled national pride now sells tickets, for a means of transportation that makes the speech's praise of England's impregnability entirely obsolete. Even without the "pelting farm," this is indeed a different ideological economy. The ironies of context have altered, but are no less piquant. Letting us hear the rhythm but not the reason of Shakespeare's verse, the United advertisement's voice-over encourages flight to a pretty, quaint Old Country, nicely deletes the "moat defensive," and once again ends without the verbs. Choosing only a few stirring phrases, the ad echoes the cost of detaching the lyric and narrative components that created Shakespeare's rich drama; it reduces vital art to nostalgic emptiness, consoling only to the comfortably numb. Or, seen from another angle by an informed audience, the advertisement reveals the impossibility of evading context without looking very silly, the revenge of words treated carelessly— the same lesson learned by the lustful lords when they callowly sonnetize in *Love's Labour's Lost*. Learning from the French ladies of that play, we need not be silencing purists who wish to prevent the borrowing and recontextualization of Elizabethan lyrical passages. But if we do not wish to be "bought" ourselves, we may wish to remember the full representation, the complex interweaving of narrative and lyric that created particular resonances. We may also wish to remember the social consequences of choosing a voice.

Invoking a historical memory and an ear attuned to reason as well as rhyme, we can discover more in Elizabethan lyrical drama than the unintended jokes provided by advertising agencies; its analogies and echoes remain copious and sometimes unexpectedly applicable. For example, Barbara Johnson has spoken to the distinction between acceptable allegorical figures of women and the disruptive presence of actual women in male domains, which in some recent cases (such as debates over men's clubs and fraternities) has led to a strategic redefinition of public and private spaces.[24] Considered in light of this subsequent history, Peele's conclusion to *The Arraignment of Paris* seems all the more striking: here the most overtly allegorical figurations—the pagan goddesses as represented by boy actors—reach outside the artistic frame of representation to offer their fruit to the queen regnant, the actual woman positioned within the traditionally male public political domain. In fusing these imaginative realms, Peele's drama counters the dominant tradition and legacy of western art. However, because his work was produced within the courtly center of state power, its representation of gender has usually been obscured and the mantle of radical innovation rewarded to the emergent drama of "new men"—Marlowe, Shakespeare, Jonson—which emphasizes the struggles and contradictions produced by an aristocratic hierarchy. At the same time, the repression of sexuality in Peele's happy ending serves as a reminder of the lasting difficulties involved in challenging traditional gender roles and confronting female sexuality simultaneously.

The works of all these playwrights still demonstrate a variety of social functions for lyric poetry, even when making it the object of satire and ridicule. Their dramatization both counters and paves the way for later conceptions of lyric, indicating the creative range of possibilities, as well as constraints, adhering in the association between lyric and the feminine. What remains necessarily elusive is the exact "fit" between Elizabethan symbolic representations and their social functions; for even when the drama is not so overtly allegorical as were the court entertainments, the mixture of readability and resistance to interpretation that characterizes art complicates all historicist endeavors. But this complexity also enriches the texts which remain, their tensions keeping them alive as rhetoric, as poetry, and as the cultural artifacts we may follow Leah Marcus in calling "puzzles."

As Dennis Kay aptly observes, "Uncertainty about where the boundary between fiction and actuality should or can be drawn—or, to put it differently, about the consequences of the permeability of literary discourse to other modes of discursive practice—can be exemplified throughout the latter part of Elizabeth's reign; it was an uncertainty that many participants in court and political affairs exploited" (20). We can hardly pretend to be more sure about the boundaries than were those who witnessed those years. Elizabeth herself saw the linkage of courtly art and politics from early on in her reign, as when she reacted to Dudley's pageant between Juno and Diana by remarking to the Spanish ambassador that "this is all against me" (Calendar of State Papers, Spanish 404). Without wishing to fall into the trap Leeds Barroll uncovers in some new as well as old historicism, of constructing a simplified causal narrative out of complicated and sparsely documented events, we can certainly acknowledge that courtly lyricism intertwined with Elizabethan politics; I have cited both specific examples and suggestive correlations throughout these chapters.[25] And those artworks which meld lyric and performance, though not so powerfully rendered or broadly appreciated as Shakespeare's, also left a legacy which need not be ignored because of the absence of a Bard and the presence of a venerated lady. Although the instititutions of criticism early worked to obscure it, the resonance of these courtly works remains: ambiguous and, from some perspectives, appealing in their complex representations of female sovereignty and subjectivity.

Elizabeth's forty years on the English throne saw the development and variation in use of lyric within drama, a rich interaction that remains to challenge easy generic or gendered preconceptions about art, and to engage and delight its audiences. Almost in spite of the historical impetus toward separate lyrical and political worlds that informs Marlowe's and Shakespeare's drama, one legacy of Elizabeth's reign, and part of her continued fascination, resides in these playwrights' complex representations of a mythic and artistic tradition created for the queen—a powerful landscape both for poetry and for female figuration. By recapturing that landscape in all its variety and complexity, we not only do greater justice to the past. We may also discover different positions for poetry within our own cultural matrix, and reclaim a lyrical passion which turns out to have been born, as well as made, public.

Notes

1. Stevens locates a split between the art forms of music and poetry at least as early as the fifteenth century (29ff.), and observes that the "idealized union of 'artistic' music and poetry" was a creation of the later sixteenth century (68); thus the notion of a more integrated past relationship, somehow destroyed by textuality, is actually less a historical than a fictional construct (in keeping with the Edenic my-

thology of Shakespeare's English history plays). On sonnets and privacy, see Ferry and Fumerton. Acknowledging the limits (and indeed potential deceptiveness) of the word "private," Fumerton's use of it to signify the unrepresentable testifies to its power in the subsequent history of lyric poetry (see " 'Secret' Arts" 126). She sees a stark contrast between "lyrical expressions of love" in sonnets and miniatures, and the "strict narrative continuity of drama" (108).

2. Despite his recognition that with the end of lyric speech comes the end of the play (107), Calderwood regards *Romeo and Juliet* as the story of Shakespeare's gradual estrangement from his "enameled, repetitive, lyrical style in favor of one that is concentrated, complex, and dramatic" (102). Recognizing that "the word never gets placed in public circulation" (118), he sees this as a flaw of the discourse itself, of Petrarchism insufficiently redeemed. Hibbard finds "something prodigal about [Shakespeare's] use of language in the early plays" ("Words" 49). See also Baxter, R. Berry, and Hill. For an excellent discussion influenced by Nancy Vickers's work, see Whittier.

3. Calderwood sees the families as resolving the play: in "this wider social marriage the play finds its formal resolution, and so it is ultimately to Shakespeare's maturing concept of dramatic form that the lovers are sacrificed" (108). Others who link the demise of the lovers with their "immature" poetic style include Baxter, R. Berry, Dickey, and Seward. Hibbard judges "true dramatic poetry" as only that which functions within the fiction to advance the narrative and characterization (*Making* 17–36).

4. See Montrose's analysis ("Shaping"); Erickson (*Patriarchal*, chap. 1) focuses on similar reinscription in *As You Like It*, as contrasted with the uneasy ending of *Love's Labour's Lost*.

5. Coleridge explicitly associates Richard with a politically disabling concept of femininity: "still he was weak and womanish, and possessed feelings, which, though amiable in a female, are misplaced in a man, and altogether unfit for a King" (Foakes 119).

6. Novy views the affinity between Shakespeare's dramatic form and his character's view in a more benign light, perhaps in part because she does not consider the specific dramatic antecedents: "In trying to get Antonio with his ascetic idealism to accept the value of marriage, Portia and Shakespeare are acting analogously to those Renaissance humanists and puritans who were writing in praise of marriage, modifying traditional devaluations of women, and criticizing the application of the ideal of celibacy" (80). Novy stresses the mutuality of love as a positive balance to patriarchal law, despite Bassanio's lightweight character. Yet his allure seems primarily attributable to good looks, Italian birth, and the ability to speak rationally (unlike her other suitors), whereas Portia, who now serves him, by contrast displays wit, generosity, intense emotion, and a subtle mind, in addition to beauty, chastity, and wealth. See Howard for a reading that stresses Portia's subversive potential, at least in comparison with Rosalind and Viola ("Crossdressing" 433, 439).

7. Much has been made of Elizabeth's "representation" as the undramatized "fair vestal, throned by the west" but as spoken by Oberon and set within the larger plot, this lyrical moment of compliment for the "imperial votress" unaffected by Cupid's "quenched" shaft may seem nearly as ironic as Marlowe's "praise" for Eliza in Iarbus's mouth. Tennenhouse remarks that at the end of *A Midsummer Night's Dream* the "grotesque body has been included within the social order without overthrowing it, indeed with the effect of invigorating that order, as the entire community . . . [is] reinscribed within a traditional hierarchy" (44). One may add that the hierarchy is not only patriarchal but headed by the male sex; in obliterating the historical reality of female sovereignty, Shakespeare's representation thus is neither a simple replication of the actual Tudor "conservative" social order nor politically "inclusive" for Hippolyta and Titania as figures of public power or sovereignty. Once again, Shakespeare's drama romanticizes marriage and male sovereignty, precisely what Elizabeth's rule countered.

8. On the legal status of married women (or absence thereof), see J. Baker, Henderson and McManus (esp. 78–80), Prior, Stone, Wrightson, and Lucas (224–26).

9. In discussing Spenser's October eclogue, Goldberg similarly discerns a monarchic threat to the artist's (presumably prior) "authority." He purposely elides his own voice with that of the character Piers, noting that "To live the poet's life means to surrender to an other, authoring swallowed in authority," and that "Authority usurps the poet's role. Celebration of authority, making the text rest in Eliza, erects a monument that turns the text into the statue made by authority, a monument whose permanence depends upon its separation from the poet and its inscription within the domain of power" (*Voice* 49). I suspect that only a post-Romantic writer would feel so overtly that his role and authority predated and took precedence over the political world in which he lived. This language of usurpation and artistic sovereignty wittily echoes early twentieth-century bardolatry, examples of which I cite below.

10. Novy does list others who have stressed social theory but, finding their claims less persuasive, does not explore how the two emphases might qualify each other. Suzuki observes that the uncertainty about historical relations between the genders in this period "reflects the contradictions between woman's legal position— *in potestate maritorum,* under the absolute power of her husband—and her actual situation, which, according to Thomas Smith, gave her 'for the most part all the charge of the house and housholde'" (31). The contemporary Smith recognized, in his *De Republica Anglorum,* the difference between theory and practice regarding women's position. Such inevitable latitude created a large space for interpretation and dramatic representation of conflict. But as Boose's account ("Scolding") of scolds' bridles demonstrates, historical practice may often have been *more* hideous than the well-known restrictiveness of legal theories and theological precedents, and in any case cannot be detached from them.

11. For related critiques, see Erickson's review in *Shakespeare Quarterly* and Sacks

(474–77). Tennenhouse similarly describes *Twelfth Night* as representing the "dilemma arising when the aristocratic female *lacks* the kind of desire that elsewhere in the comedies provides the glue for a social world that is both homogeneous and hierarchical," his word choice reinscribing the male perspective on female experience (53). A woman's perspective on Petrarchan fantasy is quite different, as Jean Howard elaborates in her analysis of Olivia's resistance ("Crossdressing"). See also Yachnin, who refers to the "inclusive social order" at the conclusion of *A Midsummer Night's Dream* (54).

12. Boose, "Scolding" 181. She discusses some of the historical practices, including ritual humiliation and torture, upholding and upheld by the sanctity of male dominance within marriage. See also Moira Ferguson's introduction on Rev. John Sprint's 1699 sermons citing marriage as both the grounds and the means for subordinating women (*First Feminists* 16ff.).

13. Tennenhouse discounts the importance of Elizabeth as female, stressing instead how she demonstrates that a woman could assume the patriarchal sovereign position (a stance finding some support in Jordan's emphasis on the queen as in part rhetorically and iconographically male); thus social positioning *absolutely* precludes sex as the basis for his gender analysis. See Sacks's criticism of Tennenhouse's stress on the "fantasy" of Elizabeth marrying (475). See also P. Berry and Bassnett. Erickson concludes that Shakespeare "dissociates himself from the royal mythology of virginity . . . and registers uneasiness with the male powerlessness to which it leads" ("Order" 135)—or is imagined to lead.

14. See particularly Novy and Rose (*Expense*), who view the ideal of companionate marriage as providing a partial escape from the dualistic representation of women as virgins or whores (though acknowledging that such dualism reemerged later). I agree with Rose that a *potentially* greater range of attitudes toward women appears in Elizabethan drama; but the idealization of marriage became just as inhibiting an orthodoxy, and as part of the dominant ideology of modern life its legacy endures.

15. Milton certainly perpetuates the ideology that the sexes have different qualities and virtues, even when the woman is more familiar and sexually available to the man. Tellingly, Coleridge's defense of *Romeo and Juliet* hinges upon the "just conception of the female character" therein achieved and upon the necessity of marriage, clearly linked by his definition of what constitutes a well-drawn woman: "there is no one character in any of his [Shakespeare's] contemporaries describing a woman, of whom a man, seriously and truly examining his heart and good sense combined in one moment, could say, 'Let that woman be my supporter in life; let her be the aid of pursuit and the reward of my success'" (Foakes 74). For Coleridge, only marriage guarantees paternal affection and indeed civilization itself: "For without marriage, without exclusive attachment, there could be no human society: herds there might be, but society there could not be: there could be none of that delightful intercourse between Father and child . . ." (92). On the historical role of women, see J. Kelly,

Stone, Wall, Wrightson, and the collections edited by Prior, Rose, Haselkorn and Travitsky, and Henderson and McManus.

16. I borrow the phrase "one-and-only" from Theweleit's materialist analysis of relations between the sexes as reflective of class interests.

17. The development of an articulated feminist movement is subject to the same charges of elitism. It is easier to be heard and to protest systemic injustice from some ground of self-enfranchisement, be it provided by sex, race, or class position; aristocratic women could provide models of female social power within the gendered hierarchy. On the important influence of the religious sovereignty of souls for initiating women's radicalism, however, see Arnoult (in Fradenburg 228ff.). In addition to Gallagher, see Mendelson, who notes that although many women were taught to read, most were not taught to write, even to sign their names (182).

18. Among the notable poems by women in praise of Elizabeth, see Mary Sidney's "A Dialogue betweene two shepheards" and her dedicatory poem prefacing the Sidney translation of the Psalms, "To the Thrice-Sacred Queen Elizabeth" (1599); Diana Primrose's "A Chaine of Pearle. Or a Memoriall of the peerles Graces, and Heroick Vertues of Queene Elizabeth, of Glorious Memory" (1630); and Bradstreet's "In Honour of That High and Mighty Princess Queen Elizabeth of Happy Memory" (1650).

19. Brief from Pius V to the rebel earls, trans. Joseph Mendham (Collins 56–57).

20. On the commercial stage and the locations of public theaters, see esp. Weimann, Mullaney, Cook (*Privileged*), Tennenhouse, and Gurr. Serious attention to this pattern may at least bring back to earth the enthusiasm often expressed for public venues as protodemocratic (as does Yachnin's emphasis on the commercialism of this not quite truly "public" theater).

21. Homans explores the gendering of Romantic poetry and its difficulties for female authorship; see also Coleridge (Foakes 46). The legacy of Hawthorne's famed scorn for lady scribblers appears in Theodore Roethke's comment that women's poetry is the embroidery of trivial themes.

22. Hence the obsession with Elizabeth's "unwomanly" treatment of Mary Stuart, not confined to Schiller's romantic dramatization though encouraged by it. For an amusing example of such drama seeping back into "historical" accounts, see *Woman,* the ambitious turn-of-the-century study of famous women from the Garden of Eden through the nineteenth century, edited by William C. King: "The darkest stain on the memory of Elizabeth is her treatment of Mary, Queen of Scots. Her execution, though clamored for by the English nation, was an act of cruelty peculiarly revolting on the part of a female sovereign and kinswoman. And Elizabeth's affected reluctance to sign the death warrant, coupled with the most flagrant duplicity following closely upon it—all of which was over-acted and disgusting—is almost as injurious to the reputation of Elizabeth as the deed itself" (256). Conversely, the myth that Elizabeth and Essex were thwarted lovers could be

invoked to create sympathy for the suffering lady; both stories frequently recur in twentieth-century movies and popularizations.

23. Garber discussed these allusions in her MLA talk (Dec. 30, 1991) and includes them in her book *Media Spectacles*.

24. See also Warner. I cite B. Johnson's lecture, "Women and Allegory." In reference to the use of the muse and other female personifications as the ground for male authority, Johnson remarked that "allegory as the Other of the public is not private."

25. Barroll examines the actual evidence linking the performance of *Richard II* with the Essex rebellion to challenge some recent interpretations and exemplify his reservations about new historical method.

Works Cited

GGS = G. G. Smith, ed. *Elizabethan Critical Essays.* 2 vols. Oxford: Clarendon Press, 1904.
Calendar of State Papers, Spanish, I, Elizabeth (1558-67). Ed. Martin A. S. Hume. London: HMSO, 1892.
Abrams, M. H. *The Mirror and the Lamp.* New York: Oxford, 1953.
Adelman, Janet. *Suffocating Mothers: Fantasies of Maternal Origin in Shakespeare's Plays, Hamlet to the Tempest.* New York: Routledge, 1992.
Allen, D. C. "Marlowe's *Dido* and the Tradition." *Essays on Shakespeare and Elizabethan Drama: In Honor of Hardin Craig.* Ed. Richard Hosley. Columbia, MO: University of Missouri Press, 1962. 55-68.
Alpers, Paul. "Pastoral and the Domain of Lyric in Spenser's *Shepheardes Calender.*" Greenblatt, *Representing* 163-80.
Altman, Joel B. *The Tudor Play of Mind: Rhetorical Inquiry and the Development of Elizabethan Drama.* Berkeley: University of California Press, 1978.
Amussen, Susan Dwyer. "Elizabeth I and Alice Balstone: Gender, Class, and the Exceptional Woman in Early Modern England." *Attending to Women in Early Modern England.* Ed. Betty S. Travitsky and Adele F. Seeff. Newark: University of Delaware Press, 1994. 219-40.
Anglo, Sydney. *Spectacle, Pageantry, and Early Tudor Policy.* Oxford: Clarendon, 1969.
Archer, John Michael. *Sovereignty and Intelligence: Spying and Court Culture in the English Renaissance.* Stanford: Stanford University Press, 1993.
Axton, Marie. *The Queen's Two Bodies.* London: Royal Historical Society, 1977.
Bakeless, John. *The Tragicall History of Christopher Marlowe.* Cambridge: Harvard University Press, 1942.
Baker, Howard. *Induction to Tragedy.* University, LA: Louisiana State University Press, 1939.
Baker, John Hamilton. *Introduction to English Legal History.* London: Butterworths, 1971.
Bakhtin, M. M. *The Dialogic Imagination.* Ed. Michael Holquist, trans. Caryl Emerson and Michael Holquist. Austin: University of Texas Press, 1981.
Baldwin, T. W. *Shakspere's Five-Act Structure.* Urbana: University of Illinois Press, 1947.

Bamber, Linda. *Comic Women, Tragic Men: A Study of Gender and Genre in Shakespeare.* Stanford: Stanford University Press, 1982.

Barber, C. L. " 'The Form of Faustus' Fortunes Good or Bad.' " *Tulane Drama Review* 8.4 (1964): 92–119.

———. *Shakespeare's Festive Comedies.* Princeton: Princeton University Press, 1959.

Barish, Jonas. *The Antitheatrical Prejudice.* Berkeley: University of California Press, 1981.

Barnet, Sylvan et al., eds. *The Genius of the Early English Theater.* New York: Mentor Books, 1962.

Barroll, J. Leeds. "A New History for Shakespeare and His Time." *Shakespeare Quarterly* 39.4 (1988): 441–62.

Bartels, Emily C. *Spectacles of Strangeness: Imperialism, Alienation and Marlowe.* Philadelphia: University of Pennsylvania Press, 1993.

Baskervill, Charles Read, Virgil B. Heltzel, and Arthur H. Nethercot, eds. *Elizabethan and Stuart Plays.* New York: Henry Holt, 1934.

Bassnett, Susan. *Elizabeth I: A Feminist Perspective.* New York: Berg, 1988.

Baxter, John. *Shakespeare's Poetic Styles: Verses into Drama.* London: Routledge and Kegan Paul, 1980.

Beckerman, Bernard. *Dynamics of Drama.* New York: Drama Book Specialists, 1979.

———. *Shakespeare at the Globe.* New York: Macmillan, 1962.

Belsey, Catherine. "Disrupting Sexual Difference: Meaning and Gender in the Comedies." Drakakis 166–90.

———. *The Subject of Tragedy: Identity and Difference in Renaissance Drama.* London: Methuen, 1985.

Berger, Harry. "Text against Performance." *Genre* 15 (1982): 49–79.

Bergeron, David. *English Civic Pageantry 1557–1642.* London: Edward Arnold, 1971.

Bernard, J. E. *The Prosody of the Tudor Interlude.* Yale Studies in English 90. 1939. New York: Archon Books, 1969.

Berry, Philippa. *Of Chastity and Power: Elizabethan Literature and the Unmarried Queen.* New York: Routledge, 1989.

Berry, Ralph. *The Shakespearean Metaphor: Studies in Language and Form.* London: Macmillan, 1978.

Bethell, S. L. *Shakespeare and the Popular Dramatic Tradition.* Durham, NC: Duke University Press, 1944.

Bevington, David. " 'Jack Hath Not Jill': Failed Courtship in Lyly and Shakespeare." *Shakespeare Survey* 42 (1989): 1–13.

Boas, Frederick S. *Christopher Marlowe: A Biographical and Critical Study.* Oxford: Clarendon Press, 1940.

———. *Queen Elizabeth in Drama and Related Studies.* London: George Allen and Unwin, 1950.

Bono, Barbara. *Literary Transvaluation: From Vergilian Epic to Shakespearean Tragicomedy.* Berkeley: University of California Press, 1984.

———. "Mixed Gender, Mixed Genre in Shakespeare's *As You Like It*." Lewalski 189–212.
Boose, Lynda E. "The Family in Shakespeare Studies; or—Studies in the Family of Shakespeareans; or—The Politics of Politics." *Renaissance Quarterly* 40 (1987): 707–42.
———. "Scolding Brides and Bridling Scolds: Taming the Woman's Unruly Member." *Shakespeare Quarterly* 42 (1991): 179–213.
Bradbrook, Muriel C. "The Artist and Society in Shakespeare's England." *The Collected Papers of Muriel Bradbrook*. Vol. 1. Totowa, NJ: Barnes and Noble, 1982.
———. *The School of Night: A Study of the Literary Relationships of Sir Walter Ralegh*. Cambridge: Cambridge University Press, 1936.
Bredbeck, Gregory W. *Sodomy and Interpretation: Marlowe to Milton*. Ithaca: Cornell University Press, 1991.
Breitenberg, Mark. "The Anatomy of Masculine Desire in *Love's Labour's Lost*." *Shakespeare Quarterly* 43 (1992): 430–49.
Brodwin, Leonora Leet. *Elizabethan Love Tragedy, 1587–1625*. New York: New York University Press, 1971.
Brooke, C. F. Tucker, and Nathaniel Burton Paradise, eds. *English Drama 1580–1642*. New York: D. C. Heath, 1933.
Bruss, Elizabeth. *Beautiful Theories: The Spectacle of Discourse in Contemporary Criticism*. Baltimore: The Johns Hopkins University Press, 1982.
Bruster, Douglas. "'Come to the Tent Again': 'The Passionate Shepherd,' Dramatic Rape and Lyric Time." *Criticism* 33 (Winter 1991): 49–72.
Bullough, Geoffrey. *Narrative and Dramatic Sources of Shakespeare*. Vol. 1. New York: Columbia University Press, 1957.
Calderwood, James. *Shakespearean Metadrama: The Argument of the Play in* Titus Andronicus, Love's Labor's Lost, Romeo and Juliet, A Midsummer Night's Dream, *and* Richard II. Minneapolis: University of Minnesota Press, 1971.
Camden, William. *Annales: The True and Royall History of the Famous Empresse Elizabeth. . . .* London, 1625–29.
Cameron, Deborah. *Feminism and Linguistic Theory*. London: Macmillan, 1985.
Campbell, O. J. *Shakespeare's Satire*. New York: Oxford University Press, 1943.
Carroll, William C. *The Great Feast of Language in* Love's Labor's Lost. Princeton: Princeton University Press, 1976.
Carter, Angela. *Wise Children*. New York: Penguin, 1991.
Case, Sue-Ellen. *Feminism and Theatre*. New York: Methuen, 1988.
———, ed. *Performing Feminisms: Feminist Critical Theory and Theatre*. Baltimore: The Johns Hopkins University Press, 1990.
Cecil, William. *The Execution of Justice in England and A True, Sincere, and Modest Defense of English Catholics by William Allen*. Ed. Robert M. Kingdon. Ithaca: Cornell University Press [for the Folger Shakespeare Library], 1965.
Clark, Eleanor Grace. *Ralegh and Marlowe: A Study in Elizabethan Fustian*. 1941. New York: Russell and Russell, 1965.

Cohen, Walter. "Political Criticism of Shakespeare." Howard and O'Connor 18–46.
Cole, Howard C. *A Quest of Inquirie: Some Contexts of Tudor Literature*. New York: Bobbs-Merrill, 1973.
Colie, Rosalie. *The Resources of Kind: Genre-Theory in the Renaissance*. Berkeley: University of California Press, 1973.
Collins, William Edward. *Queen Elizabeth's Defence of Her Proceedings in Church and State*. London: Sidney Press [SPCK], 1958.
Cook, Ann Jennalie. *Making a Match: Courtship in Shakespeare and His Society*. Princeton: Princeton University Press, 1991.
———. *The Privileged Playgoers of Shakespeare's London, 1576–1642*. Princeton: Princeton University Press, 1981.
Cope, Jackson. "Marlowe's Dido and the Titillating Children." *English Literary Renaissance* 4 (1974): 315–25.
Corthell, Ronald J. " 'The Secrecy of Man': Recusant Discourse and the Elizabethan Subject." *English Literary Renaissance* 19 (1989): 272–90.
Crewe, Jonathan. *Trials of Authorship: Anterior Forms and Poetic Reconstruction from Wyatt to Shakespeare*. Berkeley: University of California Press, 1990.
Cutts, John P. *The Left Hand of God: A Critical Interpretation of the Plays of Christopher Marlowe*. Haddonfield, NJ: Haddonfield House, 1973.
Daniel, Carter A. "*The Arraignment of Paris*." *Notes and Queries* 29 (April 1982): 131–32.
Danson, Lawrence. "Jonsonian Comedy and the Discovery of the Social Self." *PMLA* 99 (1984): 179–93.
Dash, Irene. *Wooing, Wedding, and Power: Women in Shakespeare's Plays*. New York: Columbia University Press, 1981.
Davis, Natalie Zemon. *Society and Culture in Early Modern France*. Stanford: Stanford University Press, 1975.
de Lauretis, Teresa. *Technologies of Gender*. Bloomington: Indiana University Press, 1987.
de Man, Paul. *The Rhetoric of Romanticism*. New York: Columbia University Press, 1984.
Dickey, F. M. *Not Wisely but Too Well: Shakespeare's Love Tragedies*. San Marino, CA: Huntington Library, 1957.
Dollimore, Jonathan, and Alan Sinfield, eds. *Political Shakespeare: New Essays in Cultural Materialism*. Ithaca: Cornell University Press, 1985.
Doran, Madeleine. *Endeavors of Art: A Study of Form in Elizabethan Drama*. Madison: University of Wisconsin Press, 1954.
Drakakis, John, ed. *Alternative Shakespeares*. New York: Methuen, 1985.
Eaton, Sara. "Beatrice-Joanna and the Rhetoric of Love in *The Changeling*." Case, *Performing* 237–48.
Ekeblad, Inga-Stina [Ewbank]. "On the Background of Peele's 'Araygnment of Paris.'" *Notes and Queries* n.s. 3 (June 1956): 246–49.
Eliot, T. S. "Christopher Marlowe." *Elizabethan Essays*. New York: Haskell House, 1964. 21–31.

———. *On Poetry and Poets*. New York: Farrar, Straus and Cudahy, 1957.
Erickson, Peter. "The Order of the Garter, the Cult of Elizabeth, and Class-Gender Tension in *The Merry Wives of Windsor*." Howard and O'Connor 116–40.
———. *Patriarchal Structures in Shakespeare's Drama*. Berkeley: University of California Press, 1985.
———. *Rewriting Shakespeare, Rewriting Ourselves*. Berkeley: University of California Press, 1991.
———. Rev. of *Power on Display: The Politics of Shakespeare's Genres*, by Leonard Tennenhouse. *Shakespeare Quarterly* 39 (1988): 508–11.
Evans, Malcolm. "Mercury versus Apollo: A Reading of *Love's Labor's Lost*." *Shakespeare Quarterly* 26 (1975): 113–27.
Ewbank, Inga-Stina. "'What Words, What Looks, What Wonders?': Language and Spectacle in the Theatre of George Peele." *The Elizabethan Theatre V*. Ed. G. R. Hibbard. Hamden, CT: Archon Books, 1975. 124–54.
Ferguson, Margaret. *Trials of Desire: Renaissance Defenses of Poetry*. New Haven: Yale University Press, 1983.
Ferguson, Margaret, Maureen Quilligan, and Nancy J. Vickers, eds. *Rewriting the Renaissance: The Discourses of Sexual Difference in Early Modern Europe*. Chicago: University of Chicago Press, 1986.
Ferguson, Moira, ed. *First Feminists: British Women Writers 1578–1799*. Bloomington: Indiana University Press, 1985.
Ferry, Anne. *The "Inward" Language: Sonnets of Wyatt, Sidney, Shakespeare, Donne*. Chicago: University of Chicago Press, 1983.
Fineman, Joel. *Shakespeare's Perjured Eye: The Invention of Poetic Subjectivity in the Sonnets*. Berkeley: University of California Press, 1986.
Finke, Laurie A. "Painting Women: Images of Femininity in Jacobean Tragedy." Case, *Performing* 223–36.
Foakes, R. A., ed. *Coleridge on Shakespeare: The Text of the Lectures of 1811–12*. Charlottesville: University Press of Virginia [for the Folger Shakespeare Library], 1971.
Foakes, R. A., and R. T. Rickert, eds. *Henslowe's Diary*. Cambridge: Cambridge University Press, 1961.
Forster, Leonard. *The Icy Fire: Five Studies in European Petrarchism*. Cambridge: Cambridge University Press, 1969.
Foucault, Michel. *Discipline and Punish*. Trans. Alan Sheridan. New York: Pantheon, 1977.
Fradenburg, Louise Olga, ed. *Women and Sovereignty*. Edinburgh: Edinburgh University Press, 1992.
Fraser, Antonia. *The Wives of Henry VIII*. New York: Knopf, 1992.
Freccero, John. "The Fig Tree and the Laurel: Petrarch's Poetics." *Literary Theory/Renaissance Texts*. Ed. Patricia Parker and David Quint. Baltimore: The Johns Hopkins University Press, 1986. 20–32.
French, Marilyn. *Shakespeare's Division of Experience*. New York: Ballantine Books, 1981.

Frye, Susan. *Elizabeth I: The Competition for Representation*. Oxford: Oxford University Press, 1993.
Fumerton, Patricia. *Cultural Aesethetics: Renaissance Literature and the Practice of Social Ornament*. Chicago: University of Chicago Press, 1991.
———. " 'Secret' Arts: Elizabethan Miniatures and Sonnets." Greenblatt, *Representing* 93–133.
Gallagher, Catherine. "Embracing the Absolute: The Politics of the Female Subject in Seventeenth-Century England." *Genders* 1 (1988): 24–29.
Garber, Marjorie. " 'Infinite Riches in a Little Room': Closure and Enclosure in Marlowe." Kernan 3–21.
———, ed. *Media Spectacles*. New York: Routledge, 1993.
Gascoigne, George. *The Complete Works of George Gascoigne*. Ed. John W. Cunliffe. 2 vols. Cambridge: Cambridge University Press, 1907, 1910.
———. *A Hundreth Sundrie Flowres*. Ed. Ruth Loyd Miller. Port Washington, NY: Kennikat Press, 1975.
Gibbons, Brian. "Unstable Proteus: Marlowe's *The Tragedy of Dido, Queen of Carthage*." B. Morris 25–46.
———, ed. Introduction. *Romeo and Juliet*. By William Shakespeare. New York: Methuen, 1980.
Gill, Roma. "Marlowe's Virgil: *Dido, Queen of Carthage*." *RES* n.s. 28, 110 (1977): 141–55.
Goldberg, Jonathan. *Sodometries: Renaissance Texts, Modern Sexualities*. Stanford: Stanford University Press, 1992.
———. *Voice Terminal Echo: Postmodernism and English Renaissance Texts*. New York: Methuen, 1986.
Golding, Arthur. *Shakespeare's Ovid*. 1567. London: Centaur Press, 1961.
Goldman, Michael. "Marlowe and the Histrionics of Ravishment." Kernan 22–40.
Gombrich, E. H. *Meditations on a Hobbyhorse*. London: Phaidon Publishers, 1963.
Grace, William. *Approaching Shakespeare*. New York: Basic Books, 1964.
Graff, Gerald. "Co-optation." Veeser 168–81.
Graham, Jorie. Interview by Ann Snodgrass. *Quarterly West* 23 (1986): 151–64.
Greenblatt, Stephen J. *Renaissance Self-Fashioning: From More to Shakespeare*. Chicago: University of Chicago Press, 1980.
———. *Shakespearean Negotiations*. Berkeley: University of California Press, 1988.
———, ed. *Representing the English Renaissance*. Berkeley: University of California Press, 1988.
Greene. Thomas. *The Light in Troy: Imitation and Discovery in Renaissance Poetry*. New Haven: Yale University Press, 1982.
———. "*Love's Labour's Lost:* The Grace of Society." *Shakespeare Quarterly* 22 (1971): 315–28.
Gurr, Andrew. *The Shakespearean Stage, 1574–1642*. Cambridge: Cambridge University Press, 1970.

Haigh, Christopher. *Elizabeth I.* New York: Longman, 1988.

———, ed. *The Reign of Elizabeth I.* Athens, GA: University of Georgia Press, 1985.

Hardison, O. B. "Speaking the Speech." *Shakespeare Quarterly* 34 (1983): 133–46.

Harrison, G. B., ed. *The Letters of Queen Elizabeth.* London: Cassell and Co., 1935.

Harvey, E. Ruth. *The Inward Wits.* London: Warburg Institute, 1975.

Haselkorn, Anne M., and Betty S. Travitsky, eds. *The Renaissance Englishwoman in Print.* Amherst: University of Massachusetts Press, 1990.

Hattaway, Michael. "Marlowe and Brecht." B. Morris 95–112.

Hebel, J. William, and Hoyt H. Hudson, eds. *Poetry of the English Renaissance 1509–1660.* New York: Crofts, 1940.

Hedley, Jane. "Allegoria: Gascoigne's Master Trope." *English Literary Renaissance* 11 (1981): 148–64.

Heilbrun, Carolyn G. *Writing a Woman's Life.* New York: Norton, 1988.

Heisch, Allison. "Queen Elizabeth I: Parliamentary Rhetoric and the Exercise of Power." *Signs* 1 (1975): 31–55.

Helgerson, Richard. *The Elizabethan Prodigals.* Berkeley: University of California Press, 1976.

Henderson, Diana E. "Female Power and the Devaluation of Elizabethan Love Lyrics." *Dwelling in Possibility: Essays in Gender, Genre, and Poetry.* Ed. Yopie Prins and Maeera Shreiber. Ithaca: Cornell University Press, forthcoming.

———. "Poetic Transformations." Diss., Columbia University, 1989.

Henderson, Katherine Usher and Barbara F. McManus. *Half Humankind: Contexts and Texts of the Controversy about Women in England, 1540–1640.* Urbana: University of Illinois Press, 1985.

Hendricks, Margo. "Managing the Barbarian: *The Tragedy of Dido, Queen of Carthage.*" *Renaissance Drama* 23 (1992): 165–88.

Hendricks, Margo, and Patricia Parker, eds. *Women, "Race," and Writing in the Early Modern Period.* New York: Routledge: 1994.

Heninger, S. K., Jr. "The Pattern of *Love's Labour's Lost.*" *Shakespeare Studies* 7 (1974): 25–53.

Herford, C. H., Percy Simpson, and Evelyn Simpson, eds. *Ben Jonson.* Vol. 8. Oxford: Clarendon Press, 1947.

Hibbard, G. R. *The Making of Shakespeare's Dramatic Poetry.* Toronto: University of Toronto Press, 1981.

———. "Words, Action, and Artistic Economy." *Shakespeare Survey* 23 (1970): 49–58.

Hill, R. F. "Shakespeare's Early Tragic Mode." *Shakespeare Quarterly* 9 (1958): 455–69.

Hollander, John. *The Figure of Echo.* Berkeley: University of California Press, 1981.

———. *Vision and Resonance: Two Senses of Poetic Form.* Oxford: Oxford University Press, 1975.

———. *The Untuning of the Sky.* Princeton: Princeton University Press, 1961.

Holmes, Charles S., Edwin Fussell, and Ray Frazer, eds. *The Major Critics: The Development of English Literary Criticism.* New York: Alfred A. Knopf, 1957.

Homan, Sidney. *When the Theater Turns to Itself: The Aesthetic Metaphor in Shakespeare.* Toronto: Associated University Presses, 1981.

Homans, Margaret. *Women Writers and Poetic Identity.* Princeton: Princeton University Press, 1980.

Horne, P. R. *The Tragedies of Giambattista Cinthio Giraldi.* Oxford: Oxford University Press, 1962.

Horwich, Richard. "'I Sing but after You': Shakespeare's Internal Parody." *SEL* 28 (1988): 219–40.

Hosek, Chaviva, and Patricia Parker, eds. *Lyric Poetry: Beyond New Criticism.* Ithaca: Cornell University Press, 1985.

Howard, Jean E. "Crossdressing, the Theatre, and Gender Struggle in Early Modern England." *Shakespeare Quarterly* 39 (1988): 418–40.

———. "The New Historicism in Renaissance Studies." *Renaissance Historicism: Selections from English Literary Renaissance.* Ed. Arthur F. Kinney and Dan S. Collins. Amherst: University of Massachusetts Press, 1987. 3–33.

———. "Women as Spectators, Spectacles, and Paying Customers." In Kastan and Stallybrass 68–74.

Howard, Jean E., and Marion F. O'Connor, eds. *Shakespeare Reproduced: The Text in History and Ideology.* 1987. New York: Routledge, 1990.

Hunter, G. K. *John Lyly: The Humanist as Courtier.* London: Routledge and Kegan Paul, 1962.

Hunter, Robert G. "The Function of the Songs at the End of *Love's Labor's Lost*." *Shakespeare Studies* 7 (1974): 55–64.

Hurston, J. Dennis. *Shakespeare's Comedies of Play.* London: Macmillan, 1981.

Ing, Catherine. *Elizabethan Lyrics: A Study in the Development of English Metres and Their Relation to Poetic Effect.* 1951. New York: Barnes and Noble, 1969.

Jankowski, Theodora A. *Women and Power in the Early Modern Drama.* Urbana: University of Illinois Press, 1992.

Jardine, Lisa. *Still Harping on Daughters: Women and Drama in the Age of Shakespeare.* Totowa, NJ: Barnes and Noble, 1983.

Javitch, Daniel. *Poetry and Courtliness in Renaissance England.* Princeton: Princeton University Press, 1978.

Jed, Stephanie. *Chaste Thinking: The Rape of Lucretia and the Birth of Humanism.* Bloomington: Indiana University Press, 1989.

Johnson, Barbara. "Women and Allegory." School of Critical Theory, Hanover, NH, July 21, 1992.

Johnson, Samuel. *Johnson on Shakespeare.* Ed. Walter Raleigh. London: Oxford University Press, 1965.

Johnson, W. R. *The Idea of Lyric: Lyric Modes in Ancient and Modern Poetry.* Berkeley: University of California Press, 1982.

Jones, Ann Rosalind. *The Currency of Eros: Women's Love Lyric in Europe, 1540–1620.* Bloomington: Indiana University Press, 1990.

Jones, Ann Rosalind, and Peter Stallybrass. "The Politics of *Astrophil and Stella*." *SEL* 24 (1984): 53–68.

Jordan, Constance. "Representing Political Androgyny: More on the Siena Portrait of Queen Elizabeth." Haselkorn and Travitsky 157–76.

Kahn, Coppélia. *Man's Estate: Masculine Identity in Shakespeare*. Berkeley: University of California Press, 1981.

Kantorowicz, Ernst. *The King's Two Bodies: A Study in Medieval Political Theology*. Princeton: Princeton University Press, 1957.

Kastan, David Scott. "Proud Majesty Made a Subject: Shakespeare and the Spectacle of Rule." *Shakespeare Quarterly* 37 (1986): 459–75.

Kastan, David Scott, and Peter Stallybrass, eds. *Staging the Renaissance*. New York: Routledge, 1991.

Kay, Dennis. "'She Was a Queen, and Therefore Beautiful': Sidney, His Mother, and Queen Elizabeth." *RES* n.s. 43. 169 (1992): 18–39.

Kelly, Joan. *Women, History, and Theory: The Essays of Joan Kelly*. Chicago: University of Chicago Press, 1984.

Kelly, Katherine E. "The Queen's Two Bodies: Shakespeare's Boy Actress in Breeches." *Theatre Journal* 42 (1990): 81–93.

Kennedy, William J. *Rhetorical Norms in Renaissance Literature*. New Haven: Yale University Press, 1978.

Kernan, Alvin, ed. *Two Renaissance Mythmakers: Christopher Marlowe and Ben Jonson*. Selected Papers from the English Institute, 1975–76, n.s. 1. Baltimore: The Johns Hopkins University Press, 1977.

Kimbrough, Robert, and Philip Murphy. "The Helmingham Hall Manuscript of Sidney's *The Lady of May:* A Commentary and Transcription." *Renaissance Drama* 1 (1968): 103–19.

King, John N. "Queen Elizabeth I: Representations of the Virgin Queen." *Renaissance Quarterly* 43 (Spring 1990): 30–74.

King, William C., ed. *Woman*. Springfield, MA: King-Richardson Co., 1900–1902.

Kocher, Paul. *Christopher Marlowe: A Study of His Thought, Learning and Character*. Chapel Hill: University of North Carolina Press, 1966.

Kuriyama, Constance Brown. *Hammer or Anvil: Psychological Patterns in Christopher Marlowe's Plays*. New Brunswick: Rutgers University Press, 1980.

Lanham, Richard. *The Motives of Eloquence*. New Haven: Yale University Press, 1976.

Lentricchia, Frank, and Thomas McLaughlin, eds. *Critical Terms for Literary Study*. Chicago: University of Chicago Press, 1990.

Lenz, Carolyn Ruth, Gayle Green, and Carol Thomas Neely, eds. *The Woman's Part: Feminist Criticism of Shakespeare*. Urbana: University of Illinois Press, 1980.

Lesnick, Henry G. "The Structural Significance of Myth and Flattery in Peele's *Arraignment of Paris*." *Studies in Philology* 65 (1968): 163–70.

Levao, Ronald. *Renaissance Minds and Their Fictions: Cusanus, Sidney, Shakespeare*. Berkeley: University of California Press, 1985.

———. "Sidney's Feigned Apology." *PMLA* 94 (1979): 223–33.
Lever, J. W. *The Elizabethan Love Sonnet.* 1956. London: Methuen, 1966.
———. "Three Notes on Shakespeare's Plants." *RES* n.s. 3 (1952): 117–29.
Levin, Harry. "Form and Formality in *Romeo and Juliet.*" *Shakespeare Quarterly* 11 (1960): 3–11.
———. *The Overreacher: A Study of Christopher Marlowe.* Cambridge, MA: Harvard University Press, 1952.
Levin, Richard. "Women in the Renaissance Theatre Audience." *Shakespeare Quarterly* 40 (1989): 165–74.
Levine, Laura. "Men in Women's Clothing: Anti-theatricality and Effeminization from 1579 to 1642." *Criticism* 28 (1986): 121–43.
Levine, Mortimer. *The Early Elizabethan Succession Question.* Stanford: Stanford University Press, 1966.
Lewalski, Barbara Kiefer, ed. *Renaissance Genres: Essays on Theory, History and Interpretation.* Cambridge, MA: Harvard University Press, 1986.
Lewis, C. S. *English Literature in the Sixteenth Century, excluding drama.* London: Oxford University Press, 1954.
Lindley, David. *Lyric.* The Critical Idiom 44. London: Methuen, 1985.
Loomba, Ania. *Gender, Race, Renaissance Drama.* Oxford: Oxford University Press, 1992.
Lowenstein, Joseph. *Responsive Readings: Versions of Echo in Pastoral, Epic, and the Jonsonian Masque.* Yale Studies in English 192. New Haven: Yale University Press, 1984.
Lucas, R. Valerie. "Puritan Preaching and the Politics of the Family." Haselkorn and Travitsky 224–40.
MacCaffrey, Wallace T. *Queen Elizabeth and the Making of Policy 1572–1588.* Princeton: Princeton University Press, 1981.
Marcus, Leah. *Puzzling Shakespeare: Local Reading and Its Discontents.* Berkeley: University of California Press, 1989.
———. "Shakespeare's Comic Heroines: Elizabeth I and the Political Uses of Androgyny." Rose, *Women* 135–53.
Marlowe, Christopher. *The Complete Poems and Translations.* Ed. Stephen Orgel. New York: Penguin Books, 1971.
———. *Dido, Queen of Carthage* and *The Massacre of Paris.* Ed. H. J. Oliver. Revels Edition. London: Methuen, 1968.
Marotti, Arthur. " 'Love Is Not Love': Elizabethan Sonnet Sequences and the Social Order." *ELH* 49 (1982): 396–428.
Martin, Richard A. "Fate, Seneca, and Marlowe's *Dido, Queen of Carthage.*" *Renaissance Drama* 9 (1980): 45–66.
Martz, Louis L. *The Poetry of Meditation.* New Haven: Yale University Press, 1962.
May, Steven W. *The Elizabethan Courtier Poets: The Poems and Their Contexts.* Columbia: University of Missouri Press, 1991.

McCoy, Richard C. "Gascoigne's '*Poëmata castrata*': The Wages of Courtly Success." *Criticism* 27 (1985): 29–55.

———. *The Rites of Knighthood: The Literature and Politics of Elizabethan Chivalry*. Berkeley: University of California Press, 1989.

McGrath, Patrick. *Papists and Puritans*. London: Blandford Press, 1967.

McLay, Catherine. "The Dialogues of Spring and Winter: A Key to the Unity of *Love's Labor's Lost*." *Shakespeare Quarterly* 18 (1967): 119–27.

McLuskie, Kathleen E. "Shakespeare's 'Earth-Treading Stars': The Image of the Masque in *Romeo and Juliet*." *Shakespeare Survey* 24 (1971): 63–69.

Mehl, Dieter. *The Elizabethan Dumb Show*. London: Methuen, 1965.

Mendelson, Sara Heller. "Stuart Women's Diaries and Occasional Memoirs." Prior 181–210.

Meyer, Arnold Oscar. *England and the Catholic Church under Queen Elizabeth*. Trans. J. R. McKee. 1911. London: Routledge and Kegan Paul, 1967.

Miller, Nancy K. "Rereading as a Woman: The Body in Practice." *The Female Body in Western Culture: Contemporary Perspectives*. Ed. Susan Rubin Suleiman. Cambridge, MA: Harvard University Press, 1985. 354–62.

———, ed. *The Poetics of Gender*. New York: Columbia University Press, 1986.

Miner, Earl. "Some Issues of Literary 'Species, or Distinct Kinds.' " Lewalski 15–44.

Mitchell, W. J. T. "Representation." Lentricchia and McLaughlin 11–22.

Mizener, Arthur. "The Tragedy of Marlowe's Doctor Faustus." *Shakespeare's Contemporaries*. Ed. Max Bluestone and Norman Rabkin. Englewood Cliffs, NJ: Prentice-Hall, 1961.

Montrose, Louis Adrian. "Celebration and Insinuation: Sir Philip Sidney and the Motives of Elizabethan Courtship." *Renaissance Drama* 8 (1977): 3–35.

———. "*Curious-Knotted Gardens*": The Form, Themes, and Contexts of Shakespeare's "*Love's Labor's Lost*." Salzburg Studies in English Literature: Elizabethan and Renaissance Studies 56. Salzburg, Aus.: Universitat Salzburg, 1977.

———. "Gifts and Reasons: The Contexts of Peele's *Araygnement of Paris*." *ELH* 47 (1980): 433–61.

———. "*A Midsummer Night's Dream* and the Shaping Fantasies of Elizabethan Culture." Ferguson, Quilligan, and Vickers, eds. 65–87, 329–34.

———. "Shaping Fantasies: Figurations of Gender and Power in Elizabethan Culture," *Representations* 1 (1983): 61–94.

Morris, Brian, ed. *Christopher Marlowe*. London: Ernest Benn, 1968.

Morris, Charles. *The Life of Queen Victoria and the Story of Her Reign: A Beautiful Tribute to England's Greatest Queen in Her Domestic and Official Life*. N.p.: W. E. Scull, 1901.

Morris, Harry. "Marlowe's Poetry." *Tulane Drama Review* 8 (1964): 134–54.

Mucedorus. Baskervill, Heltzel, and Nethercot 526–52.

Muir, Kenneth. *Elizabethan Lyrics: A Critical Anthology*. 1952. Granger Index Reprint Series. Freeport, NY: Books for Libraries Press, 1969.

———. *The Sources of Shakespeare's Plays*. New Haven: Yale University Press, 1978.

Mullaney, Steven. *The Place of the Stage: License, Play, and Power in Renaissance England.* Chicago: University of Chicago Press, 1988.

Nathan, Leonard. "Gascoigne's 'Lullabie' and Structures in the Tudor Lyric." *The Rhetoric of Renaissance Poetry: From Wyatt to Milton.* Eds. Thomas O. Sloan and Raymond B. Waddington. Berkeley: University of California Press, 1974.

Neale, J. E. *Elizabeth I and Her Parliaments, 1559–1581.* London: Jonathan Cape, 1953.

———. *Queen Elizabeth I: A Biography.* Garden City, NY: Doubleday, 1934.

Neely, Carol Thomas. *Broken Nuptials in Shakespeare's Plays.* New Haven: Yale University Press, 1985.

———. "Constructing the Subject: Feminist Practice and the New Renaissance Discourses." *English Literary Renaissance* 18 (1988): 5–18.

Nicholl, Charles. *The Reckoning, or the Murder of Christopher Marlowe.* New York: Harcourt Brace and Company, 1993.

Nichols, John. *The Progresses, and Public Processions of, Queen Elizabeth.* 3 vols. London: John Nichols and Sons, 1823. Reprint, New York: Kraus, 1960.

Novy, Marianne. *Love's Argument: Gender Relations in Shakespeare.* Chapel Hill: University of North Carolina Press, 1984.

Orgel, Stephen. "Making Greatness Familiar." *Genre* 15 (1982): 41–48.

———. "Nobody's Perfect: Or, Why Did the English Stage Take Boys for Women?" *South Atlantic Quarterly* 88 (1989): 7–29.

Osborne, June. *Entertaining Elizabeth I.* London: Bishopsgate Press, 1989.

Ovid. *Heroides and Amores.* Ed. Grant Showerman. 1921. Cambridge, MA: Harvard University Press, 1947.

———. *Metamorphoses.* Trans. Rolfe Humphries. Bloomington: Indiana University Press, 1955.

———. *Metamorphoses.* Vol. 2. Trans. Frank Justus Miller. Cambridge, MA: Harvard University Press, 1977.

Parker, Patricia. *Literary Fat Ladies: Rhetoric, Gender, Property.* New York: Methuen, 1987.

Patterson, Annabel. *Censorship and Interpretation.* Madison: University of Wisconsin Press, 1984.

———. "Constructing and Reconstructing Sixteenth-Century Literature: The Problem of Golden Thinking." Modern Language Association, San Francisco, Dec. 27, 1991.

———. "Lyric and Society in Jonson's *Under-wood*." Hosek and Parker 148–63.

Peele, George. *The Life and Works of George Peele.* Gen. ed. Charles Tyler Prouty. Vol. 1: *The Life and Minor Works of George Peele.* Ed. David H. Horne. Vol. 3: *The Dramatic Works of George Peele.* Ed. Mark Benbow et al. New Haven: Yale University Press, 1952, 1970.

Peterson, Douglas L. *The English Lyric from Wyatt to Donne: A History of the Plain and Eloquent Styles.* Princeton: Princeton University Press, 1967.

Pinsky, Robert. *Poetry and the World.* New York: Ecco Press, 1988.

Platz, Norbert H., ed. *English Dramatic Theories.* Vol. 1: *From Elyot to the Age of Dryden, 1531–1668.* Tübingen: Max Niemeyer, 1973.

Porter, Carolyn. "Are We Being Historical Yet?" *South Atlantic Quarterly* 87 (1988): 743–86.

Powell, Jocelyn. "Marlowe's Spectacle." *Tulane Drama Review* (1964): 195–210.

Preminger, Alex, ed. *Princeton Encyclopedia of Poetry and Poetics.* Princeton: Princeton University Press, 1974.

Preston, Thomas. *Cambises, King of Persia.* Baskervill, Heltzel, and Nethercot 143–70.

Pringle, Roger, ed. *A Portrait of Elizabeth I, in the Words of the Queen and Her Contemporaries.* Totowa, NJ: Barnes and Noble, 1980.

Prior, Mary, ed. *Women in English Society, 1500–1800.* New York: Methuen, 1985.

Prouty, C. T. *George Gascoigne: Elizabethan Courtier, Soldier, and Poet.* New York: Columbia University Press, 1942.

Puttenham, George. *The Arte of English Poesie.* Ed. Gladys Willcock and Alice Walker. Cambridge: Cambridge University Press, 1936.

Rackin, Phyllis. "Androgyny, Mimesis, and the Marriage of the Boy Heroine on the English Stage." *Speaking of Gender.* Ed. Elaine Showalter. New York: Routledge, 1989. 113–33.

Ramsey, Paul. *The Fickle Glass: A Study of Shakespeare's Sonnets.* New York: AMS Press, 1979.

Read, Conyers. *The Tudors.* New York: Henry Holt and Co., 1936.

Reeves, John D. "The Judgment of Paris as a Device of Tudor Flattery." *Notes and Queries* 199 (1954): 7–11.

Reiss, Timothy J. *Tragedy and Truth.* New Haven: Yale University Press, 1980.

Ribner, Irving, ed. *The Complete Plays of Christopher Marlowe.* New York: Odyssey Press, 1963.

Righter [Barton], Anne. *Shakespeare and the Idea of the Play.* New York: Barnes and Noble, 1962.

Roche, Thomas P. *Petrarch and the English Sonnet Sequence.* New York: AMS Press, 1989.

Roesen, Bobbyann [Anne Barton]. "Love's Labour's Lost." *Shakespeare Quarterly* 4 (1953): 411–26.

Rollins, Hyder E., and Herschel Baker, eds. *The Renaissance in England.* Lexington, MA: D. C. Heath and Company, 1954.

Rose, Mary Beth. *The Expense of Spirit: Love and Sexuality in English Renaissance Drama.* Ithaca: Cornell University Press, 1988.

———. "Sexual Love in Elizabethan Comedy." *Renaissance Drama* 15 (1984): 1–29.

———, ed. *Women in the Middle Ages and the Renaissance.* Syracuse: Syracuse University Press, 1986.

Rosmarin, Adena. *The Power of Genre.* Minneapolis: University of Minnesota Press, 1985.

Rousseau, G. S. "Marlowe's *Dido* and a Rhetoric of Love." *English Miscellany* 19 (1968): 25–49.

Sacks, David Harris. "Searching for 'Culture' in the English Renaissance." *Shakespeare Quarterly* 39 (1988): 465–88.
Sanders, Norman, et al. *The Revels History of English Drama, 1500–1576.* London: Methuen, 1980.
Saslow, James M. *Ganymede in the Renaissance.* New Haven: Yale University Press, 1986.
Schwartz, Murray M., and Coppélia Kahn, eds. *Representing Shakespeare: New Psychoanalytic Essays.* Baltimore: The Johns Hopkins University Press, 1980.
Sedgwick, Eve Kosofsky. *Between Men: English Literature and Male Homosocial Desire.* New York: Columbia University Press, 1985.
Seward, James H. *Tragic Vision in Romeo and Juliet.* Washington, DC: Consortium Press, 1973.
Shakespeare, William. *Hamlet.* Ed. Harold Jenkins. London: Methuen, 1982.
———. *King Richard II.* Ed. Andrew Gurr. Cambridge: Cambridge University Press, 1984.
———. *Love's Labour's Lost.* Ed. Richard David. London: Methuen, 1956.
———. *A Midsummer Night's Dream.* Ed. Harold Brooks. London: Methuen, 1979.
———. *The Riverside Shakespeare.* Ed. G. Blakemore Evans. Boston: Houghton-Mifflin, 1974.
———. *Romeo and Juliet.* Ed. G. Blakemore Evans. Cambridge: Cambridge University Press, 1984.
Shapiro, Michael. "Boying Her Greatness: Shakespeare's Use of Coterie Drama in *Antony and Cleopatra.*" *Modern Language Review* 77 (1982): 1–15.
Sidney, Sir Philip. *Apology for Poetry.* Ed. Forrest G. Robinson. Indianapolis: Bobbs-Merrill, 1970.
Silberman, Lauren. "Singing Unsung Heroines: Androgynous Discourse in Book 3 of *The Faerie Queene.*" Ferguson, Quilligan, and Vickers 259–71.
Smith, Bruce R. *Homosexual Desire in Shakespeare's England: A Cultural Poetics.* Chicago: University of Chicago Press, 1991.
———. "Landscape with Figures: The Three Realms of Queen Elizabeth's Country-house Revels." *Renaissance Drama* 8 (1977): 57–109.
Smith, Hallett. *Elizabethan Poetry.* Cambridge, MA: Harvard University Press, 1952.
Spearing, A. C. *Medieval to Renaissance in English Poetry.* Cambridge: Cambridge University Press, 1985.
Spenser, Edmund. *The Poetical Works of Edmund Spenser.* Ed. J. C. Smith and E. De Selincourt. 1912. London: Oxford University Press, 1947.
Spurgeon, Carolyn. *Shakespeare's Imagery and What It Tells Us.* Cambridge: Cambridge University Press, 1936.
Stallybrass, Peter. "Patriarchal Territories: The Body Enclosed." Ferguson, Quilligan, and Vickers 123–42.
Steane, J. B. *Marlowe: A Critical Study.* London: Cambridge University Press, 1964.
Stevens, John. *Music and Poetry in the Early Tudor Court.* Lincoln: University of Nebraska Press, 1961.

Stone, Donald. *French Humanist Tragedy: A Reassessment.* Manchester: Manchester University Press, 1974.
Styan, J. L. *Shakespeare's Stagecraft.* Cambridge: Cambridge University Press, 1967.
Suzuki, Mihoko. "Gender, Class, and the Social Order in Late Elizabethan Drama." *Theatre Journal* 44 (1992): 31–45.
———, ed. *English Sixteenth-Century Verse: An Anthology.* 1974. New York: Norton, 1984.
Tayler, Edward W. *Milton's Poetry: Its Development in Time.* Pittsburg: Duquesne University Press, 1979.
———, ed. *Literary Criticism of Seventeenth-Century England.* New York: Knopf, 1967.
Tennenhouse, Leonard. *Power on Display: The Politics of Shakespeare's Genres.* New York: Methuen, 1986.
Theweleit, Klaus. *Male Fantasies.* Vol. 1. Minneapolis: University of Minnesota Press, 1987.
Traub, Valerie. *Desire and Anxiety: Circulations of Sexuality in Shakespearean Drama.* New York: Routledge, 1992.
Turner, W. Craig. "Love and the Queen of Carthage: A Look at Marlowe's Dido." *Essays in Literature* 11 (1984): 3–9.
Veeser, H. Aram, ed. *The New Historicism.* New York: Routledge, 1989.
Venezky, Alice. *Pageantry on the Shakespearean Stage.* New York: Twayne, 1951.
Vickers, Nancy. "'The Blazon of Sweet Beauty's Best': Shakespeare's Lucrece." In *Shakespeare and the Question of Theory.* Ed. Patricia Parker and Geoffrey Hartman. New York: Methuen, 1985. 95–115.
———. "Diana Described: Scattered Woman and Scattered Rhyme." *Critical Inquiry* 8 (1981): 265–80.
———. "The Mistress in the Masterpiece." Miller 19–41.
———. "'This Heraldry in Lucrece's Face.'" *The Female Body in Western Culture.* Ed. Susan Rubin Suleiman. Cambridge, MA: Harvard University Press, 1985. 209–22.
Viguers, Susan T. "Art and Reality in George Peele's *The Araygnement of Paris* and *David and Bethsabe.*" *CLA Journal* 30 (1987): 481–500.
Von Hendy, Andrew. "The Triumph of Chastity: Form and Meaning in *The Arraignment of Paris*" *Renaissance Drama* n.s. 1 (1968): 87–101.
Wall, Alison. "Elizabethan Precept and Feminine Practice: The Thynne Family of Longleat." *History* 75.243 (1990): 23–38.
Wall, Wendy. *The Imprint of Gender: Authorship and Publication in the English Renaissance.* Ithaca: Cornell University Press, 1993.
Waller, Gary. *English Poetry of the Sixteenth Century.* New York: Longman, 1986.
Warner, Marina. *Monuments and Maidens: The Allegory of the Female Form.* New York: Atheneum, 1985.
Wayne, Valerie, ed. *The Matter of Difference: Materialist Feminist Criticism of Shakespeare.* Ithaca: Cornell University Press, 1991.

Weil, Judith. *Christopher Marlowe: Merlin's Prophet.* Cambridge: Cambridge University Press, 1977.
Weimann, Robert. "Bifold Authority in Shakespeare's Theatre." *Shakespeare Quarterly* 39 (1988): 401–17.
Welsford, Enid. *The Court Masque: A Study in the Relationship between Poetry and the Revels.* Cambridge: Cambridge University Press, 1927.
Whigham, Frank. *Ambition and Privilege: The Social Tropes of Elizabethan Courtesy Theory.* Berkeley: University of California Press, 1984.
Whittier, Gayle. "The Sonnet's Body and the Body Sonnetized in *Romeo and Juliet.*" *Shakespeare Quarterly* 40 (1989): 27–41.
Wickham, Glynne. "*Love's Labor's Lost* and *The Four Foster Children of Desire,* 1581." *Shakespeare Quarterly* 36 (1985): 49–55.
Wilders, John. "The Unresolved Conflicts of *Love's Labor's Lost.*" *Essays in Criticism* 27 (1977): 20–33.
Williams, Raymond. *The Country and the City.* New York: Oxford University Press, 1973.
Winters, Yvor. *Forms of Discovery: Critical and Historical Essays on the Forms of the Short Poem in English.* [Denver]: Alan Swallow, 1967.
Wollstonecraft, Mary. *A Vindication of the Rights of Women.* Ed. Carol H. Poston. New York: W. W. Norton, 1975.
Woolf, Virginia. *A Room of One's Own.* New York: Harcourt Brace Jovanovich, 1957.
———. *To the Lighthouse.* New York: Harcourt Brace Jovanovich, 1981.
Wrightson, Keith. *English Society, 1580–1680.* New Brunswick, NJ: Rutgers University Press, 1982.
Yachnin, Paul. "The Politics of Theatrical Mirth: *A Midsummer Night's Dream, A Mad World, My Masters,* and *Measure for Measure.*" *Shakespeare Quarterly* 43 (1992): 51–66.
Yates, Frances. *Astraea: The Imperial Theme in the Sixteenth Century.* London: Routledge and Kegan Paul, 1975.
———. *A Study of "Love's Labour's Lost."* Cambridge: Cambridge University Press, 1936.
Zimmerman, Susan, ed. *Erotic Politics: Desire on the Renaissance Stage.* New York: Routledge, 1992.

Index

Abrams, M. H., 22
Absolon, 81n3
Achates, 128, 140
Adonis, 156
Adventures of Master F.J., The, 28n10, 46, 49, 52, 62, 79, 82n11
Aeneas (Marlowe's): characterization, 120–21, 131–32; associated with Elizabeth I, 147–48, 159n3; role of costume, 160n10; mentioned, 126–44 passim, 146, 148–50 passim, 153, 161n13, 161n14, 161n18, 162–65 passim
Aeneas (Virgil's): contrasted with Marlowe's Aeneas, 121; mentioned, 92, 114, 131, 132, 159n3, 159n4, 160n10, 169, 220
Aeneid, 114, 132, 135, 160n10, 161n18
"Aged Lover Renounceth Love, The," 54
Albert, Prince, 238
Alchemist, The, 235
Alençon. *See* Anjou, duke of
Alfield, Thomas, 115n6
Allen, D. C., 160n11
Allen, William, 115n6
Alpers, Paul: on pastoral lyric, 95–96, 116n15; mentioned, 25
Althusser, Louis, 9
Amadine, 161n17
Ambidexter, 34, 176
Amores, 122
Amoretti: discussion of *Amoretti* 75, 59–60; mentioned, 98
Amussen, Susan Dwyer: on Elizabeth I, 27n5
Anacreon, 41
Anatomie of Absurditie, The, 37

Anglo, Sydney, 71, 72
Anjou, duke of: courtship of Elizabeth I, 28–29n12; mentioned, 87, 137
Anna (in *Dido*), 135, 137, 140, 163n25, 165n34
Antonio (in *The Merchant of Venice*), 245n6
Antony, 137
Antony and Cleopatra, 29n14, 133, 161n14
Apollo, 100, 210, 213n26
Apology for Poetry, 36, 38–40, 50, 124, 191
Aquinas, Thomas, 160n8
Arcadia, 116n15, 161n17
Archer, William: denigration of lyric, 31n24
Aristotle: on lyric, 36, 40
Armado, Don Adriano de: compared with Berowne, 186–87; mentioned, 168, 173, 177, 178, 186, 187, 198–200 passim, 203–7 passim, 212n19, 212n21, 213n23
Arraignment of Paris, The: discussion of, 85–86, 89–90, 93–94; gender issues in, 85–86, 88–95, 99–107, 112–14; sovereignty in, 85–89, 112–14; in political context, 86–88; use of lyric in, 88–98, 100, 102–6, 114; use of song in, 90–94; subjectivity of author, 96–99; contrasted with *Dido,* 114; date of publication, 114n4; pastoral characters in, 116n17; Diana's importance in, 116n19; mentioned, 25, 51, 62, 71, 77, 80, 84n21, 109, 111, 117n22, 119n34, 128, 144, 146, 158, 208, 216, 218, 224, 226, 228, 232, 243,
Arte of English Poesie: discussion of poems in, 110; mentioned, 36
Arthur, King, 75, 92
As You Like It, 17, 19, 245n4
Ascanius, 126, 162n19, 163n27
Ascham, Roger, 63, 81n3

Ashe's *Elizabeth's Farewell to the Army*, 148, 164n32
Astraea, 101
Astrophil, 53, 175, 178, 180, 185, 191
Astrophil and Stella, 38–40 passim, 125, 170, 175, 190, 208
Ate, 88, 92, 102, 104, 105, 112, 177n22
Athena, 231
Atrides, 134
Aumerle (in *Richard II*), 219
Avicenna, 160n8
Axton, Marie: on Kenilworth pageant, 78; mentioned, 9, 73

Bacon, Lord Francis, 23
"Bait, The," 160n7
Bakeless, John, 165n34
Baker, Howard: on the *Arraignment*, 112
Bakhtin, Mikhail, 192
Baldwin, T. W., 211n4
Barabas, 156
Barber, C. L., 165n37, 166n37, 210n2
Barish, Jonas, 159n5
Barnfield, Richard, 152
Barroll, J. Leeds, 244, 249n25
Barton, Anne: on *Love's Labour's Lost*, 170; mentioned, 200
Bassanio, 188, 245n6
Bassnett, Susan: on Elizabeth I, 27n5
Beatrice, 1, 91
Beckerman, Bernard, 32n28
Bellamira, 156
Bembo, Pietro, 38
Benbow, Mark, 114n4, 115n10
Benedick, 181, 223
Bernard, J. E.: on Thomas Preston, 34–35
Berowne: as satirist, 174–76; complexity of voice, 185–92, compared with Don Adriano de Armado, 186–87; mentioned, 53, 171–72, 174–93 passim, 196–205 passim, 211n10, 212n13, 212n16, 217
Berry, Philippa: on Kenilworth pageant, 74, 83n19; on Elizabeth I, 84n20, 92; mentioned, 148
Bethell, S. L.: on *Romeo and Juliet*, 2; on *Love's Labour's Lost*, 29n15

Bevington, David: on *Love's Labour's Lost*, 213n22; on misogyny in court culture, 227–28; mentioned, 212n21
blank verse, 35, 155
Bloom, Harold, 12
Boas, Frederick S.: on Elizabeth I, 239; mentioned, 164n30, 240
Bobadil, 17
Boccaccio: on poetry as allegory, 42; mentioned, 84n23
Boleyn, Anne, 118n30
Bolingbroke, 219
Bono, Barbara: on *As You Like It*, 19; mentioned, 161n18
Boose, Lynda: on *The Taming of the Shrew*, 227; mentioned, 246n10, 247n12
boy actors: in *Love's Labour's Lost*, 195, 201
Boyet, 193, 198, 201, 212n16
Boyle, Mary, 229
boys' companies: gender issues, 117n24; mentioned, 80–81, 144, 159n2, 164n30
Bradbrook, M. C.: on "Zabeta" skit, 75
Bradstreet, Anne, 232, 248n18
Breitenberg, Mark, 19, 30n19
Bremo, 161n17
Briscoe, Lily, 214
Brodwin, Leonora Leet, 162n22
Brooks, Harold, 211n6
Browning, Elizabeth Barrett, 237
Bruno, Giordano, 211n10
Bruse, Sir, Sans pittie, 75
Bruss, Elizabeth: on Harold Bloom, 12
Bruster, Douglas: on Marlowe's lyric, 126, 159n5, 160n12; mentioned, 143, 153, 159n5, 234
Brute, 92
Burbage, James, 33

Calderwood, James: on Shakespeare's poetic styles, 29n14, 169; on *Romeo and Juliet*, 245n2, 245n3; mentioned, 211n5, 211n7, 213n24
Callimachus, 41
Cambises: discussion of, 33–35; courtly pastoral and song in, 34; mentioned, 70, 176

Camden, William: on Elizabeth I, 110–11
Cameron, Deborah, 30n19
Campion, Edmund: torture and execution of, 87; mentioned, 92, 104, 111, 114n4, 118n31
Campion, Thomas, 26
Carew, Thomas, 14
Carroll, William C., 185, 191, 201, 207, 212n13, 212n18, 234
Carter, Angela, 234
Cary, Sir Lucius, 39
Case, Sue-Ellen, 231
Castiglione, Baldassare, 38, 43
Catullus, 41
Cavendish, Margaret, 230
Cecil, William, 87, 115n6
"Celebration of Charis," 161n16
"Chaine of Pearle, A . . . ," 248n18
Changeling, The, 19
Chapman, George, 211n8
Chaucer, Geoffrey: Gascoigne's allusion to, 51–52; mentioned, 46, 154
Churchyard, Thomas, 48
Cinthio, Giraldi, 165n34
Circe, 130
Clark, Eleanor Grace, 164n32, 165n34
Cleopatra, 137
Clifford, Lady Anne, 232
Coghill, Nevill, 239
Cole, Howard C.: on Kenilworth pageant, 78, 84n22; mentioned, 82n6, 116n17
Coleridge, Samuel Taylor: on Shakespeare's manliness, 14; chronology of Shakespeare's plays, 16, 29n14; nationalistic use of Shakespeare, 241–42; on marriage, 247n15; mentioned, 22, 23, 237, 245n5
Colie, Rosalie, 31n24, 123
Colin (Peele's): contrasted with Colin Clout, 96–99; mentioned, 86, 92–95 passim, 107, 114, 116n17
Colin Clout, 93, 115n10, 118n27, 148
"Colin Clout's Come Home Again," 99
Collier, John Payne: quoting Coleridge, 29n14; mentioned, 14, 241
"Come my Celia," 235
"Complaint of Philomene, The," 64

"Convent of Pleasure, The," 230
Cope, Jackson, 126
Cordelia, 223
Corinna, 122
Coronation entry of Elizabeth I, 71–72
"Coronet for His Mistress Philosophy," 211n8
Cortegiano, Il, 38, 44
Corthell, Ronald J., 118n31
Costard, 177, 186–87, 198–200, 203, 207, 212n21
Costume: Marlowe's stress on, 160n10
Country and the City, The, 236
Courtly love: contrasted with marriage, 5
Cressida, 220
Crewe, Jonathan: on Surrey's poems, 46; on Wyatt, 58; on "Gascoigne's Woodmanship," 83n13
Cupid, 126, 127, 202, 246n7
Cupid-as-Ascanius, 150
Cutts, John P., 160n10
Cynthia: associated with Elizabeth I, 6, 101; Ralegh's, 15
Cynthia's Revels, 235

Dan Bartholmew of Bathe, 52, 80, 82n10
Dan Bartholmew of Bathe, 51–52
Dane, Clemence, 239
Daniel, Carter A., 114n4
Daniel, Samuel, 17, 109, 218
Dante, 1, 52, 91
Dark Lady of the Sonnets, The, 239
David, Richard, 179
Davies, Sir John, 122
De genealogia deorum gentilium, 42
de Lauretis, Teresa, 9
de Man, Paul: on lyric, 22
De Republica Anglorum, 246n10
Deborah, 72
Deepe Desire: acted by Leicester, 77; mentioned, 73, 79, 83n19, 95
Descensus Astraea, 84n21
Devereux, Robert. *See* Essex, Robert Devereux, Earl of
"Dialogue betweene two shepherds, A," 248n18

Diana: in "Zabeta" skit, 76, 244; in the *Arraignment*, 87, 90, 91, 100, 104, 112, 116n19, 117n23; associated with Elizabeth I, 92, 101; mentioned, 84n20, 148

Dido (Marlowe's): her stylistic shifts, 135–40; associated with Elizabeth I, 146–51, 153; parody of, 150, 165n35; mentioned, 48, 126–53 passim, 157, 159n4, 161n13, 161n14, 161n18, 162–65 passim, 169, 220

Dido, Queen of Carthage: contrasted with the *Arraignment*, 114; gender issues in, 120–21, 137–40, 145–54, 162n22; use of lyric in, 125–29, 131–35; court theater devices in, 126; use of song in, 126, 160n9; lyric versus heroic rhetoric, 135–46, 161n18, 164n30; eros incompatible with politics, 136–37, 150; female sovereignty in, 137, 146–54, 162n22; temporality in, 138, 153; opening scene, discussion of, 140–46; gods (Olympians), discussion of, 140–46; allusion to Spenser, 148–49, 165n33; conclusion, discussion of, 150–51; date of production, 159n2; twentieth-century criticism of, 160n11, 163n24; absence of nationalism in, 162n19; mentioned, 25, 58, 80, 92, 99, 113, 119n33, 122, 155, 157, 158, 161n13, 163n23, 164–65n32, 167, 169, 216, 218, 222

Dido play: in *Hamlet*, 164n30

Dido (Virgil's), 147

Dido/Elissa: as pseudonym for Elizabeth I, 148

Didon se sacrifiant, 130

Discovery of a gaping gulf . . . , 28–29n12, 87

Doctor Faustus, 138, 142, 153, 163n23, 165n37, 166n37

Dol Common, 235

Dolce, Lodovico, 163n27

Donne, John, 14, 15, 39, 81n4, 160n7, 179, 211n8

Doran, Madeleine, 212n18

Drake, Sir Frances, 86, 115n8

Drayton, Michael: on lyric, 41

Drummond, William, 235

Duchess of Malfi, 231

Dudley, Robert. *See* Leicester, Robert Dudley, Earl of

Dulce bellum inexpertis, 50

Dumain: his sonnet, 182–84; mentioned, 171, 181–84 passim, 199, 206

E. K., 48, 98

Eaton, Sara: on lyric in *The Changeling*, 19

Echo, 94

echo song: at Kenilworth, 74; in the *Arraignment*, 94

Edward II, 70, 146, 156–58 passim

Edward II: use of lyric in, 156–57; mentioned, 224

Edward VI: Elizabeth's petition to, 31n21; mentioned, 70

Ekeblad, Inga-Stina. *See* Ewbank, Inga-Stina

Elegies, 122, 125

Eliot, T. S.: on Shakespeare, 29n14; mentioned, 149, 165n33

Elizabeth I: marital issues, 5, 28–29n12, 117–18n27; cult of, 6, 69, 150, 116n19; as audience, 7–13, 43–45, 67–80, 83n17, 111–13, 117n23, 150, 165n34; gender issues, 7–13, 27n5, 43–44, 117n26, 118n30, 208–10, 235–38; literary representations of, 7–13, 92, 101, 116n19, 146–51, 153, 159n3, 195–96, 238–40, 246n7, 248–49n22; as author, 20, 31n21, 209; her reign, 33, 86–88, 113, 115n8, 118n28, 208–10; praise of, 100–114, 116n19, 148, 237–38; aging of, 150, 152–53, 205, 208–10; her literary and historical influence, 232–33, 237–39, 240, 248n18

Elizabeth II, 239

Endimion, 92, 101, 222, 225

England's Helicon, 171

Epistle to Posterity, 63

"Epithalamion," 98, 148, 149, 165n33

Erickson, Peter, 245n4, 247n13

Eroticism: Marlowe's use of, 127–30, 147, 161n14

Essex, Robert Devereux, Earl of, 209, 210n3, 213n25

Euripides, 144

Evans, Malcolm, 213n26
Ewbank, Inga-Stina (Ekeblad): on Elizabeth I, 106; on the *Arraignment,* 118n32, 119n34; mentioned, 109
Execution of Justice in England, 87

F. J., 13, 54, 80
Faerie Queene, The, 7, 35, 59, 98, 149, 160n8
Falstaff, 211n12
Fates, 98, 105
Female sovereignty: fear of, 12–13; and subjectivity, 13; Peele's view of, 100–114; of Elizabeth I, 117n26, 208–10, 237–38; in *Dido,* 137, 146–54, 162n22; and lyric, 215, 235
Feminist criticism: as critical methodology, 10; of erotic praise, 18; of staged lyric, 19–20; of Shakespeare, 201, 225–26; mentioned, 211n11, 218
Ferguson, Moira, 247n12
Fineman, Joel: on Petrarchism and subjectivity, 19; mentioned, 30n18, 171, 191, 203
Finke, Laurie A., 30n19
"First Anniversarie . . . ," 39, 81n4
Fitton, Mary, 239
Flora, 102
Florio, John, 210n3
Foakes, R. A.: on Collier, 29n14
Forster, E. M., 202
Foucault, Michel, 9, 87, 88, 104, 118n31
Fraser, Lady Antonia: on Elizabeth I, 7
Freccero, John: on Petrarch, 18–19; mentioned, 39, 181
French, Marilyn, 201
Freud, Sigmund, 218
Friar Bacon and Friar Bungay: compared with *Cambises,* 34
Frye, Susan, 119n34
Fucilla, Joseph: on Petrarchism, 2
Fumerton, Patricia, 245n1

Galatea, 128, 161n17
Gallagher, Catherine: on seventeenth-century women and power, 13

Ganymede, 141–45 passim, 161n13, 164n28, 164n31
Garber, Marjorie: on Dido's demise, 151; mentioned, 153, 240
Gascoigne, George: critical views of, 11–13, 28n9, 28n10, 63, 83n15; his social standing, 46, 48–49, 82n6; literary antecedents, 46, 51–52, 63; contemporary praise of, 47–48, his poetic practice, 47, 51–52, 58–59, 80; plain speech versus lyricism, 49–51, 57, 60–61; his personas, 49–52, 74; use of irony, 52–53; temporality in, 53–62; gender issues in, 59, 61–66; his later works, 62–66; and Kenilworth pageant, 69–70, 72–77, 79, 84n23; echo song, 74; mentioned, 7, 8, 15, 23, 35, 41, 43, 81n5, 83n19, 170, 176, 201, 208, 210n1, 223, 224
"Gascoigne's Woodmanship": discussion of, 60–62; mentioned, 80, 83n13
Gender issues: sixteenth-century stereotypes, 14; in twentieth-century criticism, 14–15, 224–28; at Elizabeth's court, 65–66, 248n17; in contemporary staging, 117n24, 214–15, 231–32; and Elizabeth I, 117n26, 118n30, 237–38; in lyric, 126–27, 233, 235, 243–44; in Marlowe, 137–40, 145–54, 158, 162n22, 164n31; in Shakespeare, 168, 179, 189, 192–97, 201–4, 208–10, 213n22, 219–28, 247n11; seventeenth-century attitudes, 228–30; in sixteenth-century marriage, 246n10
Gerard's *Herball,* 206
Gibbons, Brian, 126, 150, 151, 160n10, 163n24
Gill, Roma, 162n22, 164n29
Gim, Lisa: on Elizabeth I, 27n5
Glasse of Government, The, 62–64
Gloucester, duchess of (in *Richard II*), 219
"Godly Medytacyon of the christen Sowle, A," 209
Gods (Olympians): Marlowe's vision of, 140–46
Goldberg, Jonathan: on Spenser's October eclogue, 246n9
Goldman, Michael, 165n36
Gombrich, E. H., 70

Gorboduc, 35, 49, 69, 73, 155
Grace, William, 210n2
Graham, Jorie, 24
Greenblatt, Stephen J.: on subjectivity, 30n18; on Marlowe, 165n36; mentioned, 16, 111, 151, 118n31
Greene, Robert, 34
Greene, Thomas, 155, 201
Greene Knight (Gascoigne's), 54, 56, 60, 72–74, 79, 83n19
"Greene Knight's Farewell to Fansie, The," 56–57, 60
Greville, Fulke: on Sidney, 39; on Lady Sidney, 215; mentioned, 15
Grey, Lord, of Wilton, 12, 60, 61

Haigh, Christopher: on Elizabeth, 107; mentioned, 117n26
Hamlet: Dido play in, 164n30; mentioned, 144
Harefield Place: Elizabeth I's visit, 67
Harington, Sir John, 209, 232
Harriot, Thomas, 212n17
Harvey, E. Ruth, 160n8
Harvey, Gabriel, 36, 210n3
Hattaway, Michael, 163n24
Hawthorne, Nathaniel, 237, 248n21
Hector (as Worthy), 199, 200
Hecuba, 149
Hedley, Jane: on *The Adventures of Master F.J.*, 82n11; on "Gascoigne's Woodmanship," 83n13
Heilbrun, Carolyn, 20, 223
Heisch, Allison, 232
Helen of Troy: in the *Arraignment*, 86, 89, 90–92, 93–95 passim, 100, 101, 105, 116n13; in Ovid, 114; in *Doctor Faustus*, 138, 142, 163n23
Helgerson, Richard: on Gascoigne, 62–63, 83n15; mentioned, 97
Hendricks, Margo: on *Dido*, 164–65n32
Henri IV (of France), 209, 213n25
Henry IV, 220, 211n12
Henry V, 181
Henry VIII, 68

Henslowe, Philip, 155
Heptameron, 209
"Her Majestie resembled to the crowned pillar," 44–45
Hercules, 141
Hercules (as Worthy), 199
Hermes: in the *Aeneid*, 132; in *Dido*, 132, 134, 139, 141, 143, 146, 161n18, 162n19
"Hero and Leander," 122, 125, 161n14
Heroides: *Heroides* 5 in, 114; *Heroides* 7 in, 114, 129; mentioned, 93, 139, 220
Heywood, Thomas, 239
Hibbard, G. R., 245n2
Hippolyta, 246n7
Hobbinol, 97, 115n10
Holofernes, 168, 177, 180, 184, 186–87, 198, 200, 207, 212n19
"Holy Sonnets," 211n8
Homan, Sidney, 212n21, 248n21
Horace, 41
Horne, P. R., 109, 114n4
Hotspur, 223
Howard, Jean: on Elizabeth I, 27n5; mentioned, 247n11
Huf, Ruf, and Snuf, 34
Humphries, Rolfe, 161n16
"Hundreth Sundrie Flowres, A," 49, 52, 82n7
Hunter, G. K., 63
Hurston, J. Dennis, 211n13

Iarbus, 135, 149, 165n34, 246n7
If You Know Not Me, You Know Nobody, 239
"In Honour of That High and Mighty Princess Queen Elizabeth of Happy Memory," 248n18
Inns of Court plays: Nashe's praise of, 37; contrasted with court entertainment, 70; mentioned, 35, 49, 69
Isabella, Queen (in Marlowe), 224
Ithamore, 156, 220

Jakobson, Roman: graphing narrative and lyric, 24
James I, 209, 236

Jane Anger, her Protection for Women, 232
Jankowski, Theodora A.: on Elizabeth I, 9; on gender issues, 28n8
Jaquenetta, 173, 177–78, 186–87, 200, 203–6
Jardine, Lisa, 201
Jason, 156, 220
Jessica (in *Merchant*), 220–22
Jew of Malta, The: parody of lyric in, 155–56; mentioned, 155, 156, 220
Jocasta, 35, 70, 81n5, 155
Jodelle, Etienne, 130, 163n25, 165n34
John of Gaunt: misuse of his speech, 241–42; mentioned, 103
Johnson, Barbara, 243, 249n24
Johnson, Samuel, 208, 234
Johnson, W. R., 31n24, 24
Jones, Ann Rosalind, 30n19
Jonson, Ben: on the "feminine" aesthetic, 14; on characterization, 16–17; on Elizabeth I, 235; mentioned, 15, 22, 29n13, 39, 55, 81n4, 82n8, 109, 161n16, 243
Jordan, Constance: on Elizabeth I, 27n5, 147–48; mentioned, 247n13
Juliet: characterization, 1–2, 5; mentioned, 171, 194, 218, 224
Juno: in Kenilworth pageant, 76, 102, 244; in the *Arraignment,* 87, 94, 100, 101, 105, 117n23; in *Dido,* 142; mentioned, 116n19
Jupiter: in the *Arraignment,* 94; in *Dido,* 135, 137, 141–46 passim, 161n13, 162n19, 163n25, 164n28; mentioned, 184
Juvenal, 82n8

Kantorowicz, Ernst, 115n7
Kastan, David Scott, 76, 166n37
Kate (in *The Taming of the Shrew*), 226
Katherine (in *Love's Labour's Lost*), 202
Kay, Dennis, 243
Kelly, Joan, 228
Kenilworth pageant: Elizabeth I as audience, 72–79, 83n17; Lady of the Lake interlude, 75; "Zabeta" skit discussed, 75–77; mentioned, 12, 46, 71, 83n19, 84n22, 87, 94, 95, 117n23, 197, 210n1
King, John N., 116n16

King, William C., 248n22
King Lear, 223
Knox, John, 108, 118n28, 235
Kocher, Paul, 161n14
Kyd, Thomas, 118n32

La Foole, Sir Amorous, 17
Lady Happy, 230
Lady of May, The, 40, 70, 71, 78, 111, 168, 172, 175, 192
Lady of the Lake (at Kenilworth), 72–75 passim
Laneham, Robert, 79
Lanham, Richard: on Petrarchism, 3
Laura, 1, 19
Lavinia, 135
Lear, King, 136
Leicester, Robert Dudley, Earl of: at Kenilworth pageant, 69, 73; mentioned, 83n18, 83n19, 94, 117n23, 147, 165n34, 244
Lever, J. W., 170, 206
Levin, Harry: on *Romeo and Juliet,* 2; mentioned, 163n24
Levine, Laura, 29n13
Levine, Mortimer: on *Gorboduc,* 83n18
Lewis, C. S.: on Elizabethan "Golden Age," 17–18; mentioned, 29–30n17, 82n7, 237
Lindley, David: on defining lyric, 21, 40; on Michael Drayton, 41; mentioned, 31n23
Longaville: his sonnet, 182; mentioned, 171, 177, 180–83 passim
Lord Mayor's shows, 108–9
Lorenzo (in *Merchant*), 220–22
Love's Labour's Lost: as satire, 167–70; courtly antecedents, 168; gender issues in, 168, 179, 189, 192–98, 201–6; opening speech of, 172–74; sonnets in, 174–92, 196–97; miscommunication in, 177, 179, 186–87; portrayal of the ladies, 193–97, 200–202; Nine Worthies pageant, 197–201; resolution of, 202, 204–10; songs in, 206–7, 213n24; rejection of Petrarchism, 216; lyric as private in, 217–18
Lucan, 162n18
Lucrece, 83n14

"Lullabie of the Lover, The," 54–56, 60
Lyly, John: his image of Elizabeth I as Cynthia, 101; mentioned, 63, 85, 92, 147, 210n3, 211n4, 222, 225, 227–28
Lyric: Shakespeare's use of, 5, 169–70, 192–98, 201–6, 217–19, 220–21; generic relationship with drama, 6, 16–17, 22–23, 25, 36, 169, 234–35; gender and, 8, 14–17, 20, 31n22, 35, 37–38, 43, 126–27, 219–24, 233–35, 243–44; sixteenth-century positioning of, 8, 14, 26, 35–42, 105, 154, 215–16, 233, 236; denigration of, 14–17, 29n14, 31n24, 37–38, 126, 169, 216, 231, 234; post-Renaissance theory of, 15–17, 22–24, 216, 234, 236–37; musicality of, 22, 244n1; temporality of, 24, 26, 67, 124–25, 129–31, 135, 218, 220–23; and court politics, 25–26, 69, 78–80, 215, 235, 243–44; twentieth-century criticism of, 29n14, 29n15, 30n19, 95–96, 126, 159n5, 216, 234; Wyatt's use of, 58; Peele's use of, 88–98, 100, 102–6, 114; Marlowe's use of, 121–29, 131–40, 147, 151–52, 154–58; Ralegh's use of, 123–24; Spenser's use of, 151

Mailer, Norman, 12
Marcade, 205, 209
Marcus, Leah: on Elizabeth I, 27n5, 115n9, 213n25, 243
Margaret, the fair maid of Fressingfield, 34
Marguerite of Navarre, Queen: linked to Elizabeth I, 209
Marlowe, Christopher: his social standing, 120–21, 159n1; his use of lyric, 121–25, 147, 151–52; sensuality in his lyric, 122–23; his metrical techniques, 125–26, 155; contrasted with Ovidean sources, 128–29, 139–40; his pessimism, 132–36, 140, 150, 154, 158, 162n21; gender issues in, 146–54, 158, 221, 224; religious issues, 149–50; his rejection of Petrarchism, 151–53; lyric versus heroic style, 153–54; his theatrical innovation, 153–55; lyric as failed rhetoric of desire, 154–58; use of lyric in public theater, 155–58; his influence on Shakespeare, 158–72. See also *Dido, Queen of Carthage*
Marriage: as opposed to courtly love, 5, 230–31; and Elizabeth I, 69, 75–77, 83–84n20, 232; in Shakespeare, 189, 194, 202, 204, 208, 218, 219, 222–28; as resolution in Shakespeare's comedies, 202, 215–16, 221–23; in sixteenth-century England, 226, 246n10, 247n12; influence of Reformation, 228, 230; seventeenth-century attitudes toward, 228–30; Coleridge on, 247n15
Martin, Richard A.: on Marlowe's erotic style, 128; mentioned, 159n2, 162n18
Mary Stuart, 239, 248n22
Mary Stuart, 239
Mary Tudor, 27n4, 137
Masque of Hope, 239
McCoy, Richard C.: on Gascoigne, 11–13, 28n9, 28n10, 50, 82n8; mentioned, 30n18, 64, 65, 109, 118
Medea, 220
Mendelson, Sara Heller: on seventeenth-century women's attitudes on marriage, 228–29; mentioned, 248n17
Merchant of Venice, The: use of lyric in, 220–22; marriage as resolution to, 221–22; mentioned, 16, 169, 188, 191, 221, 224, 245n6
Mercury: in "Zabeta" skit, 76; in *Love's Labour's Lost*, 210, 213n26; mentioned, 209
Mercutio, 27n3, 186, 196
Meres, Francis, 174, 207
Merlin, 75
Metamorphoses, 128
Metrical practice: rapid development of, 35; Gascoigne's, 47; Wyatt's, 47; Peele's, 117n22; Marlowe's, 125–26, 155; mentioned, 81n2
Middleton, Thomas, and William Rowley, 19
Midsummer Night's Dream, A: gendered lyric in, 222; Elizabeth I's representation in, 246n7; mentioned, 6, 16, 107, 169, 185, 198, 210n2, 211n6, 219, 239, 247n11

Miller, Nancy K.: on gender issues, 28n11; mentioned, 20
Milton, John, 247n15
"Mine Own John Poins," 62
Mirror for Magistrates, 47
Mizener, Arthur: on *Dido,* 163n23
Montrose, Louis Adrian: on Elizabeth I, 43, 117–18n27; on the *Arraignment,* 116n19; on *Love's Labour's Lost,* 213n24, 224–25; mentioned, 6, 107, 113, 116n15, 118n29, 211n4
Moon imagery, 222
Morris, Brian: on gender issues in Dido, 161n13
Morris, Charles: his comparison of Elizabeth I and Victoria, 237–38; mentioned, 239, 240
Morris, Harry, 149, 165n33
Moth, 178, 189, 190, 198, 199, 206, 212n19, 213n23
Mucedorus, 161n17
Much Ado about Nothing, 178, 181, 194, 214
Muir, Kenneth: on sixteenth-century lyric, 6
Munda, Constantia, 232

Nashe, Thomas: his disparagement of sonnets, 37–38; on Sidney, 40; on Gascoigne, 47; collaboration with Marlowe, 159n2; mentioned, 39, 43, 49, 156, 159n2, 165n34, 170, 210n3
Nathan, Leonard: on Gascoigne, 54
Nathaniel, Sir, 198, 207
Nationalism: in the *Arraignment,* 92; absence in *Dido,* 162n19; Elizabeth used as source for, 237–39; mentioned, 28–29n12
Navarre, prince of, 172–76, 179–80, 187, 193, 198, 207, 220
Neale, J. E., 69
Neeley, Carol Thomas: on gender, 9; mentioned, 232
Neville, Alexander, 81n3
New historicism: and gender issues, 10–11, 111; mentioned, 244
Nichols, John: on "Zabeta" skit, 84n21

"Nimph's reply to the Sheepheard": discussed, 123–24
Nine Worthies pageant: interplay of social classes, 197–201; mentioned, 170, 202, 207
Niobe, 90
Norton, Thomas, 35
Novy, Marianne: on Shakespeare's conclusions, 225–26; on *The Merchant of Venice,* 245n6; mentioned, 246n10, 247n14

Oberon, 222, 224, 246n7
Oedipus, 81n3
Oenone: her poetic voice, 89–90; mentioned, 92–96 passim, 103, 106, 114, 115n11, 116n13, 223
"Of Proportion," 44–45
Oliver, H. J., 148, 149, 159n2, 159n3, 160n10, 163n22
Olivia (in *Twelfth Night*), 232, 247n11
"On Monsieur's Departure," 31n21
Ophelia, 202
Orgel, Stephen: on Marlowe's *Elegies,* 122; on Elizabeth's aging, 152
Orlando (in *As You Like It*), 19
Osborne, June, 67
Othello, 136
Ovid: as source for Marlowe, 128–29; mentioned, 23, 93, 114, 122, 139–40, 150, 161n15, 163n27, 165n35

Pageant, court: temporality in, 67–68; in political context, 69–70; use of lyric in, 69–71, 80; Elizabeth I as audience for, 71–79; authors of, 84n23. *See also* Kenilworth pageant and Theater, court
Pallaphilos, 73
Pallas: in the *Arraignment,* 87, 100, 102, 105
Pandarina, 63
Paradise Lost, 228
Paris: in the *Arraignment,* 89–90, 92–95 passim, 99, 100, 107, 112, 115n11, 116n13, 116n19, 117n22, 119n33, 218
Parker, Patricia, 162n20
Passionate Pilgrim, The, 171

"Passionate Shepherd to His Love, The," 95, 122–26, 128, 143, 155–56, 160n6, 165n33
Pater, Walter, 187
Patterson, Annabel: on Jonson's lyricism, 22
Peele, George: contrasted with Spenser, 96–99; his use of lyric, 96–97, 108; gender issues and, 99–114, 117n21; complexity of his vision, 104–5; and subjectivity, 106; as influence on Shakespeare, 108; his praise of Elizabeth I, 118n27; his use of genres, 118–19n32; mentioned, 6, 8, 24, 25, 49, 51, 62, 71, 77, 80, 81, 84n21, 92–95 passim, 108, 109, 115n8, 115n10, 116n13, 116n19, 118n32, 121, 126, 128, 138, 140, 144–48 passim, 154, 155, 158, 169, 170, 208, 216–18 passim, 223–28 passim, 232, 243. *See also Arraignment of Paris*
Petrarch, 1, 23, 30n19, 42, 46, 52, 63, 91, 93, 115n12, 117n21, 148, 164n27, 170, 176, 218
Petrarchism: and Shakespeare, 2, 217–18; sixteenth-century attitudes toward, 2, 15–16, 212n16; and gender issues, 7–8, 15–21; opposed to plain style, 15; and Marlowe, 151–53; linked to money, 187–88, 193, 195; mentioned, 146, 147, 154, 169, 171, 180, 188–89, 199, 203, 215, 216, 226, 240, 245n2
Petruchio, 226
Phantasia, 160n8
Phantasmata, 160n8
Philip II (of Spain), 86, 137
"Philo to his Lady Calia sendeth this Odelet . . . ," 44–45
Philomel, 61, 68, 223
Piers, 246n9
Pilgrim sonnet (in *Romeo and Juliet*): discussed, 1–3; complexity of, 217; mentioned, 6, 108, 171
Pindar, 22, 41
Pinsky, Robert: on Thomas Campion's lyric, 26
Pius V, Pope, 235
Pléiade, the, 176
Poetics, 40
Polyphemus, 128, 129, 161n17, 165n35
Pompey (as Worthy), 199, 200
Porter, Carolyn: on power, 88

Portia (in *Merchant*), 188, 220–22, 224, 245n6
Posies, The: discussed, 49–50; mentioned, 12, 41, 46, 51, 54, 63, 65, 69, 72, 74, 80, 82n5, 82n7, 83n19
Potter, Lois: on metrical practice, 81n2
Powell, Jocelyn, 163n24
Preston, Thomas, 33–35
Primrose, Diana, 248n18
Princely Pleasures at Kenilworth, The, 69, 80. *See also* Kenilworth pageant
Prosopopoeia, 123, 160n7
Protestantism: negative attitude regarding lyric, 41; influence on marital ideals, 228; mentioned, 189
Proteus, 17, 20
Prouty, C. T.: on Gascoigne, 49, 50
Puck, 222
Puttenham, George: his literary aims, 35; on court language, 36, 43; his definition of lyric, 41; his shape poems, 44–45, on Gascoigne, 47; mentioned, 69, 118n30, 211n7
Pygmalion, 163n27
Pyramus, 220

Ralegh, Sir Walter: his use of love lyric, 123–24; mentioned, 7, 95, 100, 130, 147, 165n34, 168, 187, 206, 210n3, 238
Ramsey, Paul, 210n1
Reiss, Timothy J., 118n31
Ribner, Irving, 159n3
Rich, Penelope Devereux, 115n13, 211n10, 213n25
Richard II, 148, 219, 245n5
Richard II: gendered lyric in, 219–20; mentioned, 57, 76, 103, 158, 169, 209, 241, 242, 249n25
Righter, Anne. *See* Anne Barton
Roethke, Theodore, 248n21
Rombus, Master, 168
Romeo, 1–3, 27n2, 171, 181, 186, 194, 218
Romeo and Juliet: use of lyric in, 1–6, 217–18; gender issues in, 5–6, 27n2, 218; mentioned, 16, 23, 27n3, 42, 70, 108, 158, 169, 170, 220, 245n2, 245n3

Rosalind: in *As You Like It*, 17, 245n6; in *The Shepheardes Calender*, 97
Rosaline: in *Romeo and Juliet*, 2, 181; in *Love's Labour's Lost*, 175, 177, 179, 187–96 passim, 202, 204, 211n10, 224
Rose, Mary Beth, 30n19, 185, 213n22, 247n14
Rousseau, G. S., 163n25
Ruins of Time, The, 211n8

Sackville, Thomas, 35, 50, 144, 164n25
Sappho and Phao, 228
Saturn, 101
Satyra/Philomel, 61, 64
Savage Man, 72–76 passim, 79, 95, 197, 210n1
Schiller, Johann Christoph Friedrich von, 248n22
Scholemaster, 81n3
Seneca, 81n3
Shakespeare, William: marriage in, 5, 189, 194, 202, 204, 208, 215–16, 218, 219, 221–23, 228; and Elizabeth I, 10–11, 238–40; Coleridge on, 16, 29n14; critical evaluations of, 29n14, 30n20, 216, 224–28, 240–42; Peele's influence on, 108; Marlowe's influence on, 158, 172; in courtly context, 167–68, 209, 210n1, 210n3; satirizing courtly love tradition, 167–70, 172–92, 208; complexity of his voice, 169–70, 176, 182–92, 207, 219–24; his use of lyric, 169–70, 191, 216, 217, 219, 224; gender issues in, 178, 192–97, 208–10, 218–19, 223–27, 247n11; Sidney's influence on, 190–92. See also *Love's Labour's Lost*
Shape poems, 44–45
Shaw, George Bernard, 239
Shepheardes Calender, The: November eclogue, 48, 93, 148; April eclogue, 148; October eclogue, 246n9; mentioned, 49, 96, 97
Sidney, Sir Philip: his poetic theory, 38–40, 50, 125; his use of lyric, 38–40, 180, 116n15; gender issues, 39–40; compared to Spenser, 116n15; contrasted with Marlowe, 125; his influence on Shakespeare, 190–92; mentioned, 5, 11, 30n20, 37, 53, 70, 71, 78, 81n4, 95, 99, 100, 105, 107, 111,

115n13, 124, 158, 161n17, 167–72 passim, 175–76, 178, 188, 201, 208, 210n3, 211n10, 213n25, 215, 218
Sidney, Lady, 215
Sidney, Mary (Herbert), 248n18
Silberman, Lauren, 30n19
Skelton, John, 48, 115n10
Smith, Thomas, 246n10
Song, use of: in early Elizabethan drama, 33–34; in the *Arraignment*, 90–93; in *Dido*, 126, 160n9; in *Love's Labour's Lost*, 205–7; mentioned, 81, 81n1
Song of Solomon, 161n17
Sonnets: subjectivity and gender, 18–19; disparagement of, 37; Italian versus English, 115–16n13, sixteenth-century popularity of, 115n12, 170–71, 211n7; in *Love's Labour's Lost*, 170–92; topics for, 211n8; as "private" literature, 245n1
Sonnets, The, 167, 173–74, 178, 210n1
Sowernam, Esther, 232
Sparagmos, 103
Spearing, A. C.: on rhetorical poetry, 42
Spenser, Edmund: temporality and gender, 59–60; contrasted with Peele, 96–99; compared with Sidney, 116n15; his use of lyric, 151; mentioned, 5, 39, 48, 49, 55, 89, 93, 95, 112, 115n10, 147–53 passim, 160n8, 165n33, 170, 211n8
Sprint, Reverend John, 247n12
Spurgeon, Carolyn: on imagery in *Romeo and Juliet*, 27n3
Steane, J. B., 153, 160n10
Steele Glas, The: compared with *The Posies*, 64; mentioned, 53, 61, 65, 66, 80
Stella, 15, 180, 190, 211n10
Stevens, John: on Tudor lyric, 216; mentioned, 244n1
Stevens, Wallace, 21
Stone, Oliver, 240
Strong, Roy, 147
Stubbes, John: torture of, 87; mentioned, 28n12 104, 111
Styan, J. L., 32n28
Subjectivity: theories of, 7–13, 118; of the poet-lover, 82n9; in the *Arraign-*

Subjectivity (*continued*)
  ment, 91–92, 106, 112; authorial, 96–99; Shakespeare's, 191; of audience, 228; of Elizabeth I, 232
Surrey, Henry Howard, Earl of, 37, 46, 47, 48
Suzuki, Mihoko: on Elizabeth I, 27n5, 232; mentioned, 246n10
Swinburne, Algernon, 239
Sychaeus, 143, 159n4, 162n22, 163n27, 164n27
Sylvanus, 77, 79, 83n19
Sylvia (in *Two Gentlemen of Verona*), 204
Symposium, 152

"Tale of Troy, A," 108
Tamburlaine, 127, 135, 157, 158, 159n3, 221
Tamburlaine: failure of lyric in, 157–58; gendered lyric in, 221; mentioned, 112, 119n33, 135, 149, 158
Taming of the Shrew, The, 226, 227
Tayler, E. W., 236
Taylor, Tom, 239
Tellus, 101
Tempest, The, 210n2
Temporality: in Marlowe, 138, 153; mentioned, 135
Tennenhouse, Leonard: on Elizabeth I, 28–29n12, 247n13; on gender issues, 29n12, 118n31; on sonnets as political, 30n20; on *The Taming of the Shrew,* 226, 227; mentioned, 13, 229, 246n7, 247n11
Tennyson, Alfred, Lord, 239
Tereus, 65
Theater, court: influence on wider public, 85, use of boys' companies in, 117n21, 117n24; its devices in *Dido,* 126; satirized by Shakespeare, 167–70, 208
Theater, public: distance from poetic theory, 33; rapid development of, 35; considered by twentieth-century critics, 165n37
Theatre, the, 33, 35, 80
Thenot, 93, 115n10
Therion, 70, 172, 175
Thestilis, 88, 92–98 passim
Theweleit, Klaus, 18, 248n16

"They flee from me," 58
Thisbe, 220
Thornton, Alice, 229
Timbre, or Discoveries, 16
Titania, 222, 239, 246n7
Titania (Dekker's), 239
"To Penshurst," 109
"To the Thrice-Sacred Queen Elizabeth," 248n18
Tottel's Miscellany, 37, 41, 46, 47, 51
Trionfi, 52, 164n27; *Trionfo della Castita,* 116n19; *Trionfi della pudicizia,* 148
Troilus, 220
Trojan genealogy: Tudor promotion of, 92; mentioned, 97, 101
True Report of the Death and Martyrdom of M. Campion, 115n6
True, Sincere, and Modest Defense of English Catholics, 115n6
Tryton, 75
Turner, W. Craig, 145, 164n28
Turnus, 135
Twelfth Night, 232, 247n11
Twixt Axe and Crown, 239
Two Gentlemen of Verona, 20, 204

Udall, Nicholas, 118n30
Under-wood, 22
United Airlines, 241–42

"Valediction: on Weeping, A," 179
Vaux, Lord, 54
Veiled women: as cultural metaphor, 214–15
Venezky, Alice: on court pageantry, 71, 73; mentioned, 210n2
Venus: in the *Arraignment,* 86–93 passim, 97, 98, 105; in *Dido,* 126, 144–47 passim, 161n18, 162n19, 163n27, 164n31
Vickers, Nancy: on gender and lyric, 8, 19; mentioned, 18, 39, 30n19, 103
Victoria, Queen, 237–38
Viguers, Susan T., 116n13
Viola (in *Twelfth Night*), 202, 245n6
Virgil, 97, 114, 128, 130, 135, 140, 148, 150, 160n10, 162n18, 163n25, 164n27
Vita Nuova, 52

Volpone, 235
Von Hendy, Andrew; on the *Arraignment*, 90, 115n11, 116n19; mentioned, 97
Vulcan, 100

Waad, Armigail, 33
Waller, Gary: on Mary Wroth's poetry, 30n19
Walsingham, Frances, 213n25
Watson, Thomas, 81n3
Webbe, William: his literary aims, 35; denunciation of lyric, 38; on Gascoigne, 48
Weil, Judith, 153
"Western Wind": as starting point for English lyric, 21
Whigham, Frank, 13
Whore of Babylon, The, 239
"Whoso list to hunt," 68
Wife of Bath, 52, 154
Wilders, John, 211n4
Will Shakespeare, 239
Williams, Raymond, 236
Wilson, Dover, 213n26
Winters, Yvor: on Renaissance lyric, 15; on Gascoigne, 50, 83n13

Wollstonecraft, Mary, 15, 237
Wolstan Dixi pageant, 108, 109, 111
Woman, 248n22
Woman on top syndrome, 12, 88, 101, 121, 232
Woolf, Virginia, 106, 214–15
Wordsworth, William: on "manly" style, 14; influence on assumptions about lyric, 22; mentioned, 17
Wortley Montagu, Lady Mary, 229
Wroth, Mary, 30n19
Wyatt, Sir Thomas: his metrical technique, 47; temporality in, 58; mentioned, 15, 37, 46, 53, 59, 60, 62, 68, 170, 218

Yachnin, Paul, 248n20
Yates, Frances, 147, 191, 211n10, 212n17
York, duchess of (in *Richard II*), 219

"Zabeta" skit: description of, 75–77; mentioned, 73, 79, 84n21, 102, 111, 117n23, 118n27, 219
Zenocrate, 158, 221

DIANA E. HENDERSON is on the faculty at the Massachusetts Institute of Technology and has taught as an assistant professor of English at Middlebury College, where she also served as codirector of the Women's Studies Program. She earned her bachelor's degree from the College of William & Mary in Virginia and her doctorate from Columbia University. Her other publications include articles on works by Thomas Heywood, James Joyce, female lyricists of the English Renaissance, and Edmund Spenser.

PR 535 .L7 H46 1995
Henderson, Diana E., 1957-
Passion made public